Fishes of the Chicago Region

Fishes of the Chicago Region

A FIELD GUIDE

Francis M. Veraldi,
Stephen M. Pescitelli,
and Philip W. Willink

With a foreword by Larry M. Page

The University of Chicago Press
Chicago and London

The University of Chicago Press, Chicago 60637
The University of Chicago Press, Ltd., London
© 2025 by The University of Chicago
All rights reserved. No part of this book may be used or reproduced in any manner whatsoever without written permission, except in the case of brief quotations in critical articles and reviews. For more information, contact the University of Chicago Press, 1427 E. 60th St., Chicago, IL 60637.
Published 2025
Printed in China

34 33 32 31 30 29 28 27 26 25   1 2 3 4 5

ISBN-13: 978-0-226-83735-2 (paper)
ISBN-13: 978-0-226-83736-9 (e-book)
DOI: https://doi.org/10.7208/chicago/9780226837369.001.0001

Library of Congress Cataloging-in-Publication Data

Names: Veraldi, Francis M., 1975– author. | Pescitelli, Stephen, author. | Willink, Philip W., author. | Page, Lawrence M., writer of foreword.
Title: Fishes of the Chicago Region : a field guide / Francis M. Veraldi, Stephen M. Pescitelli, and Philip W. Willink ; with a foreword by Larry M. Page.
Description: Chicago : The University of Chicago Press, 2025. | Includes bibliographical references and index.
Identifiers: LCCN 2024033911 | ISBN 9780226837352 (paperback) | ISBN 9780226837369 (ebook)
Subjects: LCSH: Fishes — Illinois — Chicago Metropolitan Area — Identification.
Classification: LCC QL628.I3 V47 2025 | DDC 597.09773/11 — dc23/eng20241007
LC record available at https://lccn.loc.gov/2024033911

♾ This paper meets the requirements of ANSI/NISO Z39.48-1992 (Permanence of Paper).

Contents

Foreword VIII
Preface X

1 **Introduction** 2
2 **Book Organization** 22
3 **Pictorial Key to the Families** 26

SPECIES ACCOUNTS

4 **Lampreys** (Petromyzontidae) 46
5 **Sturgeons** (Acipenseridae) 58
6 **Paddlefishes** (Polyodontidae) 62
7 **Gars** (Lepisosteidae) 66
8 **Bowfins** (Amiidae) 74
9 **Freshwater Eels** (Anguillidae) 78
10 **Mooneyes** (Hiodontidae) 82
11 **Shads and Herrings** (Clupeidae) 88
12 **Suckers** (Catostomidae) 98
13 **Barbs and Carps** (Cyprinidae) 136
14 **Sharpbellies** (Xenocyprididae) 142
15 **True Minnows** (Leuciscidae) 150
16 **Loaches** (Cobitidae) 238
17 **North American Catfishes** (Ictaluridae) 242
18 **Pikes** (Esocidae) 262
19 **Mudminnows** (Umbridae) 270

20 **Salmon, Trout, Chars, and Whitefishes** (Salmonidae) 274

21 **Smelts** (Osmeridae) 308

22 **Trout-perches** (Percopsidae) 312

23 **Pirate Perches** (Aphredoderidae) 316

24 **Hakes, Lings, Rocklings, and Burbots** (Lotidae) 320

25 **Gobies** (Gobiidae) 324

26 **New World Silversides** (Atherinopsidae) 328

27 **Topminnows and Killifishes** (Fundulidae) 332

28 **Livebearers** (Poeciliidae) 340

29 **Sunfishes** (Centrarchidae) 344

30 **Temperate Basses** (Moronidae) 372

31 **Drums and Croakers** (Sciaenidae) 380

32 **Darters and Perches** (Percidae) 384

33 **Sticklebacks** (Gasterosteidae) 418

34 **Sculpins** (Cottidae) 426

Acknowledgments 436
Appendix: Fish Identification 440
Glossary 450
References 454
Photo Credits 466
Taxonomic Index 468
Subject Index 474

Foreword

The *Chicago Region* as defined herein includes an area in north-eastern Illinois dominated by one of the largest cities in the world, as well as southern Lake Michigan and adjacent areas of Indiana, Michigan, and Wisconsin. This region has a rich diversity of aquatic habitats that formed as the Pleistocene glaciers receded to the north and left behind rivers flowing through prairies and wetlands, small lakes, and the foremost feature of the region: massive Lake Michigan — the fifth-largest lake in the world.

This excellent book continues the long history of documenting the changing fish fauna in the Chicago Region. Illinois has an especially rich history of studies of its fishes, including *The Fishes of Illinois* (1908) by Stephen A. Forbes and Robert E. Richardson, *Fishes of Illinois* (1979) by Philip W. Smith, and *An Atlas of Illinois Fishes: 150 Years of Change* by Brian A. Metzke and colleagues (2022). Few other US states or global regions of similar size can boast of anything like the exceptional information available for fishes in the "Land of Lincoln." Wisconsin, too, can boast of excellent tomes on its fish fauna — most notably, George C. Becker's (1983) 1052-page treatise, *Fishes of Wisconsin*. The fishes of Indiana and Michigan have received less attention, although Shelby D. Gerking summarized in 1945 the first statewide surveys of the fishes of Indiana, and Reeve M. Bailey, William C. Latta, and Gerald R. Smith gave us in 2004 an atlas of distributions of fishes in Michigan.

This new book, *Fishes of the Chicago Region*, treats 31 families and 164 species, updates all previous information for the 13 major river drainages in the Chicago Region, and provides a large amount of new information for fishes in a rapidly changing area. It informs readers which fishes are native and were present when Europeans settlers arrived, which have been introduced from elsewhere and are now reproducing in the region, and which species, unfortunately, have been lost as part of the native fauna. The book is full of the morphological, ecological, and distributional information readers expect from a faunal monograph. We also learn about life histories of fishes, their value as commercial and sport fishes, and their conservation status.

Books that summarize information on large groups of organisms in a geographic area are of tremendous utility to scientists and others seeking information validated by experts. Francis Veraldi, Stephen Pescitelli, and Philip Willink have produced an excellent addition to that important assemblage of scientific contributions.

Larry M. Page, PhD
CURATOR OF FISHES, FLORIDA MUSEUM OF NATURAL HISTORY

Preface

The main goal of this book is to provide scientists, managers, teachers, students, naturalists, anglers, and other interested citizens with a comprehensive list and description of fishes within a colloquially acknowledged study area called the Chicago Region. Our prime focus was updating the distributions for all Chicago Region fish species. This book provides a centralized, geospatial database of fishes updating occurrence, distribution, and status of 164 fish species. More than 10,000 fish collections were included in our evaluation to provide one cohesive database for naturalists and scientists, documenting spatial distributions, frequency of occurrence, and temporal shifts in distribution and status. The maps featured here integrate volumes of records and help tell the history of the ichthyofauna within an area that has seen massive changes over the last 150 years, such as redirected waterways and extensive urban growth, as well as monumental improvements in water quality resulting from the Clean Water Act.

Also included is a pictorial family key, descriptions of each family, and descriptions of each species of fish, along with a summary of natural history with observations unique to the Chicago Region taken from nearly a hundred years of combined field experience by us, the authors. Comments on current and historic distribution of fishes also integrate the rich history of ichthyological study within the state and the region with this extensive experience. Photographs of each fish species were taken mostly from live or recently sampled fishes collected within the Chicago Region. Local museum specimens were used for extirpated or extremely rare species.

There is no official publication series for Chicago Region biota; however, there have been many publications that have focused on this unique ecological area, which has been recognized as "Globally Significant" (Chicago Wilderness 2011). Some of these publications include the seminal, widely used publication *Plants of the Chicago Region* by Floyd Swink and Gerould Wilhelm (1994) (recently updated as *Flora of the Chicago Region* by Gerould Wilhelm and Laura Rericha [2017]), *A Natural History of the Chicago Region* by Joel Greenburg (2002), as well as *Birds of the Chicago Region* by Edward R. Ford (1956).

Unlike the other taxonomic groups listed above, there is no publication dedicated to the fishes of the Chicago Region. Seth E. Meek and Samuel F. Hildebrand published "A Synoptic List of the Fishes Known to Occur within 50 Miles of Chicago" in 1910. Other books covering parts of the Chicago Region include: *The Distribution of the Fishes of Indiana* (Gerking 1945); *The Fishes of Illinois* (P. W. Smith 1979); *The Fishes of Wisconsin* (Becker 1983); *Fishes of the Great Lakes Region*, revised edition (Hubbs, Lagler, and Smith 2004); *An Atlas of Michigan Fishes* (R. M. Bailey, Latta, and Smith 2004); *Peterson Field Guide to Freshwater Fishes of North America* (Page and Burr 2011); *Fishes of Indiana* (Simon 2011); "An Updated Annotated List of Wisconsin's Fishes" (Lyons and Schmidt 2022); *Fish of Michigan* (Bosanko 2021); and *An Atlas of Illinois Fishes* (Metzke, Burr, et al. 2022). For those interested about local fish assemblages of the globally unique area surrounding Chicago — whether professional or another party — *Fishes of the Chicago Region* provides a comprehensive compilation covering portions of all 4 states with up-to-date information on status and distribution, photos, descriptions, and local authors' insights covering the diverse ichthyofauna in wide variety of habitats, including Lake Michigan, rivers and streams, wetlands, glacial lakes, and artificial reservoirs.

1

Introduction

Chicago Region Setting

The Chicago Region embraces the southern tip of Lake Michigan within the states of Illinois, Indiana, Wisconsin, and Michigan. It covers all or portions of 34 counties and spans an area of approximately 16,600 square miles, including Lake Michigan (figure 1.1). Swink and Wilhelm (1994) and Greenberg (2002) previously defined the Chicago Region using political boundaries to accommodate natural history records cited on a countywide basis. In 2007, the Chicago Wilderness Alliance redefined the Chicago Region (Chicago Wilderness 2011) to incorporate natural watersheds with county boundaries and is the resulting geographic area used for this book.

The climate of the Chicago Region is classified as humid continental, characterized by warm summers, cold winters, and frequent and sometimes extreme daily, monthly, and yearly fluctuations in temperature and precipitation. Average midsummer temperatures range from 60 to 80°F (15.6 to 26.7°C), whereas midwinter temperature ranges from 0 to 60°F (−17.8 to 15.6°C). Extreme low and high temperatures of record for the Chicago Region are −27°F (−32.8°C) and 104°F (40°C). Average annual rainfall is approximately 37.9 inches (96.3 cm), with the most rain falling between May and August. Snowfall averages 38.5 inches (97.8 cm) annually, with a high of 90 inches (228.6 cm). Natural vegetation communities include but are not limited to upland forest, floodplain forest, flatwoods, woodland, savanna, shrubland, prairie, marsh, bog, fen,

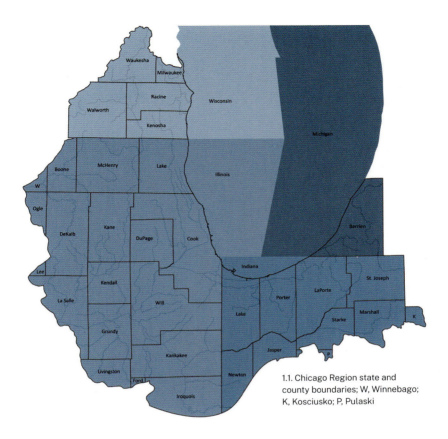

1.1. Chicago Region state and county boundaries; W, Winnebago; K, Kosciusko; P, Pulaski

sedge meadow, panne, seep, spring, cliff, ridge/swale, knob/kettle, and dune (Swink and Wilhelm 1994; Chicago Wilderness 2011). However, with almost 8 million residents, much of the natural lands have been converted for agriculture and urban development.

There are 13 major watersheds within the Chicago Region (figure 1.2) — namely, the St. Joseph River, the Galien River, the Calumet River, the Chicago Lake Plain, the Chicago River, the Pike River, the Root River, Lake Michigan (Grand Mere, Trail Creek, North Shore), the Kankakee River, the Des Plaines River, the Fox River, the Rock River, and the Illinois River. Most are entirely within the boundaries of the Chicago Region, with only portions of the St. Joseph, Illinois, and Rock River watersheds located within. Rivers and major tributaries are shown in figure 1.3.

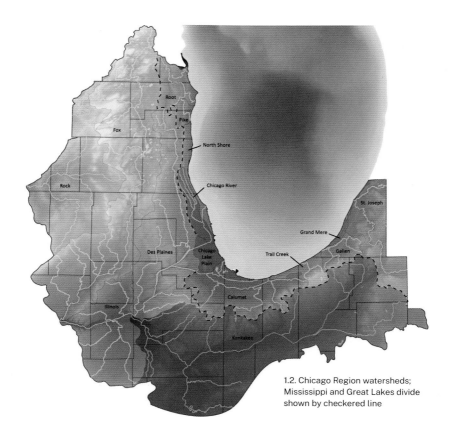

1.2. Chicago Region watersheds; Mississippi and Great Lakes divide shown by checkered line

Historically, the Illinois River basin naturally had seasonal yet substantial wetland connections with the Great Lakes basin (see figure 1.2), shown as the gap in the natural basin divide. This condition allowed for the migration of certain fish species between the 2 basins. It was extensive, allowing fishes to recolonize the Great Lakes basin post-glaciation from refugia in the Mississippi River basin. This condition allowed the Chicago and Calumet Rivers, as well as portions of the lower Des Plaines and upper Illinois Rivers, to be modified extensively from their natural hydrography. These waterways are now part of what is known as the Chicago Area Waterway System. This major modification is commonly known as the reversal of the Chicago River and is considered one of the largest engineering projects ever completed. Although the reversal of the Chicago River is credited for saving area residents from health and disease problems, the result of sending massive amounts of sewage and animal waste downstream impacted

1.3. Major streams of the Chicago Region; arrows indicate direction of flow

the entire Illinois River and the Mississippi River as far south as St. Louis. The Clean Water Act of 1972 led to improvement in wastewater control and treatment; in recent years, water quality has vastly improved across the Chicago Region. However, the current state of water-treatment methods and overflows during large storms still causes issues in every major watershed.

Dams also have a substantial negative impact within the Chicago Region as they have throughout the country. More than 180 dams and fish-migration barriers have been identified in the Chicago Region and can be found in every major watershed. These barriers fragment stream corridors, preventing natural migration and recolonization. Combined with historic habitat and water-quality degradation, the dams have contributed to extensive extirpation of localized fish and mussel species. Although the habitat and water quality have improved in many of these streams and the streams could support additional species, dams have continued to block migration back into these upstream areas. Fortunately, governmental agencies and nongovernmental groups have made partnerships and progress after many years of struggle against dam-removal opposition. Leadership provided by the Illinois Department of Natural Resources, the US Army Corps of Engineers, and county forest preserves have recently led to the removal of many dams within the St. Joseph, Des Plaines, Chicago, Kankakee, Fox, and Root River watersheds. Evaluation of some of these older connectivity projects have documented substantial riverine habitat improvements in former dam pools, as well as the reestablishment of missing fish species in upstream areas (Pescitelli 2018; Pescitelli and Widloe 2018; Deegan 2022).

Other major impacts to riverine systems include those that prevent meandering and migration within the stream's floodplain. Natural processes associated with moving streams and rivers create and sustain dynamic habitats over time, such as riffles, pools, sand and gravel bars, islands, oxbows, backwaters, and sidestream wetlands. The moving river is also able to sequester habitat-valuable large woody debris and substrates from banks through natural erosive and depositional processes. When a river is not allowed to move and erode its banks, it eventually forms a static channel that becomes homogeneous or devoid of useful fish habitats. Lakes are similar — the shoreline–water interface is most diverse when natural erosional and depositional processes are left unchecked. Just like dams in a river, shoreline armoring halts natural processes and in turn homogenizes and degrades littoral fish habitats.

Fish Habitats

Natural aquatic systems supporting fishes in the Chicago Region include marshes, swamps, glacial lakes, small coldwater rivulets, seasonal headwater creeks, warmwater streams, and wide, deep warmwater rivers. Unnatural and modified aquatic systems such as canals, reservoirs, abandoned quarries, impoundments, farm ponds, and ditches support fish as well. The Chicago Region once boasted both fish-diverse and geologically unique natural features such as Lake Michigan, the Grand Calumet River wetland complex, the Saganashkee Slough, Mud Lake, the Grand Kankakee Marsh, and Beaver Lake, as well as tallgrass-prairie streams and a multitude of clear glacial lakes that dotted the region. Most of these natural features have been modified to varying degrees or in some cases destroyed.

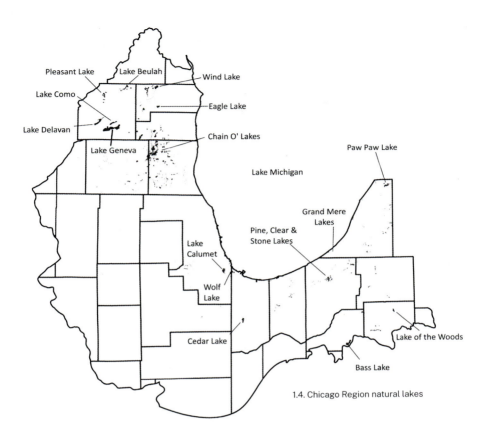

1.4. Chicago Region natural lakes

Categorization of aquatic systems is rather arbitrary in some instances, since there is a continuum of many habitats or an interlaced habitat mosaic. Considering this mosaic, the following section describes each of the regionally occurring habitats, giving local examples of fish species that may occupy each habitat.

Lakes

Natural lakes within the Chicago Region are shown in figure 1.4. Most of these natural lakes were sculpted by the last glaciation, during the Wisconsin glacial episode that took place 75,000–11,000 years ago, and are typically termed glacial lakes. Glacial lakes are generally located along the drainage-basin divides of the Fox and Des Plaines Rivers, between the Lake Michigan basin and the Kankakee River, and throughout Berrien County, Michigan. Colonization by fishes was made possible through historic connectivity of glacial meltwater bodies and recent connectivity through wetlands and streams. As these connective waters subsided, fish were trapped, and the species that endured are present today in some of the higher-quality lakes. Lakes with stream and river connections may have lake species as well as transient riverine species.

Lakes typically follow a succession from oligotrophic (lower-nutrient) to eutrophic (higher-nutrient) condition, eventually succeeding to wetland and ultimately prairie or forest. This process of succession, studied by Henry Cowles and Victor Shelford in the early 1900s, is driven by sediment, detrital, and nutrient exchange. Oligotrophic lakes are clear and usually deep — for example, Lake Michigan (figure 1.5) and Lake Geneva. Indicative fish species of oligotrophic lakes are deep-basin dwellers such as sculpins, whitefishes, and Lake Chars (Trout), which can tolerate temperatures as low as 35.6°F (2°C). The food chain these fishes depend on start with primary production near the surface and littoral zone, which mixes down to lower depths during the fall-to-winter turnover, when thermally stratified water layers intermix. Habitat structure may consist of clay mounds, rock outcrops, woody debris, and micro-topography of the bottom. The shallower littoral zone lies near the shoreline and has a much greater diversity of fishes. Habitat here consists of rock outcrops, cobble, gravel, and sand bottoms with quiescent areas able to support aquatic vegetation. Indicative species of an oligotrophic lake's littoral zone include Mimic Shiner, Bluntnose Minnow, Rock Bass, and Smallmouth Bass. Associated with vegetated areas you will find a greater diversity, including Pugnose Shiner, Blacknose Shiner, Lake Chubsucker, sunfish, Iowa Darter, Least Darter, and Western Banded Killifish.

In contrast to oligotrophic lakes, eutrophic lakes have a rich supply of nutrients typically supporting denser levels of aquatic vegetation and algal growth, leading to higher fish productivity. Eutrophic lakes are typically shallower and may have primary production throughout very large littoral zones. Here you'll find habitat structure consisting primarily of rooted and floating aquatic macrophytes over gravel, sand, or organic sediment. Root wads, undercut banks, and fallen trees also provide habitat. Indicative species of healthy eutrophic lakes are Blackchin Shiner, Blacknose Shiner, Pugnose Shiner, Starhead Topminnow, Warmouth, Iowa Darter, and Least Darter. Examples of healthy eutrophic lakes are Cross and Camp Lakes of the Fox River drainage and the Grand Mere Lakes in Berrien County, Michigan.

1.5. Lake Michigan, Ft. Sheridan, Lake County, Illinois

A hypereutrophic lake occurs naturally over geologic time through the accumulation of detritus, nutrients, and sediment. This type of lake becomes shallow and extremely dense with aquatic vegetation (figure 1.6), moving toward the next succession of aquatic habitats: the wetland. Many lakes within our region have already reached this point due to anthropogenic modifications, also called cultural eutrophication. This condition may require measures such as lake dredging and/or dam building to deepen the lake for recreational purposes.

Most natural lakes in the Chicago Region were first impacted by agricultural practices, followed by influences from extensive urbanization. Causes of lake degradation include the removal of native-fringe wetland and buffering vegetation, the introduction of invasive species, excessive nutrient inputs, recreational boating, the development of shorelines, and intentional fish kills to improve conditions for sport fishes. Temporary or isolated ponds found in forests or prairies are known as ephemeral or vernal ponds and

INTRODUCTION   9

1.6. Huntley Lake, Lake County, Illinois: Iowa Darter, Tadpole Madtom, Black Crappie

typically do not support fish, due to seasonal drying and freezing. In the absence of predatory fish, these habitats are quite important for amphibians such as salamanders and frogs.

Wetlands

Riverine backwaters, floodplain swamps, headwater marshes, and bogs are classified as wetland habitats that also support fish populations. High-quality examples of these habitats are very rare in the Chicago Region nowadays, but were historically vast, including the sidestream marshes of the upper Fox River, the floodplain swamps of the Grand Kankakee Marsh (figure 1.7), the backwaters of the Illinois River, and the headwater marshes of the upper Des Plaines River. The Calumet River system itself was a large marshy expanse with no defined river channel. The disappearance and degradation of these habitats generally resulted from hydrologic alteration, filling, and dredging. Specific reasons for these alterations included the need to provide drainage for agriculture and urban development; channelization for increased drainage, flood control, and navigation; the construction of berms and dikes for flood control; and the raising of water levels through damming for recreation. Some backwaters where sustaining riverine processes were halted for human uses are artificially maintained via dredging and water-control structures, but access by migrating fishes may be variable.

1.7. Seining a side-channel wetland, Kankakee River, Kankakee County, Illinois: Starhead Topminnow, Ironcolor Shiner, Pirate Perch

Wetlands were once common along Lake Michigan in quiescent and inland connected areas such as Wolf Lake and Lake Calumet. However, nearly all these areas have been developed, as they are prime conditions for boat harbors and recreation. Recent efforts have restored small fragments of lakeside marsh (figure 1.8).

The fish species currently found in wetland habitats are typically adapted to extreme seasonal changes in water levels and water-quality conditions. Some species leave backwaters and take refuge in main-channel habitats during low-water conditions (sunfish and Northern Pike), while some endure low-water/low-oxygen conditions (Central Mudminnow and Bluntnose Darter). These habitats are important, as they are rich in food, provide areas for spawning, and act as nurseries for juvenile fishes. Valuable fish habitats in wetlands include an abundance of high-

1.8. Northerly Island Lacustuary Marsh, Cook County, Illinois: Northern Pike, Black Buffalo, Silver Redhorse

quality native plants such as Pickerelweed (*Pontederia cordata*), pondweeds (*Potamogeton* spp.), and Buttonbush (*Cephalanthus occidentalis*), which provide diverse cover, substrate, and food (aquatic macroinvertebrates).

Ephemeral Streams

Intermittent headwater streams seasonally become devoid of water or have isolated pools with no flow during parts of the year (figure 1.9). Spring freshets and summer storms are the primary sources of hydrology where these systems occur near drainage-basin fringes. These small streams have substrates of clay hardpan, gravel, cobble, silt, and muck and are frequently colonized by terrestrial plants such as sedges (*Carex* spp.). The terrestrial plants provide spawning habitat for Brook Stickleback, Fathead Minnow, Western Blacknose Dace, and Grass Pickerel. These species migrate upstream during spring freshets and storms to take advantage of habitat with reduced predator density. After spawning, fish will migrate downstream to a permanent water source or may remain in isolated pools within the headwater stream. Many of these streams have been channelized for agricultural drainage and are recognizable as ditches or canals. Typically, the nonnative Reed Canary Grass (*Phalaris arundinacea*) becomes the dominant land cover, causing impairment.

1.9. Ephemeral stream with dry streambed, Little Rock Creek, Kendall County, Illinois

Cold Headwater Streams

Cold water conditions often occur in the small, first-order streams in the Chicago Region where groundwater discharge or seeps are abundant (figure 1.10). Keep in mind, though, that there can be cold groundwater upwellings in any given stream, river, or lake. Coldwater streams predominantly occur in Berrien County, Michigan, but may also be found in the Fox River drainage in Wisconsin and Illinois and in the northeast portion of the Kankakee River drainage in Indiana. These small streams are of 2 types: 1 having substrates of cobble, gravel, and sand with woody debris, the other having a substrate of sand, woody debris, detritus, and aquatic vegetation. These streams are relatively nutrient poor and typically support lower fish-species richness compared to warmer, nutrient-rich streams. Fishes indicative of cold headwater streams include American Brook Lamprey, Brook Char (Trout), Western Blacknose Dace, Southern Redbelly Dace, Brook Stickleback, and Mottled Sculpin. Coldwater stream habitats are declining due to increases in water temperature through agricultural and urban development of recharge zones, groundwater depletion, stormwater conveyance, the introduction of European Brown Trout, and the removal of riparian vegetation. Warming temperatures resulting from climate change may also change these streams.

1.10. Coldwater stream with groundwater input, Little Calumet River Headwater, LaPorte County, Indiana: Chestnut Lamprey, Creek Chubsucker, Western Blacknose Dace

1.11. Low-gradient stream, upper Somonauk Creek, DeKalb County, Illinois: Ozark Minnow, Common Shiner

Perennial Streams

The perennial stream habitat is dynamic and quite diverse in structure and species composition. Stream types range from low-gradient, well-vegetated streams (figure 1.11) to medium-gradient streams of gravel and cobble (figure 1.12). Stream substrates include bedrock, boulder, cobble, gravel, sand, clay hardpan, and silt. Habitat consists of undercut banks, deep pools, tree-root masses, herbaceous-root masses, logs, woody debris, detritus, and aquatic macrophytes. The presence of fish species varies, depending on geographic location and longitudinal position within the stream. For example, the St. Joseph, Fox, and Kankakee River systems flow over diverse geomorphology and glacial deposition, providing a multitude of different habitats and flow velocities and so supporting high fish-species richness. Some perennial streams, like Tyler and Big Rock Creeks of the Fox River in Illinois, and Christiana Creek of the St. Joseph River in Michigan, have high groundwater input producing what could be termed coolwater habitats. The lower water temperatures favor species such as the Mottled Sculpin and the Greenside Darter. Fish assemblages in the

upper Des Plaines, Chicago, and Calumet River systems naturally have lower fish-species richness due to low topographic relief and the relatively young age of the stream valleys, which provide less habitat and hydrologic diversity. Dominant habitat features are deep pools and runs with aquatic macrophytes and large woody debris. Although most streams have suffered from degradation, lower-gradient streams are vulnerable to sedimentation and are more often channelized than higher-gradient channels. Due to difficulties in restoring streams, the preservation of high-quality reaches should be a high priority. Simply providing streams the sufficient space to allow fluvial processes is a first step to maintaining and restoring diverse channel morphology and habitats.

Rivers

Riverine habitats typically have the highest fish-species richness due to the overall volume of habitat area and increased diversity of habitats. For example, the largest river habitat is the Illinois River near Channahon, Illinois, in which nearly 80 fish species have been recorded. Lower portions of the Des Plaines, Kankakee, and Fox (figure 1.13) Rivers in Illinois and the lower sections of the St. Joseph River in Michigan are considered larger-river habitats.

1.12. (*opposite*) High-gradient stream, Horse Creek, Will County, Illinois: Eastern Sand Darter, Slenderhead Darter, Rosyface Shiner
1.13. (*above*)Midsize-river habitat, Fox River, Kendall County, Illinois: Shorthead Redhorse, Highfin Carpsucker, Flathead Catfish

Midsize rivers include middle and upper portions of the Fox, Des Plaines (figure 1.14), Kankakee, St. Joseph Rivers, and the lower DuPage River. Smaller rivers include the Yellow River (figure 1.15) and the Mazon River and Aux Sable Creek as well as the uppermost portions of the larger rivers.

1.14. Low-gradient upper Des Plaines River, Lake County, Illinois: Blackchin Shiner, Logperch, Hornyhead Chub

Riverine systems provide highly diverse channel habitat structure due to high flows and associated power that sculpt the landscape. In-channel habitats consist of deep pools, large woody debris, large cobble and boulder riffles, undercut banks, vegetated backwaters, and large floodplains. River substrates are dependent on the underlying glacial deposits and stream power, and may include bedrock, boulder, cobble, gravel, sand, clay hardpan, silt, and detritus. Many sections of the Fox, Kankakee, and Root Rivers (figure 1.16) have large riffle and pool sequences that support fishes such as suckers (Catostomidae), madtoms (Ictaluridae), darters (Percidae), and Smallmouth Bass. Riverine habitats have some of the rarer species of the Chicago Region, which include the Pallid Shiner, the River Redhorse, the Greater Redhorse, the Freckled Madtom, and the Bluntnose Darter.

1.15. (*above*) Yellow River, Marshall County, Indiana: Northern Brook Lamprey, Mottled Sculpin, Silverjaw Minnow
1.16. (*over*) Root River, Racine County, Wisconsin: Longnose Sucker, Stonecat, Bigmouth Shiner

2

Book Organization

Family Accounts

There are 31 families recorded from the Chicago Region including those for established nonnative species. The family accounts are generally presented in 3 parts, providing information on global distribution, identifying characteristics, shared natural history traits, and ecology. Other interesting aspects are noted, including their commercial and recreational use.

Species Accounts

There are currently 164 established species recorded from the Chicago Region, of which 147 are native and 17 are nonnative. Species in this book are organized alphabetically within each family account, first by genus, then species name. Nomenclature and hierarchical listing of families follows the most up-to-date publications on the subject matter (Page and Burr 2011; Metzke, Burr, et al. 2022). However, this is an evolving science, and based on current trends, we anticipate taxonomic and nomenclature changes.

The etymology of the scientific names was included to add interest and additional information for each species. Names are usually derived from Latin or Greek, some from Native American languages, referring to some characteristic, location, or behavior of the fish. Quite often fish are named for scientists who initially described them, or in honor of mentors or significant others.

Description

Prominent characteristics useful in identifying each species are presented in this section. Characteristics include body shape and size, size and configuration of the mouth and eyes, coloration and pigmentation patterns, fin position and fin ray counts, number of scales, and size, as well as other physical attributes. Similar species are also noted, along with descriptions of distinguishing characteristics.

An aid to fish identification with anatomical figures is provided as an appendix at the end of the species accounts. Scientific terms are used in some cases but defined in the text when first appearing in the accounts or multiple times for uncommonly used terms. (A glossary is included in the back matter to define descriptive terminology.)

Natural History

This section provides typical natural history traits and behaviors, including preferred habitats, food and eating habits, reproductive strategies, and age and growth. We've attempted to provide a regional perspective by including personal observations in addition to well-established information on species' life histories and habitats.

Distribution and Status

The global distribution of each species is provided for a broader context, followed by details on Chicago Region occurrences using georeferenced maps. Additional information of interest is offered for some species' records to paint a historical picture. Status statements may include comments on relative abundance, frequency of occurrence, environmental sensitivity, and nativity, as well as use by commercial fisheries and recreational sport fishing. Official threatened or endangered species status for each state in the Chicago Region is indicated, along with comments based on our experience.

A geospatial database of Chicago Region fish records and observations was assembled to map the occurrences of all recorded fishes. A significant effort was expended between 1998 and 2023 to collect and incorporate every possible source of fish-locality data for the region. Although the intent was to make this database as inclusive as possible, it is difficult to capture all data, and new fish records will be generated.

All data presented on maps included in *Fishes of the Chicago Region* consists of collections with museum-voucher specimens or those identified in reports and surveys from reliable sources. Museum collections include the Field Museum of Natural History (FMNH), the Illinois Natural History Survey (INHS), Southern Illinois University (SIU), the Milwaukee Public Museum (MPM), the University of Michigan (UM), the California Academy of Sciences (CAS), and Auburn University (AU). Databases include the Illinois Department of Natural Resources (ILDNR), the Indiana Department of Natural Resources (INDNR), the Wisconsin Department of Natural Resources Fish Mapping Application (WDNR), the Michigan Fish Atlas Database (MIFA), the Illinois Environmental Protection Agency (IEPA), the Indiana Department of Environmental Management (IDEM) (Werbianskyj 2023), the Lake County (Illinois) Forest Preserves (LCFP), and the City of Elkhart (Indiana). Important historic data contributions include Jordan (1877–1890), E. W. Nelson (1878), Evermann and Jenkins (1892), Eigenmann and Beeson (1894), Hay (1896), Blatchley and Ashley (1901), Forbes and Richardson (1908), Meek and Hildebrand (1910), Koelz (1929), T. L. Hankinson (1919), Greene (1935), Dolley (1937), Hubbs and Trautman (1937), Shelford (1937), Ricker and Gottschalk (1941), Gerking (1945), Smith (1979), Becker (1983), and Page (1979–1998). There has also been significant effort on our parts to collect additional field data, verify dubious records, and update species nomenclature for which there are preserved and catalogued specimens to confirm identification. Records considered uncertain or dubious were excluded from these hard-copy maps.

All fish collections made within the Chicago Region are shown in figure 2.1. There are more than 10,100 collection records that span from 1869 to 2022. Each dot on the map represents a collection of fishes made at a particular place on a specific date. The collective grouping of all dots presented for each species indicates its general distribution within the Chicago Region. Species records that are ubiquitous through time are depicted by a solid-colored dot (●), as there was no depictable temporal pattern in the data. Some species warranted showing multiple symbols using different colored solid dots (●/●/●) to depict a visual difference in temporal distribution, a change in species classification, or a dispersal pattern of a migrating species. Date ranges associated with a given

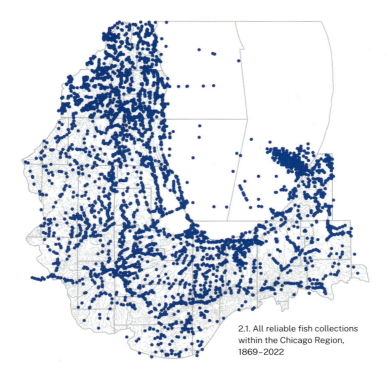

2.1. All reliable fish collections within the Chicago Region, 1869–2022

dot encapsulate the data from the first collection made to the last one made.

References

The list of references for each species includes all publications used to characterize each species for well-established information on descriptions, habitats, and life histories. Individual references are cited within the text for unique or new information, and to provide occurrence-record credit in the "Distribution and Status" section. Any information provided without reference is from our knowledge or is already established as common knowledge.

3

Pictorial Key to the Families

1a Snake-like or eel-like body; pelvic and pectoral fins absent; jaws absent, with an oral suction disk; 7 external gill openings per side
→ **Lampreys (Petromyzontidae)**

1b Pectoral fins present; pelvic fins usually present; jaws present; 1 external gill opening per side → **2**

2b Pelvic fins present; body not snake-like → **3**

3a 10 or more barbels surrounding mouth; elongated cylindrical body → **Loaches (Cobitidae)**

3b 8 or fewer barbels surrounding mouth; body shape variable → **4**

4a Dorsal fin single, extending much over half of body length; anterior nostrils tubular, but not extending to or over bottom mandible; gular plate present → **Bowfins (Amiidae)**

4b Dorsal fin single or double; anterior nostrils not tubular; gular plate absent → **5**

5a Caudal fin deeply forked; backbone clearly extending into upper tail → **6**

5b Caudal fin forked or other; backbone not clearly extending into upper lobe of tail fin → **7**

→ **Paddlefishes (Polyodontidae)**

b   Rostrum conical or shovel-like; subterminal mouth well behind eye; 4 conspicuous ventral barbels → **Sturgeons (Acipenseridae)**

a   Elongated jaws with many teeth; body completely covered with hard, plate-like, diamond-shaped scales (ganoid) → **Gars (Lepisosteidae)**

b   Jaws not elongated; scales absent, or flexible and overlapping (ctenoid or cycloid) → **8**

8a Adipose fin present → **9**

8b Adipose fin absent → **12**

9a Body with no scales; barbels present; first spine of pectoral fin resistive and prominent → **North American Catfishes (Ictaluridae)**

9b Body scaled; barbels absent; first spine of pectoral fin flimsy and flexible → **10**

0a Axillary process at base of pelvic fin present → **Salmon, Trout, Chars, and Whitefishes (Salmonidae)**

0b Axillary process at base of pelvic fin absent → **11**

a Scales ctenoid; body moderately translucent; mandible and maxilla relatively flush; pearl organs present along lower jaw and cheek; mouth does not extend well past front of eye → **Trout-perches (Percopsidae)**

b Scales cycloid; body silvery; lower jaw strongly protuberant; pearl organs absent; mouth extends well past front of eye → **Smelts (Osmeridae)**

PICTORIAL KEY TO THE FAMILIES 31

12a Anus located on ventral side of head in adults; body dark purple brown → **Pirate Perches (Aphredoderidae)**

12b Anus located immediately anterior to anal fin → **13**

13a Second dorsal and anal fins each with 60 or more rays; barbel p on tip of chin → **Burbots (Lotidae)**

4a Dorsal fin consisting of 2 or more spines not connected by a membrane
→ **Sticklebacks (Gasterosteidae)**

4b Dorsal fin without spines or with spines always connected by membrane
→ **15**

5a 1 dorsal fin → **16**

5b 2 dorsal fins → **26**

PICTORIAL KEY TO THE FAMILIES   33

16a Dorsal fin with stout, serrated spine → **Barbs and Carps (Cyprinidae)**

16b Dorsal fin without stout, serrated spine → **17**

Anal fin long, 15 or more anal rays, ventral portion of abdomen with sharp keel; adipose eyelid present (may be poorly developed) → **19**

3b Anal fin short; 14 or fewer anal rays; ventral portion of abdomen without sharp keel; adipose eyelid absent → **20**

9a Ventral portion of abdomen with sharp, sawtooth keel; origin of dorsal fin well in advance of origin of anal fin → **Shads and Herrings (Clupeidae)**

9b Ventral portion of abdomen with sharp, smooth keel; origin of dorsal fin slightly posterior to or slightly anterior of origin of anal fin
→ **Mooneyes (Hiodontidae)**

PICTORIAL KEY TO THE FAMILIES   35

20a Lips thick; lips plicate or papillose; 9 or more dorsal rays; when anal rays are pressed against the body, they reach or almost reach caudal fin origin → **Suckers (Catostomidae)**

(usually 85 or less in lateral line); pectoral fin not reaching to pelvic fin → **22**

22a Distance from tip of snout to origin of anal fin (A) 3 times longer than distance from origin of anal fin to base of tail fin (B) → **Sharpbellies (Xenocyprididae) B**

22b Distance from tip of snout to origin of anal fin (A) 2.5 times or less than distance from origin of anal fin to base of tail fin (B) → **True Minnows (Leuciscidae)**

23a (from 17b) Upper and lower jaws form a duck-like beak; jaws with large canine teeth → **Pikes (Esocidae)**

PICTORIAL KEY TO THE FAMILIES 37

24a Origin of anal fin well behind origin of dorsal fin base; mouth terminal; premaxillaries not protractible → **Mudminnows (Umbridae)**

24b Origin of anal fin anterior to or about even with origin of dorsal fin; mouth superior; premaxillaries protractible → **25**

25a Body with dark vertical bars or dark longitudinal stripe, anal fin of male without gonopodium; female without black spot on body near origin of anal fin → **Topminnows (Fundulidae)**

25b Body without dark vertical bars or dark longitudinal stripe; scales larger (30 or less in lateral line) and outlined with pigment; dark spot below eye; anal fin of male with gonopodium → **Livebearers (Poeciliidae)**

26a Pelvic fins fused together to form 1 suction disc → **Gobies (Gobiidae)**

PICTORIAL KEY TO THE FAMILIES   39

26b Pelvic fins separate → **27**

27a Body dorsally compressed; 4 or fewer pelvic rays; no scales; very large pectoral fin → **Sculpins (Cottidae)**

27b Body laterally compressed or conical; 5 or more pelvic rays; body completely scaled → **28**

8a Anterior and posterior dorsal fins situated over anal fin; body extremely slender; first dorsal fin with 6 or fewer spines → **Silversides (Atherinopsidae)**

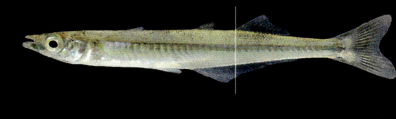

8b Anterior dorsal fin situated well in advance of anal fin origin; body not extremely slender; first dorsal fin with 6 or more spines → **29**

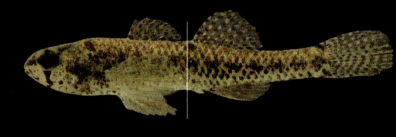

9a Lateral line extends onto caudal fin; 24 or more soft rays in second dorsal fin → **Drums (Sciaenidae)**

PICTORIAL KEY TO THE FAMILIES   41

29b Lateral line, if present, does not extend onto caudal fin; 23 or fewer soft rays in second dorsal fin → **30**

30a 1 or 2 anal spines; body more conical → **Perches (Percidae)**

30b 3 or more anal spines; body slab sided → **31**

31a Sharp spine on opercle present; dorsal fins separate or slightly connected; rear edge of gill cover serrated → **White Basses (Moronidae)**

31b Sharp spine on opercle absent, dorsal fins connected, rear edge of gill cover smooth → **Sunfishes (Centrarchidae)**

PICTORIAL KEY TO THE FAMILIES

Species
Accounts

4

Lampreys

Petromyzontidae

Species within the family Petromyzontidae are characterized by an eel-like body with external muscle segmentation (myomeres), a cartilaginous skeleton, distinct genital papillae, and 7 pore-like gill openings. All lampreys lack jaws, median fins, scales, pelvic and shoulder girdles, and ribs. Adults have an oral suction disc that may contain many or few keratinous teeth. Figure 4.1 shows the distinctive oral hoods and dentition that lampreys typically have. The larvae have the long eel-like body but lack the distinctive oral disk (figure 4.1, A) developed in adults.

Lampreys have an interesting life cycle that includes the long larval stage of the ammocoete. The elusive ammocoete remains burrowed in sand or soft sediments of a stream and filter feeds on phytoplankton and zooplankton from the water column and substrate. After metamorphosis into the adult stage around mid-summer, parasitic species of lampreys will begin to feed on fishes, while nonparasitic species may not feed at all. Parasitic lampreys will attach to a host fish with its oral disc teeth and suction by the oral hood; the rough tongue rasps an open wound so that bodily fluids may be drawn out as food.

Spawning takes place in spring, when lampreys locate suitable areas with adequate water velocities and rocky substrates. Nests are constructed by 1 or both sexes by moving gravel and pebbles around with the oral disc. The female latches on to a cobble or boulder with her oral disc so the genital vent is oriented over the nest. Usually lampreys are monogamous — only 1 male will attach to the nape of the female, dangling his body over the nest to release milt (sperm fluid) simultaneous to egg release. Released eggs and milt penetrate the interstitial spaces of the gravel, where incubation occurs. Once the eggs incubate and hatch, the ammocoete will float downstream to a suitable area where it can burrow and filter feed.

Lampreys are a very ancient group of Agnathans (jawless fishes) appearing in the fossil record more than 500 million years ago. They are the precursors to the ray-finned fishes (Class: Actinopterygii). There are 40 species of lamprey worldwide within 6 genera that inhabit coastal and inland waters, with some species living at sea and spawning in freshwater (anadromous), and inland species living entirely in freshwater. This group has an anti-tropical distribution, meaning they are found in cooler waters north of the Tropic of Cancer and south of the Tropic of Capricorn where 4 species are found in South America, New Zealand, and Australia. There are 23 species in North America, 5 of which can be found within the Chicago Region.

Lampreys are ecologically important due to their role in the food chain. During the ammocoete stage, they convert energy derived from tiny organisms that are unable to directly nourish larger fish; in turn, they become prey items for large game and predatory fishes. Parasitic lampreys influence the genetics and health of fish populations and are driving part of natural selection. A weak fish that is parasitized by a lamprey would most likely perish or become unable to reproduce, promoting healthy genetics from that species' gene pool.

Native lampreys are consumed by humans under the culinary term *lampfries* and are utilized by anglers as bait. Native freshwater lampreys are a group of concern due to their staged life cycle's dependency on habitat connectivity, functional riverine processes, and good water quality.

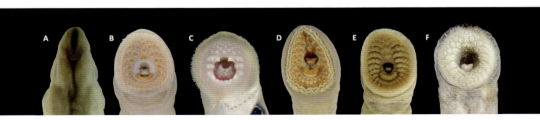

4.1. Lamprey oral hoods and dentition: (A) *P. marinus* ammocoete, (B) *P. marinus*, (C) *L. appendix*, (D) *I. unicuspis*, (E) *I. castaneus*, (F) *I. fossor*

Chestnut Lamprey

Ichthyomyzon castaneus • *Ichthyomyzon* means "fish sucker" in Greek; *castaneus*, Latin, means "chestnut," referring to the adult coloration.

Description: The adult Chestnut Lamprey has a large oral disc with 2–3 teeth directly above the mouth (supraoral), 1–10 (usually around 6) endolateral teeth, and a weakly bilobed or linear transverse lingual laminae (bottom part of tongue) (figure 4.1, E). The color is variable — usually chestnut, but ranging from grayish to tan. Both adults and ammocoetes have dark pigmentation in the lateral line organ. The adult Chestnut Lamprey can be distinguished from other species within the genus *Ichthyomyzon* by its dentition and a larger oral disc–to–total length ratio (6.3:9.1), and from the Sea Lamprey and the American Brook Lamprey by having fewer myomeres (49–56) and a continuous dorsal fin. This species can reach up to 15 inches (380 mm) long.

Natural History: The adult Chestnut Lamprey inhabits large rivers and lakes; ammocoetes and their young are found in smaller headwater streams. The natural history of this species is similar to other parasitic lampreys: spawning takes place in small headwater streams, in cobble and gravel riffles. The ammocoetes burrow in silt or sandbars with sufficient organic debris. During this period, the larvae will feed on detritus and phytoplankton via filtration. Once the Chestnut Lamprey matures, it feeds by parasitizing most large-bodied fish species, rarely causing death of the host.

Distribution and Status: The Chestnut Lamprey occurs naturally within the Red River, Mississippi River, Great Lakes, and St. Lawrence

Chestnut Lamprey records, 1878–2022

basins, and in a few Gulf slope drainages. Records for the Chicago Region are primarily from Lake Michigan and tributary streams — principally, the St. Joseph River and Calumet Rivers. The earliest recorded specimen of the Chestnut Lamprey within the Chicago Region is from Lake Michigan at Whiting, Indiana, in 1900 (FMNH). Reproduction is noted from the Little Calumet River system, with ammocoete records taken from the headwaters in LaPorte County, Indiana, in 2010. There is 1 record for the Illinois River, LaSalle County, Illinois (INHS 1998), where it is also native but much rarer. The Chestnut Lamprey is in danger of becoming extirpated throughout the Great Lakes due to management practices targeted at the nonnative Sea Lamprey, including dams and habitat degradation. The Chestnut Lamprey is still common in the St. Joseph River in Indiana in reaches where no species-specific lampricides are applied (Cochran et al. 2015). We consider this a species of special concern within the Chicago Region.

References: Cochran et al. 2015; Hubbs and Lagler 1964; Hubbs and Trautman 1937

Lamprey

Ichthyomyzon fossor • *Ichthyomyzon* in Greek means "fish sucker"; *fossor* is Latin for "digger," in reference to the burrowing or nest-building habits of lampreys.

Illinois Natural History Survey Specimen #90911

Description: The adult Northern Brook Lamprey has an oral disc much narrower than the width of its body, where the oral disc diameter–to–total body length ratio is 3.6:4.9. The dentition of this species is weak, with a thin layer of skin covering some teeth. There are 1 to 2 supraoral teeth, a row of unicuspid endolateral teeth, and a moderately to strongly bilobed transverse lingual lamina (figure 4.1, F). Ammocoete and immature adults are generally gray to brown on the back and sides and yellow on the belly and fins. Spawning adults observed from Marshall County, Indiana, were completely slate blue. The adult Northern Brook Lamprey can be distinguished from other species within the genus *Ichthyomyzon* by their weak dentition, and from the Sea Lamprey and the American Brook Lamprey by having fewer myomeres (47–56) and a continuous dorsal fin. This species may reach lengths up to 6.5 inches (170 mm).

Natural History: The Northern Brook Lamprey occurs in small rivers, preferring clear, cool water. Adults of this species are nonparasitic and likely do not feed, living only long enough to spawn. Early life stages require silt or sandbars with organic matter, usually covered by aquatic vegetation. Spawning takes place in swift current over boulders, cobble, and gravel. On May 1, 2001, 5 adult Northern Brook Lamprey were observed spawning in the Yellow River of Marshall County, Indiana. The lampreys attached to a large boulder in a very swift portion of a riffle; however, they were attached in a turbulence-free zone (eddy) directly behind the boulder that deflected the current to the sides. Immediately below the boulder, Northern Brook Lampreys were spawning in gravel and pebbles. Adults die within a few days after spawning. There was likely groundwater discharge at this site, as the water was very cold and adjacent to a riparian fen.

Distribution and Status: The Northern Brook Lamprey occurs naturally in the Hudson Bay, Great Lakes–St. Lawrence Seaway, Mississippi River, and Ohio River basins, and the Ozarks. Throughout this distribution, populations are localized and disjunct, suggesting a once more common and wider distribution throughout the Midwest. The Northern Brook Lamprey was documented for the first time within the Chicago Region in 1919 from the Galien River, Berrien County, Michigan (UM). Since then, it has been observed only 40 times. We last observed this species from the Yellow River in Marshall County, Indiana, in 2001 (INHS). Although the Northern Brook Lamprey is very rare in the Chicago Region, recent collections were made in the Mukwanago River, Wisconsin (WIDNR 2021), and the Yellow River system, Indiana (IDEM 2017). This species is listed as endangered in Illinois, and of special concern in Indiana.

References: Cochran et al. 2015; Hubbs and Lagler 1964; Hubbs and Trautman 1937; Willink and Dreslik 2023a

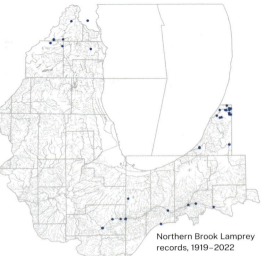

Northern Brook Lamprey records, 1919–2022

LAMPREYS (PETROMYZONTIDAE)　51

Field Museum Specimen #73646

Description: The adult Silver Lamprey has a large oral disc diameter–to–total body length ratio (5.9:11.8). All teeth are typically unicuspid, but this species can have up to 2 bicuspid endolateral teeth, with 1–4 supraoral teeth (almost always 1), and a moderately to strongly bilobed transverse lingual lamina (figure 4.1, D). Ammocoete and immature adults are yellowish tan on the back and sides. Spawning adults darken to a blue-gray and become black by the time spawning is complete. The lateral line organ is pigmented with black in specimens over 6 inches (150 mm). The adult Silver Lamprey can be distinguished from other species within the genus *Ichthyomyzon* by its unique unicuspid dentition, and from the Sea Lamprey and the American Brook Lamprey by having fewer myomeres (47–55) and a continuous dorsal fin. Adults grow up to 13 inches (328 mm) long.

Natural History: The adult Silver Lamprey inhabits rivers and connected lakes. The natural history of this species is similar to other parasitic lamprey; however, little is known about specifics within the Chicago Region.

Distribution and Status: The Silver Lamprey occurs naturally in the Hudson Bay, Great Lakes–St. Lawrence Seaway, Mississippi River, and Ohio River basins. Records for the Chicago Region are few (12) and sporadic, with most from Lake Michigan and its tributaries. The

Silver Lamprey records, 1878–2022

earliest recorded specimen from the region is from the Milwaukee River, Milwaukee County, Wisconsin (USGSWI 1900). This rare and sporadically occurring lamprey may quite possibly be extirpated throughout the Lake Michigan drainage, due in part to use of lampricides and other management practices targeting the nonnative Sea Lamprey. Dams and habitat degradation have also contributed to their decline. The only likely extant population is from the St. Joseph River in Berrien County, Michigan (MIFA 2002), and the Kankakee River, Kankakee County, Illinois (INHS 2016). We consider this a species of special concern within the Chicago Region.

References: Hubbs and Lagler 1964; Hubbs and Trautman 1937

American Brook Lamprey

Lethenteron appendix • *Lethenteron* is of Latin origin, likely meaning "forgetting intestine," referring to the degenerate intestine of the adult; *appendix* in Latin refers to the long genital papilla of breeding males — an "appendage" or "addition."

Description: The adult American Brook Lamprey has a small oral disc-to-total body length ratio (4.0:7.2). Teeth are primarily dull, with 2 widely separated supraoral teeth, 3 bicuspid endolateral teeth, 1 row of posterior teeth, and a linear transverse lingual lamina (figure 4.1, C). Individuals from the Chicago Region have 2 high, separated, but touching dorsal fins. Ammocoetes and immature adults are grayish brown on the back and sides and yellow on the belly and fins. Spawning adults are darker brown and become black as spawning is completed. The lateral line organ completely lacks pigment. Myomeres range from 66–74. See other lampreys for distinguishing characteristics. This species can reach up to 8.5 inches (220 mm).

Natural History: The American Brook Lamprey inhabits cold rivers, streams, and headwater creeks with groundwater discharge. This species is described as nonparasitic, but it also has been reported to grow after larval transformation, which indicates some type of feeding. It is unknown if the adult becomes parasitic, consumes other organisms, or continues to feed on plankton. The ammocoete burrows into silt, sand, or organic debris in medium to small rivers where in Great Lake populations it resides for about 7.5 years. Spawning usually begins in March, migrating to

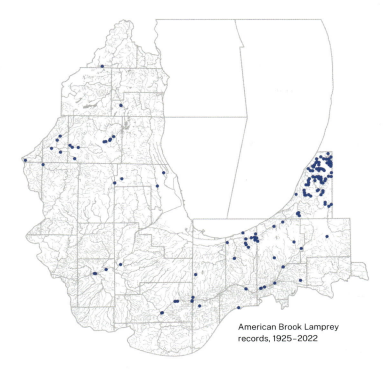

American Brook Lamprey records, 1925–2022

swifter currents over cobble and gravel substrates. Nests are made by both males and females, with 1 pair or multiple pairs spawning in the same nest.

Distribution and Status: The natural distribution of the American Brook Lamprey in North America is quite disjunct. Populations occur in Alaska, the Northwest Territory of Canada, the Atlantic slope drainages, the Great Lakes–St. Lawrence Seaway basin, the Ozark Highlands in the Mississippi drainage, and the southeastern drainages of the Ohio River system. This is the most frequently found lamprey within the Chicago Region, with about 220 records, which are concentrated in the Paw Paw River of Berrien County, Michigan, the Kankakee River in Indiana, and the Kishwaukee River in Illinois. It is a useful indicator of groundwater discharge, good water quality, and connectivity. The American Brook Lamprey is listed as threatened in Illinois.

References: Hubbs and Lagler 1964; Hubbs and Trautman 1937; Vladykov and Kott 1978

Sea Lamprey

Petromyzon marinus · *Petromyzon*, of Greek origin, means "stone sucker"; *marinus*, of Latin origin, means "of the sea."

(*Top*) Sea Lamprey adult; (*bottom*) Sea Lamprey ammocoete

Description: The adult Sea Lamprey has a large oral disc–to–total body length ratio (7.1:13.2). Dentition is well developed, having 2 supraoral, 4 bicuspid endolateral, 8–10 posterior circumoral, and 7–8 infraoral lamina teeth; the transverse lingual lamina is bilobed and strongly developed for rasping flesh (figure 4.1, B). Body coloration is quite variable, where ammocoetes are gray to dark brown and recently metamorphosed individuals are blue-gray to blue-black; large adults may be tan with dark brown blotches or slate blue; spawning adults are marbled dark brown and olive. The ventral area is usually white to silver in all individuals. The Sea Lamprey differs from *Ichthyomyzon* species by having 2 widely separated dorsal fins and more myomeres (67–74); and from the American Brook Lamprey by having a larger oral disc–to–total body length ratio and different dentition (figure 4.1). This species can reach up to 47 inches (1,200 mm) long in the ocean but is usually between 14 and 23 inches (355 to 610 mm) in Lake Michigan.

Natural History: In the Chicago Region, Sea Lampreys begin life in Lake Michigan tributaries, where they spend 3–8 years as nonparasitic larvae, filter feeding in soft substrates. After metamorphosis to the adult stage, they migrate at night to Lake Michigan, where they have been found swimming freely or attached to other fish, both nearshore and in depths up to 120 feet (36 m). Generally, the larger host fish are not killed by Sea Lampreys, but this species can cause death in smaller or diseased individuals, especially if there are multiple lampreys on the same fish. Adults spend about 2 years in Lake Michigan, then migrate into tributary streams during their second spring to spawn over nests built in sand and gravel just below or in riffles. After a total life span of around 8–10 years, they are presumed to die after spawning.

Sea Lamprey records, 1937–2022

Distribution and Status: The Sea Lamprey occurs naturally throughout the North Atlantic Ocean, the Baltic Sea, the Mediterranean Sea, and most confluent freshwater rivers and lakes. The first Sea Lamprey observed from the upper Great Lakes was from Lake Erie in 1921, 88 years after the Welland Canal, which bypasses Niagara Falls, was completed. The first record taken in the Chicago Region was from Lake Michigan in Berrien County, Michigan, waters in 1937 (MIFA). Although this species is non-indigenous and considered a nuisance within the upper 4 Great Lakes, it has been recorded only 58 times between 1937 and 2022 within the Chicago Region. The application of lampricides to spawning tributaries and the use of low-head dams to block spawning runs are 2 invasive methods that have reduced Sea Lamprey abundance. Although these methods have reduced nonnative Sea Lamprey

numbers, they have adversely impacted amphibians, mussels, macroinvertebrates, native lampreys, and other native fishes directly or by fragmenting their habitats. Noninvasive methods of preventing reproduction are trapping and removal, the release of sterile males, and pheromone signatures to confuse reproductive behavior. Commercial catch records on the Great Lakes suggest that fisheries collapsed before the colonization of the Sea Lamprey. This species is considered nonnative to the Chicago Region, and not much of a nuisance.

References: Applegate 1950; R. M. Bailey and Smith 1981; Brussard et al. 1981; Bryan et al. 2005; Christie 2000; Goode 1887; Hubbs and Lagler 1958, 1964; Lawrie 1970; Potter and Beamish 1977; Radforth 1944; Smiley 1882; Vladykov and Kott 1980; Waldman et al. 2004; Wigley 1959

LAMPREYS (PETROMYZONTIDAE)   57

5

Sturgeons

Acipenseridae

Sturgeons are characterized by the longitudinal rows of well-developed bony plates (scutes, bucklers), and an inferior, protractible mouth without teeth. The snout is short and broad or flat with elongated, fleshy lips and a row of 4 barbels anterior to the mouth. The tail differs from most fishes due to its longer top ray giving it asymmetrical form (heterocercal). There is a single large gill cover with a pair of openings behind the eyes (spiracles) that allow water to pass directly to the gills. They have a corkscrew-shaped lower intestine and a skeleton composed primarily of cartilage, although some of the bones become hardened in older individuals of some species.

Fully grown sturgeons can range in size from the tiny Syr Darya Sturgeon (*Pseudoscaphirhynchus fedtschenkoi*) at 11 inches (280 mm) to the largest published record of a Beluga Sturgeon (*Huso huso*) at 20 feet long (6 m) and weighing more than 4,500 pounds (2,040 kg). Sturgeons grow slowly and do not reproduce until they are between 5 and 28 years of age, depending on the species. Adults spawn at two-to five-year intervals, increasing in length with age.

Many sturgeon species are anadromous, migrating from marine or saltwater bodies to freshwater rivers to complete reproduction. Others remain in freshwater rivers and lakes their entire life but can be very migratory within these systems. This ancient order

(Acipenseriformes) of fishes first appeared in the fossil record about 225 million years ago. Worldwide distribution of the family is largely restricted to north of 22°N latitude along ocean coastlines, large rivers, estuaries, inland lakes, and inland seas. There are 25 species worldwide, 8 of which are native to North America. Three species reside in Illinois and only one in the Chicago Region: Lake Sturgeon.

Historically, sturgeons were among the most important commercial fishes in the world. Bony scutes were used to fashion spear tips and tools by early cultures. Sturgeons were not only a food source but an industrial resource as well, used to make glues and gelatins (isinglass). Due to a slow reproduction rate, heavy commercial exploitation, and the blockage and destruction of their spawning habitats, many species of sturgeon are threatened or endangered. Sturgeons are now being cultured for commercial use; native populations are being reestablished through dam removal, strict harvest regulations, and habitat restoration.

Lake Sturgeon

Acipenser fulvescens • *Acipenser* is Latin for "sturgeon"; *fulvescens* is Latin for "yellowish color."

Description: Although not closely related, the Lake Sturgeon generally has the guise of a shark, with a similar body shape, a heterocercal tail, a spiracle (a small opening that is a precursor to the gill slit), rough skin (no scales), and a primarily cartilaginous skeleton. The body is large and robust, with a slender caudal peduncle rounded in cross-section. There are 3 rows of 5 distinct bony plates, or scutes — 1 ventrally along the back and 1 laterally on each side of the fish. The head and snout are conical in adults and flatter and shovel-like in juveniles. The toothless mouth is subterminal and has a lower lip consisting of 2 smooth lobes. Four smooth barbels arranged in a straight, evenly spaced row are located about midlength between the mouth and the tip of the snout. The coloration is primarily sandy yellow, olive, or gray dorsally and cream to off-white ventrally. Juveniles are the same coloration but have dark brown to gray blotches and flecks to provide camouflage. The largest Great Lakes individual was recorded from the Chicago Region in 1943 just north of Benton Harbor, Michigan. The specimen was 8 feet (2,438 mm) long and weighed 1,385 pounds (682 kg).

Natural History: Lake Sturgeon are benthic dwellers of large rivers and glacial lakes. This species requires extensive areas less than 30 feet (9.1 m) deep over a sand or silt bottom with plentiful food. Juveniles primarily occupy sandy areas of rivers and lakes. Spawning is typically associated with rock rapids, boulder-strewn riffles, rocky outside bends of large rivers, or rocky shoal areas of large lakes. Spawning depths range between 1 and 90 feet (0.3 and 27 m). Moving water is essential for spawning substrates to remain silt free. Although foraging habitat is plentiful in the southern basin of Lake Michigan, the only potential for spawning habitat within the Chicago Region would be the St. Joseph River in Michigan, the Root River in Racine, Wisconsin, and the natural limestone shoals along the Lake Michigan shoreline.

Distribution and Status: There are 10 historical anecdotal and floating carcass records of Lake Sturgeon occurrence in the Chicago Region, all of which are from Lake Michigan. The Lake Sturgeon was noted as abundant in the southern basin of Lake Michigan by E. W. Nelson (1876), Jordan (1878), and Forbes (1885). Prior to the late 1800s, anglers regarded the Lake Sturgeon as a nuisance and burned the carcasses on the beaches, but soon thereafter the roe and flesh of this fish became a coveted delicacy. Forbes and Richardson (1920) indicated a significant fishery in 1885 off the shores of Waukegan, Chicago, and South Chicago, Illinois. The fishery crash in Lake Michigan is illustrated with the following statistics on Lake Sturgeon harvest: 1880, 3.84 million pounds (1,741.8 metric tons); 1885, 1.41 million pounds (517.1 metric tons); 1890, 947,000 pounds (429.6 metric tons); 1893, 312,000 pounds (141.6 metric tons); 1899, 109,000 pounds (49.5 metric tons) (Smiley 1882). Becker (1983) notes that in 1966 only 2,000 pounds were taken from Lake Michigan. This sharp decline in the southern Lake Michigan population coincides with observations throughout the Great Lakes and the Mississippi River basin. Meek and Hildebrand (1910), Greene (1935), and Becker (1979) indicated Lake Sturgeon presence in the Chicago Region. Nonconfirmable sitings have been made in recent years. In the summer of 2023, a floating carcass was recorded nearshore of Jeorse Park Beach, East Chicago, Indiana, by US Army Corps fisheries biologists. A recent effort to restore populations in the Great Lakes by federal, state, and local agencies includes habitat restoration, dam removal, and the reintroduction of native Lake Sturgeon stocks. This species is listed as threatened in Michigan and endangered in Illinois and Indiana.

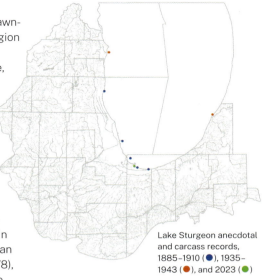

Lake Sturgeon anecdotal and carcass records, 1885–1910 (●), 1935–1943 (●), and 2023 (●)

References: Becker 1979; Forbes and Richardson 1920; Great Lakes Fishery Commission 1962; Greenberg 2002; Peterson, Vecsei, and Jennings 2007; Pflieger 1975; Smiley 1882; Smith 1979; Willink 2017

6

Paddlefishes

Polyodontidae

Easily recognized by their long, flat, paddle-like snout, these primitive fishes lack scales and have a very large, gaping mouth below the snout. The paddle contains sensory nerves (figure 6.1) to detect prey and may help stabilize the fish as it feeds. Living primarily in large rivers and connected lakes and backwaters, the Paddlefish feeds by swimming with its mouth open to capture small zooplankton and invertebrates in the water column, filtering them with modified gill structures called gill rakers (figure 6.2). Like sturgeons, paddlefishes have a cartilaginous skeleton, an asymmetric (heterocercal) tail fin, and a corkscrew-shaped lower intestine. Paddlefishes grow up to 60 inches (1,500 mm).

Paddlefishes are an ancient family dating back to the late Cretaceous (80 million years ago) that is closely related to sturgeons. The family Polyodontidae contains 2 genera, each with 1 species. The 2 species are similar in appearance with elongated, paddle-like snouts. The Chinese Paddlefish (*Psephurus gladius*) lived in central China, preyed on other fishes, and could exceed 21 feet (6.5 m) in length. It has not been seen alive since 2003 and has recently been declared extinct. American or Mississippi Paddlefish occupy the Mississippi and Gulf Coast drainages and were once present in the Great Lakes.

Paddlefishes are fished commercially in some larger rivers, primarily for their caviar. In recent years, they have come under increased

6.1. Paddlefish sensory pores

6.2. Gill rakers

harvest pressure for their eggs due to the decline of sturgeons. This has prompted more stringent harvest regulations in some states. Paddlefish farming has also become more prevalent in recent years. Although paddlefishes remain fairly common, populations have been reduced by pollution, dams, and overfishing.

PADDLEFISHES (POLYODONTIDAE)   63

Paddlefish

Polyodon spathula · *Polyodon* is Greek, meaning "many teeth," possibly referring to the numerous gill rakers, as adults lack teeth, although young Paddlefish have many small teeth; *spathula* refers to the snout, which resembles the kitchen utensil.

Description: Paddlefish are unique and do not resemble any other Chicago Region fish, easily recognizable by the elongated, flat, paddle-like snout and long triangular gill cover. The snout, head, and gill cover are spotted with sensory pores (see figure 6.1). The mouth is large and adapted for filter feeding with long, slender gill rakers (see figure 6.2). The dorsal fin is situated near the rear of the fish. The tail fin is large and asymmetrical, with vertebrae continuing through the upper lobe. The body is covered with smooth, scaleless skin, although scattered scales are sometimes present near the tail. Adults can reach up to 7 feet (2.2 m) in total length.

Natural History: The Paddlefish lives in large rivers, lakes, and impoundments where it strains plankton with its large mouth. It typically inhabits backwaters and oxbow lakes in the summer and fall, moving to the main channel in winter and spring. Spawning adults migrate to large sand and gravel shoals below riffles with a relatively fast current. Required large-river habitats within the Chicago Region are limited to the upper Illinois River. In places where many historical migratory paths are impeded by dams, the Paddlefish migrates extensively during lower river stages rather than during large floods. The elongated snout is not only an important part of this fish's electro-sensory system but may also be used to stabilize its body when swimming with the mouth open while feeding on plankton.

Distribution and Status: The Paddlefish can be found throughout the Mississippi River basin from Montana to New York to Louisiana, and in the Gulf slope drainages from the Mobile River basin to the Galveston River basin. It is extirpated from the Great Lakes, and only a few old records exist over the entire basin. Since the Paddlefish was able to cross the shallow seasonal connections between the Mississippi drainage and Great Lakes, it is likely that these 2 Paddlefish populations were isolated since the natural closing of the Lake Chicago Outlet 4,000 years ago. The 1 Chicago Region record from the Great Lakes basin is from 1869, from the St. Joseph River near Niles, Michigan. The specimen was on display in Clement L. Barron's museum but was lost when the museum closed. Another unconfirmed report is from the Calumet River, and at the time was believed by Forbes (1884) to have been an individual that wandered through the Illinois and Michigan Canal. Meek and Hildebrand (1910) claim that the Paddlefish had been seen in Lake Michigan, but also believed it was not native to the Great Lakes. There are 2 recent records from the Illinois River, at the mouth of the Fox River (ILDNR 2012). The Paddlefish is listed as threatened in Wisconsin and extirpated from Michigan, and is considered naturally rare within the Chicago Region.

Paddlefish records, 1869 (●) and 2022 (●)

References: R. M. Bailey, Latta, and Smith 2004; Becker 1983; Bemis, Findeis, and Grande 1997; Grande and Bemis 1991; Hoxmeier and Devries 1997; Hubbs and Lagler 1964; J. S. Nelson 2006; Purkett 1961; Wuepper 2001

7

Gars

Lepisosteidae

Gars are characterized by an elongated, cylindrical body, a long snout with many small, needle-like teeth, and bony, non-overlapping ganoid scales armoring the body. This group is piscivorous and often occupies vegetated backwaters and sloughs as well as areas of slow current in the mainstem channel. One interesting primitive feature is that the gar's esophagus is still connected to the air bladder (physostomus). Therefore, gars can survive in oxygen-depleted habitats by gulping air their gas bladder can absorb oxygen from.

Spawning takes place in the spring, with the larger female and several males broadcasting adhesive eggs and sperm over vegetation or gravel. Young gars can attach themselves to vegetation or other objects with an adhesive disc on their snouts. Juveniles feed on invertebrates, but quickly convert to an almost exclusively piscivorous diet, which they maintain throughout their adult lives. The gar waits motionlessly for its prey to approach, then captures the fish with a sweeping motion of its long snout. After waiting for the prey to cease struggling, the gar repositions the captive fish by moving back and forth to swallow it headfirst.

Gars are a very ancient family, dating back to the early Jurassic period 200 million years ago. Worldwide there are 7 species ranging from eastern North America to Costa Rica and Cuba; 3 are found within the Chicago Region. The rare Alligator Gar

(*Atractosteus spatula*) formerly occupied the upper Mississippi and Illinois Rivers; however, due to modification of these large rivers for navigation, they are seldom seen farther north than central Illinois. Alligator Gar can be identified by having 2 rows of teeth on upper jaw (versus 1 row of teeth in the 3 *Lepisosteus* gar species in the Chicago Region). It is uncommon, but gar species can hybridize, producing offspring that cause identification confusion (Herrington et al. 2008; Lyons and Schmidt 2022).

Although gars are not a popular sport fish, they are targeted by some anglers, including bowfishers. They can be eaten but are not widely used as a food fish, and their roe is poisonous to humans. They are often maligned by uninformed anglers, who often throw incidentally captured fish on the bank to die, believing gars compete with piscivorous game fishes. However, gars play an important ecological role in a balanced fish community — for example, they can consume extremely spiny fishes and survive internal puncture wounds from such prey, allowing them to eat nonnative juvenile Common Carp.

Spotted Gar

Lepisosteus oculatus • In Greek, *lepis* means "scale" and *osteus* means "bone," referring to the hard, bony scales; *oculatus*, Latin, means "having eyes," in reference to the large spots.

Description: The adult Spotted Gar has distinctive dark spots on its snout, head, body, and fins. The body is long and cylindrical, with a moderately long snout about the length of the head. The non-overlapping ganoid scales are hard and bony. Although the spotted adults are readily distinguishable from other gar species, the young are similar by sharing a dark lateral stripe and a fleshy appendage on the upper part of the caudal fin. The snout length of the Spotted Gar is much shorter and wider than the Longnose Gar's but similar in length to the Shortnose Gar's, which lacks spots. Spotted Gar are known to attain a length of 44 inches (1,115 mm).

Natural History: The Spotted Gar inhabits large rivers and lakes, often associated with clear, vegetated pools and runs in rivers. It typically avoids faster-moving water except during the spawning period. Life-history characteristics are very similar to Shortnose and Longnose Gars.

Distribution and Status: The Spotted Gar occurs in the lower Mississippi River and Gulf slope drainages, with a disjunct population in southern Michigan. This species is relatively rare in the Chicago Region, with only 9 observations since 1945. There are 2 records from the St. Joseph River, 1 from Gerking (1945) and from a 2003 specimen curated by the City of Elkhart, Indiana. The records for various glacial lakes shown on the map below were recorded from Indiana DNR fisheries surveys but are not validated with curated specimens or photos. The recent record (ILDNR 2014) documented from the North Shore Channel in Chicago may illustrate the potential for these fishes to

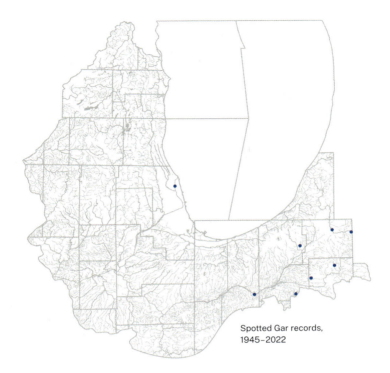

Spotted Gar records, 1945–2022

migrate long distances — perhaps across Lake Michigan or along its shores. The Spotted Gar is considered naturally rare within the Chicago Region.

References: Eddy and Underhill 1974; Grande 2010; Hubbs and Lagler 1964; Page and Burr 2011; Smith 1979; Trautman 1957

Longnose Gar

Lepisosteus osseus · In Greek, *Lepis* means "scale" and *osteus* means "bone," referring to the hard bony scales; *osseus* means "bony" in Latin.

Description: The Longnose Gar has an elongated cylindrical body and a rounded tail. Spots are absent on the top of the head but often occur on the lower jaw. Larvae and very young individuals have a fleshy protuberance at the top of the caudal fin, which is an extension of the spinal cord. A dark black lateral stripe is present on juveniles; it becomes broken and discontinuous as the fish ages, eventually developing into dark blotchy spots, especially on the fins. This species can be distinguished from other Chicago Region gar species by having a long, thin snout about 15 times longer than the width. Adults can grow up to 72 inches (1,830 mm) long.

Natural History: The Longnose Gar lives in large to medium rivers and lakes. It is often associated with slower-moving waters such as backwaters or oxbows, but it also appears commonly in faster-moving current where prey fish are abundant. Spawning takes place in mid to later spring in shallow, slower areas of rivers and at the mouths or lower areas of larger creeks. We have observed them swimming in schools, breaking the water's surface with their long snouts.

Distribution and Status: The Longnose Gar occurs in Great Lakes, Mississippi River, and Ohio River basins and Gulf and Atlantic slope drainages. Records within the Chicago Region are concentrated in the St. Joseph River, the upper Illinois River area, and the glacial lakes in Wisconsin. This species appears to be fragmented in the Kankakee River by the Kankakee dam. Although the Longnose Gar is tolerant of water-quality degra-

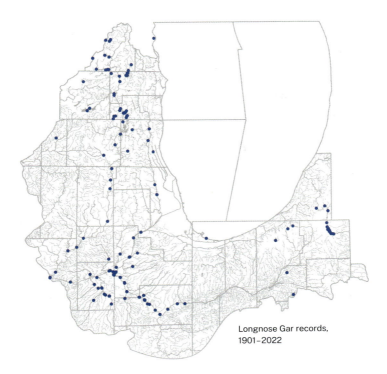

Longnose Gar records, 1901–2022

dation, its distribution is naturally limited by its affinity for larger rivers. It is considered stable within the Chicago Region.

References: Eddy and Underhill 1974; Grande 2010; Hubbs and Lagler 1964; Page and Burr 2011; Smith 1979; Trautman 1957

Shortnose Gar

Lepisosteus platostomus · In Greek, *Lepis* means "scale" and *osteus* means "bone," referring to the hard bony scales; *plato* is Greek for "broad"; *stomus* is Greek for "mouth."

Description: The Shortnose Gar, as the name implies, has a comparatively short, broad snout. Although the snout size is similar to the Spotted Gar, the lack of distinct black spots on the head and snout differentiates the 2 species. The Shortnose Gar also lacks spots on the pectoral and pelvic fins and has a higher lateral line count (60–64) compared to the Spotted Gar (54–58). The young of the 2 species are very similar in appearance. The adult Shortnose Gar can reach up to 33 inches (830 mm) in length.

Natural History: The Shortnose Gar occupies small to large rivers as well as swamps and lakes. This species is often associated with large woody debris or aquatic vegetation. The food habits of the Shortnose Gar differ somewhat from the other species in that it often feeds on invertebrates, including insects and crayfish, although fish still compose a large portion of its diet. Spawning takes place in the spring in faster water.

Distribution and Status: The Shortnose Gar occurs in the Mississippi and Ohio River basins. It was not observed within the Chicago Region until the 1980s, with only 12 records total. All records are from the upper Illinois River and confluent river mouths, except for on the Kankakee River at the Illinois–Indiana

Shortnose Gar records, 1980–2022

state line and on the Fox River in Racine County, Wisconsin (WDNR 2010). This species is considered naturally rare within the Chicago Region but can be locally abundant.

References: Eddy and Underhill 1974; Grande 2010; Hubbs and Lagler 1964; Page and Burr 2011; Smith 1979; Trautman 1957

8

Bowfins

Amiidae

Bowfins are distinguished by a long, stout, cylindrical body with a large terminal mouth. Primitive characteristics include a hard plate in the throat area (gular plate) and a rounded, heterocercal tail fin. As with the gars, the gas bladder of the bowfins is still connected to the esophogus, which allows them to gulp air and survive in low-oxygen conditions or even out of water for long periods. Bowfins in North America are a midsize predatory fish, 15–20 inches (375–500 mm) in length. Fossils indicate that the largest extinct Bowfin from Africa attained a size of 11.5 feet (3.5 m) long.

Bowfins are currently found only in the drainages of eastern and midwestern United States, although the fossil records indicated they were once widespread in Europe, Asia, Africa, Japan, the Middle East, China, South America, and western North America. Bowfins are sometimes referred to as "living fossils," an ancient group of fishes closely related to the gars. The order Amiiformes was a species-rich group of fishes that dates to the late Jurassic period (150 million years ago). In 1912, Oliver Perry Hay of Chicago's Field Museum reported a nearly complete skeleton of a bowfin in clay deposits of the Pleistocene age near Chicago. Historically, only 1 species of extant bowfins was recognized, *Amia calva*. Recently, a second species was described and named the Eyetail Bowfin (*Amia ocellicauda*) (Wright et al. 2022; Brownstein et al. 2022). The western part of this species' range includes the Chicago Region.

Although not frequently targeted by anglers, Bowfins — or Dogfish, as they are commonly called — do take bait and lures. They are voracious feeders and offer a good fight for their size. Bowfins may be similarly maligned as gars, ending up thrown on the bank to die. They are not often harvested for eating, and their roe is poisonous to humans.

Eyetail Bowfin

Amia ocellicauda · *Amia* is an old Greek name for some type of fish, possibly a bonito; *ocellicauda* is a Latin term referring to the ocellus, or spot, on the caudal peduncle. *Bowfin* refers to the long and undulating dorsal fin.

Description: The Eyetail Bowfin is a cylindrically robust fish with cycloid scales. The mouth is full of sharp teeth. Body coloration is a bronze-brown with mottling. Adult males become brilliant turquoise during breeding season. This is the only native North American freshwater fish that possesses a gular plate — a thin bony plate in the throat area between the lower jaws. Other distinctive features include an elongated dorsal fin, tubular barbels protruding from the nostrils, a nonprotrusible maxilla, an abbreviated heterocercal caudal (tail) fin, a spot on the caudal fin, and a vascularized and subdivided gas bladder that serves as a functional lung. Young hatchlings have an adhesive organ on the nose that allows them to attach to aquatic vegetation. Adults are typically in the 15–20-inch (375–500-mm) range but can grow up to 30 inches (750 mm).

Natural History: The Eyetail Bowfin lives in low-gradient areas like sloughs, lakes, and marsh systems. It is also found in large-river backwater and oxbow areas associated with dense submergent and emergent vegetation. In lake systems, they can be found in shallow fringe marshes and weedbeds. The Eyetail Bowfin primarily eats fish but can also consume ducklings and small mammals. Spawning takes place in late spring

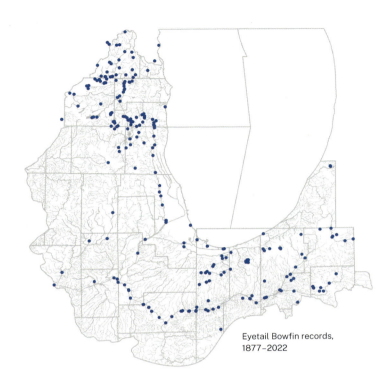

Eyetail Bowfin records, 1877–2022

with males constructing nests in the soft bottom silts of aquatic weed beds, dislodging plants to expose roots. The newly hatched young form dense schools and are protected by the male.

Distribution and Status: The Eyetail Bowfin occurs in North America in the Great Lakes basin, Mississippi River, New England, and Texan drainages. Most records for the Chicago Region occur in the upper Fox River watershed and the backwaters and main channel of the Kankakee River. The Eyetail Bowfin morphologically resembles the invasive and nonnative Snakehead (Channidae). Many reports of Snakehead occurrences were discredited when specimens were identified as the native Eyetail Bowfin. This species may be important to lake and river sport fisheries by helping keep prey fish from becoming overabundant, although it is not the direct target of anglers. The status of the Eyetail Bowfin within the Chicago Region is stable; however, its low-gradient habitats are very susceptible to degradation from shoreline and hydrologic alterations.

References: Brownstein et al. 2022; Grande and Bemis 1998; Schultze and Wiley 1984; Wright et al. 2022

9

Freshwater Eels

Anguillidae

Eels are distinguished by a long slender body and an absence of pelvic fins; they have very small scales, not visible to the naked eye. Freshwater eels are a very interesting family due to their unique life history, which for the most part is still unknown. The American Eel, for example, spawns in the Sargasso Sea near Bermuda. The newly hatched leptocephalus (leaf-like larvae) migrate to the coastal regions, transform into a small translucent stage known as glass larvae, then to a dark phase called elvers, finally maturing into the long, snake-like adult. This process may take a year or more. It was once thought that males remain in the brackish coastal areas, while the female migrates up freshwater rivers, but that now appears to be an oversimplification. Some individuals and populations move long distances upstream and can remain for 10 or more years before returning to the Sargasso Sea, where they spawn and die; some remain in the ocean their whole lives. The spawning behavior has never been observed and is currently being studied by ichthyologists.

There are 19 species of freshwater eels occurring on all continents of the globe. Only one, the American Eel, occurs in North America and the Chicago Region.

Eels as a group are a very important commercial food fish worldwide. In some areas of heavy migration, elaborate traps are constructed to capture them as they move upstream. Smoked eel is a popular food in areas of Europe and as cooked sushi in Japan. Glass larvae are considered a delicacy in some countries as well. Eels have a strong cultural significance in some countries as well. Adult eels are very hard to handle with bare hands due to their strong, muscular bodies and slippery skin.

American Eel

Anguilla rostrata · Anguilla is Latin for "eel"; *rostrata* is Latin for "beaked."

(*Left*) side view; (*right*) top view

Description: The American Eel has an elongated, serpentine body and head. The superior positioned mouth is studded with many small teeth. The rear tip of the mouth reaches to or extends beyond the eye. The pectoral fins are rounded and the only paired fins present. The dorsal fin originates roughly one-third along the length of the body and is continuous with the caudal fin. The anal fin originates roughly between the front of dorsal fin and mid-body and is continuous with caudal fin. Similar-looking species are the freshwater lampreys, but American Eels have jaws and pectoral fins. This fish possesses very small scales embedded in the skin, which are not noticeable except on careful examination. Within the Chicago Region, adult total body lengths typically range from 12 to 40 inches (300–1,000 mm).

Natural History: The American Eel can be found in larger rivers or lakes. It can move over land, breathing through its skin and a modified gas bladder. It is predominantly a nocturnal predator, feeding on fishes, small vertebrates, and invertebrates. Terrestrial movements are most common in damp areas such as marshes, partially flooded areas, or even lawns after heavy rains. It can climb over or around dams if the incline is not too steep. This species displays both amphidromy (moving between saltwater and freshwater) and facultative catadromy (living in freshwater and spawning in saltwater), but many individuals stay in saltwater. Fry are hatched thousands of miles from the Chicago Region in the Atlantic Ocean, somewhere in or near the Sargasso Sea; the exact area has yet to be discovered.

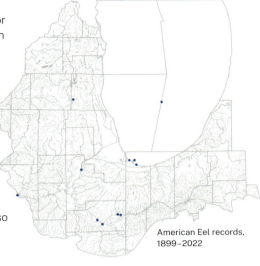

American Eel records, 1899–2022

Distribution and Status: The American Eel occurs throughout the Atlantic Ocean and tributary streams, including the Great Lakes. Most American Eels in the Chicago Region are found in the Illinois River, Kankakee River, or Lake Michigan. Possible migration routes include the Mississippi River and the St. Lawrence Seaway. Conventional fish survey techniques (e.g., electofishing, seines, etc.) do not appear to be very effective at catching eels, so they could be more common than as indicated on the distribution map. Anglers using baited hooks occasionally report catching eels. Locks and dams presumably hinder the movement of eels, so it is assumed that there are fewer eels now than in the past. One large specimen (30 inches/ 750 mm) was captured in a strip mine lake in the Mazonia–Braidwood State Fish and Wildlife Area (Grundy County, Illinois), presumably migrating from the Illinois River up the Mazon River. Eels are uncommon but appear to be stable in the Chicago Region. It is listed as a species of special concern in Indiana.

References: Graham 1997; Grande and Bemis 1998; J. S. Nelson 2006; Schultze and Wiley 1984; W. B. Scott and Crossman 1973; Smith 1979; Tiemann, Taylor, et al. 2015

10

Mooneyes

Hiodontidae

Mooneyes are a large-river fish, not well known to most people. They are flat sided and silvery, with large, prominent eyes, growing up to 15 inches (375 mm). They superficially resemble herrings and shads but differ in having teeth on their "tongue"; they also have a lateral line, and a dorsal fin right above the anal fin, as opposed to the far-forward position found in herrings and shads. All fins are soft and lack spines. The belly is keeled but not saw toothed. As with the whitefish family (Salmonidae: Coregoninae), fish in the mooneye family have a small, bony triangular structure located just above the pelvic fin, called the axillary process, but are different by lacking an adipose fin.

Mooneyes are part of an interesting group of primitive fishes called Osteoglossomorphs because their tongues are bony and have teeth. As such, they are related to some well-known aquarium fishes, including the South American Arawana (*Osteoglossum bicirrhosum*) and the strange African Elephant Fish (*Gnathonemus petersii*). The mooneye family consists of 2 species found only in North America. Both occur within the Chicago Region but are quite rare, limited by their preference for large-river habitats.

Mooneyes are occasionally taken by hook and line, although they are not usually abundant enough to be of recreational or commercial interest near the Chicago Region.

Goldeye

Hiodon alosoides • *Hiodon* is Greek, referring to the toothed bone in the mouth; *alosoides* is Latin and Greek for "shad like."

Description: The Goldeye has a very laterally compressed, silvery body and large eyes with golden irises. The Goldeye has a large mouth, with the back end reaching beyond the pupil. The midbelly keel of the Goldeye is smooth and extends forward from the anal vent, all the way to the pectoral fins — longer than the Mooneye keel, which terminates at the pelvic fins. In addition to the eye coloration, this species can be distinguished from the Mooneye by having a dorsal fin situated just behind the anal fin, with 9–10 rays. Adults may reach up to 20 inches (510 mm).

Natural History: The Goldeye is primarily a large-river fish but can also be found in smaller tributary rivers, impoundments, and connected lakes. The habitats of the Goldeye are very similar to the Mooneye, typically associated with large, deep pools and sluggish currents with silty substrates. They have also been observed in swifter currents of power plant discharge, likely feeding on smaller fishes. They can feed in low-light, turbid waters and eat aquatic and terrestrial insects, crayfish, and fish. Spawning takes place in spring: eggs are broadcast in shallow water over a variety of substrates, including silt, muck, and gravel. This species is adapted to naturally turbid waters and is quite sensitive to chemical pollution. Details of its life history are

Goldeye records, 1976–2022

not well documented within the Chicago Region.

Distribution and Status: The Goldeye occurs naturally in the Arctic and Mississippi River basins and is not recorded from the Great Lakes. Its preference for large rivers with connected lakes and backwaters restricts this species to the upper Illinois River within the Chicago Region, where it is considered naturally rare, having been recorded only 15 times since 1976. Where abundant in the more northern waters of Minnesota and Canada, this species is fished commercially and by hook and line to be smoked and eaten. Goldeye is listed as endangered in Wisconsin.

References: Eddy and Underhill 1974; Page and Burr 2011; Trautman 1957

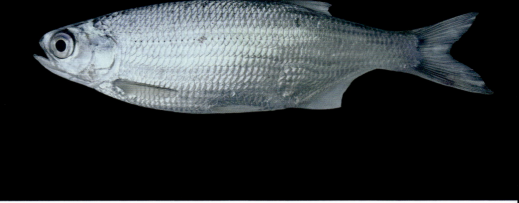

Description: The Mooneye has a very laterally compressed, silvery body, with a large eye containing a silver iris. The mouth is small, the maxillary reaching the front or middle of the pupil. The smooth midbelly keel extends forward from the anal vent to the pelvic fins. In addition to the silver eye coloration, this species can be distinguished from the Goldeye by having a dorsal fin situated just in front of the anal fin, with 11–12 rays. Adults can reach about 20 inches (508 mm).

Natural History: The Mooneye occurs primarily in large rivers and confluent lakes. These fish prefer areas of sluggish or quiet waters, typically over silt or muck, but have also been reported feeding in swifter waters where minnows were abundant. They feed primarily on aquatic invertebrates, crayfish, and fish. Gravid females have been collected in early spring, and spawning is believed to take place in smaller tributary streams where currents are swifter, which presumably suspend the fertilized eggs and early larvae in the water column. Mooneyes typically grow to 9–11 inches and are sexually mature in their third or fourth year. This species is adapted to naturally turbid waters but is quite sensitive to chemical pollution. Details of its life history are not well documented within the Chicago Region.

Mooneye records, 1901–2022

Distribution and Status: The Mooneye occurs naturally in the Hudson Bay, Great Lakes, and Mississippi River basins. Due to their preference for large rivers and confluent lakes, Mooneyes are uncommon in the Chicago Region, being recorded only 15 times since 1979, and once in 1901. They are found occasionally in the upper Illinois River and lower reaches of the Fox and Kankakee Rivers but have never been taken in abundance. The species is listed as endangered in Michigan.

References: Eddy and Underhill 1974; Page and Burr 2011; Trautman 1957

11

Shads and Herrings

Clupeidae

Shads are common in local waters and often seen in large schools. Members of this family are generally torpedo shaped and laterally compressed, ranging in size from 1 to 30 inches (from 25 to 750 mm). Their heads are without scales. The eyes have conspicuous adipose eyelids. Some species have a jaw without teeth and some with minute teeth. A single small dorsal fin is located near the midpoint of the body, with the pelvic fins roughly below the dorsal fin base. The dorsal and pelvic fins are absent in some species. There are no spines in the fins, only soft rays. The lateral line is absent. The scales are cycloid, with the abdominal scales usually forming thickened, horny plates (scutes), resulting in a sawtooth keel. An axillary process (a small triangular bone) is present above the pelvic fin. Species within this group primarily shoal or school, with some species migrating from the sea to freshwater for spawning.

The earliest known fossils of Clupeids are from the Cretaceous period, with many species represented in the Eocene Green River Formation of western North America. There are approximately 210 living species in 64 genres within the family. Most species are marine, including sardines and pilchards. These fishes are found globally in fresh, brackish, and marine waters. There are 4 species in the Chicago Region: 2 native and 2 nonnative.

Herrings and shads are extremely important globally. Although the species within the Chicago Region are not commercially harvested, many Clupeid species are highly valued commercial fishes, processed for food, oil, and fish meal. They not only provide a direct food source to humans, but also are a significant food source for large commercial fish populations such as tuna and mackerel (Scombridae) and salmon. The 2 native Chicago Region species, Skipjack Herring and Gizzard Shad, are an important forage base for popular game fishes.

Description: The Skipjack Herring is a silvery, streamlined fish with a large terminal mouth. This species may be distinguished from the Alewife by having a more horizontal, larger mouth with the maxilla protruding beyond the mandible; an axillary process more than half the length of the pelvic rays; and a dorsal ray count that is usually 17–18. This fish can grow to 23 inches (580 mm) but is most commonly around 12 inches (300 mm). Reports from the Mississippi River by anglers indicate that Skipjack Herring can reach 3.5 pounds (1600 g).

Natural History: The Skipjack Herring occurs in medium to large rivers in moderate to swift currents. It can also be found in reservoirs and lakes connected to rivers. This species is known to travel in large schools, but when collected in the Chicago Region, it is usually only an individual or 2 nested among a large school of Gizzard Shad or Threadfin Shad. It is called the Skipjack due to its behavior of breaking the water surface when chasing minnows. Food consists of plankton, small insects, and fish. Skipjack Herring can complete their entire life cycle in freshwater. Spawning takes place in the spring, with adults often making long upstream migrations. Maturity occurs after 2 or 3 years of growth.

Skipjack Herring records, 1958–2022

Distribution and Status: The range of the Skipjack Herring includes the Mississippi River basin, Gulf slope drainages, and the Red River of the North. This species is considered extirpated from the upper Mississippi River due to lock and dam construction. In the Chicago Region, it may be found in the Illinois River, the Kankakee River up to the Wilmington dam, and the Des Plaines River up to the Salt Creek confluence. The status of the Skipjack Herring in the Chicago Region is secure, but with dam removal and water-quality improvements, this species could become more widely distributed. It is listed as endangered in Wisconsin. The Skipjack Herring can be angled with light tackle and is said to provide excellent sport.

References: Hubbs and Lagler 1964; Page and Burr 2011; Pflieger 1975; Smith 1979; Trautman 1957

SHADS AND HERRINGS (CLUPEIDAE)

Description: The Alewife is a small, laterally compressed fish that possesses an oblique mouth about 45 degrees to the horizontal. The dorsum is slate gray to bluish-black, with silvery sides and a whitish belly. This species may be distinguished from the Skipjack Herring by its much smaller, oblique mouth; an axillary process half the length of the pelvic rays; and a dorsal ray count that is usually 14–16. Alewife may attain lengths of up to 15 inches (380 mm), but on average are around 8 inches (200mm).

Natural History: The Alewife occurs naturally in open waters of the Atlantic Ocean and confluent rivers. In the Great Lakes it prefers open lake waters, and infrequently migrates into tributary rivers and streams. The Alewife is described as a riverine spawner in its natural range; however, within the Chicago Region, reproduction is known to take place only in Lake Michigan. During the colder months, Alewives occupy deep waters and return to the shallows between June and August to spawn over sand flats and beaches. This species plays a pivotal role as an invasive species in the current Great Lakes food web. As a planktivorous species, it strongly influences planktonic and nektonic

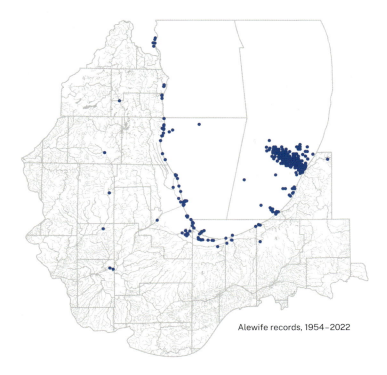
Alewife records, 1954–2022

(larvae) communities while providing ample food for piscivorous fishes. Massive die-offs of Alewives were once common along Lake Michigan shores. Possible causes include sudden water cooling, lack of food, incomplete adaptation to freshwater, or carrying-capacity limits. Since the introduction of salmon into Lake Michigan, Alewife populations have decreased and die-offs are less common.

Distribution and Status: The Alewife is native to the Atlantic continental shelf from South Carolina to Red Bay, Labrador, including the St. Lawrence River and Lake Ontario. The creation of the Welland Canal in the 1820s allowed for this fish to enter the upper Great Lakes in 1931, which were naturally isolated by Niagara Falls. The first official Chicago Region record of the Alewife was from Waukegan, Illinois, in 1954 (FMNH). Since the Whitefish populations were fully exploited by then, it was easier for the Alewife to fill the open planktivore niche in Lake Michigan. The Alewife is considered nonnative and invasive within Lake Michigan and the Chicago Region.

References: Hubbs and Lagler 1964; Page and Burr 2011; Trautman 1957

Gizzard Shad

Dorosoma cepedianum · *Dorosoma*, Greek, means "lance body" from the body shape of young shad; *cepedianum* is in homage to the French naturalist Citoyen Lacepede.

Description: The Gizzard Shad is very laterally compressed, with a long anal fin, blunt snout, and a long filamentous dorsal ray. Juveniles and small adults have a distinct dark spot behind the gill opening, which can be faint or absent in larger adults. Adult riverine forms of this species look different than the variation found in Lake Michigan, where small (here, >10 inches/250 mm) individuals look similar, but larger specimens change from sleek silver to gray and dusky. An individual taken from Lake Michigan, Lake County, Indiana, measured 20 inches (509 mm) and 3.5 pounds (1.6 kg). These larger fish in Lake Michigan and Lake Calumet may be the source of erroneous sharpbelly (Xenocyprididae) observations due to their similar body types, sawtooth keel, and jumping habits. The Gizzard Shad can be distinguished from the nonnative Threadfin Shad by having 52–70 lateral line scales, 25–34 anal rays, and lack yellowish fins.

Natural History: The Gizzard Shad prefers large to medium lowland rivers and lakes where there is quiet open water. Turbidity and poor water quality seem to have no ill effects on this species in the Chicago Region, as it can be found in canals, ditches, reservoirs, and ponds. The Gizzard Shad is a filter feeder, primarily filtering protozoan and microcrustacea

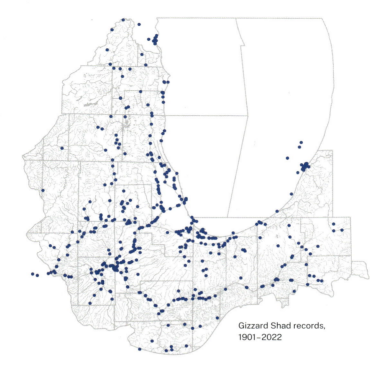

Gizzard Shad records, 1901–2022

from silty and muck-like sediment. Gizzard Shads broadcast their eggs over a variety of substrates between late March and early August.

Distribution and Status: The natural distribution of the Gizzard Shad includes the Mississippi basin, Atlantic slope drainages, and Gulf drainages. In the Chicago Region, it would not be a surprise to find this fish in any larger body of water. It is commonly perceived that abundant Gizzard Shad populations were introduced and are the cause of unbalanced fish assemblages. However, Gizzard Shads often become abundant in streams or lakes with high nutrient levels, silt, and mud, driving the planktonic food source. They are an important link in the food chain, converting basal nutrients into biomass for other fishes, reptiles, birds, and mammals. The status of this fish within the Chicago Region is stable and it can be extremely abundant.

References: Eddy and Underhill 1974; Hubbs and Lagler 1964; Page and Burr 2011; Trautman 1957

Threadfin Shad

Dorosoma petenense · *Dorosoma*, Greek, means "lance body," from the body shape of young shad; *petenense* is derived from the type locality of this species at Lake Petén Itzá, Guatemala.

Description: The Threadfin Shad is very silvery and laterally compressed. It has faint yellow pigmentation in the fins and black spots on the lower jaw and floor of mouth, both lacking in the Gizzard Shad. The lateral line scale count of the Threadfin is usually 40–48, and the anal ray count is usually 17–25. The lower jaw protrudes beyond the upper jaw, which makes the snout more pointed and distinguishes it from the Gizzard Shad, whose jaws are of equal length. The adult is typically small in the Chicago Region, with most observations in the 4-inch (100-mm) range.

Natural History: This species prefers the warm effluent discharge of the Chicago Sanitary and Ship Canal and the lower Des Plaines River, which is above 50°F (10°C) year-round. Its spawning and feeding habits are similar to the Gizzard Shad's, with the exception that the Threadfin Shad feeds on phytoplankton and zooplankton from the water column rather than the substrate. The Threadfin Shad cannot tolerate water temperatures under 45°F (7.2°C), which is evident by mass die-offs in the Mississippi River north of the Ohio River confluence.

Distribution and Status: The literature on the distribution of the Threadfin Shad is conflicting. Some believe it was a Central American

Threadfin Shad records, 1981–2022

species that was introduced into the Mississippi River and Gulf drainages, but others say it was native to the southern states. Within the Chicago Region, the Threadfin Shad's distribution is limited by its inability to adapt to colder water temperatures. The population sustained in the Chicago Region is due to the thermal pollution provided by several electricity-generating power plants on the Chicago Sanitary and Ship Canal and upper Illinois River. It has been stocked in some cooling lakes to provide forage. This fish is considered nonnative and survives by relying on Chicago's thermal pollution.

References: Page and Burr 2011; Pflieger 1975

SHADS AND HERRINGS (CLUPEIDAE) 97

12

Suckers

Catostomidae

In higher-quality rivers, suckers are often one of the most abundant family groups and as such are considered a good indicator. They can be distinguished from other family groups by several distinctive characteristics. The most prominent trait and basis for the family name is the subterminal or bottom placement of the mouth that is adapted for bottom feeding. Other common characteristics include thickened lips, cycloid scales, abdominal pelvic fins, ventrally oriented pectoral fins, and an elongated anal fin. The dorsal fin, although variable in length, is inserted well in advance of the pelvic fin in all species. Sucker species also lack spinous fins, barbels, and adipose fins. Body coloration can be silver, brassy, gold, or purple and green, as in the buffaloes. Some species have bright red or orange fin coloration during spawning or juvenile life stages. Juveniles tend to exhibit saddle-like banding of pigmentation on the dorsal surface, but in most adults, patterns are subtle or absent. Nuptial tubercles are present on the anal fin of some species, while others have small tubercles over most of the body. A few species have larger snout tubercles, which is especially prominent in the chubsuckers.

Worldwide, the sucker family comprises 10 genera with 82 species. Most species are limited to the Western Hemisphere, except for the Chinese Sucker (*Myxocyprinus asiaticus*), which occurs as a relic in some rivers of China, and the Longnose Sucker, whose range extends from North America into Siberia. Although species occur from the Arctic Circle to Mexico, the greatest diversity is found in midwestern and southeastern United States. The Chicago Region contains a diverse assemblage of catostomids: 18 species from 7 genera.

Suckers are not an important commercial or sport fishery within the Chicago Region; further south, though, in the Mississippi and Illinois Rivers, buffalo species are fished commercially. Suckers can be taken by hook and line using earthworms or other live baitfish on the bottom. Despite their reputation as an inedible rough fish, most suckers have a mild, flavorful taste, although the flesh contains many bones. Some of the redhorse *Moxostoma* species have large spring spawning runs into smaller creeks and establish small territories that are defended. Poor water quality, habitat degradation, and dams have had a significant effect on the abundance and distribution of some sucker species.

River Carpsucker

Carpiodes carpio · *Carpiodes* means "carp-like" in Latin; *carpio* is Latin for "carp," indicating this fish's similarity to the Common Carp.

Description: The River Carpsucker has a slab-sided body with large silvery scales and slate-colored fins. This species can be distinguished from the Quillback by having a nipple on the center of the lower lip. The River Carpsucker also has a very short quill on the dorsal fin and an elongated body. The Highfin Carpsucker, which also has a nipple on the lower lip, has a very long dorsal fin quill and a shorter, laterally compressed body. On the River Carpsucker, the sum of the pelvic and anal fin rays totals 17; on other carpsucker, the total is 18 or more. Other characters include a short, rounded snout, the jaw extending past the margin of eye, and 33–36 lateral line scales. River Carpsucker can reach a length of over 20 inches (500 mm).

Natural History: The River Carpsucker inhabits medium to large rivers. It prefers quieter pools over silt, sand, or finer gravel and often feeds in large schools. Its food selection reflects a preference for slow-water habitat, consisting of bottom muck with diatoms, algae, and desmids, but also including some aquatic insect larvae, mollusks, and small crustaceans. The River Carpsucker spawns in early spring, primarily within the river mainstem in large schools over sand and gravel

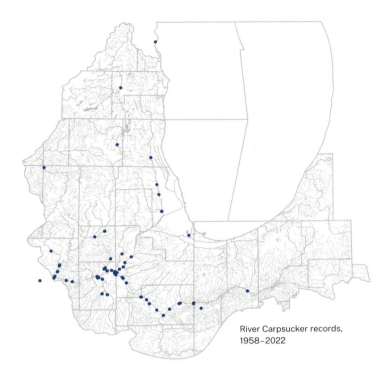

River Carpsucker records, 1958–2022

shoals with moderate flows. Eggs are broadcast randomly and adhere to the substrate.

Distribution and Status: The River Carpsucker occurs naturally in the Mississippi and Ohio River basins and Texas Gulf slope drainages. This species does not occur naturally in the Great Lakes basin. Persistent records within the Chicago Region are from the lower Fox, Kankakee, and upper Illinois Rivers, all in Illinois. Like the Quillback's, the range of the River Carpsucker has recently expanded from the upper Illinois to the lower Des Plaines River, likely due to water-quality improvements. Transient individuals are occasionally captured in the Chicago Area Waterway System.

Reference: Page and Burr 2011

SUCKERS (CATOSTOMIDAE) 101

Quillback

Carpiodes cyprinus · *Carpiodes* means "carp-like" in Latin; *cyprinus* is the same as the generic name of the Common Carp, due to its superficial similarity in appearance and habits.

Description: The Quillback has a slab-sided body with large silvery scales and slate-colored fins. This species can be distinguished from the Highfin and River Carpsuckers by lacking a nipple on the lower lip. Other helpful characters include a quill-like anterior ray extending beyond middle of the dorsal fin base, a long, rounded snout, the jaw not extending past the eye margin, 36–37 lateral line scales, and the sum of anal and pelvic fin rays of 18 or more. Like other *Carpiodes* species, the spawning Quillback male develops fine, sandpaper-like tubercles over most of the body, where the female's tubercles are much less developed. Adults can grow to more than 20 inches (500 mm), but average size ranges from 15 to 18 inches (375 to 450 mm). Juvenile Carpsuckers can be distinguished from juvenile buffaloes by having a triangular versus rounded subopercle on the gill cover.

Natural History: The Quillback inhabits large rivers mostly but can also be found in smaller streams and lakes. It prefers slower-moving water in deeper pools, although it can be found in a variety of current and habitat conditions. Food items are like other carpsuckers', including bottom muck, detritus, algae, and a variety of invertebrates. Although some reproduction may take place in the main river channel, large numbers of

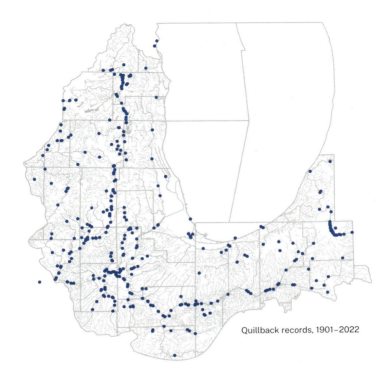

Quillback records, 1901–2022

Quillbacks ascend the lower reaches of tributary creeks to spawn. Spawning was observed in Ferson Creek (Kane County, Illinois) in April, with eggs broadcast over cobble and gravel runs in 2–3 feet (about 1 m) of water. Large numbers of Quillback have also been observed ascending Big Rock Creek (Kendall County, Illinois) from the Fox River in April and May, concurrent with the Shorthead Redhorse spawning migration. Quillbacks are noted to spawn in the lower reaches of tributaries, within 2–3 miles (3.2–4.8 km) of the river mouth.

Distribution and Status: The natural distribution of the Quillback includes the Hudson Bay, Mississippi River, Ohio River, Great Lakes, Gulf slope, and some Atlantic slope drainages. It is the most widely distributed and abundant species of the *Carpiodes* species within the Chicago Region, where records are concentrated along the mainstems of all the larger rivers. Records on Lake Michigan are associated with river mouths or enclosed harbors. Its status is stable, and in recent years it has expanded its range from the upper Illinois River into the Des Plaines River, likely due to water-quality improvements.

Reference: Page and Burr 2011

Description: The Highfin Carpsucker has a slab-sided body with large silvery scales and slate-colored fins. This species can be distinguished from the Quillback and the River Carpsucker by its shorter, more compressed, sunfish-like body and the quill-like anterior ray extending beyond rear of the base of the dorsal fin. Other helpful characteristics include a nipple on the lower lip, a proportionally smaller head and deeper body, a blunt snout, and the jaw, which does not extend past margin of eye. Like the River Carpsucker, it has 33–36 lateral line scales. Adult Highfin Carpsuckers are smaller in length compared to the other 2 species, typically around 12 inches (300 mm).

Natural History: The Highfin Carpsucker is the least tolerant of 3 *Carpiodes* species. Its habitat preference is larger rivers with intact fluvial functions, in areas of faster current with gravely or rocky substrate and no silt. Food habits are like the River Carpsucker and Quillback. Spawning takes place in large aggregations

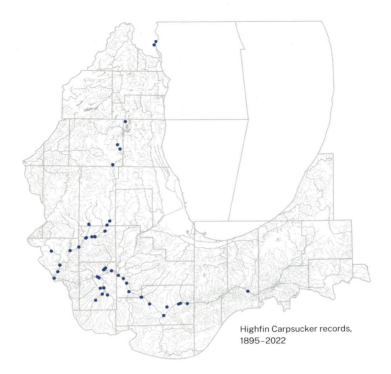

Highfin Carpsucker records, 1895–2022

where eggs are broadcast over gravely substrate in late spring.

Distribution and Status: The Highfin Carpsucker is distributed sporadically throughout the Mississippi River, Ohio River, Gulf, and Atlantic slope drainages. This species was reported from the Lake Michigan watershed but does not occur in the Great Lakes basin within the Chicago Region. All records for this species are from the Kankakee River and upper Illinois River and tributaries in Illinois, including the lower Fox River. The Highfin Carpsucker may also be limited due to fragmentation by dams and its sensitivity to water-quality and habitat degradation, but it appears to persist where habitat is favorable and could expand its range if habitat and water quality continue to improve.

References: Hubbs and Lagler 1964; Page and Burr 2011; Pflieger 1975

Longnose Sucker

Catostomus catostomus • *Catostomus* means "mouth below" in Greek.

Description: The Longnose Sucker has a distinctly cylindrical and bicolored body, with a dark olive or tan color above and white on the bottom surface. As the name implies, the snout is long, extending well beyond the tip of the upper lip. The lips are large and covered with small bumps (papillose), with the rear edge of the lower lip strongly bilobed. The scales are very small, with 90–120 scales in the lateral line series. During breeding season, the male has a crimson-colored lateral band and develops small tubercles on body and fins. The Longnose Sucker is superficially similar to the White Sucker but is different by having an elongated snout and higher lateral line scale count (90–120 versus 53–74). Adults can reach a length of 25 inches (640 mm).

Natural History: The Longnose Sucker is a northern coldwater species, occupying large, clear lake habitats, ascending confluent tributary streams only to spawn or overwinter. It typically inhabits waters 30–90 feet (9–27 m) deep, moving into the shoreline to feed at night or when temperatures decline. In Lake Superior, specimens were taken by commercial fishers in 600 feet (183 m) of water. This species prefers temperatures between 38 and 59°F (3 and 15°C), with a lethal temperature recorded at 80°F (27°C). Food consists of invertebrates and plant matter. We often observed the Longnose Sucker in Lake Michigan in currents at the ends of rocky breakwaters, foraging through periphyton, as well as over cobble shoals. This species typically lives up to 11 years but has been recorded as old as 19.

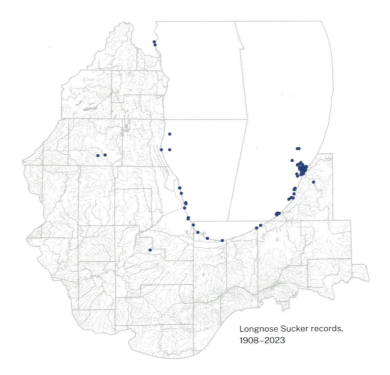

Longnose Sucker records, 1908–2023

Spawning takes place when springtime water temperatures reach between 33 and 59°F (10 and 15°C) in both lakes and tributary streams. In streams, shallow gravel riffles and gravel shoals are used where eggs are buried in the substrate. In lakes, Longnose Suckers spawn along wave-driven shores over gravel and sand. Some lake populations migrate into tributary streams to spawn, often returning to the same stream.

Distribution and Status: The Longnose Sucker has a Holarctic distribution (around the North Pole), occurring in Europe, Siberia, and North America. The Chicago Region is at this species' southern limits, with nearly all records taken from Lake Michigan. There is 1 old riverine record from the St. Joseph River, Berrien County, Michigan (MIFA 1937), likely captured during a former spawning run. In 2012, a spawning run was observed in the Root River, Racine County, Wisconsin, by the Wisconsin DNR. The Longnose Sucker is listed as threatened in Illinois. The Lake Michigan population within the Chicago Region is stable. Although it has many small bones and is not readily caught by hook and line, it is considered a flavorful fish.

References: Becker 1983; Edwards 1983; Page and Johnston 1990b; Willink 2016

SUCKERS (CATOSTOMIDAE) 107

Description: The White Sucker has a cylindrical body with slate-gray, bronze, or brownish coloration above, fading to white on the belly. Adults range in size from 10 to 15 inches (250 to 375 mm), but larger individuals up to 20 inches (500 mm) are not uncommon. Scales are very small, increasing in size in the rear portion of the body, with 53–74 scales in the lateral line series. Lips are large, bilobed, and covered with small bumps (papillose). Nuptial males develop a rose-colored lateral stripe flanked by darker stripes, and tubercles on the body and fins. Young White Suckers have a somewhat mottled appearance, most often with 3 distinct darker blotches along the lateral margin. The White Sucker lacks an elongated nose, readily distinguishing it from the Longnose Sucker. Juvenile White Suckers superficially resemble small redhorses but can be distinguished by the papillose lips and smaller scales.

Natural History: The White Sucker inhabits a large range of habitats, from fast-flowing, gravel-bottom riffles to sluggish, silt-covered pools and lakes. It is found in all sizes and types of rivers, streams, and lakes, and is one of the most pollution-tolerant fishes. The life history of this widespread species has been well studied. Its food consists largely of

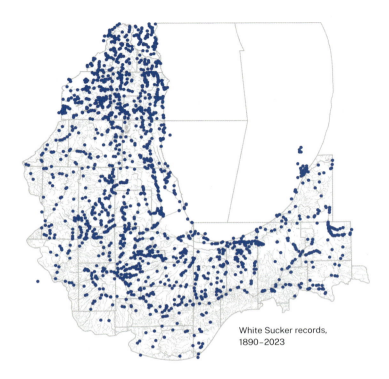

White Sucker records, 1890–2023

insect larvae, primarily midges, as well as other small crustaceans. Large volumes of detritus have also been found in this species' gut contents, suggesting intentional rather than incidental ingestion. Upstream spawning migrations take place in mid to late April. Lake populations migrate into tributary streams to spawn, often returning to the same stream in successive years. Mating behavior is like that of other suckers, randomly burying the eggs and sperm in gravel substrate — a behavior known as brood hiding (Page and Johnson 1990b).

Distribution and Status: The White Sucker occurs in Canada and the US from the Mackenzie River system south to Texas, and from the Rockies to the Atlantic slope; it has been introduced elsewhere. This species is ubiquitous throughout the Chicago Region, boasting over 3,100 records. It is tolerant and is usually more abundant in degraded or marginal-quality streams. This fish can be taken by hook and line and is edible from clean waters. It is a popular bait among Muskellunge anglers, widely sold and distributed as a bait-bucket fish. This species' status is abundantly secure.

References: Page and Burr 2011; Page and Johnson 1990b

Western Creek Chubsucker

Erimyzon claviformis • *Erimyzon* means "to suck" in Greek; *claviformis* is Latin for "club shaped," referring to the body shape.

Description: The body of the Western Creek Chubsucker is cylindrical, robust, and somewhat laterally compressed. The mouth is small and terminal, and the lips are relatively thin, forming a distinct V shape at the rear margin. The body coloration is olive green, with 5–8 dark pigmented blotches along the side. The blotches also appear on the dorsal surface but are often weaker and are not continuous with the lateral markings. Young individuals have a solid dark line along their lateral surface. In breeding males, the anal fin becomes bilobed and large, and hook-like tubercles develop on the side of the snout. This species can be distinguished from most other suckers by lacking a lateral line. It can be difficult to discern the Western Creek Chubsucker from the similar Lake Chubsucker, but helpful distinguishing characteristics include 14 or more predorsal scales, 9–11 dorsal rays, 39–45 lateral scales, and a lesser body depth at the dorsal fin origin. Adults in the Chicago Region rarely exceed 6 inches (150 mm).

Natural History: The Western Creek Chubsucker lives in low- to moderate-gradient streams and headwater creeks. We have observed this species in the headwaters of the Little Calumet River in moderate flow, clear water, sand, and gravel substrates with sparse vegetation, woody debris, and undercut banks as cover. The diet of the Western Creek Chubsucker has not been extensively examined but may be similar to the Lake Chubsucker, foraging on planktonic instead of benthic organisms. This habit is suggested by the terminal location of its small mouth. Spawning is described in detail by Page and Johnston (1990b) from central Illinois, occurring in midspring (May) in relatively warm water, 75°F (24°C). Spawning habits are divergent from other sucker species, including aggressive territorial defense by the male employing its well-developed tubercles. Also, unlike other sucker species, spawning can take place between 1 female and 1 male only. The Western Creek Chubsucker deposits its eggs and sperm into the sand and gravel, often in nests previously constructed by the Central Stoneroller or the Creek Chub.

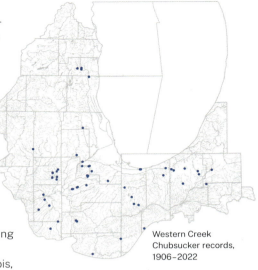

Western Creek Chubsucker records, 1906–2022

Distribution and Status: The Western Creek Chubsucker occurs in the Mississippi River basin, the lower Great Lakes basin, and some Gulf slope drainages. This species has been recorded 65 times within the Chicago Region, which lies in the northernmost part of its range. Records for Wisconsin are old, and it is uncertain if that subpopulation is still extant. The Western Creek Chubsucker is listed as endangered in Michigan. Given the low abundances and low frequency of occurrence, we consider this a species of special concern within the Chicago Region. The reliance on smaller headwater creeks for spawning, and intolerance to sedimentation and habitat modifications, make this species highly vulnerable to agricultural practices.

References: Lyons and Schmidt 2022; Page and Burr 2011; Page and Johnston 1990b; Trautman 1957

Lake Chubsucker

Erimyzon sucetta · *Erimyzon* means "to suck" in Greek; *sucetta* is French for "sucker."

Juvenile Lake Chubsucker

Description: The body of the Lake Chubsucker is cylindrical, robust, and somewhat laterally compressed. The mouth is terminal, and the lips are relatively thin, forming a distinct V shape at the rear margin. Body coloration is olive green, with 5–8 dark pigmented blotches along the side. Older individuals tend to lose markings and become a solid brassy color. Young individuals have a solid dark line along their lateral surface that is wider and more prominent than the juvenile Western Creek Chubsucker. In breeding males, the anal fin becomes bilobed and large, and hook-like tubercles develop on the side of the snout. This species can be distinguished from most other suckers by lacking a lateral line. It can be difficult to discern from the similar Western Creek Chubsucker, but helpful characteristics include 13 or fewer predorsal scales, 10–13 dorsal rays, 34–40 lateral scales, and a greater body depth at the dorsal fin origin. Adults rarely exceed 10 inches (250 mm) in the Chicago Region but can grow up to 16 inches (405 mm) in southern US populations.

Natural History: Lake Chubsuckers inhabit clear, vegetated glacial lakes, and well-vegetated, low-gradient streams and ditches, especially where marshes formally existed. We

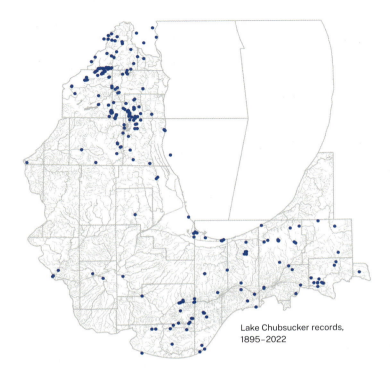

Lake Chubsucker records, 1895–2022

have found this species almost exclusively in dense aquatic vegetation in lakes and wetland sloughs. Its food reportedly consists of planktonic microcrustaceans, aquatic insect larvae, mollusks, algae, and detritus. Many individuals are sexually mature at age 1 and rarely live beyond age 4. In the Chicago Region, spawning takes place in spring, with eggs broadcast over vegetation.

Distribution and Status: The Lake Chubsucker occurs in Gulf slope and southern Atlantic slope drainages, with sporadic occurrences throughout the Great Lakes and Mississippi River basins. Chicago Region records are concentrated in the glacial lakes and tributary streams of Wisconsin and in the historic Beaver Lake area of the Kankakee and Iroquois Rivers in Illinois and Indiana (Kankakee Sands). It is sporadic elsewhere in the region, and not recorded from Berrien County, Michigan. Although its abundance and distribution has been diminished compared to historic levels due to extensive draining of wetlands, its status is stable based on the persistency of records over time.

References: Page and Burr 2011; Page and Johnston 1990b; Trautman 1957

Sucker

Hypentelium nigricans · *Hypentelium* is Greek, meaning "below five lobes," referring to structure of the lower lip; *nigricans*, which means "blackish" in Latin, refers to the dark black mottled areas found across the dorsal surface.

Description: The Northern Hog Sucker is one of the most easily distinguishable species in the Chicago Region due to its large, concave-shaped head, large protruding lips covered with small bumps (papillose), and large pectoral fins. It is also rare among the sucker family in having a distinct pigmentation pattern consisting of 5 dark bands, or saddles, across the top surface (sometimes faded), with dark speckles across the entire body. The ventral surface is flattened, especially near the head. The body narrows considerably toward the tail region, giving this unusual fish an out-of-proportion appearance. Adults are typically in the 10–12-inch (250–300-mm) range, with females generally growing larger. Individuals measuring up to 20 inches (500 mm) can be found in larger rivers.

Natural History: The preferred habitat of the Northern Hog Sucker is high- to moderate-gradient streams with rocky substrate. Its flattened body and large pectoral fins help it stay in place and navigate these areas of higher water velocities. It can be found in streams ranging from small creeks to larger rivers if riffle habitat is present. The most abundant populations seem to occur in larger streams and small rivers. This species is very sensitive to siltation and channelization. Food consists of

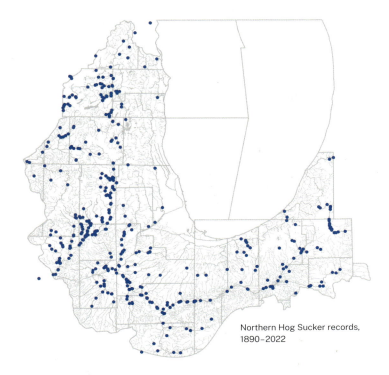

Northern Hog Sucker records, 1890–2022

a variety of aquatic invertebrates, including small-shelled animals. The Northern Hog Sucker spawns in the late spring in medium-size gravel bars at the downstream end of riffles with higher water velocities. The larger female is often closely escorted by multiple males (3–12) for a prolonged period, prior to simultaneously burying the eggs and sperm — a behavior known as brood hiding.

Distribution and Status: The Northern Hog Sucker occurs in Hudson Bay, Great Lakes, Mississippi River, and Ohio River basins, and in the Gulf and Atlantic slope drainages. Records for this species occur throughout the Kankakee, Fox, Rock, and St. Joseph Rivers, in both the mainstem and larger tributaries. It is typically not found or is rare in lowland areas, in reaches impacted by dams, or in manmade waterways like the Chicago Area Waterway System. Although sensitive to habitat and water-quality degradation, its status is stable where it occurs.

References: Page and Burr 2011; Page and Johnston 1990b; Smith 1979

Smallmouth Buffalo

Ictiobus bubalus · In Greek, *Ictiobus* means "bull fish," referring to its robust, bulky body; *bubalus* is Greek for "buffalo."

Description: The Smallmouth Buffalo is a robust, slab-sided fish with a relatively small head and large eyes. This species can be distinguished from other buffaloes by having a deep, laterally compressed body with a highly arched nape that is somewhat keeled. In addition, the mouth is smaller and subterminal, with thick, heavily grooved lips. Similar to that of the other buffaloes, the dorsal fin is long and sickle shaped, with 26–31 rays. The lateral line is complete with 36–38 scales. Body coloration is bronze-green on the back and sides, fading to slate or whitish color in the lower body. Lower fins are usually well pigmented. Breeding males become darker, with bluish-black gunmetal coloration and small tubercles over the body. The Smallmouth Buffalo is the smallest species of the *Ictiobus* genus, reaching an average of 15–17 inches (375–425 mm) as adults. The juvenile Smallmouth Buffalo is distinguished from the other buffaloes by its mouth position and deeper body but is very difficult to distinguish from the Black Buffalo. The juvenile Smallmouth Buffalo also resembles small carpsuckers, which have triangular subopercles (lower gill cover margin) compared to buffalo species, which a have semicircular subopercle.

Natural History: The Smallmouth Buffalo primarily inhabits larger-river habitats and lakes near river mouths. It generally prefers firm-bottomed substrate, but as an opportunistic feeder will occupy a large range of habitats. This species has been observed in vegetated backwaters and oxbow lakes, in large, healthy rivers, and in highly degraded navigation and sanitary canals. It is usually associated with silty flats in about 1–6 feet (0.3–1.8 m) of water, or rocky shorelines with steep drop-offs. Its food consists of a variety of benthic organisms, attached algae, and detritus. Spawning takes place in late spring in relatively shallow areas with minimal current. Eggs are broadcast randomly and fertilized by several males, adhering to any surface and hatching after 8–14 days. The Smallmouth Buffalo can live for 8 or more years.

Distribution and Status: The Smallmouth Buffalo occurs in the Mississippi River, Ohio River, and Gulf drainages; it has been introduced elsewhere. The only Great Lakes basin records are from the Chicago Region. Records from the Calumet River, Lake County, Indiana (FMNH 1908), and Wolf Lake, Cook County, Illinois (INHS 1903), are from before the permanent Cal–Sag Channel arti-

Smallmouth Buffalo records, 1903–2022

ficial connection; therefore, it is likely to have naturally dispersed through the seasonally connected wetlands between the Des Plaines and Calumet Rivers. Records for the Smallmouth Buffalo are concentrated in the upper Illinois River area and throughout the Kankakee River mainstem. In recent years (1996–2022), this species has dispersed upstream of the Brandon Road Lock near Joliet, Illinois, where it was previously absent. Smallmouth Buffalo is usually more abundant than the other buffalo species. Its status is stable, with some range expansion into previously degraded waters of the greater Chicago area.

References: Page and Burr 2011; Pflieger 1975; Smith 1979; Trautman 1957; Willink 2009

Bigmouth Buffalo

Ictiobus cyprinellus · In Greek, *Ictiobus* means "bull fish," referring to its robust, bulky body; *cyprinellus* is Latin for "small carp."

Description: The Bigmouth Buffalo has a stout body, but rounder in cross-section and less laterally compressed than those of the other 2 buffalo species. Unlike other species in the sucker family, it has a large terminal mouth with thin lips. This species shares most of the same characteristics as the other 2 buffaloes, including a long, falcate dorsal fin and a semicircular subopercle. Body coloration is variable, ranging from bluish green on top to bronze, coppery green laterally, fading to a slate gray on the bottom. Although the body form and terminal mouth help distinguish it from the other buffaloes, field identification can still be a bit challenging for the inexperienced observer. Bigmouth Buffalo adults commonly reach 25 inches (625 mm), with individuals weighing up to 50 pounds (23 kg) frequently captured in large-river commercial catches.

Natural History: The Bigmouth Buffalo is a large-river species, preferring slow-moving or standing water in backwaters, oxbows, and connected lakes. It can tolerate shallow enriched waters with silty, organic substrate. With its larger terminal mouth, this species feeds more in the middle zone of the water column rather than the bottom feeding typical for most suckers. Its food consists of plankton and drifting insect larvae, occasionally picking

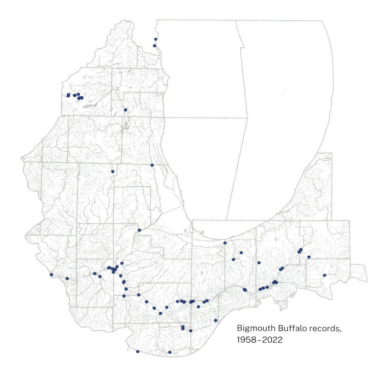

Bigmouth Buffalo records, 1958–2022

food items from rocks, logs, and other structures. The Bigmouth Buffalo spawns generally in April or May, in flooded backwater areas in large schools. A single female is pushed to the surface by a pair of males and broadcasts the adhesive eggs and sperm randomly. Hatching occurs in 8–14 days, with no nesting or parental care observed. Growth is very rapid and large females are quite fecund, releasing several hundred thousand eggs at a time.

Distribution and Status: The Bigmouth Buffalo occurs in the Mississippi River, the Ohio River, Lake Erie, and the Red River of the North; it has been introduced elsewhere. Records are concentrated in the Kankakee and upper Illinois Rivers. This species was found to occur in the upper Des Plaines River by Southern Illinois University in 2002, before any of the Des Plaines River dams were removed. Records from the Rock River system include Lake Delavan, Lake Comus, and the confluent Turtle Creek, Walworth County, Wisconsin (USGSWI 1970–1975). There is a relatively recent record from the Fox River in Kenosha County, Wisconsin (USGSWI 1996). It appears to be stable in the Chicago Region.

References: Page and Burr 2011; Pflieger 1975; Smith 1979; Trautman 1957

Description: The Black Buffalo is a robust fish with a conical head and small eyes. While not as laterally compressed or deep bodied as the Smallmouth Buffalo, it is more elongated. The mouth is large and inferior, with thick, heavily grooved lips. Otherwise, this species shares most of the same characteristics as the other 2 buffaloes, including the long, falcate dorsal fin and the semicircular subopercle. Body coloration is usually dusky bronze to gray. Juveniles of the Black and Smallmouth Buffalo species are very similar. The Black is the largest of the 3 buffalo species, weighing up to 80 pounds (36 kg). One individual taken on Lake Michigan during US Army Corps surveys of Burns Harbor (2000) measured 30 inches (770 mm) long and 18 pounds (8 kg).

Natural History: The Black Buffalo inhabits large rivers and lakes. Its habitat preference is similar to the Smallmouth Buffalo; they quite often occur together. The food of the Black Buffalo includes primarily insects and mollusks but also crayfish, algae, and other plant material. Spawning takes place during spring in swampy, vegetated flooded areas. Although it reportedly spawns in groups like most other suckers, a gravid female and several males have been observed to segregate from the larger group to spawn, randomly

Black Buffalo records, 1903–2022

broadcasting the adhesive eggs and sperm. We noted this fish spawned successfully and recruited juveniles in Northerly Island lagoon adjacent to Lake Michigan, which at the time was devoid of vegetation with nearly a 100% sand bottom. It is unknown whether spawning took place in the outlet channel where there is current and sandy gravel, or if eggs were broadcast over the calm sand flats, where young were captured. Young captured were between 4 and 5 inches (100 and 127 mm).

Distribution and Status: The Black Buffalo occurs naturally in the Mississippi River, Ohio River, and the lower Great Lakes; introduced elsewhere. Like the other buffalo species, most records are throughout the Kankakee River mainstem and upper Illinois River. There is also a relatively disjunct population in the Calumet River system and associated Lake Michigan shoreline. Wisconsin has listed the Black Buffalo as threatened. Populations are stable within the Chicago Region.

References: Page and Burr 2011; Pflieger 1975; Smith 1979; Tiemann, Taylor, et al. 2015; Trautman 1957

Description: The Spotted Sucker is a rather unique sucker due to the spotted pattern appearing along the lateral surfaces in parallel lines. In addition, it can be distinguished from most other suckers by lacking a lateral line. Its body form is elongated and torpedo shaped, like the redhorses. The dorsal fin is short (11–12 rays) and slightly concave. The subterminal lips are rather thin and striated (plicate) and U shaped along the rear margin. Coloration is pale olive in the dorsal region, fading to silvery white in the lower body; some individuals can be quite dusky. The fins are slate colored. Spawning males have pronounced tubercles on the snout, head, and anal fin, and develop a rosy-pink coloration along the lateral surface. Adults are typically in the 12–16-inch (300–400-mm) range.

Natural History: The Spotted Sucker is found in a wide variety of habitats but is most abundant in medium to large lowland rivers. Its preferred habitat is lower-gradient areas with finer substrates and aquatic vegetation. Food includes algae and a variety of invertebrates and plant material. Spawning takes place in April and May, with males defending territories over gravel shoals below riffles. Eggs are buried into the substrate, with the female attended to by 2 males. Other males try to inter-

Spotted Sucker records, 1890–2022

fere and sometimes ram the mating couple.

Distribution and Status: The Spotted Sucker occurs in the Mississippi River, Ohio River, southern Great Lakes, Gulf slope, and southern Atlantic slope drainages. Records within the Chicago Region are primarily in the Kankakee and upper Des Plaines Rivers in Illinois and the St. Joseph River in Indiana. It is absent from higher-gradient rivers and tributary streams. Interestingly, the Spotted Sucker was not found in the Illinois portion of the upper Des Plaines River prior to the 1990s, although it was historically recorded from the Wisconsin section. Its status is stable; however, it is rarely abundant at any locations except those in the upper Des Plaines River.

References: Page and Burr 2011; Page and Johnston 1990b; Trautman 1957

Description: The Silver Redhorse has a robust body profile that is deepest at the dorsal fin origin. This species can be distinguished from all other Chicago Region redhorses by having a bumpy (papillose), strongly bilobed, and V-shaped lower-lip margin and a convex dorsal fin with 14–17 (usually 15) rays. There are usually 40–42 lateral line scales and 12 scales around the caudal peduncle. Body coloration can be silvery, bronze, or olive above with a white belly. The tail coloration is slate gray and the lower fins are yellowish. Breeding males develop small tubercles on the anal and tail fins. One individual taken on Lake Michigan during US Army Corps surveys of Chicago Harbor (1995) measured 32 inches (820 mm) and 7 pounds (3.2 kg).

Natural History: The Silver Redhorse lives in medium to larger rivers and clear lakes. In streams, this species prefers deeper, firm-bottomed pools. In Lake Michigan, it has been observed on rocky shorelines, breakwaters, and sand flats in water over 6 feet (1.8 m) deep. The diet is composed largely of insect larvae, but crayfish, mollusks, and algae are also consumed. The Silver Redhorse spawns earlier in spring than most other redhorse species do, thus the alternate common name March Horse. Spawning was recounted from Iowa and Missouri as taking place

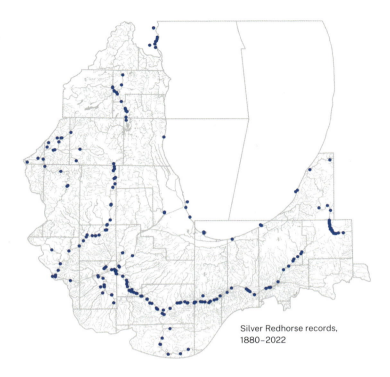

Silver Redhorse records, 1880–2022

over gravel and cobble in shallow riffles. As described for other redhorses, 1 female was attended to by 2 or more males. No territorial behavior was noted.

Distribution and Status: The Silver Redhorse occurs in the Hudson Bay, Mississippi River, Ohio River, and Great Lakes basins. The preference for big-river and lake waters is reflected in the distribution pattern for this species within the Chicago Region. Abundant populations are found throughout the St. Joseph, Kankakee, Mazon, Fox, and Kishwaukee Rivers. This species is found in the lower Fox River in Illinois and in the Wisconsin portion above the Chain O' Lakes; however, it is absent in McHenry and Lake Counties, Illinois, possibly due to fragmentation by several dams. The Silver Redhorse is very rare in the Des Plaines River upstream of the Brandon Lock at Joliet, Illinois, with only 2 existing records. Abundance is very low when found in smaller tributary streams. Although this species is commonly found along the shoreline of Lake Michigan, it is usually taken in low abundances (≤2) where individuals are quite large. The Silver Redhorse can be taken by hook and line, and like other redhorse species, is quite edible. Its status is secure.

References: Hubbs and Lagler 1964; Page and Burr 2011; Pflieger 1974

SUCKERS (CATOSTOMIDAE)   125

River Redhorse

Moxostoma carinatum · *Moxostoma* is Greek, meaning "mouth to suck"; *carinatum*, from Latin, means "keeled," referring to the low ridges on the dorsal aspect of the skull.

Description: River Redhorse has a thick, heavy body with a cylindrical cross-section. The head is very large proportionally, and the bulbous snout extends well past the upper lip. Distinguishing characteristics include grooved (plicate) lips with a nearly straight posterior edge, a concave dorsal fin with 12–13 rays, 42–44 lateral line scales, and 12–13 scales around the caudal peduncle. The pharyngeal arch is very thick, with 6–8 molar-like teeth; all other redhorses within the Chicago Region have slender arches with blade-like teeth. Body coloration can be bronze to olive above with a white belly. There are prominent dark spots at the base of each scale on the back and sides. The tail coloration is red, and the anal fin can be red to orange. Breeding males develop tubercles on the head and the anal and tail fins. The River Redhorse is different from the Silver, Black, and Golden Redhorses by having a red tail. This species is most similar to the Greater Redhorse, which can be distinguished by a smaller, blunter head; also, the Greater Redhorse's scale count around the caudal peduncle is higher (15–16). The similar Shorthead Redhorse can be distinguished by the much smaller tapered head, the falcate dorsal fin, and transverse divisions in the striations (papillae) on posterior edge of the bottom lip. The River Redhorse is one of the larger redhorses within the Chicago Region and can attain a length of 30 inches (770 mm).

Natural History: As the name implies, the River Redhorse occupies only large to medium rivers. It is typically found in deep, often swiftly flowing riffles, runs, and pools. It is not typically associated with cover such as large woody debris. This species will consume macroinvertebrates like other redhorses but is unique in consuming larger freshwater mollusks and mussels. The large molariform teeth in the throat (pharyngeal teeth) are used to crush the hard shells. Spawning habits were detailed by Hackney, Tatum, and Spencer (1967), in which the River Redhorse male prepares substrates before spawning by building a nest (redd) in sand and gravel shoals in runs or pools. The male fans away finer substrates with his tail or sucks them away by mouth, and arranges stones with his snout. The nest-building male is joined a female and typically 1 or more males. The eggs and sperm are simultaneously buried in the nest's gravel. Little is known about spawning sites in the Chicago Region; however, radio-tagged adults in the Kankakee River in Illinois moved into fast-moving mainstem riffles in March (Butler and Wahl 2017). We have not observed movement into tributary streams, and neither juveniles nor subadults have been encountered during local fish surveys.

River Redhorse records, 1958–2022

Distribution and Status: River Redhorse distribution covers the St. Lawrence River, lower Great Lakes, Ohio River, Mississippi River, and Mobile River basins. It is relatively limited in the Chicago Region and throughout most of its range due to the need for high-quality larger-river habitat. This species was not recorded from the Chicago Region until 1958 by the INHS (Fox River, Kane County, Illinois), likely due to an improvement in fish collection techniques and wider use of boat electrofishing. It is most abundant in the Kankakee River in Illinois, where populations have been relatively stable for the last 30 years. Although widely distributed throughout the Kankakee River system, it is much less abundant in the sandy, channelized segments in Indiana. Records are relatively rare in the fragmented Fox River in Illinois and Wisconsin. The River Redhorse is listed as threatened in Michigan, Wisconsin, and Illinois. It is considered a species of special concern throughout the Chicago Region, based on its specific needs of natural riverine function. Further study of its life history and spawning requirements is needed.

References: Butler and Wahl 2017; Hackney, Tatum, and Spencer 1967; Jenkins and Burkhead 1994; Page and Johnston 1990b; Willink and Dreslik 2023d

Description: The Black Redhorse has a slender, elongated body that tapers to a slender caudal peduncle — the area just in front of the tail. The head and body are the most streamlined among the redhorse species in the Chicago Region. Other distinguishing characteristics include plicate (grooved) lips, a moderately curved posterior edge of the lower lip, a concave dorsal fin with 12–13 rays, 44–47 lateral line scales, and 12–14 scales around the caudal peduncle. The coloration is dusky black on top, silver/gray on the sides, and white on the belly. Pectoral, pelvic, and anal fins can be slightly orange in coloration, especially in juveniles. The dorsal and tail fin are slate colored and become darker during spawning. Spawning individuals develop minute tubercles on the body, anal fin, and tail fin. The similar Golden Redhorse differs by having larger scales with 40–42 in the lateral line series, 9 pelvic rays, a thicker caudal peduncle, and a more acutely angled posterior edge of the lower lip. The Black Redhorse is smaller than most redhorse species, reaching 10–14 inches (250–350 mm).

Natural History: The Black Redhorse inhabits small to medium rivers. It prefers higher-gradient segments with riffles and clean-bottomed pools. Black Redhorses feed primarily on aquatic insects and other

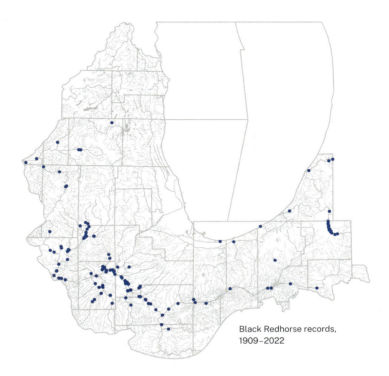

Black Redhorse records, 1909–2022

invertebrates, although algae and detritus may be ingested. Spawning takes place in April and May in deeper, swifter areas of riffles over coarser substrate. Territoriality is not displayed. One female is attended by 2 males as they bury eggs and sperm into the substrates. The Black Redhorse is very intolerant of siltation and other habitat and water-quality degradation.

Distribution and Status: The Black Redhorse occurs in the Great Lakes, Ohio River, Mississippi River, and Mobile River basins. Due to its sensitivity to degraded conditions and affinity for small rivers, this species is absent from most of the Chicago Region. Records are concentrated and persistent over time in the Kishwaukee, Kankakee, lower Fox, and upper Illinois River tributaries in Illinois, and the St Joseph River in Indiana and Michigan. The first reliable record for the Chicago Region is from the Galien River, Berrien County, Michigan (MIFA 1919), taken by T. L. Hankinson. The Black Redhorse is listed as endangered with a very limited distribution in Wisconsin. Its status in the Chicago Region appears stable, but distribution is likely reduced compared to historic records.

References: Jenkins and Burkhead 1993; Kwak and Skelly 1992; Page and Johnston 1990b

SUCKERS (CATOSTOMIDAE) 129

Golden Redhorse

Moxostoma erythrurum · *Moxostoma* is Greek, meaning "mouth to suck"; *erythrurum* is also Greek, meaning "red tail" — a misnomer, since this species has a slate-colored tail as an adult.

Description: The Golden Redhorse has a fusiform (oval cross-section) body that is slightly compressed, with a thickened tail region (peduncle). Distinguishing characteristics include plicate lips, a moderately angled posterior edge of the lower lip, a concave dorsal fin with 12–14 rays, 40–42 lateral line scales, and 12 scales around the caudal peduncle. The coloration is golden to bronze on the back and sides, and white on the belly. Pectoral, pelvic, and anal fins can be slightly orange in coloration, especially in juveniles. The dorsal and tail fin are gray, becoming darker during spawning. Nuptial males develop a dark midlateral stripe, and large tubercles on the head with finer tubercles on the body, anal fin, and tail fin. Adults are typically 12–16 inches (300–400 mm) but can reach up to 20 inches (500 mm) in length. This species can be distinguished from the River, Greater, and Shorthead Redhorses by having a slate- or gray-colored tail. See the Black Redhorse and Silver Redhorse accounts for differences among similar slate-tailed redhorse species.

Natural History: Occupying a wide range of habitats, including smaller creeks and larger rivers, the Golden Redhorse is one of the more tolerant species of the genus in relation to channel gradient, siltation, and water quality. Adults occupy deeper pools and runs, whereas juvenile seek shallower, slower-current areas. Food habits are like other redhorses, including aquatic insect larvae, other invertebrates, detritus, and algae. Spawning takes place in April and May over gravel and cobble. Vigorous tail motion during multiple spawning acts creates nest-like cavities in which finer gravel is displaced, exposing coarser, cobbly substrate where the fertilized eggs are deposited. Males display aggressive behavior using their large head tubercles. Females are typically attended by 2 or more males in the spawning act.

Golden Redhorse records, 1880–2022

Distribution and Status: The Golden Redhorse occurs in the southern Great Lakes, Mississippi, Ohio River, and Mobile River basins. Within the Chicago Region, it is very common throughout the Kishwaukee, Fox, upper Illinois, Kankakee, and St. Joseph Rivers, and their tributary streams. This species is rare or absent in the impaired lower-gradient Lake Plain streams, in particular the Des Plaines, Chicago, and Calumet Rivers. Although it does not inhabit Lake Michigan, it can be found venturing out from confluent river mouths. The Mazon River and Aux Sable Creek also hold abundant populations of Golden Redhorse, despite low summer-flow conditions. Golden Redhorse is moderately widespread and can be very abundant where it occurs, making its status secure.

References: Jenkins and Burkhead 1993; Kwak and Skelly 1992; Page and Johnston 1990b

Shorthead Redhorse

Moxostoma macrolepidotum · *Moxostoma* is Greek, meaning "mouth to suck"; *macrolepidotum* is Greek for "large scaled."

Description: The Shorthead Redhorse has a slender, elongated body, nearly round in cross-section. The head is proportionally very small and tapered compared to other redhorses. Other distinguishing characteristics include plicate lips with lateral divisions that appear as papillae near the posterior edge. The posterior edge of lower lip is straight; the dorsal fin is slightly falcate, with 12–13 rays. This species has 42–44 lateral line scales and 12–13 scales around the caudal peduncle. Body coloration can be bronze to olive above with a white belly. There are dark spots at the base of each scale on the back and sides. The tail coloration is red, and the anal fin can be red to orange. Breeding males develop tubercles on the anal and tail fins, with all fins becoming deep red. The Shorthead Redhorse differs from the Golden, Black, and Silver Redhorses by having a red tail. Greater and River Redhorse also have a red tail fin but both species have much larger, rounded heads and curved lower-lip margins. Adults in Lake Michigan and larger rivers can reach a length of 21 inches (554 mm) but they are typically smaller.

Natural History: The Shorthead Redhorse inhabits medium to large rivers and clear lakes. In rivers, this species is associated with swiftly flowing runs and moderately flowing pools, ranging from sand to rocky substrates. In Lake Michigan, it is associated with river mouths, rocky shorelines, and manmade breakwaters. Food includes insect larvae and other macroinvertebrates. Spawning typically initiates in late March or early April, with large migrations into tributary creeks. Spawning is not reported from Lake Michigan but may likely occur in tributary streams. Like Golden Redhorse, Shorthead Redhorse also creates spawning depressions in the substrate by vigorous tail motion during multiple spawning acts. Large aggregates of up to 40 nest-like depressions have been observed in Big Rock Creek (Fox River, Illinois). No aggressive behavior was noted. Juvenile Shorthead typically exit the tributaries, returning to the river mainstem by late fall.

Shorthead Redhorse records, 1880–2022

Distribution and Status: The Shorthead Redhorse occurs in the Hudson Bay, Great Lakes, Mississippi River, Ohio River, and Atlantic slope basins. Within the Chicago Region, records are concentrated in the lower Fox, Kankakee, upper Illinois Rivers in Illinois and St. Joseph River in Indiana where it is quite abundant. It is common along the shores of Lake Michigan, but not very abundant and individuals are typically quite large. This species is rare or absent in the impaired lower-gradient Lake Plain streams, like the Des Plaines, Chicago, and Calumet Rivers. The Shorthead Redhorse is considered stable within the region.

References: Jenkins and Burkhead 1993; Kwak and Skelly 1992; Page and Johnston 1990b

Greater Redhorse

Moxostoma valenciennesi · *Moxostoma* is Greek meaning "mouth to suck"; *valenciennesi* after Achille Valenciennes, a French naturalist who first described this species.

Description: Greater Redhorse have a torpedo-shaped, somewhat laterally compressed body. The head is large and rounded with a blunt snout. Distinguishing characteristics include plicate lips with a slightly curved posterior edge, a convex/concave dorsal fin with 13–14 rays, 42–45 lateral line scales, and 15–16 scales around the caudal peduncle. Body coloration can be bronze to olive above with a white belly. There are dark spots at the base of each scale on the back and sides. In all live adult specimens that we have observed, the tail is red, the anal and dorsal fins have prominent red margins, and the pectoral and pelvic fins are orange with a yellowish white line on the first ray. Breeders develop minute tubercles on the head, anal and tail fins; all fins turn red. Adults are larger, typically 18–22 inches (457–560 mm). We captured and released an adult from the Lake Michigan drainage in Michigan that was 28 inches (711 mm). The Greater Redhorse is different from the Golden, Black, and Silver Redhorses by having a red tail. The red-tailed Shorthead Redhorse has a much smaller head and mouth with a straight lower-lip margin. The Greater and River Redhorse are very similar but differ by head length and shape, with caudal peduncle scale count being the most reliable (15–16 versus 12–13, respectively).

Natural History: The Greater Redhorse inhabits large creeks to medium rivers and clear lakes throughout its range. In the St. Joseph River, Indiana, it was found to be associated with moderately flowing runs and pools over sand or gravel shoals. This type of habitat corresponds to those we found in Aux Sable Creek, Grundy County, Illinois, and the Mukwonago River, Waukesha County, Wisconsin. Overall, the ecology and life history of this rare species has not been well documented. Limited information suggests that its diet consists of insect larvae and other crustaceans, which is consistent with the comb-like structure of the pharyngeal teeth. Spawning appears to be like that of other redhorse species, taking place in moderate flows over gravel and cobble. Females are attended to by multiple males who do not exhibit aggressive behavior. Collection of juveniles is rare in the Chicago Region, with the only occurrence in Aux Sable Creek, a small to midsize direct tributary to the Illinois River.

Distribution and Status: The natural range of the Greater Redhorse includes the upper Mississippi River and Great Lakes–St. Lawrence Seaway basins. This species has a limited distribution in the Chicago Region and can be found only in the St. Joseph River in Indiana and the upper Illinois River, Aux Sable Creek, and Fox River in Illinois. There is a population just to the north in the Milwaukee River, Milwaukee County, Wisconsin. The only specimen from the Des Plaines River system was

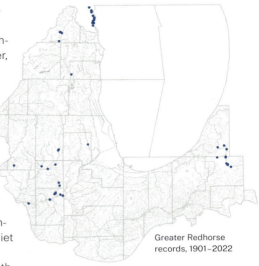

Greater Redhorse records, 1901–2022

taken in Salt Creek, DuPage County, Illinois, by Forbes and Richardson (INHS 1901). The specimen was originally mislabeled as Golden Redhorse and later identified as a Greater Redhorse by R. E. Jenkins (Smith 1979). As such, this species was previously thought to be extirpated from Illinois; however, its absence in historic collections may be due to the reliance on seining as the primary collection technique, which selects against larger, more mobile species. The advance of mobile electrofishing techniques has resulted in a more accurate account of its distribution. Still, it remains one of our rarest and least-studied species. The Greater Redhorse is listed as endangered in Illinois and Indiana and threatened in Wisconsin.

References: Cook and Bunt 1999; Page and Johnston 1990b; Smith 1979; Willink and Dreslik 2023c

SUCKERS (CATOSTOMIDAE)   **135**

13

Barbs and Carps

Cyprinidae

The Common Carp was introduced to North American freshwaters in the early 1800s by German immigrants to establish a sport fishery in the Hudson River, New York. It was subsequently widely stocked around the country by well-meaning, uninformed fisheries managers. The Goldfish, being a very popular aquarium and feeder fish, made its way into North American freshwaters via release. Both the Goldfish and the Common Carp are very tolerant of water-quality and habitat degradation. Goldfish are typically most abundant in highly degraded waters, whereas the Common Carp can thrive in a range of habitats. Distinctive characteristics include large scales, a long, single dorsal fin with 1 stout serrated spine, and a robust body. Many but not all species have barbels on their mouths. Barbs and carps can be found in fresh and brackish waters throughout Africa and Eurasia.

There are about 1,700 species within the Cyprinid family, some of which become brightly colored with tubercles during the spawning period. Both the nonnative Common Carp and Goldfish are well established and reproduce within the Chicago Region. Some species are quite large, exceeding 40 inches (1,000 mm). Until recently, this family included smaller minnows, which are now classified in the family Leuciscidae. Another group, commonly known as Asian, or bigheaded carps, were also split from Cyprinidae and are now in the family Xenocyprididae.

This group of fishes is economically important in the aquaria and food industries. In Europe, Common Carp and barbs are highly valued as sport fishes, with many anglers practicing catch and release only. These large-bodied fish are fun to catch and are targeted by anglers throughout the Chicago Region. We observed a single specimen of Tinfoil Barb (*Barbonymus schwanenfeldii*) from the Des Plaines River, Cook County, Illinois (Field Museum specimen 130065). This is an example of aquaria release in which this tropical species likely perished during the cold winter months.

Goldfish

Carassius auratus · *Carassius* is the Latinized version of *karass*, this fish's common name in Eurasia; *auratus* means "gilded" in Latin.

Description: Goldfish have a very stout body with large scales and a thick caudal peduncle. The mouth is terminal, slightly upturned, and without barbels. The anal fin has a stout spine that is serrated on the posterior edge. Recently released ornamental varieties can vary in color, but are predominantly brilliant orange, often intermixed with white. The coloration in reproducing populations eventually reverts to the wild type, which is typically a uniform brass brown. The Goldfish differs from the Common Carp in having no barbels and fewer lateral line scales (26–30 versus 32–38). Goldfish and Common Carp can hybridize — most often in degraded habitats. These hybrids are generally intermediate in shape and morphological counts (lateral line scales, gill rakers, etc.) and often have only a single barbel on the mouth. Typical length for the adult Goldfish is 12 inches (300 mm) or less.

Natural History: Goldfish prefer slow-moving or still water and are often associated with aquatic vegetation. They are typically found in larger streams and rivers and tend to be less associated with the bottom than Common Carp. This species is highly tolerant of pollution, temperature extremes, turbidity, and degraded habitats; however, their abundance is usually low in the presence of native fishes, indicating they are poor competitors. Goldfish feed on crustaceans, plant matter, and aquatic insect larvae. Smaller, brightly colored Goldfish are very vulnerable to predators like bass, pike, catfish, turtles, and herons. Goldfish start spawning in late spring and continue throughout the summer. Males will crowd around a female, with simultaneous release of gametes (eggs and sperm) over plants and roots. The scattered eggs are adhesive, sticking to any available substrate.

Goldfish records, 1909–2022

Distribution and Status: The native range of the Goldfish includes the freshwaters of East Asia. It was one of the first nonnative species to be introduced into the Chicago Region, already being reported in several Illinois rivers by 1876. Goldfish were on exhibit in lagoons at the 1893 World's Fair in Chicago and then released or escaped into Lake Michigan. This species was still abundant in ponds and lagoons in Chicago parks in 1910. Historically, before water-quality improvements due to the Clean Water Act, the Goldfish was very abundant in Chicago waterways, the Des Plaines River, and downstream to the Illinois River. Recently released pet Goldfish are not uncommon in large urban areas such as park lagoons along the Chicago lakefront. In Indiana and Michigan, the collection records are concentrated near Lake Michigan. Many other records have resulted from the release of aquaria specimens.

References: Becker 1983; Meek and Hildebrand 1910; E. W. Nelson 1876; Schofield et al. 2005; Smith 1979; Willink 2002; Woods 1960

BARBS AND CARPS (CYPRINIDAE)   139

Common Carp

Cyprinus carpio · *Cyprinus* is Greek for "carp"; *carpio* is a Latinized version of *carp*.

Description: The Common Carp has a robust body with a high back and very large scales. The dorsal fin is long, stretching to near the caudal fin, having 15–23 rays. The fronts of the dorsal and anal fins have a stout spine, serrated on the posterior edge. The mouth is terminal, protrusible, and relatively small for the body size. Two barbels are found in the corners of the mouth, along the upper lip. Body color is typically golden brown, sometime with an orange hue. Adults can range from 25 inches (625 mm) to more than 30 inches (750 mm) in length. Some individuals have very few scales, either scattered about the body or sometimes concentrated in a single row along the lateral line. These variants, known as Mirror or Leather Carp, are just variations of the Common Carp. The Common Carp can be confused with the Goldfish but has barbels on the mouth and more lateral line scales (32–38 versus 26–30). Common Carp are also similar to buffaloes and carpsuckers, but these species lack barbels and spines on the dorsal and anal fins. For many years, Koi (ornamental fishes that can be bright gold, red, white, black, or any combination of these, sometimes with long, flowing fins) was considered domesticated varieties of Common Carp. Koi is now recognized by some as domesticated varieties of Amur Carp (*Cyprinus rubrofuscus*).

Natural History: Common Carp is a very adaptable fish and can be found in any type of water body. It can live in almost any aquatic habitat with sufficient water, with a preference for slow-moving water over a mud bottom. Food consists primarily of aquatic insect larvae, but also includes plants, mollusks, and other crustaceans. One manner of feeding is to ingest mud and insects, sometimes even driving their head into the bottom of the river, then ejecting the mud out their gills while selectively retaining the insects. This foraging behavior has the unintended consequence of uprooting vegetation, destroying patches of native plants, and increasing water turbidity. Common Carp spawn in the spring to early summer, usually in shallow, nearshore areas with aquatic vegetation. Several to dozens can congregate in a single area where the females cast the eggs into the water column, with males simultaneously releasing milt. In shallow water, the spawning activity creates a great deal of thrashing and splashing. The eggs are adhesive and stick to plants, rocks, or any nearby objects. A single female can release 500,000 to over 2 million eggs.

Distribution and Status: Native to freshwaters throughout Europe and Asia, it was widely introduced and distributed within freshwaters of the US and Canada. Common Carp from Germany were introduced into the US around 1831, to Illinois in 1879, and the Chicago Region starting in 1890. It is very widespread and abundant in the Chicago Region and can account for the majority of biomass in some localities. This species is nonnative, invasive, and highly tolerant of polluted waters and habitat degradation. Common Carp can be taken by hook and line and provides great sport fishing due to its large body and brute-force fighting ability.

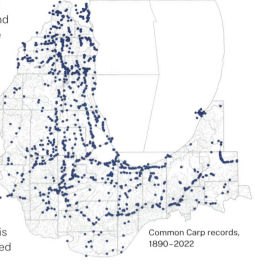

Common Carp records, 1890–2022

References: Balon 1995; Becker 1983; Cole 1905; Forbes and Richardson 1920; Kottelat and Freyhof 2007; Smith 1979; Willink 2002

14

Sharpbellies

Xenocyprididae

Sharpbellies are large-bodied fish closely related to Common Carp, and until recently were placed in the Cyprinidae family with carps and barbs (Tan and Armbruster 2018). These introduced fishes, known as Asian or bigheaded carp, can grow quite large, up to 48 inches (1,219 mm). Some have a ventral keel and low-positioned eyes with fine scales (Silver and Bighead Carps), while others have larger scales and a more rounded bodied without a ventral keel (Grass and Black Carps).

The sharpbelly family includes 160 species native to East Asia. The 4 species in the Midwest were imported to the United States for use in southern aquaculture ponds, in which 3 species escaped from the floodplain ponds during flood events within the Mississippi River basin and one (Grass Carp) intentionally introduced throughout the region for aquatic weed control. Three of the species have been found in the Chicago Region: Grass Carp, Silver Carp, and Bighead Carp. To date, Black Carp have not been recorded as far north as the Chicago Region.

These fishes are highly valued for food in their native range in Asia and are overfished and somewhat depleted. The flesh is white and lightly flavored, unlike Common Carp's, although sharpbellies are also quite bony, making it somewhat unpalatable for the American consumer. They are commercially fished in some areas on the Mississippi and Illinois River where they are very abundant; however, due to their lack of acceptance as a food fish (due in part to their association with the Common Carp), they are used primarily for pet food and fertilizer. Efforts are being made to rebrand and promote them for increased human consumption within the US. This would help raise their market value and commercial harvest, hopefully reducing their populations, which in some areas outnumber those of native fish species. The Illinois Department of Natural Resources, with support from federal agencies, has been hiring commercial fishermen to remove Sharpbellies, primarily Bighead and Silver Carp, from the upper Illinois River. These efforts have been ongoing since 2010 and have resulted in the reduction of populations at the leading edge of the "invasion," which has lessened upstream migration pressure. This area is not normally open for commercial harvest so the fish are used for fertilizer and pet food.

Description: Grass Carp have a large, elongated, cylindrical body with very large scales. The head is short and blunt, with eyes that are relatively low on the side of the head. The dorsal fin is short (8 rays) and pointed. The caudal peduncle is also short and very thick. Dorsal coloration is olive green, fading to silver on the sides and white on the bottom. The large scales are outlined in pigment, giving a distinct crosshatched appearance. Within the throat are relatively thin and comb-like (pharyngeal) teeth with ridges along their surface used for grinding plant material. Grass Carp are most similar to Black Carp (which does not occur in the Chicago Region but is spreading northward from the lower Illinois River). Black Carp have a darker, bronze color compared to the much lighter-colored Grass Carp, with distinctively molar-like pharyngeal teeth evolved for eating mussels. Grass Carp can grow up to 48 inches (1,219.2 mm). A recent capture in Lake Calumet, Cook. County, Illinois, measured 57 pounds (25.9 kg).

Natural History: The Grass Carp lives in lakes or portions of rivers with little or no current. It is associated with aquatic plants, which it consumes in large quantities. For this reason, it is often stocked in ponds to

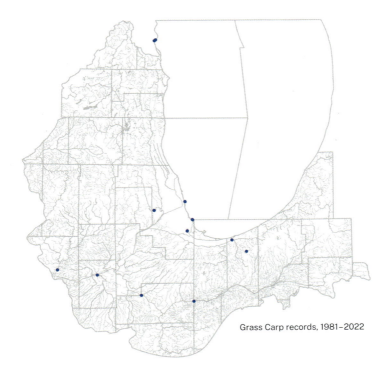

Grass Carp records, 1981–2022

control "weeds." Only triploid Grass Carp are allowed to be stocked, which have 3 sets of genes and are reportedly unable to reproduce; however, there is some evidence that not all triploids are sterile. Grass Carp spawn in the spring when river levels rise. It typically swims upstream to an area with turbulent, flowing water where eggs are broadcast and fertilized in the water column. The buoyant embryos float downstream until they hatch.

Distribution and Status: The Grass Carp is native to East Asia. Within the Chicago Region it is most common in the upper Illinois River, the Chicago Area Waterway System, and Lake Calumet. Although reproduction is possible in these systems, juveniles have not been observed. Adult fish are often found in ponds and park lagoons where they were stocked. Grass Carp is also often sold in regional fish markets. In the Chicago Region, there is no indication it reproduces in large numbers. Although not extremely abundant, it can potentially adversely impact native aquatic plant communities.

References: Nico, Williams, and Jelks 2005; Page and Burr 2011; Schofield et al. 2005

SHARPBELLIES (XENOCYPRIDIDAE) 145

Silver Carp

Hypophthalmichthys molitrix · *Hypophthalmichthys* is Greek for "eye under the fish"; *molitrix*, Latin, means "grinder" (possibly referring to the pharyngeal teeth)

Description: The Silver Carp has a fusiform, somewhat laterally compressed body and a relatively large head. The eyes sit low on the side of the head, at the lower edge of the mouth. The mouth is moderately large and curved downward, with the lower jaw extending beyond the upper jaw. The dorsal fin is short, with 8 rays. Both the dorsal and anal fins are pointed (falcate). Scales are relatively small, with a scaleless keel that runs along the belly from the back of the gills to the anal fin. The body is silvery gray in color without spots or blotches. The most similar species are the Bighead Carp and the large adult Gizzard Shad. The Bighead Carp can be distinguished by the belly keel extending only as far forward as the pelvic fins and its mottled, darker pigment along the sides. The Gizzard Shad has a comparatively tiny mouth, an extremely laterally compressed body, and a long filament on its dorsal fin. Adult Silver Carp are typically between 24 and 48 inches (600 and 1,200 mm) in length.

Natural History: The Silver Carp occupies large rivers and lakes, preferring habitats with little or no flow, such as bays, backwaters, and floodplain lakes. The Silver Carp also prefers impounded rivers with nutrified waters, as this provides the coupled lake and river components they prefer. It is not often found in midchannel or other areas with swifter currents. It tends to jump in response to motorboats and other loud noises, presumably a fright response. The Silver Carp feeds by pumping water over its gill rakers, straining out primarily phytoplankton (microscopic plants and algae). Foraging is often near or at the surface. Spawning takes place when river levels rise in the spring and early summer in areas of turbulent water. Eggs and milt are broadcast near the surface; the fertilized eggs must float downstream long enough to hatch before sinking (60 miles/96.6 km or 30 hours). A single female can produce up to 2 million eggs.

Silver Carp records, 2005–2022; red line indicates authors' observed range

Distribution and Status: The Silver Carp is native to East Asia and was originally brought into the southern United States in the early 1970s to control algae and provide another fish crop in catfish culture ponds. In 1994 a mass escape from farm ponds in Arkansas occurred and these fish began spreading through the Mississippi up into Illinois River. It is very abundant in the upper Illinois River up to the Starved Rock Dam, becoming less abundant upstream, due in part to lack of reproduction as well as large-scale removal efforts by commercial fishers contracted by resource management agencies. There is great concern these fish will invade the Great Lakes through the Chicago Area Waterway System; however, their upstream progress is currently stalled in the Dresden Pool of the lower Des Plaines River, about 50 miles from Lake Michigan.

Reference: Kolar et al. 2007

SHARPBELLIES (XENOCYPRIDIDAE)   147

Description: Bighead Carp have a fusiform, somewhat laterally compressed body and a large head. The eyes are low on the side of the head, almost below the mouth. The mouth is large and terminal with the lower jaw protruding slightly beyond the upper jaw. A scaleless keel runs along belly from anal fin to pelvic fins. The dorsal fin is short (8 rays) and the pelvic fin has a forward placement, just behind the pectoral fin. The pelvic fin is long, stretching to the pelvic fin. The upper surface is gray with a pinkish hue. The sides are gray, mottled with darker blotches, fading to dull white on the belly. The scales are relatively small. Adults can grow up to 48 inches (1,200 mm) in length. The most similar species is the Silver Carp, which has a smaller head, shorter pectoral fins, and a longer belly keel extending forward to the gill opening. The Silver Carp is also lighter in color and lacks darker blotches along the sides. Grass Carp have relatively low eyes, but their scales are much larger than those of the Bighead Carp with a visible crosshatch pattern.

Natural History: Bighead Carp lives in large rivers and lakes. It prefers habitats with little or no flow, such as side bays, backwaters, and flood plain lakes, where abundance can be very high. Bighead Carp is not often found in mid-channel or other areas with swifter current. It feeds by straining plankton (microscopic plants and animals) out of the water as it passes through their gills. Foraging is often near or at the surface of the water. Spawning takes place during rising river levels in the spring and early summer. It congregates in areas of turbulent water and broadcasts eggs and milt near the surface. The fertilized eggs must float downstream long enough to hatch before sinking (60 miles or 30 hours). A single female can have up to 2 million eggs.

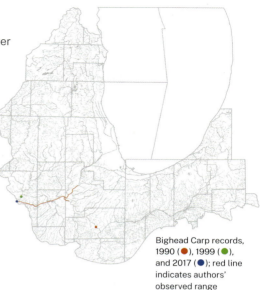

Bighead Carp records, 1990 (●), 1999 (●), and 2017 (●); red line indicates authors' observed range

Distribution and Status: The Bighead Carp was originally brought into the southern United States from its native East Asia in the early 1970s to clean algae out of culture ponds and serve as an aquaculture food fish. It escaped in 1994 along with Silver Carp from farm ponds in Arkansas and these fish began spreading through the Mississippi up into Illinois River. Reproducing populations stretch upstream to the Starved Rock Dam. Sporadic occurrences outside the waterway happen from time to time, as this fish is released by people for religious practices. Hence it has been caught in the Kankakee River in 1990 (INHS) and several Chicago area ponds since 2003 where isolated introductions are apparent. In 2009, a single Bighead Carp was found in Lockport, Illinois, several miles downstream from the electric barriers in the Chicago Sanitary and Ship Canal. There is great concern that they will invade the Great Lakes through the Chicago Area Waterway System; however, their upstream progress has been stalled in the Dresden Pool of the lower Des Plaines River, 50 miles from Lake Michigan for several years.

Reference: Kolar et al. 2007

15

True Minnows

Leuciscidae

The family Leuciscidae includes all native North American minnows and is a quite diverse group. These fishes used to be part of a large Cyprinidae family, which also included carps, barbs, and sharpbellies (Tan and Armbruster 2018). Minnows are typically small fishes, with 1 dorsal fin and paired abdominal pelvic fins, lacking hard spines. The mouths of minnows vary widely from large to very small, with many different configurations, often useful in species identification. Body shapes are also very diverse, ranging from tall and laterally compressed to oval, round, or cylindrical.

Minnows can be found in the full range of habitats in the Chicago Region, from very small headwater streams to the largest rivers, and from small, vegetated ponds to the clear waters of Lake Michigan. While many species feed on aquatic invertebrates, some also include fish in their diet; others may eat only fresh or decaying plant material. Most species are relatively short lived (2–5 years), maturing after 1–2 years. Some breeding males display a range of brilliant colors and textures, from bright red and orange to iridescent blue.

Worldwide there are 667 species in the family Leuciscidae — mostly smaller fishes with very diverse life histories and habits. The largest minnow is the Colorado Pikeminnow (*Ptychocheilus lucius*), which can attain a length of 6 feet (1.8 m) and a weight up to 80 pounds (36 kg). In the Chicago Region, 43 of the 251 native

North American minnow species have been recorded. Two other species have had very limited historic occurrences in the Chicago Region and do not seem to have viable, extant populations currently; therefore, full species accounts are not included here. The Bigeye Chub (*Hybopsis amblops*) (eye length roughly equal to snout length, a small barbel in corner of the mouth, a rounded snout protruding anterior of the mouth) has a few records in the Iroquois watershed. The Bigeye Shiner (*Notropis boops*) (eye length greater than snout length, a black peritoneum, a black stripe along body that wraps around the snout and darkens the tips of the upper and lower jaws) has several historical records in the Illinois River.

In the Chicago Region, minnows are not of high economic value except as baitfish used by anglers and on a more limited basis as food in sport fish hatcheries or rearing. However, most bait minnows are sourced from out of state or raised in hatcheries or ponds, particularly the Fathead Minnow and the Golden Shiner. Some anglers seine for their own minnows in local waters. Minnows are of high ecological value, providing a vital link in the food chain as forage for predatory game fishes, birds, reptiles, and some mammals.

Central Stoneroller

Campostoma anomalum · *Campostoma* is Greek for "curved mouth," referring to its crescent-shaped mouth; *anomalum* is Latin for "extraordinary."

(*Top*) nonbreeding male/female; (*bottom*) breeding male

Description: The Central Stoneroller is a rather robust minnow, with a brownish, somewhat bronze stippled or mottled appearance. The unique characteristic for this species is a crescent-shaped subterminal mouth with a hard cartilaginous ridge on the lower lip. A dusky lateral band is present on younger fish and sub-adults. A dark band is also present on the dorsal and anal fins, the pigment becoming more intense and thicker in spawning males. The large breeding males also develop very large head tubercles and intense pigmentation that includes mottling, orange and black median fins, and large white lips. Females and smaller males develop these display features to a lesser degree. This species is distinguishable from the very similar Largescale Stoneroller by the scale count around the body just in front of the dorsal fin — due to slightly smaller scales, the circumferential count is greater on the Central Stoneroller, usually 37–48, versus 31–36 for the Largescale Stoneroller. Adult Central Stonerollers can reach up to 7 inches (175 mm) in length.

Natural History: The preferred habitat of the Central Stoneroller is moderate-to higher-gradient reaches of streams and small rivers. This species is typically found over coarse, rocky substrate in faster currents, avoiding low-gradient streams and manmade canals, although it has been observed in some agricultural ditches where flow is present. Food consists primarily of algae, which the Central Stoneroller scrapes off rocks using the hard plate on its lower lip. This herbivorous technique is unique among Chicago Region minnows. This species also has an elongated gut, which aids in digestion of the algae. We have observed spawning males building nests by pushing or moving stones with the mouth to create a shallow depression. Males attempt to defend the nest, but when a female enters the nest, other males rush in to create a communal spawning frenzy. Spawning takes place early in the spring, usually March to May.

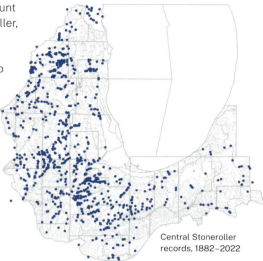

Central Stoneroller records, 1882–2022

Distribution and Status: The Central Stoneroller occurs in the Mississippi River, Ohio River, and Great Lakes basins. This species is widespread throughout the Chicago Region. The first time it was observed in the Chicago Region was in 1882 from a Fox River tributary near Plano, Illinois (INHS Kendall County, Illinois), perhaps taken by Stephen A. Forbes. Its status is secure, often occurring in high abundance where habitat is favorable.

References: Smith 1979; Trautman 1957

TRUE MINNOWS (LEUCISCIDAE)   153

Stoneroller

Campostoma oligolepis · *Campostoma* is Greek for "curved mouth," referring to its crescent-shaped mouth; *oligolepis* is also Greek, meaning "few scales."

(*Top*) nonbreeding male/female; (*bottom*) breeding male

Description: The Largescale Stoneroller is very similar in appearance to the Central Stoneroller in coloration and form, with the same hard cartilaginous ridge on the lower lip. As the name implies, the Largescale Stoneroller has larger scales, which are more apparent in older individuals when placed side by side with the Central Stoneroller. As discussed in the Central Stoneroller account, a scale count around the body is quite often necessary to distinguish the 2 species. Differences in nuptial characteristics have also been noted between the 2 species, with the Largescale Stoneroller having fewer head tubercles and lacking a dark band on the anal fin. Adults can reach up to 7 inches (175 mm) in length.

Natural History: The Largescale Stoneroller prefers the same habitat and has similar habits to the Central Stoneroller but appears to be more intolerant of degraded conditions. Our observations indicate this species is found in reaches that have cooler water temperatures, where groundwater becomes an input component; however, additional study is needed. Spawning habits are like the Central Stoneroller's in that males build nests. Since the 2 species occur together in many streams and both appear to be early spawners, some separation/recognition mechanism exists, although hybridization is apparent, based on observations of overlapping scale counts and other characteristics.

Distribution and Status: The Largescale Stoneroller occurs in disjunct populations within the Mississippi and Mobile River basins. The distribution of the Largescale Stoneroller within the Chicago Region overlaps the Central Stoneroller's, but with a much less frequency of occurrence. Most occurrences are documented from the lower Fox River system and the Rock River system, with Lake Michigan drainage occurrences in

Largescale Stoneroller records, 1901–2022

Wisconsin. Big Rock Creek (Fox River, Illinois) has optimal Largescale Stoneroller habitat, with rocky substrate and cooler water. This species is not typically found in large numbers like the Central Stoneroller. We consider its status to be stable. The Largescale Stoneroller is a good candidate for additional study regarding its specific habitat and temperature preferences.

References: Smith 1979; Trautman 1957

Northern Redbelly Dace

Chrosomus eos · *Chrosomus* means "colored body" in Greek, referring to its bright coloration; *eos* is Greek for "dawn," referring to its red color.

Description: The Northern Redbelly Dace is fusiform minnow that has a distinctive pattern of coloration along the sides, marked with 2 distinctive dark lateral bands with gold in between. The belly is a yellowish red that fades to cream. It has very fine scales, with usually 85 in the lateral line. Both anal and dorsal fins typically have 8 rays. The gut is long and is surrounded by a black peritoneum (stomach lining). Breeding males intensify in color patterns, becoming reddish on the lower head, red and/or yellow on the belly, and yellow on the fins; this happens with the females to a lesser extent. This species can be distinguished from the similar Southern Redbelly Dace by having a smaller and more oblique mouth and a more rounded snout, and breeding males being more yellow than red. The Northern Redbelly Dace rarely exceeds 3 inches (75 mm) in length.

Natural History: The Northern Redbelly Dace is found in small creeks and bog ponds. This species prefers cool, clear, shallow water with vegetation and very little current. It feeds on zooplankton, algae, plants, and small insects. It is a communal spawner, breeding throughout the summer months in smaller groups among plants and algal beds. The eggs are left unattended.

Northern Redbelly Dace records, 1906–2022

Distribution and Status: The Northern Redbelly Dace occurs in the northern forest ecoregion throughout Canada and dips down into the upper Mississippi River and Great Lakes basins. This species has a very limited occurrence in the Chicago Region, which is at the southern extent of its natural distribution — it is found only in Wisconsin, at a relatively limited number of sites. The first time this species was recorded in the Chicago Region was from 1906 in Barnes Creek, Kenosha County, Wisconsin (USGSWI). We consider this species naturally limited within the region, but stable.

References: Eddy and Underhill 1974; Hubbs and Lagler 1964

Southern Redbelly Dace

Chrosomus erythrogaster · *Chrosomus* is likely Greek, meaning "colored body," referring to bright coloration; *erythrogaster* is Greek meaning "red belly."

Description: The Southern Redbelly Dace is fusiform minnow that has a stunning pattern and coloration like the Northern Redbelly Dace. It has very fine scales, with usually 85 in the lateral line. Both anal and dorsal fins typically have 8 rays. The gut is long and surrounded by a black peritoneum. The dorsal region is dark, the sides are marked with 2 distinctive lateral bands with gold between, and the belly is a reddish that fades to cream. Breeding males intensify these color patterns, becoming crimson red on the lower head, red and/or orange on the belly, and orange on the fins; this happens with the females to a lesser extent. The Southern Redbelly Dace can be distinguished from the Northern by having a larger and less oblique mouth and a more pointed snout, and breeding males are more red than yellow. Adults rarely exceed 3 inches (75 mm) in length.

Natural History: The Southern Redbelly Dace primarily occupies small streams and headwater areas with clear water, continuous flow, and silt-free substrate for spawning. We have also observed this species in agricultural ditches where the waters are deep and cool. Occasionally, limited numbers are encountered in larger streams or rivers. In its preferred habitat, large schools swim near the bottom, feeding mainly on

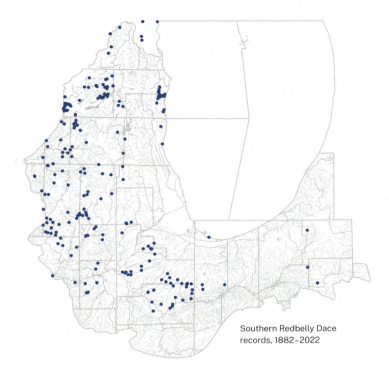

Southern Redbelly Dace records, 1882–2022

plant material and small crustaceans. Breeding takes place in large aggregations, often over the nests of other minnow species, such as the Hornyhead Chub.

Distribution and Status: The Southern Redbelly Dace occurs in the mid–Mississippi River, Ohio River, and southern Great Lakes basins. It occurs more frequently in the western half of the Chicago Region in Illinois and Wisconsin, is limited in Indiana, and is absent from Michigan. Two records in eastern Indiana are for lakes (Koontz Lake, Starke County, USGS 1986; Mill Pond, Marshall County, INDNR 1995), which are atypical habitats for this species, but both have inflowing and outflowing streams. Since this species has been observed in bait buckets, these atypical occurrences may have resulted from unintentional introduction. The Southern Redbelly Dace is considered stable within the Chicago Region but is listed as endangered in Michigan.

References: Smith 1979; Trautman 1957

Lake Chub

Couesius plumbeus · *Couesius* is named in honor of Dr. Elliott Coues, an American ornithologist who collected the type specimens; *plumbeus* means "lead colored" in Latin.

Description: The Lake Chub is a grayish-silver minnow, often appearing very pale, with some darker scales intermixed. The scales are relatively small, with usually 60–67 lateral line scales. The most distinguishing characteristics are the inconspicuous barbel in the rear corner of the mouth, the lack of pigment in the dorsal and anal fins, and a smaller mouth that does not extend past the front of the eye. These characteristics distinguish this species from the Creek Chub. The adult Lake Chub is known to reach 9 inches (225 mm) in length.

Natural History: The Lake Chub is most often encountered in cold, clear lakes and the mouths of confluent streams. Individuals were typically observed over sand and gravel often in association with rubble. This species occupies lower areas of the water column, feeding on aquatic insects and crustaceans. Spawning takes place in the spring in shallow water, and maybe deep water too, over a variety of habitats along lakeshores or in the mouths of tributaries. We took large gravid females exceeding 8 inches (200 mm), in gill nets in 90 feet (27 m) of water, 3 miles (4.8 km) off the coast of Chicago Harbor in the winter of 1999, courtesy of a US EPA survey vessel. We also took large gravid females off the coast of Waukegan, Illinois, in gill

Lake Chub records, 1919–2022

nets intended for Whitefish and Yellow Perch in April 2000 in 75 feet (22 m) of water.

Distribution and Status: The Lake Chub occurs in the boreal forest region of Canada and North America, inclusive of the Great Lakes. Its Chicago Region distribution includes Lake Michigan and the glacial lakes in Wisconsin. In Lake Michigan, it has been found from the shoreline to about 100 feet (30 m) deep. The Lake Chub can be found entering confluent streams as well, especially during spring spawning season. This species is uncommon in the Chicago Region, with only 57 records here at the southern extent of its distribution. The recent collections in Wisconsin (WDNR 2010–2022), the presence of gravid females in deep waters of Lake Michigan, and juveniles in the northern Illinois ravine mouths and beaches may indicate that the population is stable.

References: Becker 1983; Eddy and Underhill 1974; Hubbs and Lagler 1964; Willink 2017

Red Shiner

Cyprinella lutrensis · *Cyprinella* is Greek, meaning "small carp"; *lutrensis*, Latin, means "of the otter" — this fish's type locality is Otter Creek, Arkansas.

Description: The Red Shiner is a silvery satin minnow with a laterally compressed body. As with all members of this genus, the scales are diamond shaped. This species can be distinguished from the Spotfin Shiner by having more diffuse dorsal fin pigmentation, a more blunted nose, and 9 anal rays. Juveniles are similar to the Spotfin Shiner, which has only 8 anal rays and a slenderer body. Breeding males turn an iridescent blue with bright red fins. The distinguishing dusky bar behind the gill cover intensifies to a purplish hue. The Red Shiner reaches a maximum size of 4 inches (100 mm).

Natural History: The Red Shiner is adapted to occupy the naturally warm and turbid streams of the Grand Prairie. It typically inhabits larger streams and small to medium rivers and is found over a diverse array of substrates and a range of stream habitats. As we have observed, it is most abundant in pools, below riffles with very short runs. Aquatic vegetation and filamentous algae appear to be a large component of its diet, which also includes small aquatic and terrestrial insects. The Red Shiner spawns throughout the season from late May through early October.

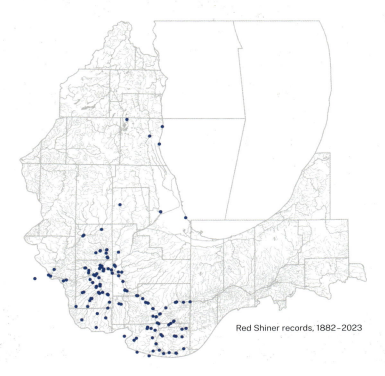

Red Shiner records, 1882–2023

Distribution and Status: Red Shiner are considered native to the Mississippi basin and not to the Great Lakes basin. Within the Chicago Region the distribution of the Red Shiner is naturally restricted to the Grand Prairie areas of Illinois, which includes the Kankakee, lower Des Plaines, and upper Illinois Rivers. Records within the Great Lakes basin are old, sporadic, and possibly the result of bait-bucket introductions.

References: Pflieger 1975; Smith 1979

Spotfin Shiner

Cyprinella spiloptera · *Cyprinella* is Greek, meaning "small carp"; *spiloptera*, also Greek, means "spot fin," referring to the dark spot on the dorsal fin.

Description: The Spotfin Shiner is a somewhat laterally compressed, silvery satin minnow. Distinguishing characteristics include diamond-shaped scales, 8 anal fin rays, and distinctive black patches or "spots" between the back few rays of the dorsal fin. Pigmentation is lacking or much reduced between the front rays on the dorsal fin. Other helpful characteristics include an oblique mouth, 35–39 lateral line scales, and 8 dorsal fin rays. The breeding males attain a steel-blue body with yellowish fins that have a satin-white edge. This species resembles the Red Shiner, which has a deeper and more laterally compressed body and 9 anal rays. Adult Spotfin Shiners reach a maximum size of about 4 inches (100 mm).

Natural History: The Spotfin Shiner occupies a wide range of water bodies, from midsize streams to large rivers and glacial lakes. It is not abundant or common in smaller headwater streams. The Spotfin Shiner is found over many types of substrates and a variety of habitats, including deep riffles, pools, runs, and backwaters. In lakes, this fish occupies the littoral zone, from the shallowest beach edge to a depth of 10 feet (3 m) among aquatic plants. It can tolerate a wide range of water-quality conditions and can be found in highly modified channels. Food items

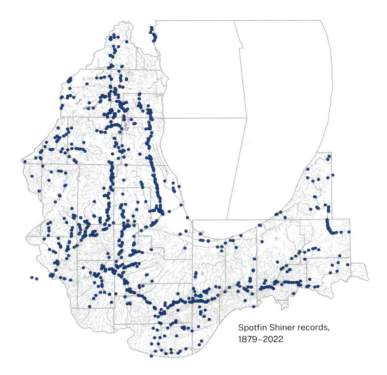

Spotfin Shiner records, 1879–2022

include terrestrial and aquatic insects, fish, eggs, and vegetation. Favorable conditions allow spawning from late May through September. This fish is a crevice spawner, meaning the female places her eggs in cracks of rocks or interstitial spaces of larger stone; the eggs are then fertilized by males. We have observed this behavior in aquaria.

Distribution and Status: The Spotfin Shiner occurs in the Mississippi River, Ohio River, and Great Lakes basins, and some Atlantic slope drainages. Distribution of this species includes every county within the Chicago Region. The records are concentrated primarily within large rivers, large streams, and glacial lakes, excluding Lake Michigan. This species is common and abundant within the Chicago Region.

References: Page and Burr 2011; Smith 1979

TRUE MINNOWS (LEUCISCIDAE)   165

Gravel Chub

Erimystax x-punctatus · *Erimystax*, Greek, means "very mustached," which pertains to the barbels; *x-punctata* is Latin, "spotted with *x*'s."

Description: The Gravel Chub is a silvery to dusky minnow with a long, slender body that is slightly compressed dorsoventrally. Main characteristics include barbels at the corners of the mouth and outlined scales that give an appearance of X- or Y-shaped patterns. Other distinctive characteristics include large eyes, a bulbous snout, and a subterminal mouth with thin lips. Breeding males develop minute tubercles on the head, body, and pectoral fins. Adults are usually less than 4 inches (100 mm) in length.

Natural History: The Gravel Chub inhabits small to large rivers in the deep, swift-flowing areas of riffles. Preferred substrate types include sand, small gravel, and sometimes large cobbles. Its diet consists of small plant particles and small aquatic insects. This species is also unique in having a high density of taste buds on its snout for prey detection. Spawning appears to take place in early spring, but the life cycle of this fish is not well known. The Gravel Chub is dependent on natural fluvial processes and the sorting of substrates associated with meandering rivers to provide required gravel bars and shoals.

Distribution and Status: The Gravel Chub is known from disjunct populations within the Mississippi River,

Gravel Chub records, 1997 and 2013

Ohio River, and Great Lakes basins. This species has been collected only three times in the Chicago Region, in 1997. The records are all from the Kishwaukee River in Winnebago County, Illinois (INHS), and the South Branch Kishwaukee River in DeKalb County, Illinois (INHS), both part of the Rock River system. The species is limited by habitat availability and may also be impacted by dams and poor water quality. The Gravel Chub is considered rare and sensitive, with potential for extirpation from the Chicago Region. This species is listed as threatened in Illinois and endangered in Wisconsin.

References: Eddy and Underhill 1974; Hubbs and Lagler 1964; Tiemann, Sherwood, and Stites 2022; Trautman 1957; Willink and Dreslik 2023b

Brassy Minnow

Hybognathus hankinsoni · *Hybognathus*, Greek, means "swollen jaw," referring to the upper jaw; *hankinsoni* is in honor of the ichthyologist T. L. Hankinson.

Description: The Brassy Minnow is a small, dusky-yellowish minnow with a fusiform (oval cross-section) body shape. The dorsal surface is olive green, fading to a brassy hue just above and below a dusky and diffuse lateral stripe. The upper jaw overhangs the lower jaw, giving it a blunt snout that is about equal to the eye diameter. The dorsal fin is rounded at the rear edge. Other characteristics include 7–8 anal rays, a straight lateral line with about 35 scales, 13–15 pectoral rays, and fins with a light, dusky pigment. The intestine is longer than most other minnows, giving it a very soft belly and a black peritoneum. According to Eddy and Underhill (1974), the best way to distinguish this species from the Silvery Minnow is the radii count on the scales, to be viewed under a microscope: 20 for Brassy Minnow and 10–12 for Silvery Minnow. Adult fish are usually 3–4 inches (75–100 mm) in length.

Natural History: The Brassy Minnow live in creeks, small rivers, lakes, and bogs. All observations within the Chicago Region are associated with riverine systems. Habitat preference includes vegetated muddy areas in slack water. This species is primarily herbivorous, feeding on detritus, diatoms, and algae. Spawning takes place in the spring over vegetation.

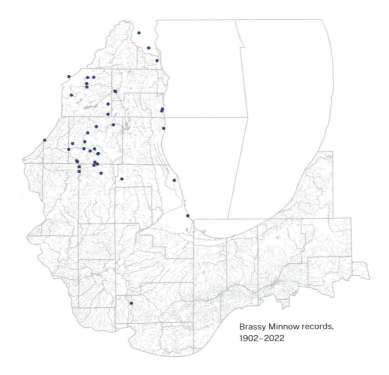

Brassy Minnow records, 1902–2022

Distribution and Status: The Brassy Minnow is typically a Grand Prairie minnow species, with some records within the northern forests of the Great Lakes region. Within the Chicago Region, known localities are predominantly in the Kishwaukee and upper Fox River drainages. The single existing disjunct population in Horse Creek of the Kankakee River, Illinois, was confirmed by the INHS in 1994. The few records from the Great Lakes basin are typically old (1902–1947), except for 1 specimen taken in 1987 (INHS) from the North Shore Channel, Cook County, Illinois. This species is listed as threatened in Illinois. Due to its very limited distribution and abundance, we consider it a species of special concern.

References: R. M. Bailey 1954; Becker 1983; Eddy and Underhill 1974; Page and Burr 2011; Smith 1979

Description: The Mississippi Silvery Minnow is a small, silvery minnow with a fusiform body shape. The upper jaw overhangs the lower jaw, giving it a blunt snout that is longer than the eye diameter. The dorsal fin is pointed (falcate) at the rear edge. Other characteristics include 7–8 anal rays, a straight lateral line with about 35–39 scales, 15–16 pectoral rays, and fins having no pigment. The intestine is longer than most other minnows', giving it a very soft belly and a black peritoneum. Breeding males develop small tubercles on the head, body, and fins. According to Eddy and Underhill (1974), the best way to distinguish this species from the Silvery Minnow is the radii count on the scales, to be viewed under a microscope: 20 for Brassy Minnow and 10–12 for Silvery Minnow. The adult Mississippi Silvery Minnow can reach a length of 5 to 6 inches (125 to 150 mm).

Natural History: The Mississippi Silvery Minnow is found primarily in larger rivers — usually in backwaters with less current, over mud or sandy bottoms. It typically forages on algae and diatoms in schools over the surface of the soft sediment. Spawning takes place in late spring, with eggs broadcast over the soft substrates.

Distribution and Status: The Mississippi Silvery Minnow has been

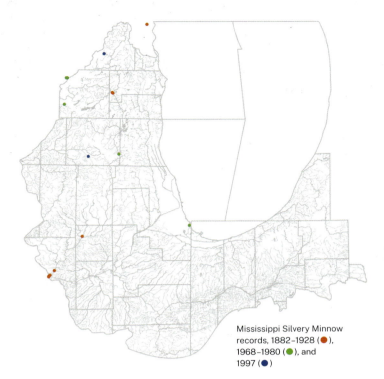

Mississippi Silvery Minnow records, 1882–1928 (●), 1968–1980 (●), and 1997 (●)

recorded at only 9 localities within the Chicago Region, most of them quite old (1882–1928). The most recent record is from the South Branch Kishwaukee River, taken by the INHS in 1997. The Calumet River, Cook County, Illinois (INHS 1980), record could be from a bait-bucket introduction, as it was collected in the deep navigation channel. Muddy slackwater habitats with native vegetation are highly vulnerable to historic and more recent degradation (channelization and drainage), which could account for the limited occurrence within the Chicago Region. We consider this a species of special concern within the Chicago Region, with potential for extirpation.

References: R. M. Bailey 1954; Eddy and Underhill 1974; Forbes and Richardson 1920; Pflieger 1975; Smith 1979

Pallid Shiner

Hybopsis amnis · *Hybopsis*, Greek, "rounded face"; *amnis*, Latin, "of the river."

Description: The Pallid Shiner is a small, pale minnow with a fusiform body, large elliptical eyes, and a rounded snout. Other distinguishing characteristics include a subterminal horizontal mouth, a diffuse lateral band evident as a bridle around the nose, and the absence of barbels. Characteristics that distinguish the Pallid Shiner from other minnows with a lateral band include lack of pigmentation on the lower lip or chin, 8 anal rays, 8 dorsal rays, and lack of pigment in the body and the fins except for diffusely outlining the dorsal scales. The diffuse lateral band is darker in preserved specimens. In some specimens, the body is deeper before the dorsal fin, giving that fin a high appearance. Adults attain a length of less than 3 inches (75 mm).

Natural History: The Pallid Shiner is found in medium to large rivers. Observations within the Chicago Region indicate its preferred habitats are the margins of riffles and runs with swift to moderate currents over sand and gravel substrates, often with aquatic or overhanging terrestrial vegetation. This species is most likely adapted to naturally turbid streams, based on its Mississippi River–centric distribution and pallid coloration. Kwak (1991) provided information on the ecological characteristics of a population of Pallid Shiner in the Kankakee River. Food and spawning habitats are unknown.

Distribution and Status: The Pallid Shiner occurs in the Mississippi River

Pallid Shiner records, 1895–2022

basin from Minnesota to Texas. Within the Chicago Region, this species is currently found in the lower Kankakee River and upper Illinois River, at the Des Plaines River confluence. The 1989 record for Braidwood Cooling Lake (INHS, Will County, Illinois) indicates entrainment from the Kankakee River. The 1971 (INDNR) record for the Yellow River, Starke County, Indiana, is dubious, as there is no preserved specimen, and similar-looking species occur within the area. This species has most likely been reduced in distribution and abundance due to large-river riffle habitats being destroyed by canal dredging and flooded out by impounding dams. In 2012, the Illinois Natural History Survey discovered this species farthest upstream on the Des Plaines River since the 1900 record at Berwyn, Cook County, Illinois (FMNH). This indicates the potential for the Pallid Shiner to migrate and spread should conditions improve elsewhere. This species is listed as endangered in Illinois, Wisconsin, and Indiana. In the Chicago Region it is a species of special concern, in need of further study regarding its distribution patterns and natural history.

References: Kwak 1991; Pflieger 1975; Smith 1979; Tiemann, Taylor, et al. 2015

Striped Shiner

Luxilus chrysocephalus · *Luxilus*, Latin, meaning "small, bright fish"; *chrysocephalus*, Greek, "golden head."

(*Top*) female or nonbreeding male; (*bottom*) breeding male

Description: The adult Striped Shiner is a deep-bodied minnow with a silvery-gray upper body and white belly. The juveniles are more slender and silvery translucent, with smaller scales. Distinguishing characteristics include large crescent-shaped scales and a dark stripe that runs along the dorsal surface from the head to the tail fin. Other helpful characteristics include 8–10 anal rays, 37–40 lateral line scales, 24–29 circumbody scales at the dorsal fin origin, fewer than 17 predorsal scales, a rounded dorsal fin, and a large and oblique mouth. Lines of pigment run down the back from the dorsal fin along both sides and converge at the caudal peduncle into a V shape. These stripes are sometimes difficult to discern in younger live specimens. Breeding males become intensely showy, their body taking on a rosy sheen, and their crescent scales becoming outlined with darker pigment. Tubercles also become prominent on the head, and the distal margin of dorsal, anal, and caudal fins develop rosy markings. The Striped Shiner is very similar to and hard to distinguish from the Common Shiner, especially juveniles. Also, these 2 species have an overlapping distribution and tend to hybridize. While discerning differences in post-dorsal stripes (converging in Striped Shiner, parallel in Common Shiner) is often difficult in the field, it is easier in preserved specimens and remains the most reliable albeit still troublesome characteristic, especially for smaller individuals. Adult Striped Shiners can reach 8 inches (200 mm) in length.

Striped Shiner records, 1890–2022

Natural History: The Striped Shiner primarily inhabits small to medium streams, and also occurs in large rivers. It is most abundant in runs and pools below riffles but can be found in a variety of stream habitats. This species is omnivorous, feeding on larger aquatic and terrestrial insects and plant material. Spawning takes place during spring in rocky runs with moderate current, sometimes over nests created by the Hornyhead Chub.

Distribution and Status: The Striped Shiner occurs in the Mississippi River, Ohio River, and southwestern Great Lakes basins. The first Chicago Region record for this species was taken by David Starr Jordan in 1890 from the Yellow River, Marshall County, Indiana. This species is widespread throughout the southern half of the Chicago Region but diminishes in a northern gradient, where it is replaced by the Common Shiner. This pattern is especially clear in the Fox River basin. In recent surveys, we have found only Striped Shiners in the Des Plaines and Kankakee watersheds. This minnow is not recorded from the Rock River system. As noted above, the Striped Shiner hybridizes with the Common Shiner where their distribution overlaps. Striped Shiner has been observed in bait buckets. It was listed as endangered in Wisconsin but may be extirpated. We consider the Striped Shiner abundant and stable within the Chicago Region.

References: Dowling, Broughton, and DeMarais 1997; Forbes and Richardson 1920; Hubbs and Lagler 1964; Lyons and Schmidt 2022; Pflieger 1975; Smith 1979

Common Shiner

Luxilus cornutus · *Luxilus* is Latin for "small, bright fish"; *cornutus* is also Latin, for "horned," perhaps referring to the tubercles on spawning males.

Description: The Common Shiner is a deep-bodied minnow with a silvery-gray upper body and white belly. Distinguishing characteristics include large crescent-shaped scales and a dark stripe that runs along the dorsal surface from the head to the tail fin. Other characteristics include 8–10 anal rays, 37–40 lateral line scales, 30–35 circumbody scales at the dorsal fin origin, more than 17 predorsal scales, a rounded dorsal fin, and a large and oblique mouth. The stripes on the back behind the dorsal fin do not converge, running parallel to the tail region. Similar to the Striped Shiner, the Common Shiner breeding male becomes more intensely pigmented with a rosy sheen, darker outlines on the crescent scales, prominent head tubercles, and rosy markings on the distal margin of its dorsal, anal, and caudal fins. Adults can grow to more than 7 inches (175 mm) in length. See the Striped Shiner account for distinguishing interspecies characteristics.

Natural History: The Common Shiner inhabits small to medium streams but can also be found in large rivers and sometimes lakes. In general, natural history, spawning, and food habitats are known to be like those of the Striped Shiner. This species spawns in late May and June over excavated

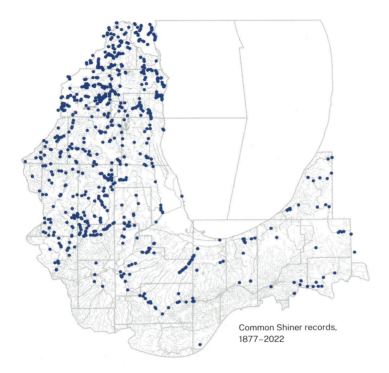

Common Shiner records, 1877–2022

nests, sometimes using nests of other fish species; the male will defend a nest against intrusion by other males.

Distribution and Status: The Common Shiner occurs in the upper Mississippi River, Great Lakes, and Atlantic slope basins to North Carolina. The first Chicago Region record for this species was taken by David Starr Jordan in 1877 from Clear and Pine Lakes, LaPorte County, Indiana. This species occurs in abundance throughout the northern half of the Chicago Region but diminishes in a southern gradient, where it is replaced by the Striped Shiner. We have observed this species in live bait markets. The Common Shiner is abundant and stable within the Chicago Region; however, additional study on its sympatric (overlapping) distribution with the Striped Shiner is needed.

References: Becker 1983; Dowling, Broughton, and DeMarais 1997; Hubbs and Lagler 1964; Lyons and Schmidt 2022; Page and Burr 2011; Pflieger 1975; Smith 1979

Redfin Shiner

Lythrurus umbratilis · *Lythrurus* means "blood tail" in Greek, in reference to the red coloration; *umbratilis*, from the Latin word *umbra*, means "shade."

Description: The Redfin Shiner is a fusiform minnow with a somewhat deep body covered by small scales. Distinguishing characteristics include a small dark blotch of pigment at the anterior base of the dorsal fin, 10–12 anal fin rays, an eye diameter larger than the mouth, and the dorsal fin origin behind the pelvic fin. Other helpful characteristics include more than 38 lateral line scales, a rounded belly, and a dusky stripe along the midline of the body. Silvery sides are speckled with fine dusky spots, and the mouth is terminal and oblique. Nuptial males develop a deep metallic blue on the sides, red with black pigment on the fins, and fine tubercles on the body and fins. The bigger males become enlarged on the nape. Typical adult size is 3 inches (75 mm).

Natural History: The Redfin Shiner prefers the lower-gradient portions of small to large streams over finer substrates. It is somewhat tolerant of warmer temperatures and higher turbidity and is often found in agricultural ditches. We found algae, seeds, copepods, macroinvertebrates, and larval fishes in the gut content of

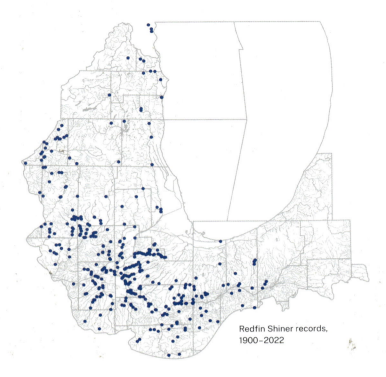

Redfin Shiner records, 1900–2022

150 individuals. Spawning activity has been observed from late April through August, with the Redfin Shiner utilizing the nests of other fishes.

Distribution and Status: The Redfin Shiner occurs from the Hudson Bay south to Texas and east to Maine. The first Chicago Region record for this species was in 1900 from the Des Plaines River at Berwyn, Illinois (FMNH). This species is found sporadically around the Chicago Region but is absent from the St. Joseph, Galien, and upper Kankakee River systems in Indiana and not present in Michigan. It is common within the upper Illinois River tributaries but is not typically found in high abundance. We have observed this species in bait buckets. We consider this species stable within the Chicago Region, but it is listed as threatened in Wisconsin.

References: Hubbs and Lagler 1964; Pflieger 1975; Smith 1979; Trautman 1957

Shoal Chub

Macrhybopsis hyostoma · *Macrhybopsis*, from the Greek for "round face"; *hyostoma* is from *hyo*, meaning "hog," and *stoma*, meaning "mouth," referring to the fish's subterminal mouth.

Description: The Shoal Chub is a delicate, translucent minnow with relatively small eyes, and black round spots scattered on its the back and sides. The upper body has a pale-yellow tint, and the lower body is silvery white. The snout is long and bulbous, extending far beyond the upper lip. Conical barbels are readily apparent, extending from the corners of its small, horizontal mouth. The dorsal fin is well in front of the pelvic fin; the anal fin ray count is 6–7. Breeding males do not display any special coloration but have small tubercles in the head region and on pectoral fin rays. Adults are less than 3 inches (75 mm) in length.

Natural History: The Shoal Chub is typically a large-river fish, inhabiting areas of sluggish flow over fine substrates. This species has adapted to turbid rivers and has external taste buds on the head, body, and fins, reducing its reliance on sight feeding. Primary food items include insect larvae, small crustaceans, small adult insects, and plant material. Spawning takes place throughout the spring and summer in faster-flowing water, where eggs develop as they drift on the current.

Distribution and Status: The Shoal Chub occurs in the Mississippi and Ohio River basins and Gulf slope

Shoal Chub records, 1981–2022

drainages. This species was recorded only 8 times within the Chicago Region, from the Illinois River. Although the Shoal Chub is common in the larger rivers of the Mississippi basin, it is rare in the Chicago Region due in part to the lack of large-river habitat. It may also be affected by locks and dams, dredging, and river channelization. We consider this a species of special concern and in need of further study. The Shoal Chub is listed as threatened in Wisconsin.

References: Metzke, Burr, et al. 2022; Page and Burr 2011; Smith 1979

Silver Chub

Macrhybopsis storeriana · *Macrhybopsis* is Greek for "round face"; *storeriana* is in homage to D. H. Storer, an early North American ichthyologist and naturalist.

Description: The Silver Chub is a large, slender minnow with no distinctive markings or spots. The coloration is mostly silver, with a faint green tinge in the dorsal region. The eye is larger than other species within this genus, its diameter nearly equal to the length of the snout. The snout is blunt and extends beyond the upper lip. A short conical barbel is located at the corners of the small horizontal mouth. The dorsal fin has 8 rays and is situated in front of the pelvic fin. The anal fin has 7–8 rays. Breeding adult males have no enhanced coloration but develop small tubercles that traverse the pectoral rays dorsally. One of the larger species of this genus, the Silver Chub may attain a length of 9 inches (225 mm) but is more commonly observed in the 4–6-inch (100–150-mm) range.

Natural History: The Silver Chub is typically found in large rivers and lakes, usually in quiet, deep pools over sand and gravel substrates. Food items include aquatic and terrestrial insects and larvae, tiny mussels, and seeds. Although this species' spawning habits are not well known, it is reported to spawn in June and July, preferring rocky substrate, with the pelagic development of embryos similar to that of the Shoal Chub.

Silver Chub records, 1901 (●) and 1981–1993 (●)

Distribution and Status: The Silver Chub occurs within the Mississippi River, Red River, and Great Lakes basins. This species has been observed only 3 times within the Chicago Region, all from the Illinois River. Although occurrence is limited regionally by lack of larger-river habitat, it may also be limited by locks and dams, dredging, and channelization. It is possible this species existed or still exists in Lake Michigan, as suggested by the large population in Lake Erie. The Silver Chub is listed as threatened in Michigan. We consider this a species of special concern. More information on its distribution and habitats is needed.

References: Hubbs and Lagler 1964; Pflieger 1975; Smith 1979; Trautman 1957

Northern Pearl Dace

Margariscus nachtriebi • *Margariscus*, Latin for "pearl"; *nachtriebi*, origin unknown.

Description: The Northern Pearl Dace is a terete (cylindrical, tapering) minnow with a small terminal mouth and a blunt snout. A small barbel can be found in the crease of the upper lip near the corners of the mouth, but this barbel is not always present. To distinguish this species from the Creek Chub, note that the mouth does not reach the eye and the anterior base of the dorsal fin is without dark pigment. The Northern Pearl Dace has 8 anal rays, 8 dorsal rays, and 60–75 lateral line scales. Upper-body coloration is variable, ranging from light gray (pearl) to mottled black and brown. A faint lateral stripe is sometimes present, which is more distinct in juveniles. Breeding males develop tiny tubercles on the head, body, and pectoral fins and become pinkish in color with a prominent red lateral stripe. Adult size is 6 inches (150 mm).

Natural History: The Northern Pearl Dace is generally restricted to cold-water streams, preferring areas of sand, gravel, and silt. We observed this species in Wisconsin in very cold water associated with overhanging fringe marsh and meadow vegetation. This fish will feed on any small aquatic or terrestrial insects, plankton, and algae. Spawning behavior is more elaborate than most minnow species, with the male defending loosely defined territories, allowing

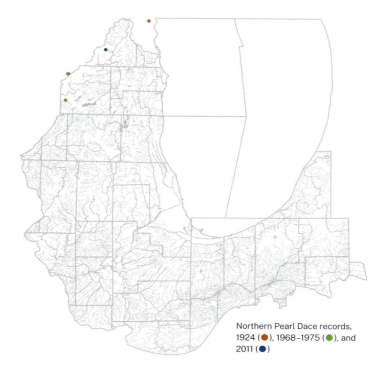

Northern Pearl Dace records, 1924 (●), 1968–1975 (●), and 2011 (●)

only females in to breed. Nest building or material moving has not been observed.

Distribution and Status: The Northern Pearl Dace occurs in disjunct populations within the upper Mississippi River, Great Lakes, Hudson Bay, and some northern Atlantic slope drainages. The Chicago Region is at the limit of its southern distribution. As such, the only 3 records for this species within the Chicago Region are from the Rock River system in Walworth County, Wisconsin (MPM 1968), and Waukesha County, Wisconsin (WDNR 2011). The 1924 record from the Milwaukee River is included out of interest. The most likely limiting factor is its necessity for coldwater streams with ample groundwater inputs.

References: Eddy and Underhill 1974; Hubbs and Lagler 1964

Hornyhead Chub

Nocomis biguttatus · *Nocomis* (or Nokomis) is Ojibwe for "daughter of the moon" or "grandmother"; *biguttatus* is Latin, meaning "two spotted."

Description: The Hornyhead Chub is a robust minnow with large, distinct scales, a relatively small eye, and a barbel in the corners of the mouth. Body coloration is brown above a diffuse black lateral stripe fading to tan below and white on the belly. The dorsal scales are outlined by dark pigment. In nuptial males, the body colors and pigmentation intensify, with the throat, belly, and pectoral fins becoming tinged with red. Breeding males also have prominent tubercles, with larger individuals developing a red spot behind the eye. Juveniles have a reddish-orange tail, and the caudal peduncle spot is more distinct. This species can be distinguished from the similar Creek Chub by a more subterminal and smaller mouth that does not extend to the front of the eye, larger scales with 48 or fewer in the lateral line, a distinct caudal spot, and the absence of a dark blotch at the anterior base of the dorsal fin. Also, the upper lip of the Hornyhead Chub is uniform in width, while the Creek Chub's is thicker at the middle portion. Adult Hornyhead Chubs can grow up to 10 inches (250 mm) but are typically smaller, ranging from 4–8 inches (100–200 mm).

Natural History: The Hornyhead Chub inhabits creeks and small rivers with clear water flowing over rubble, gravel, or bedrock. It is tolerant of moderate turbidity but less common under these conditions, requiring clean substrates to reproduce. It forages on aquatic insect larvae, small crayfishes, small fishes, snails, worms, and plant matter. Spawning takes place in early summer, with the male choosing an area clear of fine sediment in the glide above or the run below a riffle. He then carries smaller gravel in his mouth and pushes the stones with his snout to build a gravel pile up to 2 feet (61 cm) in diameter and several inches tall. The male will spawn with multiple females while building a nest, hence eggs are distributed throughout the layers of gravel. As we have observed, and well noted in the literature, other species of minnows and darters spawn over Hornyhead Chub nests. With many minnow species spawning in proximity over the nest, the potential for hybridization is high. The Common Shiner will even help guard the nest for a time.

Hornyhead Chub
records, 1895–2022

Distribution and Status: The Hornyhead Chub occurs in the Mississippi River, Ohio River, and Great Lakes basins. This species is common and widespread throughout the Chicago Region, and usually abundant where conditions are favorable. It is not found in highly degraded streams and is less common in low-gradient areas. It is absent from the Chicago and Calumet Rivers due to the absence of riffle-run habitats. The Hornyhead Chub status is stable and is considered somewhat of a keystone species due to the use of its nests by other fish species.

References: Becker 1983; Cahn 1927; Forbes and Richardson 1920; Hankinson 1920, 1932; Hubbs and Cooper 1936; Smith 1979

Golden Shiner

Notemigonus crysoleucas · *Notemigonus*, Greek, means "angled back"; *crysoleucas*, also Greek, means "golden white."

Description: The Golden Shiner has a very deep and thin (laterally compressed) body. It differs from all other native minnow species in having an unscaled ventral keel between the anus and pelvic fins, and a strongly downcurved lateral line. The dorsal fin has 8 rays and is set back toward the caudal fin. The anal fin is moderately pointed (falcate), with 11–14 rays. The mouth is terminal, upwardly curved, and proportionally small. There are typically 42–54 lateral line scales. Adults are silvery gold, darker on the dorsal region; the fins are often yellowish in color. Breeding males develop a more golden hue with orange to reddish fins. Juveniles are less laterally compressed, with a silvery body and a diffuse black stripe from the gill cover to the base of the tail. Sometimes the Golden Shiner breeding male is misidentified as the invasive Rudd (*Scardinius erythrophthalmus*). The Rudd can be distinguished from the Golden Shiner by having a scaled (versus unscaled) keel and 36–45 lateral line scales (versus 42–54); further, if fins are colored, they are bright red (versus more orange). The adult Golden Shiner can reach up to 7 inches (175 mm) but is usually smaller.

Natural History: The Golden Shiner lives in ponds, lakes, streams, rivers, and other connected aquatic systems.

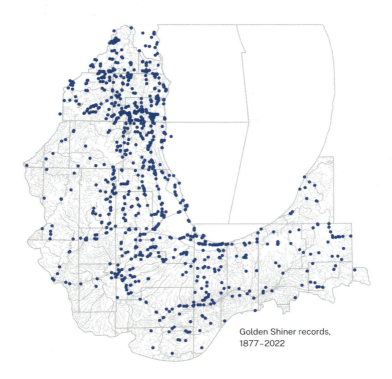

Golden Shiner records, 1877–2022

Preferred habitat includes moderately flowing to still waters, often associated with aquatic vegetation when present. We have observed this species in nearly all types of habitats, including polluted streams with low dissolved oxygen and general habitat degradation. The Golden Shiner is omnivorous, feeding on aquatic insects, terrestrial insects, crustaceans, mollusks, algae, and plant matter. Spawning takes place in the spring and sometimes in late summer when temperatures recede. The eggs are broadcast over plants or the nests of other fishes.

Distribution and Status: The Golden Shiner occurs naturally from the Rockies to the Atlantic slope in the US and Canada. This species can be found in most water bodies within the Chicago Region. It is widely traded and transported as baitfish and will continue to be introduced into many systems. This species is considered common and tolerant to pollution and habitat degradation. Although the similar-looking Rudd is reported in the Chicago Region, there are no known established populations or official records.

References: Burkhead and Williams 1991; Forbes and Richardson 1920; Page and Burr 2011

Pugnose Shiner

Notropis anogenus • *Notropis*, Greek, means "keeled back"; *anogenus*, also Greek, means "without chin."

Description: The Pugnose Shiner is a small fusiform or spindle-shaped minnow, straw colored above a dark lateral band and translucent to white below. Distinguishing characteristics include a small, vertical, superior mouth, and a dark lateral band continuing around the nose. A dark triangular spot at the tail appears separate from the lateral band. Characteristics that help distinguish the Pugnose Shiner from other laterally banded minnows include pigmentation on the lower lip but not the chin, 7–10 anal rays, 8 dorsal rays, diffuse pigment at the base of the anal fin, and dorsal scales outlined in pigment. This small minnow rarely reaches 2 inches (50 mm) in length.

Natural History: The Pugnose Shiner is typically found in glacial lakes and connected sloughs with abundant aquatic vegetation and clear water. Historically it may have been more abundant in clear, sluggish streams and rivers. We have observed small schools foraging primarily in the middle of the water column feeding on crustaceans and algae at Cross Lake, Antioch, Illinois. When startled, the Pugnose Shiner dives to the bottom and hides in vegetation, making it very difficult to catch with nets or electrofishing methods. Spawning

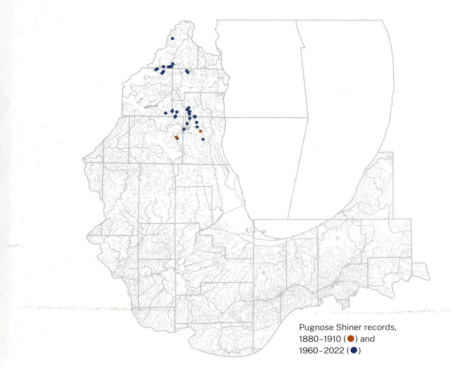

Pugnose Shiner records, 1880–1910 (●) and 1960–2022 (●)

takes place in the late spring to early summer.

Distribution and Status: This species is found within the glacial lakes and northern forest ecoregion of the Red River, the upper Mississippi River, and the Great Lakes. This species is currently restricted to the glacial lakes of northern Illinois and Wisconsin within the Chicago Region. These lakes have been widely altered by human activities, which has led to the species' disappearance. The presence of the Pugnose Shiner within the Chicago Region was confirmed in the late 1990s and early 2000s by Southern Illinois University and Wisconsin DNR inventories. It is listed as endangered in Illinois and Michigan, threatened in Wisconsin, and of special concern in Indiana. Although the Chicago Region is at the southern distribution limit of the Pugnose Shiner, we consider it a species of special concern. Its presence is indicative of healthy native aquatic plants and clean water.

References: R. M. Bailey 1959; Becker 1983; Eddy and Underhill 1974; Forbes 1885; Greenberg 2002; Hubbs and Lagler 1964

Emerald Shiner

Notropis atherinoides · *Notropis*, Greek for "keeled back"; *atherinoides*, Greek for "silverside-like," due to a similarity to the silverside family.

Description: The Emerald Shiner is a long, fusiform, and laterally compressed minnow with a greenish hue when viewed from above. The body is silver; the dorsal scales are lightly outlined in pigment. Distinguishing characteristics include 8 dorsal rays, 10–13 anal rays, a terminal and oblique mouth, and the dorsal fin's origin behind the pelvic fin. Breeding individuals do not display coloration but do develop tiny tubercles on the head. This species can be distinguished from the similar Rosyface and Carmine Shiners by a more rounded, shorter snout that is equal to or less than the eye diameter. Adults grow to a length of 4–5 inches (100–125 mm).

Natural History: The Emerald Shiner occurs in medium to large rivers and large oligotrophic lakes. There appears to be no specific substrate preference as it is a pelagic fish, continually moving in schools that feed primarily on zooplankton. Spawning was observed during the night from late May to late June, with eggs broadcast in open water over sandy beaches. Little else is known about this species' spawning habits and requirements within the Chicago Region.

Distribution and Status: The Emerald Shiner occurs from Saskatchewan to Texas, inclusive of the Mississippi River, Ohio River, and

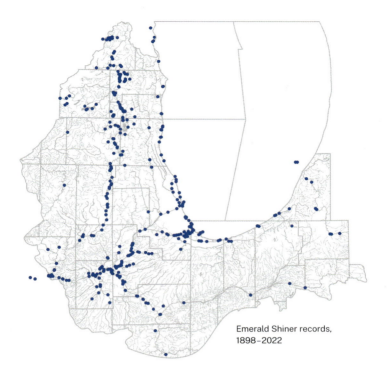

Emerald Shiner records, 1898–2022

Great Lakes basins. It is widely distributed within the Chicago Region in larger rivers and Lake Michigan. It is also found sporadically in smaller streams. Historic accounts indicate it used to be abundant in immense schools within the Great Lakes, indicating a keystone role as a forage fish. The Emerald Shiner is stable and often very abundant where found.

References: Hubbs and Lagler 1964; Smith 1979; Trautman 1957; Woods 1957a

Description: The River Shiner is a rather large, slender minnow lacking distinctive markings. It has a large, oblique mouth and larger scales. The dorsal area is tan colored, fading to white on the underside. A wide predorsal stripe runs along the length of the dorsal surface. The River Shiner is one of only a few minnow species with 7 anal rays. The lateral line runs along the entire length but lacks pigmentation. Smaller specimens may be confused with the Sand Shiner, which also has 7 anal rays; however, the Sand Shiner has a wedge of pigment in front of the dorsal fin and a distinctly pigmented (punctate) lateral line. The Sand Shiner's mouth is also smaller, not exceeding the diameter of the eye. Adults attain a length of 4–5 inches (100–125 mm).

Natural History: The River Shiner, true to its name, lives almost exclusively in large rivers. It prefers areas sheltered from the main current, usually with a sand, rubble, or mud bottom. Vegetation is usually absent. This species feeds on aquatic insect larvae and spawns during the summer over sand and gravel.

Distribution and Status: The River Shiner is found primarily in the upper Illinois River, with some individuals entering the lower Fox, Des Plaines,

River Shiner records, 1878–2022

and Kankakee Rivers. Records beyond these areas are sporadic and/or questionable. Historically, Sand Shiners, Mimic Shiners, Bigmouth Shiners, and others have often been misidentified as River Shiners, inaccurately portraying the actual range.

This species requires further investigation of its ecology and distribution.

References: Becker 1983; Forbes and Richardson 1920; Hubbs and Lagler 1964; Pflieger 1975; Smith 1979

Silverjaw Minnow

Notropis buccatus · *Notropis*, Greek, means "keeled back"; *buccatus*, Latin, means "cheek," referring to the depressions in the fish's lower cheek.

Description: The Silverjaw Minnow has a fusiform body with a slightly depressed head, a small subterminal mouth, and large, upward-looking eyes. The body coloration is pale and silvery with a tan back and white belly. This minnow is distinct from all others in having a row of pearl organs appearing as slight indentations on the snout, between the eye and the upper jaw and wrapping around the lower margin of the eye. The pearl organs are divided by walls into cavernous chambers that are part of the sensory system. The Trout-perch is the only other species in the Chicago Region to have pearl organs but can be distinguished by having an adipose fin. The adult Silverjaw Minnow is typically less than 3 inches (75 mm) in length.

Natural History: The Silverjaw Minnow inhabits small streams, including headwaters with perennial flow. As well, we have found this species in older, naturalized agricultural ditches with good base-flow water quality. It prefers shifting-sand-and-pea-gravel bars below riffles and in runs, where it schools and feeds on cladocerans and midge larvae, and to some extent detritus. The pearl organs are thought to be sensory structures that help the Silverjaw Minnow find food on or in sandy substrate. We have observed this species spawning over coarse sand below

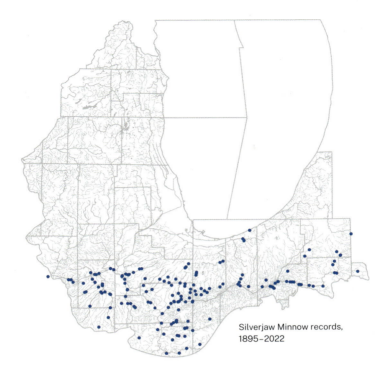

Silverjaw Minnow records, 1895–2022

riffles, which is similar to reported studies.

Distribution and Status: The Silverjaw Minnow occurs from Illinois to Maryland in the Ohio River basin and southern tip of the Great Lakes basin, south to the Cumberland River in Tennessee. Most of the Chicago Region records for this species are from the Kankakee River system and upper Illinois River tributaries.

The records for the Lake Michigan drainage are old (1937–1947), from Coffee Creek, Porter County, Indiana (Gerking 1945). This species may be extirpated from the Great Lakes drainage within the Chicago Region but is stable within the Kankakee River system.

References: Etnier and Starnes 1993; Gerking 1945; Page and Burr 2011; Smith 1979; Trautman 1957

TRUE MINNOWS (LEUCISCIDAE)

Description: The Ghost Shiner has a fusiform body that is slightly deeper just in front of the dorsal fin. As suggested by the name, its body coloration is light and translucent with only scattered pigmentation. Other distinguishing characteristics include falcate (sickle-shaped) dorsal and anal fins, and long pelvic fins reaching back to the origin of the anal fin when collapsed. The lateral line scales just behind the gill are higher than wide (elevated). The snout is rounded, with a slightly subterminal oblique mouth. The dorsal and anal fins usually have 8 rays. Adults are typically less than 2 inches (50 mm) in length.

Natural History: The Ghost Shiner is a large-river species, occupying deep pools and backwaters. This species prefers slow-moving and sluggish waters over silt substrates and can be tolerant of turbid and polluted waters. We have observed this species in the Cal–Sag Channel in water 10–14 feet (3.0–4.3 m) deep along the bottom, primarily among small woody debris, detritus, muck, algal mats, and rubbish. Little is known of its food and spawning habits.

Distribution and Status: The Ghost Shiner occurs in the Mississippi and Ohio River basins and the Gulf drainages in Texas. There is an isolated

Ghost Shiner records, 1957–2022

population between Lakes Huron and Erie. This species is considered nonnative to the Lake Michigan drainages, although access can now be gained through the artificial Chicago Area Waterway System. We have taken this species by means of deepwater trawling from the Cal–Sag Channel and the Calumet River in the navigation canal portions (INHS 1999; FMNH 2010). Most records are from the Kankakee and Illinois Rivers. A large collection was made in the Little Calumet River in 2013. The Ghost Shiner is stable within its natural Illinois River system range. More information is needed on this elusive species.

References: Page and Burr 2011; Smith 1979; Trautman 1957

Ironcolor Shiner

Notropis chalybaeus · *Notropis* means "keeled back" in Greek; *chalybaeus* is Greek for "iron-colored."

Description: The Ironcolor Shiner is a fusiform, straw-colored minnow with a dark lateral band extending around the snout. Body coloration is very light and translucent below the lateral band. Characteristics distinguishing the Ironcolor Shiner from other laterally banded minnows include a small, oblique mouth with pigmentation on the lower lip and chin, dark pigment at the base of the anal fin, and dorsal scales well outlined in pigment. There is also pigmentation inside the mouth. It has 8 anal rays and 8 dorsal rays. The top edge of the lateral band is diffuse, whereas the bottom margin has a clean distinct edge. Adults can reach up to 2.5 inches (65 mm).

Natural History: The Ironcolor Shiner is found in small creeks to medium rivers, where they prefer areas of moderate to slow current, with sandy substrates, aquatic vegetation, and woody debris, often near confluences of streams and backwaters. A mixed school of Ironcolor and Weed Shiners was observed in moderate current at the discharge channel of a Kankakee River backwater in Newton County, Indiana. The Ironcolor Shiner is an omnivore, eating detritus and various invertebrate prey. Although it spawns primarily in spring or early summer, we have found gravid females in August in the Kankakee River system.

Ironcolor Shiner records, 1895–2022

Distribution and Status: The Ironcolor Shiner occurs in disjunct populations from Wisconsin south to Texas in the Mississippi basin, and Atlantic and Gulf slope drainages. It does not occur in the Great Lakes basin. All records for this species within the Chicago Region are from the eastern sand basin of the Kankakee River system. There is 1 old record from the Des Plaines River at Berwyn, Cook County, Illinois (INHS 1901). The Ironcolor Shiner is listed as threatened in Illinois and extinct in Michigan. Within the Chicago Region it is rare, but it appears to be stable in the Kankakee River system.

References: Page and Burr 2011; Smith 1979

Bigmouth Shiner

Notropis dorsalis · *Notropis* means "keeled back" in Greek; *dorsalis*, Latin, pertaining to the back.

Description: The Bigmouth Shiner has a fusiform body and a dorsally flattened head. Distinguishing characteristics include a large (length greater than eye diameter) subterminal, nearly horizontal mouth and a complete lateral line punctuated by pigment on either side. The color is drab brown above and silvery below. It usually has 8 anal fin rays and a dark, uniform dorsal stripe. The Bigmouth Shiner is very similar to the Sand Shiner, which has 7 anal rays, a smaller mouth, and a wedge of pigment in front of the dorsal fin. This species vaguely resembles the Silverjaw Minnow but lacks pearl organs below the mouth. Adult Bigmouth Shiners grow up to 3 inches (75 mm).

Natural History: The Bigmouth Shiner occupies perennial headwater creeks, streams, and small rivers. It is found most often in areas of slower current over sand and/or silt. This species is tolerant to habitat alternation and has been observed in abundance in channelized streams. Its food consists mostly of benthic aquatic invertebrates, but it will consume detritus and plant material. Spawning takes place primarily in June and July.

Distribution and Status: The Bigmouth Shiner occurs in the upper Mississippi River basin and some smaller disjunct populations in the Great Lakes basin. It was recorded in

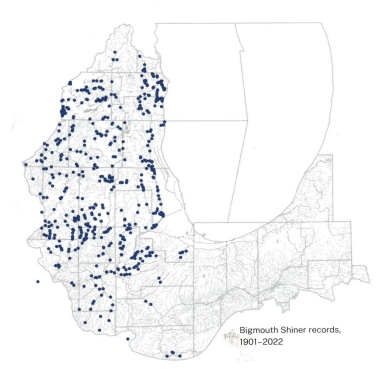

Bigmouth Shiner records, 1901–2022

the Chicago Region for the first time in 1901 from the Fox River at Millbrook, Kendall County, Illinois (INHS). Within the Chicago Region it is found in most watersheds in Illinois and Wisconsin. It is largely absent from the Kankakee River drainage and is overall rare or absent in Indiana, where it is a species of special concern. In Michigan it is listed as threatened. It is stable within the Chicago Region.

References: Eddy and Underhill 1974; Page and Burr 2011; Smith 1979

Blackchin Shiner

Notropis heterodon · *Notropis* means "keeled back" in Greek; *heterodon*, also Greek, means "varying teeth."

Description: The Blackchin Shiner is a fusiform minnow that is straw to olive colored above a dark lateral band, and translucent to white below. The lateral band continues around the nose above a small terminal and oblique mouth. To distinguish the Blackchin Shiner among other laterally banded minnows, these characteristics are useful: pigmentation present on the lower lip and the chin, 8 anal rays, 8 dorsal rays, dark pigment at the base of the anal fin, and dorsal scales well outlined in pigment. Another unique identifying feature is the distinct zigzag pattern in the front portion of the lateral band. In addition, there is no pigmentation inside the mouth. Adults are typically less than 3 inches (75 mm) in length.

Natural History: The Blackchin Shiner is usually found in natural lakes with abundant aquatic vegetation and clear water. We have also observed this species in streams and rivers with slow currents and aquatic vegetation. The Blackchin Shiner feeds on small crustaceans, amphipods, and midge larvae, foraging in submerged plants in midwater or at the surface. It spawns in the late spring to summer among aquatic plants.

Distribution and Status: The Blackchin Shiner occurs in the upper

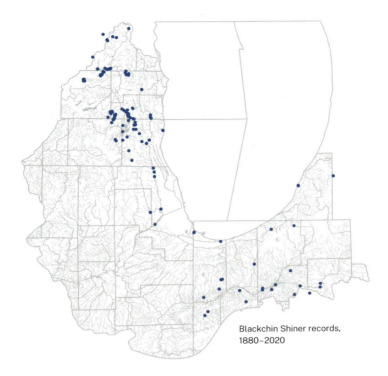

Blackchin Shiner records, 1880–2020

Mississippi River and Great Lakes basins. Within the Chicago Region, this species occurs sporadically within the Lake Michigan drainages, with centers of abundance in the glacial lakes of the upper Fox River system and in the upper reaches of the Kankakee River watershed. The Kankakee River population is the southernmost extent of its distribution in North America. It is relatively sensitive to water quality and habitat degradation, especially impacts to native aquatic vegetation. This species is listed as threatened in Illinois. There are recent collections in the Des Plaines River indicating range expansion there. Further study is needed regarding its distribution and status throughout the region.

References: Becker 1983; Burr, Santucci, et al. 2005; Forbes and Richardson 1920

Blacknose Shiner

Notropis heterolepis · *Notropis* is Greek for "keeled back"; *heterolepis* is also Greek, meaning "various scales," referring to its different-size scales.

Description: The Blacknose Shiner is a terete (cylindrical, tapering at both ends) minnow with a silvery-straw color above a dark lateral band extending around the nose. Its body is translucent to white below, and it has a slightly subterminal horizontal mouth. In comparison to other laterally banded minnows, there is no pigmentation on the lower lip or chin and the dorsal scales are heavily outlined in pigment. There is a band of unpigmented scales just above the lateral line and below the pigmented dorsal scales. There is also pigment at the base of the anal fin, which contains 8 rays. The lateral black stripe contains crescent-shaped patterns— another unique feature of this species. Adults are typically 3 inches (75 mm) or less in length.

Natural History: The Blacknose Shiner is usually found in glacial lakes and sluggish streams with abundant aquatic vegetation and clear water. Our most recent observations indicate its preferred habitat is in the shallow littoral zone, 2–4 feet (0.6–1.2 m) deep among tall pondweeds and milfoils. The substrates were primarily muck and sand. We have not observed this species in stream habitats, but it could occur if lake-like habitat conditions are present. The Blacknose Shiner spawns

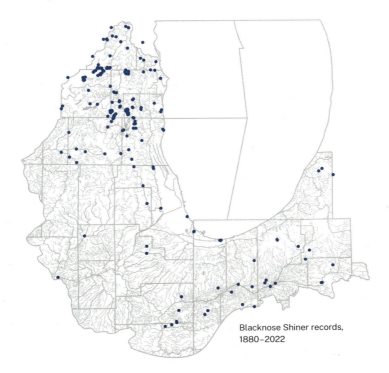

Blacknose Shiner records, 1880–2022

in late spring to early summer and feeds primarily on crustaceans.

Distribution and Status: The Blacknose Shiner is a species of the northern forest and glacial lakes ecoregions with the Chicago Region at its southern limit. It is most persistent in the glacial lakes and connected sloughs in Wisconsin, northern Illinois, and Berrien County, Michigan. An intensive survey by Southern Illinois University and the Wisconsin DNR in the late 1990s and early 2000s confirmed population stability in the northern glacial lakes.

Recent records from Stone Lake, LaPorte County, Indiana, and Lawrence Lake, Marshall County, Indiana (IDEM 2022), confirm this species' persistence in Indiana. The Blacknose Shiner is listed as endangered in Illinois. Within the Chicago Region, additional information on its distribution is needed — especially within the Kankakee Sands area, where it appears to be relatively stable.

References: Burr, Santucci, et al. 2005; Forbes and Richardson 1920; Roberts, Burr, and Whiles 2006

Spottail Shiner

Notropis hudsonius · *Notropis* means "keeled back" in Greek; *hudsonius* refers to the Hudson River, where it was originally described.

Description: The Spottail Shiner is a fusiform, robust minnow with a silvery body. Distinguishing characteristics include a black spot at the base of its tail, a diffuse predorsal stripe with no wedge, 8 anal rays, a rounded snout, and an eye diameter longer than the mouth. The mouth is terminal and slightly oblique, without barbels. The dorsal and anal fins are strongly pointed. The distinct tail spot and lack of lateral banding sets this minnow apart from other similar species. The tail spot is also present on very young individuals. A rather large minnow, the Spottail Shiner often reaches 6 inches (150 mm) in length.

Natural History: The Spottail Shiner lives primarily in large lakes and large rivers. It is sometimes found in smaller tributaries that flow into larger bodies of water, but never far upstream. In Lake Michigan, this species typically inhabits sandy beaches; it can also be found along rock revetments and in deep pelagic waters. In rivers, it is usually found in deep pools and runs. The Spottail Shiner has a relatively broad diet, feeding on aquatic insects, crustaceans, algae, and plant matter. Spawning takes place in late spring to early summer over gravel or sandbars in rivers, and on sandy beaches in lakes.

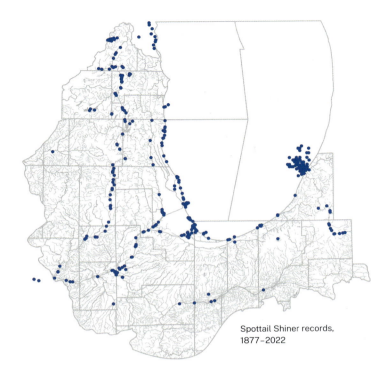

Spottail Shiner records, 1877–2022

Distribution and Status: Occurring from the Northwest Territories to the Hudson Bay in Canada, the Spottail Shiner also occupies the upper Mississippi River basin, the Great Lakes basin, and the Atlantic slope drainages. Within the Chicago Region it can be found most abundantly along the shoreline of Lake Michigan, the upper Illinois River, the Fox River in Illinois, and the St. Joseph River in Indiana. The earliest record of this species was taken by David Starr Jordan in 1877 from Pine and Clear Lakes, LaPorte County, Indiana. The only record for the Rock River system is old (1880), from the Kishwaukee River, Boone County, Illinois (INHS). We consider this species stable within the Chicago Region.

References: Becker 1983; Forbes and Richardson 1920; Smith 1979; Wells 1968

Ozark Minnow

Notropis nubilus · *Notropis* means "keeled back" in Greek; *nubilus* means "cloudy" in Latin.

Description: The Ozark Minnow is a terete (cylindrical, tapering) minnow with a dusky-straw color above a dark lateral band that extends to the snout. The dorsal scales are heavily outlined in pigment, with little or no pigment below the lateral band. Coloration at the fin origins and head is typically yellow/orange, which intensifies in breeding individuals. The terminal mouth is oblique and small, extending only back to the front of the eye. The Ozark Minnow is unique among other laterally banded minnows and among the *Notropis* genus overall in having a long-coiled gut. The lack of pigmentation on the chin and at the base of the anal fin also helps in distinguishing this species from other laterally banded minnows. It has 8 anal fin rays and 8 dorsal fin rays. Adults are typically 3 inches (75 mm) in length.

Natural History: The Ozark Minnow typically occupies clear, high-gradient streams with gravel or rocky substrates and persistent groundwater discharge. Our observations revealed a slightly different habitat usage in a stream segment in Somonauk Creek that has a relatively low gradient with substrates of fine gravel and sand. As this fish's long gut suggests, its food consists of bottom ooze, periphyton, algae, and

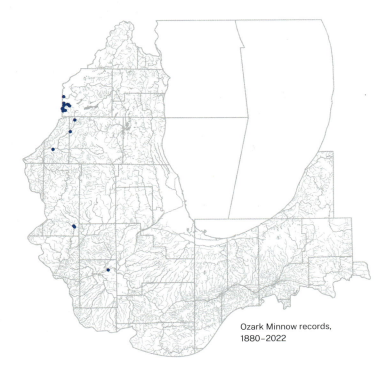

Ozark Minnow records, 1880–2022

detritus. Spawning takes place in May and June, often associated with the nests of the Hornyhead Chub.

Distribution and Status: The Ozark Minnow occurs within the Mississippi River basin from Minnesota to the Ozarks. All records within the Chicago Region for this species are from the Rock River drainage, with 1 exception: we discovered a disjunct population from Somonauk Creek, DeKalb County, Illinois, in 2007 (FMNH), outside its known distribution in upper northwestern Illinois. The Ozark Minnow is listed as threatened in Wisconsin and Illinois. We consider the Ozark Minnow a species of concern within the Chicago Region and in need of more detailed information on distribution and natural history.

References: Page and Burr 2011; Smith 1979; Willink 2017

Description: The Carmine Shiner is morphologically identical to the Rosyface Shiner (see account below) and can be distinguished only by genetic analysis.

Natural History: This species appears to have natural history characteristics similar to the Rosyface Shiner.

Distribution and Status: The Carmine Shiner occurs in the Red River of the North, the upper Mississippi River, and the Ozarks region. It was recently found to be genetically distinct from the Rosyface Shiner. As such, this genetic distinction indicates that the Carmine Shiner occurs only in the

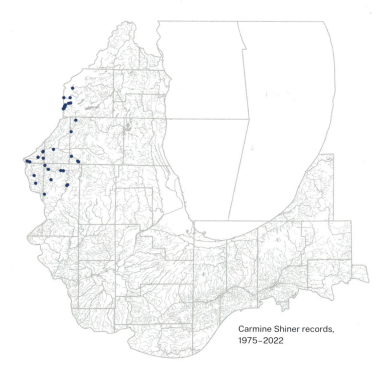

Carmine Shiner records, 1975–2022

Rock River system within the Chicago Region. We consider the Carmine Shiner stable within the region. Further study is needed to determine if this genetically distinct species has similar ecological requirements and habits compared to the closely related Rosyface Shiner.

References: Page and Burr 2011; R. J. Scott, Willink, and Norton 2018; Willink 2017

Rosyface Shiner

Notropis rubellus • *Notropis* means "keeled back" in Greek; *rubellus* is of Latin origin, meaning "red," referring to the breeding coloration of the male.

Description: The Rosyface Shiner is a long and slender minnow. The dorsal region is dark, usually with an olive, emerald, or blueish hue. The sides are silvery and the belly white. A dusky lateral band is present but is often faint or lacking in small individuals and some adults outside the breeding season. The dorsal fin is positioned well behind the pelvic fin origin — a characteristic useful for identification. It has a complete lateral line and an anal fin with 9–11 rays. The Rosyface Shiner differs from the similar Emerald Shiner in having a longer, more pointed snout and a more slender body. Breeding males display a bluish body hue, as well as red/orange pigment at the bases of the fins and lower head region. They also develop fine tubercles on the head and nape. Females show similar breeding attributes but to a much-diminished level. Adults are 3–4 inches (75–100 mm) in length.

Natural History: The Rosyface Shiner occurs in larger streams and small to medium rivers. We have collected it primarily in fast-water habitats over bedrock, boulder, cobble, and gravel. It is intolerant of water-quality degradation and siltation. Food consists primarily of aquatic and terrestrial invertebrates. Spawning takes place in late spring, with eggs and milt released in flow-

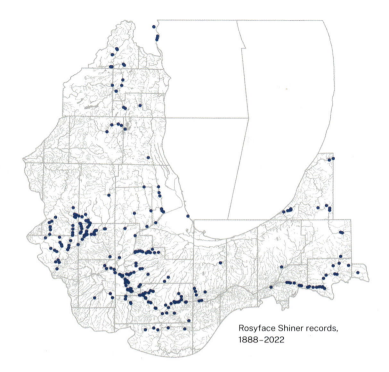

Rosyface Shiner records, 1888–2022

ing water over gravel or rubble. Like most minnows, this species is sexually mature in the first year and has a life span of about 3 years.

Distribution and Status: The Rosyface Shiner occurs in the Great Lakes and Ohio River basins. Records within the Chicago Region are concentrated in the higher-gradient reaches of the St. Joseph, Yellow, and Kankakee Rivers, and upper Illinois River tributary streams. In 2012, a population of Rosyface Shiner was found for the first time in the Des Plaines River near Riverside, Illinois. Following the removal of the Hofmann Dam and 10 other mainstem dams, the species has dispersed upstream, north to Indian Creek in Lake County, Illinois, as well as the undammed reaches downstream. The appearance in the Des Plaines River indicates improved water quality within the system. The expanding distribution of the Rosyface Shiner resulting from dam removals on the Des Plaines River demonstrates the importance of connectivity. This species is stable and expanding within the Chicago Region and is a useful indicator of good habitat and water quality.

References: Eddy and Underhill 1974; Page and Burr 2011; R. J. Scott, Willink, and Norton 2018; Willink 2017

Sand Shiner

Notropis stramineus · *Notropis*, Greek, means "keeled back"; *stramineus*, Latin, means "of straw," referring to the pale body color.

Description: The Sand Shiner is a fusiform minnow with a large eye, a bluntly rounded snout, and a terminally oblique mouth. The coloration is silvery gray with a straw-colored hue in the dorsal area, but sometimes can be very washed out. Characteristics distinguishing the Sand Shiner from other Chicago Region minnows include 7 anal fin rays, a lateral line slightly decurved and punctate (studded with dots of dark pigment), and a distinct predorsal wedge of pigment. There is also typically a short interruption of the dorsal stripe on either side of the dorsal fin; the stripe then resumes to the caudal fin. Adults can reach slightly over 3 inches (75 mm).

Natural History: The Sand Shiner occurs in small creeks, large rivers, and glacial lakes. Based on historic descriptions and our observations, this species prefers water that is moving over sand and or sandy gravel. In riverine habitats, it is found at the margins of riffles and in runs, and in lakes, along wave-swept beaches. This species can tolerate water-quality degradation if clean sandy habitats are available. Food habits are somewhat general, consisting of immature aquatic insects, small crustaceans, detritus, and some plant material. Spawning takes place in its first and second years over sand or small gravel, with peak activ-

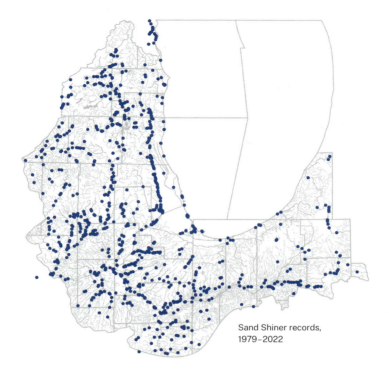

Sand Shiner records, 1979–2022

ity during mid to late summer when stream flows are moderate to low. Gravid females were observed in Lake Michigan at Calumet Beach, Cook County, Illinois, in mid-July.

Distribution and Status: The Sand Shiner occurs in the Mississippi River, Ohio River, and Great Lakes basins; there is also a disjunct population in Texas. This species is widespread throughout the Chicago Region and can usually be found in streams with clean sandy habitat and good to moderate water quality. One of the earlier records taken from the Chicago Region was by Oliver Perry Hay in 1879 from the Kankakee River, Lake County, Indiana. The status of the Sand Shiner is considered stable.

References: Cochran 2014; Eddy and Underhill 1974; Page and Burr 2011; Smith 1979; Trautman 1957

Weed Shiner

Notropis texanus · *Notropis* means "keeled back" in Greek; *texanus* refers to Texas.

Description: The Weed Shiner is a small fusiform minnow that is straw colored above a dark lateral band and translucent to white below. Distinguishing characteristics include a small terminal and oblique mouth and a dark lateral band evident as a bridle around the nose. This species differs from other minnows by a dark lateral band due to pigmentation on the lower lip and chin, and by having 7 anal rays. There is diffuse pigment at the base of the anal fin, and the dorsal scales are outlined in pigment. The bottom and top edges of the lateral band are more diffuse than other banded minnows. Adults are typically less than 3 inches (75 mm) in length.

Natural History: The Weed Shiner is found in small creeks to medium rivers, especially near confluences and backwater mouths. This species commonly occurs in areas of moderate to slow current with sandy substrates and woody debris. We have observed a mixed school of Weed and Ironcolor Shiners in moderate current at the discharge channel of a Kankakee River backwater in Newton County, Indiana. The Weed Shiner is an omnivore, eating detritus and various invertebrate prey. It spawns primarily in spring and early summer.

Distribution and Status: The Weed Shiner has a wide distribution within

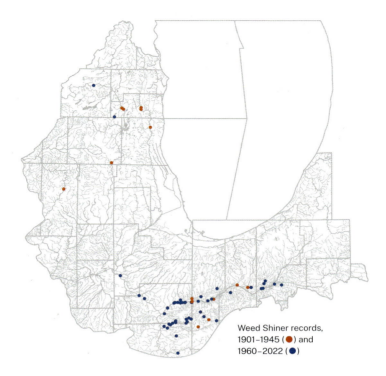

Weed Shiner records, 1901–1945 (●) and 1960–2022 (●)

the United States, from Minnesota to Texas to the East Coast. Within the Chicago Region, the Weed Shiner is found persistently in the Kankakee River and Beaver Creek systems of the Kankakee Sands ecoregion. Records for the upper Rock, Fox, and Des Plaines River systems are old (1901–1941) except for a specimen reported from Sugar Creek, Walworth County, Wisconsin, in 1999 by the USGS Wisconsin Fish Database. Collection data suggests that the range of the Weed Shiner has diminished over time. The Weed Shiner is designated as endangered in Illinois and is believed to be extirpated in Michigan.

References: Page and Burr 2011; Pflieger 1975; Smith 1979

Mimic Shiner

Notropis volucellus • *Notropis* means "keeled back" in Greek; *volucellus* is Latin for "winged or swift."

Description: The Mimic Shiner is a terete, somewhat laterally compressed minnow with large eyes, a bluntly rounded snout, and a subterminal oblique mouth. The coloration is silvery gray, with an olive hue in the dorsal area. The combination of characteristics distinguishing the Mimic Shiner from most other minnows include 8 anal fin rays, lateral line scales that are slightly elevated (taller than wide), a lateral line that is slightly punctate with pigment, and no distinct pigment wedge in front of the dorsal fin. The Mimic Shiner is very similar to the Sand Shiner, but lacks the predorsal wedge and has 8 rather than 7 anal rays. The Mimic Shiner rarely exceeds 3 inches (75 mm) in length.

Natural History: The Mimic Shiner can be found in any size stream or river but is most abundant in larger-river habitats in the Chicago Region. It also occurs in oligotrophic lakes. A multitude of habitat preferences have been reported for this species. We have observed it in high abundance along the sandy beaches of Lake Geneva, pelagic schools in Lake Michigan, vegetated sandy runs in the St. Joseph River, and in silty pools of the upper Illinois River. The Mimic Shiner eats a wide array of foods, including dipteran larvae, zooplankton, amphipods, small terrestrial insects, and plant matter. It spawns throughout the late spring and summer, with peak spawning in midsummer.

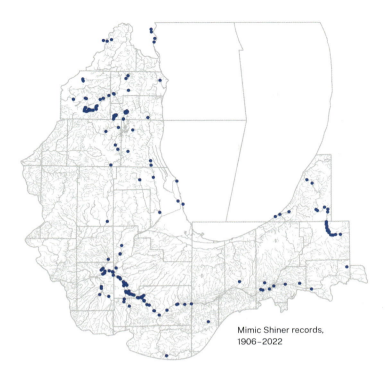

Mimic Shiner records, 1906–2022

Distribution and Status: The Mimic Shiner occurs in the drainages of the Great Lakes, Mississippi River, Ohio River, and the Gulf slope, and other disjunct populations. Most records within the Chicago Region occur in the upper Fox River, the lower Kankakee River, the St. Joseph River, and Lake Geneva. This species also occurs to a lesser degree along the sandy beaches of Lake Michigan and confluent streams. It is becoming more prevalent in recent stream and lake surveys, most likely owing to a better understanding of species identification and improved collection techniques. Based on the wide variety of habitat preferences, the Mimic Shiner — true to its name — may have been confused with other similar species throughout its North American range. It is possible that it is a complex of several similar species that have not been adequately distinguished yet. We consider the Mimic Shiner to be stable within the Chicago Region.

References: Black 1945; Eddy and Underhill 1974; Hubbs and Lagler 1964; Page and Burr 2011; Trautman 1957

Pugnose Minnow

Opsopoeodus emiliae • *Opsopoeodus*, Greek, "teeth for delicate feeding"; *emiliae* is in honor of Emily Hay, wife of the species describer, Oliver Perry Hay.

Description: The Pugnose Minnow is a small, fusiform minnow that is dusky gray in color above and below a dark lateral band that continues around the nose. The lateral band and the small superior and vertical mouth help distinguish it from most other minnows. Additional features of the Pugnose Minnow, which are unique among other dark-banded minnows, include pigmentation on the lower lip and chin, 7–8 anal rays, 9 dorsal rays, and a clear interruption in the middle of the otherwise pigmented dorsal fin. Adults are typically less than 3 inches (75 mm) in length.

Natural History: The Pugnose Minnow is almost exclusively found in riverine habitats with abundant aquatic vegetation and slow-moving water, including marshes, backwaters, and side channels of rivers; however, it can also be found in some lakes. In the Kankakee River it has been observed along island shores with the plant American Water Willow (*Justicia americana*), but it has mostly been found in clear water over fine mucky substrates. Little is known of this species' natural history. It has been observed in the Chicago Region spawning in early summer and eating crustaceans and midge larvae.

Distribution and Status: The Pugnose Minnow has a wide distribution within the United States but is

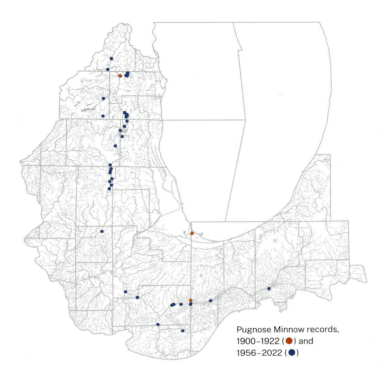

Pugnose Minnow records, 1900–1922 (●) and 1956–2022 (●)

usually found in low abundance. Most Chicago Region records are located within the upper Fox River and the Kankakee River. The 2 Wolf Lake, Lake County, Indiana, records are old (FMNH 1900; Meek and Hildebrand 1910), and presumably this population was extirpated due to dredging Wolf Lake from a marsh into a lake. Due to its limited abundance, it could be considered vulnerable; however, its persistence in collections over many years indicates it is stable in some areas. The Pugnose Minnow is listed as endangered in Michigan. We considered it a species of concern within the Chicago Region.

References: Forbes and Richardson 1920; Gilbert and Bailey 1972; Page and Johnston 1990a; Willink 2009

Suckermouth Minnow

Phenacobius mirabilis · *Phenacobius* is Greek, meaning "deceptive life," referring to its sucker-like appearance; *mirabilis*, Latin, means "wonderful."

Description: The Suckermouth Minnow has an elongated but rather flattened top to bottom (dorso-ventrally compressed) form with a fleshy subterminal mouth resembling a sucker (Catostomidae), which is unique among minnow species. The following characteristics distinguish this species from suckers: a prominent spot at the base of the tail, a narrow lateral line stripe with small dark spots, a short dorsal fin (8 rays), and a short anal fin (6–7 rays) that does not extend to the tail fin. Dorsal scales are outlined with pigment, while the ventral surface is mostly white. Breeding males develop small tubercles and intensify in black pigment around the scales and lateral line band, giving it a dark, dusky look. Adults grow up to 4 inches (100 mm) in length.

Natural History: Suckermouth Minnow prefers the fast waters of riffles in small streams to large rivers. As a Great Plains species, it is typically tolerant of turbidity in the water column, but requires clean, gravely substrates for foraging and reproduction. Its food consists primarily of aquatic insect larvae. Spawning likely occurs throughout the spring and summer months, as we have observed gravid females during this time.

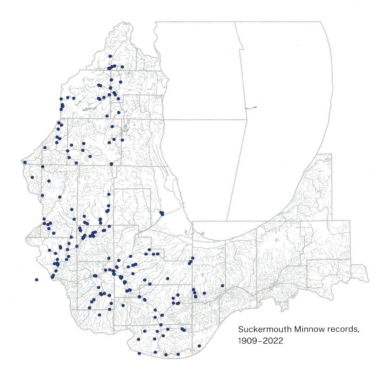

Suckermouth Minnow records, 1909–2022

Distribution and Status: This Great Plains species occurs within the Mississippi and Ohio River basins. Within the Chicago Region it occurs most frequently in the lower Kankakee, lower Des Plaines, Fox, and Rock River systems. It is absent in the eastern areas of Indiana and Michigan. The first time this species was recorded from the Chicago Region was in 1909 in Marley Creek, Will County, Illinois (FMNH). The Suckermouth Minnow is considered sensitive and indicative of high-quality, unmodified habitats; however, its populations are generally stable.

References: Page and Burr 2011; Pflieger 1975; Smith 1979

Bluntnose Minnow

Pimephales notatus · *Pimephales* is Greek for "swollen head"; *notatus*, Latin, means "marked with spots."

Description: The Bluntnose Minnow has a terete body with a subterminal mouth and overhanging snout that gives it the bluntnose look. Its body color can be dusky olive, silvery, or translucent, depending on water clarity. It has a black stomach lining, which often gives the outside surface a dusky appearance. The dorsal fin is rounded, with a dark blotch at the front with 8 rays. The anal fin is also rounded and has 7 rays. Spawning males become dark with an enlarged head and prominent tubercles on the snout. This species can be distinguished from other minnows by the small, crowded scales on the nape just behind the head, and the short and thickened first dorsal ray. It differs from the congeneric Fathead and Bullhead Minnows by having a subterminal horizontal mouth, a dark lateral stripe, a caudal spot, and body scales strongly pigmented that create a crosshatch pattern. Mature males can grow up to 3 inches (75 mm), whereas females tend to be smaller.

Natural History: The Bluntnose Minnow is found in a wide range of habitats. We have observed this species in sluggish and fast-velocity streams and on lakeshores. Although the Bluntnose Minnow is somewhat tolerant, we have not typically found it in highly degraded streams, and it can be very abundant in high-quality

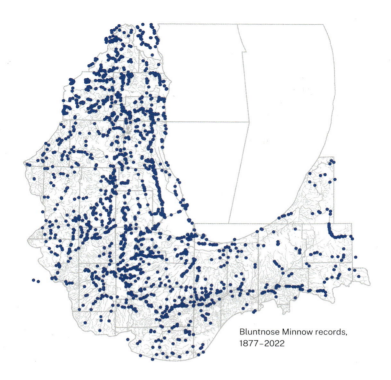

Bluntnose Minnow records, 1877–2022

streams. An omnivorous feeder, it ingests plant material and detritus as well as small aquatic invertebrates. Spawning takes place throughout the summer. Females deposit eggs in clusters on the underside of rocks, sticks, rubbish, and other structures. Males guard the eggs and tend the nest by removing debris and aerating the eggs.

Distribution and Status: The Bluntnose Minnow occurs in the Mississippi River, Ohio River, and Great Lakes basins, and some northern Atlantic slope drainages. This species is ubiquitous and abundant throughout the Chicago Region, with a current tally of 3,290 records. Being so abundant, it is likely this was the very first species ever officially recorded within the Chicago Region, in 1877 by David Starr Jordan from Clear and Pine Lakes, LaPorte County, Indiana. It is typically one of the last minnows (Leuciscidae) to disappear from a degrading stream and is stable throughout the Chicago Region.

Reference: Page and Burr 2011

Fathead Minnow

Pimephales promelas · *Pimephales* is Greek for "swollen head"; *promelas* is also Greek, meaning "black in front," referring to the black head of spawning males.

Description: The Fathead Minnow is a stout-bodied fish that is very familiar due to its wide culture and use as a baitfish. Body color can be dusky olive to washed out, depending on water clarity. Like the Bluntnose Minnow, the Fathead Minnow has a black stomach lining (peritoneum). The dorsal fin is rounded, with pigmentation in the front portion, and has 8 rays. The anal fin has 7 rays. This species can be distinguished from other minnows by the small, crowded nape scales, and the rudimentary and thickened first dorsal ray. It differs from the related Bluntnose and Bullhead Minnows by having a small superior, oblique mouth, an incomplete lateral line, a diffuse lateral stripe, no caudal spot, and herring bone lines along its sides. Spawning Fathead Minnow males become dark with a slightly enlarged head and prominent tubercles on the snout. Adults attain a length of 3 inches (75 mm) but are typically smaller.

Natural History: The Fathead Minnow is found in a range of water-body types, including creeks, rivers, ponds, and lakes. It generally avoids currents, preferring pooled areas of creeks, backwater areas, and slow-moving ditches and canals, generally thriving in soft-bottomed habitats. Its diet consists mostly of detritus, muck, aquatic vegetation, and algae. It can

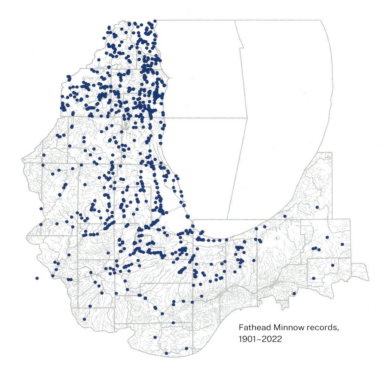

Fathead Minnow records, 1901–2022

be very abundant in some locations, due in part to its prolific reproductive habits that include multiple spawning events throughout the season. Females lay eggs in an individual nest, typically on the underside of rocks or other objects. The males exhibit parental care, guarding from predators and tending to the eggs by aerating and debris removal.

Distribution and Status: The Fathead Minnow occurs from the Rockies to the Appalachians, and from the Hudson Bay to the Rio Grande in Mexico. This species is widely distributed and stable within the Chicago Region. Releases from bait buckets are likely frequent.

Reference: Page and Burr 2011

TRUE MINNOWS (LEUCISCIDAE)

Description: The Bullhead Minnow has a cylindrical body. Typical of this genus, it has small, crowded nape scales and a short, thickened first dorsal fin ray. Body color can be dusky olive, silvery, or translucent, depending on water clarity. Spawning males become darker, with an enlarged head and prominent tubercles on the snout. The dorsal fin has 8 rays and a dark blotch in the front portion. The anal fin has 7 rays. The Bullhead Minnow can be distinguished from the Fathead and Bluntnose Minnows by having a terminal and slightly oblique mouth, a thin lateral stripe, a diffuse caudal spot, a silvery peritoneum, and weakly pigmented body scales creating a vague crosshatch pattern. Mature males can grow up to 3 inches (75 mm) or more, whereas females tend to be smaller.

Natural History: The Bullhead Minnow is a large-river species, rarely found in tributary streams and even less frequently in lakes. This species prefers slow to moderate currents over silt or sand with aquatic vegetation. Its food habits are widely varied, but probably incorporate more invertebrates than either the Bluntnose Minnow or the Fathead Minnow does, as indicated by the terminal mouth. Spawning behavior is similar to the Bluntnose Minnow, where the eggs are attached to

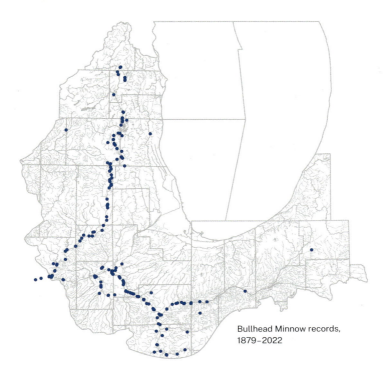

Bullhead Minnow records, 1879–2022

a stone or log and are cared for by the male.

Distribution and Status: The Bullhead Minnow occurs in the Mississippi River basin, Ohio River basin, and Gulf drainages, but is not native to the Great Lakes basin. This species is restricted primarily to the mainstem Fox, Mazon, and Kankakee Rivers of Illinois within the Chicago Region. There are 2 records that may be bait-bucket introductions or misidentifications, as the habitat at the localities are atypical and connectivity to downstream populations limited: Des Plaines River, Lake County, Illinois (SIU 1985), and Potato Creek, St. Joseph County, Indiana (INDNR 1979 no specimen). It is stable throughout the region.

References: Eddy and Underhill 1974; Smith 1979; Trautman 1957

Longnose Dace

Rhinichthys cataractae · *Rhinichthys* means "fish snout" in Greek; *cataractae*, Latin, means "from the cataracts."

Description: The Longnose Dace is a fusiform minnow with a ventrally compressed head. The snout is rounded, with barbels in the corner of a subterminal mouth. The center of the upper lip is connected to the snout by a ridge of flesh known as a frenum. The long nose and mouth barbels set this fish apart from most other minnows. The Longnose Dace can be distinguished from the somewhat similar Western Blacknose Dace by having a subterminal mouth, an overhanging snout, and a slenderer body. Body coloration can be bronze to dusky, depending on water clarity; the belly is pale white, the fins yellowish orange. Breeding individuals become dark on the back and sides, with a mix of red, orange, and yellow on the belly and lower fins. Adults are typically 2–4 inches (50–102 mm) but are known to reach 5.5 inches (140 mm).

Natural History: The Longnose Dace requires strongly moving waters associated with riffles, rapids, or powerful shoreline waves of lakes. Substrates are typically composed of large boulders, cobble, and gravel within these habitats, which in the Chicago Region are usually found on the tops of high moraines and along the shoreline of Lake Michigan. The Longnose Dace is known to feed on aquatic insect larvae and midges. Spawning takes place over the shift-

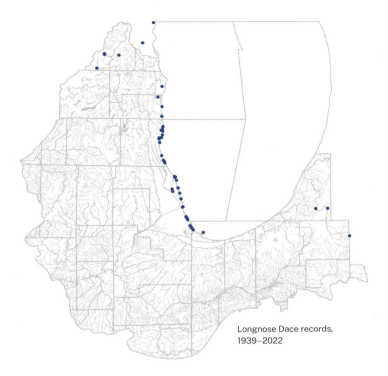

Longnose Dace records, 1939–2022

ing gravel and sand on Lake Michigan beaches in late spring.

Distribution and Status: The Longnose Dace occurs throughout Canada and the northern United States, only extending south along the Rocky and the Appalachian Mountains. All Chicago Region records for this species occur along the shoreline of Lake Michigan except for 7 records: 3 from the St. Joseph River system in Berrien County, Michigan (MFA), and 4 from the upper Fox River system in Waukesha, Wisconsin (USGSWI). The Longnose Dace was voted the official fish of the city of Chicago in 2002 due to its prevalence along the Chicago shoreline. Its status is stable within the Chicago Region, but it is listed as a species of special concern in Indiana.

References: Becker 1983; Eddy and Underhill 1974; Hubbs and Lagler 1964; Trautman 1957; Willink 2017

Western Blacknose Dace

Rhinichthys obtusus • *Rhinichthys* is Greek, meaning "fish snout"; *obtusus* is Latin, meaning "blunt," referring to the rounded snout.

Description: The Western Blacknose Dace is fusiform minnow with a ventrally compressed head and a barbel at each corner of its mouth. The snout is somewhat rounded, and the mouth is terminal, with a slight downward curve. The center of the upper lip is connected to the snout by a frenum. This species can be distinguished from the Longnose Dace by having a more terminal mouth, a less overhanging snout, and a stouter body. The back is heavily pigmented above the lateral line; the belly is pale white. There is a faint black stripe along the side that extends from the base of tail to the nose. Small dark blotches are present along the sides and dorsal surface. Breeding individuals develop a distinct red lateral band and small tubercles on the dorsal and anal fins. The juvenile Western Blacknose Dace can be distinguished from Stonerollers by lacking cartilaginous ridge on the lower lip, and from Hornyhead Chubs by having much smaller scales with 60–75 in the lateral line. Adults are typically 2–4 inches (50–102 mm) but are known to reach 5 inches (125 mm).

Natural History: The Western Blacknose Dace is found in cold to cool headwater and small streams, usually over gravel and cobbles in fast-running water. It lives primarily on the bottom in riffles and runs,

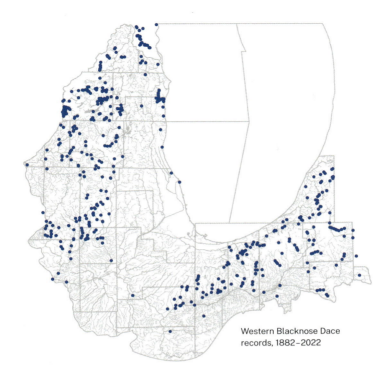

Western Blacknose Dace records, 1882–2022

where it forages on aquatic insect larvae and diatoms; it has been observed in midwater-column foraging as well. Spawning takes place during the late spring and includes building piles of small gravel for nests.

Distribution and Status: The Western Blacknose Dace occurs in the upper Mississippi River, Ohio River, and Great Lakes basins. This species is found in the upper reaches of the Kankakee River, Fox River, Rock River, and Great Lakes tributary streams. It is absent or less frequently encountered in the warmer, low-gradient streams of the Iroquois and upper Illinois Rivers. The Western Blacknose Dace is stable within the region.

References: Becker 1983; Eddy and Underhill 1974; Forbes and Richardson 1920; Hubbs 1936; Smith 1979; Trautman 1957

Creek Chub

Semotilus atromaculatus · *Semotilus* is Greek, meaning "spotted banner," referring to the dorsal fin; *atromaculatus* means "blackspotted" in Latin.

Description: The Creek Chub is a medium to large minnow with a stout, cylindrical body, a triangular black dot at the base of the anal fin, and a blotch of pigment at the base of the dorsal fin. The mouth is horizontal and proportionally large, extending past the front of the eye. Like most minnow chubs, it has a barbel, but it is hidden in the fold of the upper lip above the corner of the mouth, not in the corners. The scales of the Creek Chub are quite small, with 51–64 in the lateral line. The dorsal and anal fins both have 8 rays. The upper lip is widened in the middle region. These characteristics can be used to distinguish the Creek Chub from the Lake Chub and the Hornyhead Chub. The upper body is shaded in light-olive pigment, and the lower surface is white with a dusky band along the lateral surface. Older fish have a purplish iridescent band. Adult males develop small bumps known as tubercles on their heads and bodies during spawning season. Adults are often 5–6 inches (125–150 mm) in length, but larger individuals up to 10–12 inches (250–300 mm) are not uncommon in larger streams.

Natural History: The Creek Chub inhabits streams of all sizes but is less common or absent in larger-river habitats. It has been observed in most types of stream habitat in the Chicago Region. This species is an

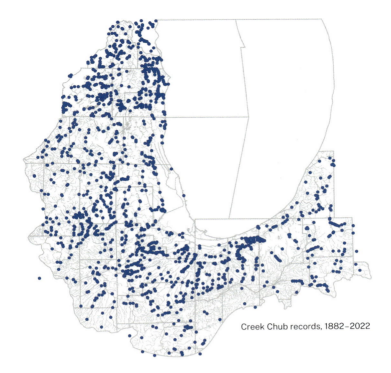

Creek Chub records, 1882–2022

adaptable omnivore, lending to its ubiquitous distribution. The larger mouth allows it to ingest a wide variety of prey types, including fish; the Creek Chub serves as the top predator in smaller streams without larger predators. It is tolerant of turbidity and poor water quality and survives in isolated pools in low-water conditions. Spawning takes place in April and May. Breeding males construct nests in gravel.

Distribution and Status: The Creek Chub occurs in the Mississippi River, Ohio River, and Great Lakes basins, and in Atlantic slope drainages. This species is one of the more ubiquitous species in the Chicago Region, with 2,500 records, and it occurs in all the drainages from Wisconsin to Michigan. High abundance of Creek Chub at a given site is often associated with low overall fish-species richness, indicating a stream with impaired water quality, still, this species requires moderate quality habitat. This fish is a good target for microfishing, as it will readily take tiny lures and baits. We consider the Creek Chub common and tolerant.

References: Smith 1979; Trautman 1957

TRUE MINNOWS (LEUCISCIDAE) 237

16

Loaches

Cobitidae

These odd-looking, nonnative fishes are small and bottom dwelling, with a subterminal mouth and up to 6 pairs of barbels. Their body shapes range from fusiform (torpedo shaped) to long and thin. Scales are absent or very small, and a small spike is found below the eye. They have only 1 row of teeth in their throats (pharyngeal teeth). An adipose fin is found on some species, and in many species, males have modified pectoral rays. Some are brightly colored and popular as aquarium fishes. They live in a diverse range of habitats, from fast-flowing streams to swamps, where they may bury their bodies in soft substrates. Most species are scavengers or omnivorous.

The family Cobitidae is related to minnows and suckers and contains at least 221 species, with the highest diversity in Southeast

Asia. They are also found in Europe and northern Africa. No species are native to North America. Due to their popularity as an aquarium fish, they have been released in many areas outside their native range, including the Chicago Region, where 1 species, the Oriental Weatherfish, has become established.

In Asia, loaches are a popular food fish and can be farm raised. Some members of the genus *Misgurnus* are called weatherfish because they are apparently sensitive to changes in air pressure and exhibit agitated behavior when the weather changes, especially when severe storms are approaching. They can be highly migratory and are affected by dams in their native range.

Oriental Weatherfish

Misgurnus anguillicaudatus • *Misgurnus* comes from the Greek word *miseo*, "to hate," and the Turkish *gür*, "loud" — a name given to this fish due to its habit of becoming very active during the barometric pressure changes prior to thunderstorms; for *anguillicaudatus*, no definitive origin is known, but *anguilla* is Latin for "eel" and *caudatus* is Latin for "tail," perhaps referring to its elongated body.

Description: The Oriental Weatherfish has a very elongated body with numerous small scales. Its most distinguishing characteristic is the presence of 10 short barbels surrounding the mouth. No other fish in the Chicago Region has an elongated body combined with 10 mouth barbels. The eyes are quite small. The dorsal, anal, and caudal fins are rounded, with the pelvic fin directly below the dorsal fin. Dark spots and mottling appear along the top and sides, which are light green and yellow and fade to cream color on the ventral surface, which lacks markings. The upper and lower tail regions have fleshy ridges just in front of the caudal fin. There is a small dark spot on the caudal peduncle near base of caudal fin, which has bands of pigment. Mature males are usually smaller than females. Mature males also have an elongated ray at the front of the pelvic fin, forming a point. Oriental Weatherfish is vaguely similar to the catfishes, which have only 8 longer mouth barbels. Catfishes also have a less-elongated body and have spines in the dorsal and pelvic fins. Freshwater eels and lamprey have elongated bodies but lack mouth barbels. Adult size for the Oriental Weatherfish is typically 6 inches (150 mm) or less.

Natural History: Oriental Weatherfish are most common in wetlands, marshes, slow-moving streams, and canals where the bottom is mud or another soft material. Often these habitats are vegetated. This species is primarily benthic, living along the bottom and burrowing into the substrate when frightened. Due to its ability to breathe air through the rear portion of its intestine, it can survive in seasonally isolated pools with very low oxygen. Air bubbles can sometimes be seen exiting the anus when this fish is taking in air from the surface. It may also breathe through its skin. These adaptations for breathing air are helpful in its native environments of ponds and marshes with periodically low oxygen levels. This ability also allows it to persist in polluted and degraded habitats in the Chicago Region. Its food consists of small crustaceans, insect larvae, worms, algae, and plant matter. Whether the plant matter and algae are ingested intentionally or incidentally with other food items is not clear. In its native range of East Asia, the Oriental Weatherfish will bury itself in the mud during the winter. Eggs are deposited on the roots and bases of plants from April to May.

Oriental Weatherfish records, 1987–2022

Distribution and Status: The Oriental Weatherfish native range is East Asia. The first record in the Chicago Region was from Cook County, Illinois, in 1987. Since this fish is a common species in the aquarium trade, it is most likely that local introductions resulted from intentional and/or accidental release. This species was initially collected from the North Shore Channel, which for several years was the only body of water with Oriental Weatherfish. The fish subsequently appeared sporadically throughout the Chicago Area Waterway System. Surveys in Will County in 2005 found a substantial number. The first record in Indiana was in the West Branch of the Grand Calumet River in 2002. It was collected in several more localities in 2005 in the Grand Calumet River (both East and West Branches) and Indiana Harbor Canal. It is possible that these fish are more common in the Chicago River system than the data indicate; due to their small size and burrowing habits, they could have evaded capture in routine surveys. Initially, the Oriental Weatherfish was found primarily in polluted or degraded habitats, where there was little competition from native fishes. In recent years, numbers have been increasing and it has spread into less degraded habitats. Small populations have also become established in Michigan, Idaho, and California. The fact that it was present in the Chicago Region in apparently low numbers for many years before increasing in abundance and range is a reason for some concern.

References: Belcik 2017; Graham 1997; Herald 1962; J. S. Nelson 2006; Norris 2015; Okada 1960; Page and Laird 1993; Simon, Bright, et al. 2006; Willink and Veraldi 2009

LOACHES (COBITIDAE) 241

17

North American Catfishes

Ictaluridae

Catfishes are quite familiar and recognizable, characterized by a dorsoventrally flattened head, 4 pairs of mouth barbels, or "whiskers," a fleshy adipose fin, stout fin spines, and an absence of scales. Some species have venom in their spines with varying degrees of potency, but nonlethal. The diminutive madtom's venom is strong enough to cause pain in humans but does not cause any lasting harm.

Catfishes are generally nocturnal and benthic, relying on their barbels for sensory input. They typically spawn in nests and exhibit parental care. Their size can vary widely from 5-inch (125-mm) madtoms up to the largest North American catfish, the Blue Catfish (*Ictalurus furcatus*), which can grow up to 60 inches (1,500 mm). The record weight for this species is 143 pounds (65 kg). Their habitats also range widely from shallow riffles to the deepest areas of large rivers and lakes.

North American catfishes' geographic range is from Canada to Guatemala. This group includes about 51 species from 8 genera. In the Chicago Region there are 4 genera, with a total of 9 species. Bullheads are distinguished by their stout bodies and rounded tail fin. Madtoms are small and slender, with a very long adipose fin. Channel Catfish and Blue Catfish have deeply forked tail fins. Flathead Catfish has a rounded tail and a lower jaw that protrudes beyond the upper jaw.

The larger catfishes are one of the more important commercial and recreational families. Channel Catfish is among the most targeted species by anglers across the country and in the Chicago Region. They are relatively easy to catch and abundant in most rivers. They are also widely stocked in ponds and lakes, where they are easy to raise and widely available to restaurants and grocery stores. Flathead Catfish can grow to up 60 inches (1,500 mm) and have become quite popular among local anglers. Blue Catfish are not native to the Chicago Region but have been stocked in local cooling reservoirs and are also popular among local anglers.

Black Bullhead

Ameiurus melas · *Ameiurus*, Greek, means "un-forked tail"; *melas*, also Greek, means "black" or "dark."

Description: The Black Bullhead has a stout body, a moderately flattened head, and a straight to slightly notched tail fin. This species can be distinguished from other bullheads by the dark chin barbels, a shorter anal fin (19–23 rays), a smoother pectoral spine (not sawtooth), and the lack of a mottled pigmentation pattern. Body coloration is variable, but is typically dusky to solid black on the back and yellow to off-white on the belly. Sometimes there are black speckles on the sides. Young typically look just like adults. This species is the largest of the bullheads, growing up to 24 inches (600 mm), although typical size is 10–14 inches (250–350 mm).

Natural History: The Black Bullhead lives in most types of slow-moving aquatic habitats, including rivers, streams, lakes, ponds, and wetlands. It is quite tolerant, withstanding low oxygen, high turbidity, and habitat degradation. It is primarily a nocturnal feeder, finding refuge under banks, logs, brush piles, thick vegetation, and other suitable structures during the day. Young primarily eat aquatic insects, whereas adults are omnivorous, foraging on mollusks, insects, worms, crayfishes, and fish. Scavenging on dead organisms has also been observed. Spawning takes place in late spring, when females scoop out small depressions in soft sediment for the eggs. After fertiliza-

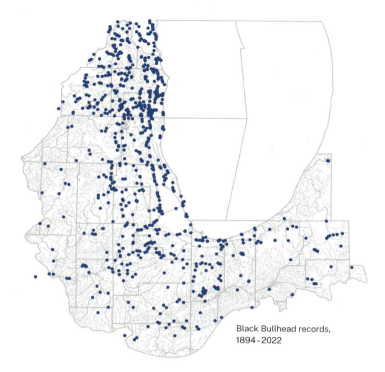

Black Bullhead records, 1894–2022

tion, the male will guard the nest. One or both parents are often observed defending large schools of fry.

Distribution and Status: The Black Bullhead occurs in Hudson Bay, Great Lakes, Mississippi River, Ohio River, and Mobile River basins. This species is very common and widespread throughout the Chicago Region and can be expected to be found anywhere. It is often found in high abundances in degraded systems and is considered common and tolerant. It can be caught by hook and line using baits like those used for other catfishes.

References: Becker 1983; Hubbs and Lagler 1964; Trautman 1957

Yellow Bullhead

Ameiurus natalis · *Ameiurus*, Greek, means "un-forked tail"; *natalis*, Latin, means "with large buttocks," probably referring to the humps that can form on males between the top of the head and dorsal fin.

Description: The Yellow Bullhead has a shape and appearance similar to the other bullhead species but can be distinguished by the yellow or cream-colored chin barbels, longer anal fin (24–27 rays), a sawtooth pectoral spine (5–8 teeth), and lack of a mottled pigment pattern. Variable body coloration ranges from olive to brown on the back and sides and white to bright yellow on the belly. Young typically look like adults. Maximum size is 19 inches (470 mm), typically 6–12 inches (150–300 mm).

Natural History: The Yellow Bullhead lives in most slow-moving riverine habitats, and to a lesser degree lakes, ponds, and wetlands. This species generally has habits like other bullhead species. Spawning takes place in late spring in natural cavities or constructed depressions near cover. Both parents participate in building the nest, where eggs are laid in a gelatinous mass.

Distribution and Status: The Yellow Bullhead occurs in the Great Lakes, Mississippi River, Atlantic slope, and

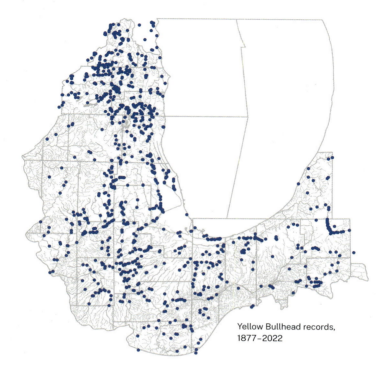

Yellow Bullhead records, 1877–2022

Gulf slope drainages. This species is very common and widespread throughout the Chicago Region, but usually observed in low abundance. It is targeted by anglers in slow-moving areas of rivers. Its conservation status is stable within the region.

References: Becker 1983; Hubbs and Lagler 1964; Smith 1979

Brown Bullhead

Ameiurus nebulosus • *Ameiurus*, Greek, means "un-forked tail"; *nebulosus*, Latin, means "clouded," referring to the mottled coloration.

Description: Having the typical bullhead body form, Brown Bullhead differs from other bullheads by having brown or dark-colored chin barbels, a comparatively short anal fin (21–24 rays), a sawtooth pectoral spine (5–8 teeth), and a distinct mottled pattern. Body coloration is variable, ranging from dark brown to bronze on the back, dark or bronze mottling on the sides, and white to yellow on the belly. Young typically look like adults. Maximum size is 21 inches (500 mm).

Natural History: The Brown Bullhead lives primarily in lakes, rivers, and backwaters with abundant vegetation and clear water. In the Chicago Region, this species has most often been observed among dense floating leaf macrophytes, including Spatterdock (*Nuphar advena*) and American Water Celery (*Vallisneria americana*). The Brown Bullhead has a natural history typical of the other bullheads, which includes omnivorous feeding, nest building, and parental care.

Distribution and Status: The Brown Bullhead occurs in the Great Lakes, Mississippi River, Atlantic slope, and Gulf slope drainages. Concentrations of records within the Chicago Region are in the glacial lakes of Wisconsin and northern Illinois, the middle Kankakee River, and portions of the

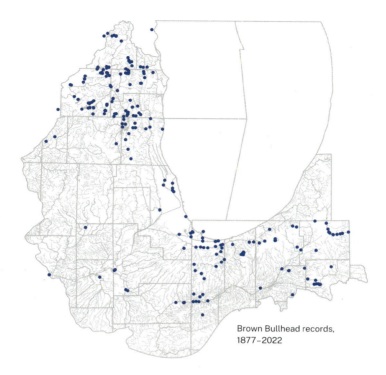

Brown Bullhead records, 1877–2022

Little Calumet River and St. Joseph River. It is far less common in the Chicago Region than the Black and Yellow Bullhead species, often occurring in higher-quality habitats. Due to low abundance and an affinity for dense vegetation, this species is not often caught by anglers. Its status is stable.

References: Becker 1983; Hubbs and Lagler 1964; Trautman 1957

Description: The Channel Catfish has a long, slender body with a deeply forked tail fin, very pointed at the upper and lower tips. The coloration is variable, ranging from grayish-silver to black, sometimes with tints of green or blue. Distinct black spots appear on the lateral surface of very young and juvenile fish, disappearing or becoming less prominent in older individuals. The upper jaw protrudes beyond the lower jaw. The anal fin is convex, with 24–30 fin rays. The adipose fin has a distinct lobe at the end. Breeding males are typically much darker, with fleshy lips and swollen heads. It is most similar to the Blue Catfish, but it lacks spots and has a longer (30–36 rays) and straighter anal fin. Flathead Catfish differ from Channel Catfish in having a much flatter head, a prominently protruding lower jaw, and a shorter anal fin. Adult Channel Catfish are usually in the range of 18–30 inches (450–750 mm) but can grow to 40 inches (1,000 mm) or greater.

Natural History: The Channel Catfish is most abundant in rivers, large streams, and lakes, but are also found in smaller streams. It has a relatively wide ecological tolerance but is not usually abundant in streams with degraded habitat. Although found throughout most riverine habitats, abundance is higher in areas with deep runs and faster-flowing water. Food habits include a wide range of items, including fish, crayfish, invertebrates, and plant material. This species also scavenges dead organisms and other organic detritus. Spawning takes place in late spring

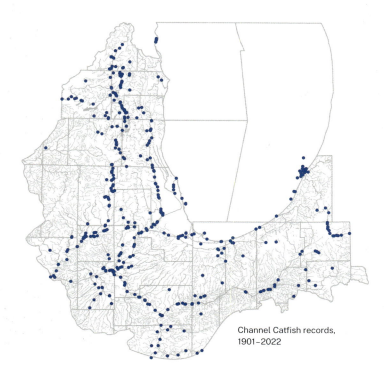

Channel Catfish records, 1901–2022

and summer. Males select secluded sites and construct nests or find existing cavities in banks or large woody debris. They guard the nests and provide care for eggs and young larvae until they leave the nest, about a week after hatching. The Channel Catfish is highly migratory. During warmer months it can be wide ranging, moving generally upstream, especially during high-water events, when it often moves into smaller tributaries. During the fall season it moves downstream and overwinters in large congregations in deeper pools.

Distribution and Status: The Channel Catfish occurs from the Rockies to the Atlantic slope, primarily within the United States. Reflecting its habitat preference, records throughout the Chicago Region are concentrated in larger rivers, plus the shoreline of Lake Michigan up to 30 feet deep. This species is actively stocked in private and public ponds and lakes for recreational fishing purposes. Extremely popular as a sport and commercial fish, it is widely introduced and cultured in warmer climates. The Channel Catfish is considered stable within the Chicago Region.

Reference: Page and Burr 2011

Slender Madtom

Noturus exilis • *Noturus* is from Greek, meaning "back tail," referring to the fusion of the tail fin and the adipose fin; *exilis* means "slender" in Latin.

Description: Madtoms are distinguished from other catfishes by the shape of the adipose fin, which is long and low and touches a well-rounded tail fin. The Slender Madtom has a dorsoventrally flattened head and an eel-like body. This species can be separated from the other madtoms by having a terminal mouth with equal jaw lengths, a sawtooth pectoral spine (6 teeth), and a lack of backward extensions on the premaxillary tooth patch. Also, there are typically black borders on the margins of the dorsal, caudal, and posterior portion of the anal fins, although they are not always evident. Overall coloration is a light orange-tan, with gray or light-yellow pigmentation in front of the dorsal fin, and white on the belly. It can grow up to 6 inches (150 mm) but is typically smaller.

Natural History: The Slender Madtom inhabits the fast-flowing riffles of streams and smaller rivers. It is adapted to live in very fast water, being dorsally compressed and having spines to lock them into crevices between cobble, boulder, or bedrock. Like other catfish, it is a nocturnal feeder, preying on small aquatic insects, copepods, and amphipods. Spawning takes place in early to mid-summer in bedrock fissures or excavated nests under slab rocks. Males guard the nests and young.

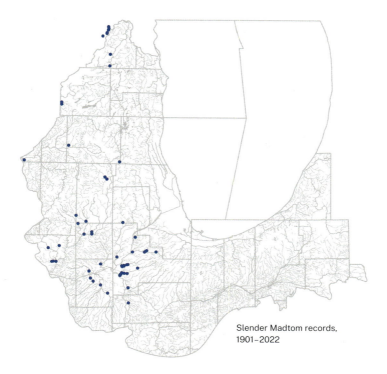

Slender Madtom records, 1901–2022

Distribution and Status: The Slender Madtom occurs in several disjunct populations within the mid– Mississippi River basin. Records within the Chicago Region are primarily in tributaries of the Rock River, Fox River, and upper Illinois River. The first record for this species within the region was in 1901 (INHS) from the DuPage River, Will County, Illinois.

The Slender Madtom is listed as endangered in Wisconsin and considered to be vulnerable within the Chicago Region. This species relies on connectivity within the upper Illinois River system.

References: Page and Burr 2011; Smith 1979

Stonecat

Noturus flavus · *Noturus* is from Greek, meaning "back tail," referring to the fusion of the tail fin and the adipose fin; *flavus*, Latin, means "yellow," in reference to its color.

Description: The Stonecat has a body form like other madtoms but differs in having a terminal mouth with a protruding upper jaw, a smooth pectoral spine, and backward extensions on the premaxillary tooth patch. Also, there are typically whitish margins on the dorsal, caudal, and posterior portion of the anal fins that are sometimes not evident. Overall coloration is a light tan to gray, with white on the belly. This species can grow up to 12 inches (305 mm).

Natural History: The Stonecat occurs primarily in medium- to high-gradient streams and rivers within the Chicago Region. They live in fast water between cobble, boulder, and bedrock. We have also observed this species associated with large woody debris. Trautman (1957) reported it from the limestone and gravel shoals and sandy beaches along the coast of Lake Erie. Prey consists of riffle-dwelling insect larvae, crayfish, and occasionally small fish. Spawning takes place in early summer to midsummer. The male guards the nest of eggs placed under large stones in or near flowing water. After hatching, parents guard young fry for a short time until they leave the nest.

Distribution and Status: The Stonecat occurs throughout the Mississippi River, Ohio River, and Great Lakes basins. Records are

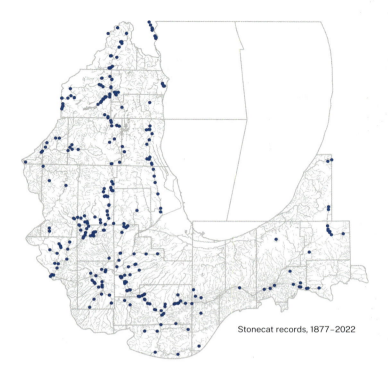

Stonecat records, 1877–2022

widespread throughout the Chicago Region, concentrated around large-river mainstems and the lower reaches of confluent streams. There are no records for the Calumet River system. The only record for a lake setting within the region was taken by David Starr Jordan in 1877 from Clear and Pine Lakes, LaPorte County, Indiana. We consider this species stable within the region.

Reference: Trautman 1957

NORTH AMERICAN CATFISHES (ICTALURIDAE) 255

Tadpole Madtom

Noturus gyrinus • *Noturus* is from Greek, meaning "back tail," referring to the fusion of the tail fin and the adipose fin; *gyrinus*, Greek for "tadpole," refers to the tadpole-like body.

Description: The Tadpole Madtom has a flattened head and body but is stouter than other madtoms. This species can be separated from the other madtoms by having a terminal mouth with equal jaws, a smooth pectoral spine, and no backward extensions on the premaxillary tooth patch. Also, a vague lateral stripe intercepted by vertical herringbone lines is typical but sometimes not evident. Overall coloration is olive to dusky, without color margins on the fins. This species can grow up to 4 inches (100 mm).

Natural History: Inhabiting a wide range of aquatic habitats, from large rivers, to lakes, and marshes, the Tadpole Madtom prefers sluggish or calm waters with abundant aquatic vegetation, small woody debris, and detritus. We have observed it living in a mix of small branches, detritus, and rubbish at the bottom of the Chicago Sanitary and Ship Canal. Prey items include small crustaceans, worms, and insect larvae. Gravid females have been observed in midsummer. This species is not known to construct nests, but eggs are guarded after being attached to sticks, stones, tin cans, or other debris.

Distribution and Status: The Tadpole Madtom occurs in the Mississippi River, Ohio River, and Great Lakes basins, and in the Atlantic and Gulf

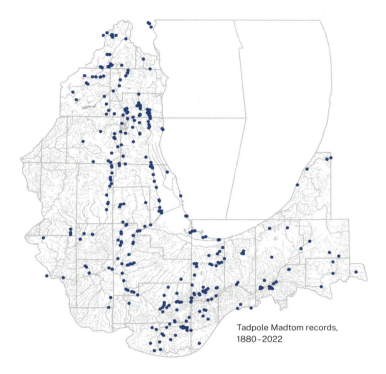

Tadpole Madtom records, 1880–2022

slope drainages. It is found in most drainages within the Chicago Region, where lowland habitats occur. We collected this species off the bottom of the Calumet–Saganashkee (Cal-Sag) Channel, Cook County, Illinois (INHS 1999), indicating its tolerance to habitat and water-quality degradation. The Tadpole Madtom is rarely found in abundance, but records are persistent through time.

Reference: Page and Burr 2011

Freckled Madtom

Noturus nocturnus · *Noturus* is from Greek, meaning "back tail," referring to the fusion of the tail fin and the adipose fin; *nocturnus* means "nocturnal" in Latin, referring to its dark color.

Description: The Freckled Madtom has the typical flattened head and body of a madtom, but is more robust than Stonecat and Slender Madtoms and slenderer than the Tadpole Madtom. Additional characteristics that differ from other madtoms are a terminal mouth with the upper jaw protruding, a sawtooth pectoral spine (3 teeth), and the lack of backward extensions on the premaxillary tooth patch. Overall coloration is dark, dusky, and speckled with tiny black melanophores. The fins are without color margins. Adults are typically 4 inches (100 mm) or less.

Natural History: In the Chicago Region, the Freckled Madtom occupies deep rocky runs with strong currents in medium to large rivers. A nocturnal feeder, it mostly consumes aquatic insect larvae and some small fish. Spawning takes place in midsummer in constructed nests or small existing cavities. Like other madtoms, it exhibits parental care of offspring during early life stages.

Distribution and Status: The Freckled Madtom occurs in the lower Mississippi River and Gulf slope drainages. Populations within the Chicago Region are somewhat disjunct from those of the Mississippi River, occurring only in the upper Illinois River and tributaries. There

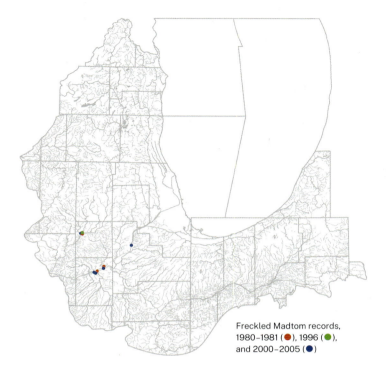

Freckled Madtom records, 1980–1981 (●), 1996 (●), and 2000–2005 (●)

are only 9 records for this species within the region between 1980 and 2005, including Aux Sable Creek, the Mazon River, the Illinois River, the Des Plaines River, and Little Rock Creek. The last record was taken by the authors from the Des Plaines River, Will County, Illinois, in 2005 (FMNH).

The Freckled Madtom is considered vulnerable and a species of concern within the Chicago Region.

References: Pflieger 1975; Smith 1979; Willink, Veraldi, and Ladonski 2006

Flathead Catfish

Pylodictis olivaris • *Pylodictis*, Greek for "mudfish"; *olivaris*, Latin, "olive colored."

Description: The Flathead Catfish has a somewhat flattened and comparatively slender body, and a broad dorsoventrally flattened head. In addition to its head shape, this species can be distinguished from other adult catfish by the protruding lower jaw and a shorter anal fin (14–17 rays). The juveniles can be distinguished from the diminutive madtoms by a large and lobed adipose fin, the backward-extending tooth patch on the roof of mouth, and a light-orange blotch on the tip of the upper caudal fin. The tail fin is rounded, with a slight central notch. Coloration is variable, depending on water turbidity, ranging from dark brown to olive to a bleached-out tan. The sides are often mottled, and the belly can be white or yellow. The adult is a very large fish, with the world-record catch of 123 pounds (56 kg).

Natural History: Although considered a large-river species, the Flathead Catfish also inhabits lakes and manmade reservoirs where it has been stocked. We have also observed mating pairs in small tributaries in the Fox River watershed. It prefers deeper water with moderate to strong currents, often associated with undercut banks, large boulders, and/or large woody debris. Bridge abutments and other manmade structures are also commonly used

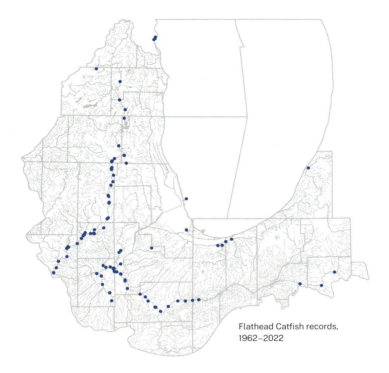

Flathead Catfish records, 1962–2022

for cover. This species is a nocturnal piscivore, often entering shallow, faster currents to feed at night. Large adults have been recorded eating waterfowl and small mammals. Juveniles prefer shallower riffle habitat and prey on macroinvertebrates. Flathead Catfish grow rapidly and can obtain a very large size, exceeding 48 inches (1,219 mm) in length. Their spawning habits are like other catfishes.

Distribution and Status: The natural distribution of the Flathead Catfish includes the Mississippi River, Ohio River, southern Great Lakes, and Gulf slope drainages. Records for this species within the Chicago Region are concentrated in the lower Kankakee River, the upper Illinois River, and the Fox River. We also have recent records (2001–2009) from Lake Michigan and its tributaries. The Flathead Catfish is stable within the region. This species is a popular target of anglers and noodlers (captured by hand) and is commercially fished in large rivers in reaches where it is abundant. As such, it has been widely introduced within and outside its natural range.

Reference: Trautman 1957

18

Pikes

Esocidae

The pike family is one of the better-known and easily recognized groups of fishes, owing to their characteristic torpedo-like body form, duckbill snout, posterior placement of dorsal fin, and sharp teeth. They typically have distinctive spotted or striped patterns, and their scales are very small. The pikes are largely piscivorous ambush predators, preferring larger lakes and sluggish backwater areas of rivers, where they are often associated with shallower weedy zones. Spawning typically occurs over vegetation or detritus; adhesive eggs are broadcast and stick to leaves, twigs, and stems. Pikes exhibit no parental care.

The pike family contains only 1 genus, with 5 species occurring worldwide. Their distribution is limited to the northern continents (Holarctic). There are 3 species found within the Chicago Region: Grass Pickerel, Muskellunge, and Northern Pike.

The Northern Pike is native to local rivers. Although they are targeted by anglers, they are not particularly abundant in the Chicago Region. They do reproduce on their own. Supplemental stocking has been largely unsuccessful. The Muskie is a highly managed sport species that has been introduced successfully into many waters outside its natural distribution, including larger local lakes. These fish do not reproduce naturally in the Chicago Region. Escapees from the stocked lakes do end up in local rivers where they are sought by anglers. Northern Pike and Muskellunge have been hybridized; however, the hybrid known as the Tiger Muskie is no longer stocked in the Chicago Region. Muskellunge-stocking programs have been successful in several Chicago Region lakes. The Grass Pickerel is quite small and not considered a sport species.

Grass Pickerel

Esox americanus · *Esox* is Latin for "pike," referring to the long-pointed snout; *americanus* refers to America.

Description: The lateral surface of the Grass Pickerel is covered with 20 or more irregular olive-green or brown vertical bars. The pattern can be mottled and quite variable. The most distinctive feature of the Grass Pickerel is the dark teardrop marking below the eyes, which is mostly uniform in width and extends to the bottom of the jaw. It is also the only *Esox* species with a fully scaled cheek and gill cover. The Grass Pickerel has 10–14 (usually 12) branchiostegal rays and 4 mandibular pores (rarely 3 or 5). This fish is a small pike, attaining a maximum length of 12 inches (300 mm).

Natural History: The Grass Pickerel is most common in the slower-moving areas of rivers and streams, and can also be found in lakes, marshes, backwaters, and sloughs, as well as agricultural ditches with sufficient perennial flow. It is often associated with aquatic grasses, overhanging vegetation, and small woody debris. Although fish are a significant portion of the adult Grass Pickerel diet, this species also will consume crayfish, tadpoles, and aquatic insect larvae. Spawning takes place during March and April, with adhesive eggs broadcast over submerged vegetation. Growth in the first year can be up to 4–6 inches (100–150 mm).

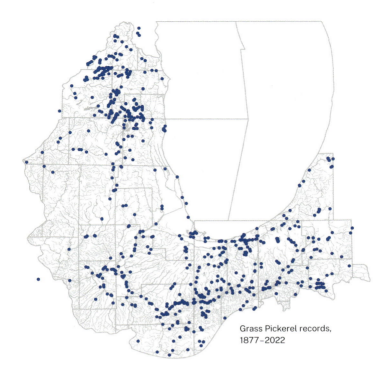

Grass Pickerel records, 1877–2022

Distribution and Status: The natural range of the Grass Pickerel includes the Great Lakes, Mississippi River, Ohio River, Atlantic slope, and Gulf slope drainages. It is noted as being introduced elsewhere. Within the Chicago Region, records are most numerous from the upper Fox and Kankakee Rivers. Its distribution reflects its preference for lower-gradient segments of streams, lakes, and marshes. It is rarely abundant; however, its status is secure. Grass Pickerel in the Great Lakes and Mississippi watersheds are often considered to be in the subspecies *Esox americanus vermiculatus* and are sometimes called *Esox vermiculatus*.

References: Eddy and Underhill 1974; Page and Burr 2011

Description: The Northern Pike is a long cylindrical fish with distinctive pigmentation patterns consisting of 7–9 irregular rows of light-colored round or oval markings extending along both lateral surfaces. The background coloration ranges from olive green to light brown. In juveniles, the pattern consists of light-colored vertical bars. The bottom, or ventral surface, is white or very light colored in both juveniles and adults. Fins usually contain dark to dusky spots between the rays. The cheek is fully scaled, and the gill cover is only partially scaled at the top. The teardrop below the eye is absent or weakly developed, which is more prominent in juveniles. The outer circumference of the lower jaw has 5 mandibular pores, rarely 4 or 6. The lower surface of the gill cover has 14–16 rays within the membranes (branchiostegal rays). The Northern Pike can be distinguished from the other 2 *Esox* species most easily by oval spots on the sides, the fully scaled cheek, the presence of scales only on the top of the gill cover, the number of branchiostegal rays, and the number of mandibular pores. Adults are typically in the 20–30-inch (500–750-mm) range but can exceed 50 inches (1,250 mm).

Natural History: The Northern Pike, like other members of the family, generally prefers lakes, and rivers with sidestream marsh and oxbow habitats. It is most often associated with shallow water and aquatic vegetation but may move to deeper areas during warmer summer months. Very young pike feed on invertebrates, but quickly become piscivorous. Like most fish, this species is opportunistic and occasionally takes crayfish, amphibians, ducklings, and even small mammals. Growth is very rapid, attaining lengths of up to 10–12 inches (250–300 mm) in the first year. The Northern Pike spawns in shallow water 0–6.5 feet (0–2 m) over vegetation in spring shortly after ice-out, when the water has warmed to 35.6–53.6°F (2–12°C). The fish tend to migrate to flooded marshes and wetlands or shallow shoreline inundations. Optimal spawning habitat includes flooded vegetation in a shallow, sheltered area, with a high affinity for sand and silty substrates (Lane, Minns, and Portt 1996). Pike spawn by broadcasting eggs over vegetation, preferably grasses and sedges. The eggs adhere to plant surfaces, suspended above the stream substrate. Nursery habitat is often contiguous with spawning habitat. Juveniles are typically associated with dense submergent and emergent aquatic plants, where they spend the spring in the shallow depths before moving out to deeper water in the fall.

Distribution and Status: The Northern Pike occurs in North American, Europe, and Asia with a circumpolar range (Holarctic). In North America, it ranges from the Arctic Circle south to Missouri, and from the Rockies east to the Atlantic slope. It is widely introduced in and outside its natural range. Records for

Northern Pike records, 1895 and 2022

the Northern Pike are numerous and widespread throughout the Chicago Region. It was even found in 35 feet (10.7 m) of water in Lake Michigan, and is becoming more common along the Chicago lakefront, especially in harbors. Although native to the Chicago Region, Northern Pike stocking has supplemented natural populations in some areas. Abundance can be quite low; it increases in a northern gradient into Wisconsin. Their status is secure but may become vulnerable due to warming temperatures combined with diminished and fragmented spawning habitats. The Northern Pike is one of the most sought-after sport and trophy fishes in North America. Despite having many bones, the flesh is delicious.

References: Casselman and Lewis 1996; Eddy and Underhill 1974; Lane, Portt, and Minns 1996; Weed 1927

Description: The Muskellunge is the largest of the pike species, with a long robust body. Coloration and markings can be highly variable. Some contain either bars, spots, or both. In some specimens, pigment patterns are absent or hard to discern. The Muskellunge also varies widely in color but is generally greenish gold to brown. No teardrop is present below the eye. Scales are found only on the top of the cheek and gill cover. There are 16–19 branchiostegal rays and 6–9 mandibular pores. The Muskellunge is best distinguished from other pikes by the scale pattern on the cheek and gill cover, branchiostegal ray count, and mandibular pore count. Adults can exceed 50 inches (1,250 mm).

Natural History: Ecologically, the Muskellunge is very similar to the Northern Pike, generally preferring lakes, marshes, backwaters, or sluggish area of rivers and larger creeks. It is also often associated with shallow water and aquatic vegetation but moves to deeper areas or to the mouths of creeks, seeking cooler water during warmer summer months. Young fish quickly convert to a piscivorous diet. Growth is very rapid, attaining lengths of up to 10–12 inches (250–300 mm) in the first year. Adults can exceed 50 inches (1,250 mm), but are generally smaller, in the 35–40-inch (875–1,000-mm) range. Muskellunge are broadcast spawners that typically spawn during the early spring season when water temperatures range from 46.4 to 64.4°F (8 to 18°C) in shallow water of 0–6.6 feet (0–2 m) with a relatively flat bottom slope (Krebs 2020). Typical substrates include a high affinity to silt and clay, with a medium affinity to sand (Krebs 2020). Cover types include submergent and emergent vegetation, along with stumps and logs. Young Muskellunge remain in the shallows among submergent vegetation, with a high affinity to silt substrate and a medium affinity to sand (Krebs 2020). The Muskellunge and the Northern Pike spawn at different times, which avoids natural hybridization of the 2 species.

Muskellunge records, 1910 (●) and 1977–2022 (●)

Distribution and Status: The natural range of the Muskellunge is centered on the Great Lakes and Ohio River basins, including the upper Mississippi River and Red River of the North. Lake Michigan and its confluent tributaries are the only part of the Chicago Region within its natural range. There is only 1 record for the native Great Lakes Muskellunge (*Esox masquinongy masquinongy*) taken by Meek and Hildebrand in 1910. The exact location was described as Edgemoor, Lake County, Indiana, and is plotted at the old Wolf Lake confluence to Lake Michigan. During the early 1900s, Wolf Lake was still connected to Lake Michigan here and retained its natural community form of a hemi-marsh. It is quite possible that Wolf Lake could have been a spawning ground for the Great Lakes Muskellunge. In the 1940s, Wolf Lake was severed from Lake Michigan by the construction of a wartime railroad line. The Lake Michigan genotypes are currently considered extirpated; due to stocking programs, various other genotypes are now present, and all other records (1977–2022) within the Chicago Region for this species are likely from these stockings. Although Muskellunge are only stocked in lakes, they escape into local river systems. The Fox River has one of the more abundant populations where records are taken most frequently at the mouths of larger tributary streams. Muskellunge have recently started to appear along the Chicago lakefront and Chicago River. It would be interesting to genetically sample those specimens found within the natural range of Lake Michigan, as native source populations still exist in northern waters.

References: Dombeck, Menzel, and Hinz, 1984; Krebs 2020; Meek and Hildebrand 1910; Smith 1979; Weed 1927

PIKES (ESOCIDAE) 269

19

Mudminnows

Umbridae

The mudminnow family is a rather secretive group of fishes, largely unknown to the general public. They are related to the pike, and through time have been placed in and out of the Esocidae family. There is little physical resemblance to pikes except for the long round body and posterior position of the dorsal fin. The local Chicago Region mudminnow has mottled brown pigmentation, with a brown bar just in front of the rounded tail fin. These fish prefer prairie sloughs, low-gradient streams, and associated wetlands with dense aquatic vegetation. Mudminnows can gulp atmospheric oxygen, which allows them to live in low-oxygen conditions, typical of wetland habitats.

The Umbridae family contains 5 species, 4 in North America and 1 in Europe. The Alaska Blackfish (*Dallia pectoralis*) is restricted to the northwest of Alaska, and the European Mudminnow (*Umbra krameria*) occurs in Eastern Europe. The Eastern Mudminnow (*Umbra pygmaea*) occurs in the southeastern United States, the Olympic Mudminnow (*Novumbra hubbsi*) in the Pacific Northwest. The only species within the Chicago Region is the Central Mudminnow.

This group of fishes is valued by humans for their attractiveness and success in aquaria culture. They are sometimes used as baitfish.

Central Mudminnow

Umbra limi · *Umbra* is Latin for "shade" or "shadowed"; *limi* is Latin for "mud."

Description: The Central Mudminnow has a distinctive, dark, and mottled pigmentation pattern along its body. The dorsal fin is rounded and situated toward the back of the body near the caudal fin, which is also rounded. The mouth is terminal. Scales are cycloid and rather large. Mudminnows superficially resemble topminnows but lack the characteristic upturned mouth and fused frenum (the groove between the upper lip and snout). They grow to only 6 inches (150 mm).

Natural History: Mudminnows are found primarily in wetlands, backwater areas, bogs, and low-gradient streams, closely associated with aquatic vegetation. They are commonly found in drainage ditches where former wetlands were drained. They can tolerate low oxygen levels and reportedly gulp air, similar to gars and bowfins. Their food consists primarily of aquatic invertebrates, but they will also consume decaying plants and organic material. Spawning takes place in early spring, laying individual eggs on aquatic vegetation.

Distribution and Status: The Central Mudminnow is widely distributed throughout the Chicago Region.

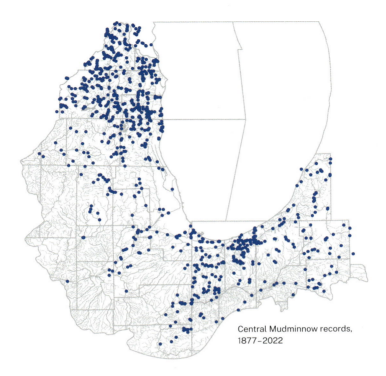

Central Mudminnow records, 1877–2022

Although this species is quite tolerant of poor water quality, vegetation beds and wetlands associated with lakes and streams are essential habitat.

References: Page and Burr 2011; Smith 1979

20

Salmon, Trout, Chars, and Whitefishes

Salmonidae

This group of fishes are thick bodied, with a fleshy adipose fin just in front of the tail fin. Their scales are smooth edged (cycloid), and the lateral line is complete. An elongated, modified scale at the base of the pelvic fin (axillary process) sets the salmonids apart from most fishes.

Salmon, trout, and chars are fine scaled, having more than 100 scales in their lateral line, 16 or fewer dorsal fin rays, and large conspicuous teeth. Depending on the age and season, they can also have body coloration, pigments, and patterns. The whitefishes and ciscoes have fewer than 15 dorsal fin rays; have large, rounded scales; have no maxillary teeth; and are silvery without coloration or patterning. Many species in this family are exclusively freshwater, while others live in the ocean and migrate long distances up freshwater rivers (anadromous), sometimes jumping over large natural barriers to spawn.

The family Salmonidae inhabits the Northern Hemisphere and comprises 3 subfamilies: Coregoninae (whitefishes and ciscoes,

85 species), Thymallinae (graylings; 14 species), and Salmoninae (chars, trout, and salmon, 75 species). Sixteen species of salmonids are known from the Chicago Region. Four of these are Pacific salmon (*Oncorhynchus* spp.) species, stocked in the Great Lakes for recreational fishing and to control the Alewife, and the European Brown Trout (*Salmo trutta*) for stream fishing. The taxonomy of ciscoes is difficult and contentious, with some researchers combining all ciscoes into 1 species, *Coregonus artedi* (Lyons and Schmidt 2022). There are occasional reports in the Chicago Region of Pink Salmon (*Oncorhynchus gorbuscha*), with its relatively large black oval spots along the back and entire tail, but these are migrants from northern Lake Michigan.

Salmonids have long been of great commercial and recreational value. Their flesh is prized for its flavor and texture; their roe is considered a delicacy worldwide. Excessive overharvest, pollution, and dams have depleted many native stocks and diminished entire populations, leading to widespread propagation and introduction, often in unexpected areas outside their native range. The Chicago Region is a prime example. Lake Michigan was once a premier resource for Lake Trout, whitefishes, and ciscoes. Due to 75 years of overfishing, the native populations of salmonids were all but eradicated by the 1940s. This brought about the introduction of nonnative salmon, when in the early 1970s, Pacific Northwest species were stocked by federal and state agencies. The stocking was initiated to provide an economically valuable sport fishery and to control the invasive Alewife. The stocking program has not been without controversy, as it conflicts with efforts to restore native fisheries.

Some restoration efforts have been focused on the native Lake Trout, with moderate success, as populations remain well below historic levels. It is believed that 6 of the 10 species of whitefishes are extirpated from Lake Michigan, with several considered extinct. Some of these ciscoes are so rare, extirpated, or extinct that descriptions and natural history information in these accounts have been summarized from Koelz (1929) and photos are of museum specimens.

Longjaw Cisco

Coregonus alpenae · *Coregonus* is derived from the Greek for "angle eye." The name *alpenae* means "of Alpena, Michigan" — this species was first described from Lake Michigan near Charlevoix, Michigan.

Field Museum Specimen #13939

Description: The Longjaw Cisco has a compressed and elongated body, with the greatest depth near the middle of the fish. Coloration is generally very pale, silvery with a faint pink to purple iridescence strongest above the lateral line and absent on the belly. The head of this species, compared to that of other species, is short and deep; the snout is broad and rounded. Premaxillaries may be slightly pigmented, but the anterior maxilla has little to none. The lower jaw is without pigment. The premaxillaries are angled down and forward 45–60 degrees. The maxilla is very long, extending beyond the anterior edge of the pupil but seldom to the center. The lower jaw is stout and usually projects beyond the upper jaw and lacks a bump on the chin (symphyseal knob). The gill rakers (33–46) are medium to long, with the longest about equal in length to the longest gill filaments. Spawning males develop 1 tubercle per scale on the lateral surfaces and 2 on each lateral line scale. Tubercles are not present on scales along the back and the belly. Small tubercles of irregular shape and size are irregularly scattered on the head and faintly on the fins and the lower jaw. Superficially, this species most closely resembles the Deepwater Cisco. The Longjaw is the largest of all the ciscoes, with a maximum length of 21 inches (533 mm) and weight of 4 pounds (1.8 kg).

Natural History: The Longjaw Cisco is a bathypelagic species, occupying the deep basins of Lake Michigan, normally found at depths between 180 and 540 feet. Mature individuals consume Opossum Shrimp (*Mysis relicta*) almost exclusively; however, other stomach contents documented included mayfly larvae, plant material, fish scales, cased invertebrate eggs, and trace amounts of sand. The Longjaw Cisco is a fall spawner in the Chicago Region, which Koelz (1929) observed firsthand 17 miles offshore of Michigan City, Indiana, on November 19, 1920. Anglers also reported to Koelz (1929) that Longjaws came into shallow water (60 feet/ 18.3 m) in the northern part of Lake Michigan to spawn in late October and November.

Longjaw Cisco records, 1920–1921

Distribution and Status: The range of the Longjaw Cisco is limited to Lakes Michigan and Huron. In the Chicago Region, it once could be found in Lake Michigan well offshore in 60–600 feet (16–160 m) of water. At one time the Longjaw Cisco constituted an important part of the commercial fishery of Lake Michigan for the smoked fish trade. It was once quite abundant offshore of Michigan City and, according to Koelz (1929), made up a third of the overall cisco catch. Surveys in which ciscoes were taken in identical gangs of gill nets set in the same areas at different periods show the dramatic decline of this species, which resulted primarily from intensive commercial fishing with continually decreasing mesh sizes. It is likely that the Longjaw Cisco formed part of the food chain that supported Lake Char (Trout) and Burbot populations. The Longjaw Cisco was listed at one point as federally endangered, then removed because it seemingly became extinct. Further investigation is needed to determine if it is still extant within the deep basin of southern Lake Michigan.

References: Bersamin 1958; Hubbs and Lager 1964; Koelz 1929; S. H. Smith 1964

Lake Herring (Cisco)

Coregonus artedi · *Coregonus* is derived from the Greek for "angle eye"; *artedi* is in homage to Peter Artedi, who is considered the father of ichthyology.

Field Museum Specimen #63396

Description: Lake Herring, or Cisco, found in Lake Michigan generally have an elongated, elliptical body that is round in cross-section. This species is extremely variable between populations. The coloration is silvery for the most part; however, sheens of iridescent purple and pink can be glimpsed along the sides. The dorsum is dark blue-gray, the abdomen white. The lower jaw is equal in length to the upper jaw. The premaxillaries are very short, not quite longer than wide. The anterior maxillary is always with dark pigment, and the lower jaw has faint pigment with a symphyseal knob. The gill rakers (41–55, usually 46–55) are usually long, rarely medium length. All males and most of the females develop small, scattered breeding tubercles on the head and a single tubercle on the posterior edge of the body scales. Juveniles may superficially resemble the Bloater. This species typically attains lengths of 12–18 inches (300–450 mm) but can reach 21 inches (525 mm).

Natural History: The Lake Herring inhabits cold glacial lakes and confluent rivers. It is a highly nomadic and pelagic species, schooling along the coastal waters of Lake Michigan. It remains nearshore in the colder months, from late September to early June, and then disperses to deeper waters where temperatures remain cold. It is most frequently associated with inshore shoals and shallow water over a wide variety of bottom types, but usually sand. The deepest this species was recorded in Lake Michigan was at 300 feet (90 m). Primary food items include small zoo-plankton, shifting to Opossum Shrimp in December following spawning. Incidental or intentional consumption of conspecific eggs has also been observed during December. During summer months, insects are a significant portion of the diet. The Lake Herring spawns from early November to mid-December when the water temperature drops to about 42°F (5.5°C), with peak activity at temperatures below 39°F (3.9°C). This species is believed to be a pelagic spawner at depths from 60–120 feet (18–36 m). Eggs are demersal and eventually sink to the bottom and stick to the sand. The very deep samples of eggs and fish may be the result of drift from the shallows. Lake Herring have also been observed spawning in rivers, such as the Oconomowoc River (Waukesha County, Wisconsin) just to the north of the Chicago Region.

Distribution and Status: The Lake Herring occurs naturally throughout the Atlantic, Arctic, upper Mississippi River, and Great Lakes basins. In the Chicago Region, it is recorded from the shallower waters of Lake Michigan and several larger glacial lakes. We have made records as recent as 2004 in Lake Michigan in 16–50 feet (5–15 m) of water at Waukegan, Illinois (FMNH). Records from Lake Geneva and Lake Beulah, Walworth County, Wisconsin, date from late 2012. Records from Lake Maxinkuckee (INDNR 1985) in Marshall County, Indiana, which is just south of the Chicago Region, are

Lake Herring records, 1890–1921 (●), 1935–1971 (●), and 1981–2022 (●)

most likely the southernmost population of this species. The last Chicago Region record for this species was taken from Lake Geneva, Walworth County, Wisconsin, in 2012 (WDNR). Historically, the distribution and abundance in glacial lakes was probably greater than it is now, due to eutrophication and overfishing. The Lake Herring is listed as endangered in Illinois and Indiana and threatened in Michigan. Its status is considered critical within the Chicago Region, requiring further research into distribution and habits. It is reported that this species can still be taken by hook and line off Michigan City, LaPorte County, Indiana.

References: Becker 1979; Cahn 1927; Dryer and Beil 1964; Eddy and Underhill 1974; Fey 1955; John and Hasler 1956; Koelz 1929; S. H. Smith 1956; Trautman 1957; Wells 1968

SALMON, TROUT, CHARS, AND WHITEFISHES (SALMONIDAE)   279

Lake Whitefish

Coregonus clupeaformis • *Coregonus* is derived from the Greek for "angle eye"; *clupeaformis* means "herring shaped" in Latin.

Description: The Lake Whitefish has a fusiform but laterally compressed body. Large individuals develop a pronounced hump from the head to the origin of the dorsal fin. The coloration is silvery, with a dark to light sheen from the dorsal to the abdomen. The pectoral, pelvic, and anal fins are white but can have a pinkish-orange tinge. The dorsal and caudal fins are a translucent gray. The mouth is small and subterminal. The lower jaw is not pigmented, nor does it have a symphyseal knob; the tip of the lower jaw extends beyond the tip of the upper. The maxillaries are always with pigment and seldom extend beyond the anterior edge of the pupil. The premaxillaries slant backward, giving the mouth a rounded and subterminal profile. Gill rakers (19–33, usually 26–28) are short, with the longest shorter than the longest gill filament. Breeder males and females both develop tubercles on the head and body. Adults can reach 31 inches (800 mm) and 26.5 pounds (12 kg).

Natural History: The Lake Whitefish inhabits cold glacial lakes and rivers. It is associated with shallower waters, usually no deeper than 180 feet (55 m). It remains nearshore during the winter when there is ice cover, moving out to deeper water at ice-out. This fish most likely moves in and out of the littoral areas as temperature, currents, and food supply dictate. It travels in schools, like most ciscoes and whitefishes. Mature Lake Whitefish generally consume aquatic insects, copepods, crustaceans, small mollusks, fish eggs, seeds, small fish, and incidental items such as sand, gravel, cinders and wood fragments. In Lake Michigan, spawning begins sometime between November and December, depending on water temperature (40–43°F/ 4.4–6.1°C), and continues for about 2–6 weeks. Spawning generally occurs at night over gravel, honeycomb rock, or small stones at 6–60 feet (2–20 m) along the shores, shoals, or reefs. Eggs are broadcast and settle to the bottom. Lake Whitefish are also known to spawn in rivers over bedrock shoals.

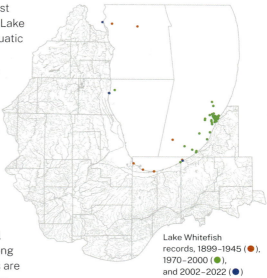

Lake Whitefish records, 1899–1945 (●), 1970–2000 (●), and 2002–2022 (●)

Distribution and Status: The Lake Whitefish is found from the Yukon Territory and British Columbia, including the Yukon, Skeena, and Fraser River systems, through the Arctic Canadian coast to Ungava Bay and Labrador, south to the Great Lakes basin and the upper Mississippi River system. It has been introduced elsewhere outside its range, such as the Pacific Northwest. In the Chicago Region, the Lake Whitefish is restricted to Lake Michigan and confluent rivers when spawning. Recent records include the nearshore waters off St. Joseph, Michigan, Michigan City, Indiana, and Waukegan, Illinois, and along the Chicago lakefront. Since the Lake Whitefish was an extremely important food commodity, it was overfished by 1922. Federal statistics from 1880 show that Lake Michigan produced over 12 million pounds (over 5.4 million kg) of Lake Whitefish, and then in 1922, the catch plummeted to 1.5 million pounds (about 680,000 kg). Lack of regulation on size limits contributed to its decline. The Lake Whitefish is considered of special concern within the Chicago Region and in need of study for details on distribution and abundance.

References: Eddy and Underhill 1974; Hubbs and Lagler 1964; Koelz 1929; Smiley 1882; Trautman 1957

Bloater

Coregonus hoyi · *Coregonus* is derived from the Greek for "angle eye"; *hoyi* is in homage to P. R. Hoy, MD, of Racine, Wisconsin, a naturalist and ichthyologist.

Juvenile Bloater

Description: The Bloater has a body with the greatest depth at its midpoint and is silvery in color with a pinkish or bluish sheen. The abdomen is silvery white. The dorsal and caudal fins are a translucent gray with a dark edge; the median fins are weakly pigmented. The snout is usually just longer than the proportionally large eye. The premaxillaries are pigmented and angled down and forward. The maxillary is pigmented and extends to the pupil of the eye. The lower jaw is clearly pigmented (except in some Lake Michigan populations). The lower jaw is longer than the upper jaw, with weakly developed mandibles. The gill rakers (41–55, usually 46–55) are typically long; the longest are usually longer than gill filaments. Pelvic fins are long but rarely reach past the anus. Breeding adults develop tubercles, usually 1–3 per scale along the sides. Adults can reach 10.5 inches (265 mm) in length, rarely exceeding 7 inches (200 mm).

Natural History: The Lake Michigan Bloater populations prefer a wide variety of depths and can be found anywhere from over 600 feet (180 m) to shallow beaches. The greatest abundances are typically found in schools between 120 and 360 feet (37 and 110 m). Mature individuals generally consume aquatic insects, copepods, crustaceans, small mollusks, and fish eggs. In Lake

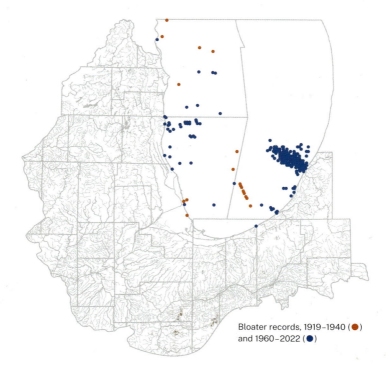

Bloater records, 1919–1940 (●) and 1960–2022 (●)

Michigan, spawning begins sometime between late February and early March and continues for about 4 weeks. Broadcast spawning takes place over sand or rock at depths of 60–180 feet (18–55 m).

Distribution and Status: The Bloater is known from Lakes Superior, Huron, Michigan, Ontario, Nipigon, and Winnipeg, and other deep Canadian Shield lakes. In the Chicago Region, it is restricted to Lake Michigan. There are 300 records for this species between 1919 and 2022. Recent records (2009, 2014) include the nearshore waters and beaches of downtown Chicago. Since the Bloater was once an extremely important food commodity, it is generally considered overfished, but currently more abundant than any of the other ciscoes. This species is of special concern within the Chicago Region and in need of study.

References: Hubbs and Lagler 1964; Koelz 1929; Willink 2017

SALMON, TROUT, CHARS, AND WHITEFISHES (SALMONIDAE)

Deepwater Cisco

Coregonus johannae · *Coregonus* is derived from the Greek for "angle eye"; *johannae* means "of Johanna" in Latin, in honor of the life companion of George Wagner, who first described the species.

Field Museum Specimen #2089

Description: The Deepwater Cisco has a fusiform body, with the greatest depth just in front of the dorsal fin. The coloration is silvery with a pinkish or bluish sheen. The abdomen is silvery white. The dorsal and caudal fins are a translucent white with a dark edge; the median fins are usually pigmented, more so along the edges. The premaxillaries are weakly or not pigmented. The maxillary is seldom pigmented and extends to the center of the eye. The snout and paired fins are comparatively long. The gill rakers (26–36, usually 27–32) are typically short. Breeding males develop a tubercle on each scale, sometimes 2 to each scale. Adults grow to 12 inches (300 mm) in length.

Natural History: The Lake Michigan Deepwater Cisco populations prefer water ranging from 180 to 600 feet (55 to 183 m) in depth but are uncommon above depths of 400 feet (122 m). This species lives in schools. Mature individuals generally consume Opossum Shrimp, *Psidium*, *Pontoporeia*, aquatic insects, copepods, crustaceans, small mollusks, and fish eggs. Fish scales have also been found in gut contents. In Lake Michigan, spawning begins sometime between late August and early September and continues for about

284   CHAPTER 20

Deepwater Cisco records, 1906–1920

4 weeks. It is unknown what substrates and depths are used for spawning, but this most likely takes place at 600 feet (183 m) or more.

Distribution and Status: The Deepwater Cisco is endemic to Lake Michigan and Lake Huron. In the Chicago Region, it is restricted to Lake Michigan. There are only 5 records for this species from 1920 by Koelz; 1 record of the type specimen described by Wagner in 1906 was taken off Racine County, Wisconsin, 150 feet (45.7 m) deep (US National Museum #87353). The Deepwater Cisco was apparently an important food commodity, with overfishing contributing to its demise. This species is of critical status within the Chicago Region; further investigation is needed to determine if the species is still extant within the deep basin of southern Lake Michigan.

References: Hubbs and Lagler 1964; Koelz 1929

Kiyi

Coregonus kiyi · *Coregonus* is derived from the Greek for "angle eye"; *kiyi* is based on a local term used by Lake Michigan anglers and commercial fishers.

Field Museum Specimen #9689

Description: The Kiyi is one of the smallest ciscoes, having a laterally compressed and thin body. The coloration is silvery, with a pink to purple sheen above the lateral line and dense pigmentation on the dorsum, mouth, head, and fins. The abdomen is silvery white. The snout is longer than the diameter of the large eye. The maxillary extends beyond the anterior edge of pupil, but never to its center. The lower jaw is weakly developed and projects beyond the upper jaw. The mandible is thin and distinctly hooked at the tip. The gill rakers (34–45, usually 36–41) are usually medium in length. The average size is 10 inches (250 mm).

Natural History: The Lake Michigan Kiyi populations prefer water depths between 120 and 600 feet (37 and 183 m) but are uncommon above depths of 240 feet (73 m). They most often occur in schools. Mature individuals reportedly consume only Opossum Shrimp. In Lake Michigan, spawning begins sometime between late October and early November and continues for about 4 weeks. It is unknown what substrates and exact depths are used for spawning, but this most likely takes place at 420 feet (128 m) or more on shoals.

Distribution and Status: The Kiyi is known from Lakes Michigan, Superior, Huron, and Ontario. In the

Kiyi records, 1920

Chicago Region, it is restricted to Lake Michigan, with only 5 records for this species by Koelz in 1920. There are records from northern Lake Michigan in the 2000s for this species (MIFA). The Kiyi was not specifically an important food commodity, due to its small size; however, many were kept or killed as bycatch with other Cisco species, especially as gill-net mesh sizes decreased. This species is of critical status within the Chicago Region, and further investigation is needed to determine if the species is still extant within southern Lake Michigan.

References: Eddy and Underhill 1974; Hubbs and Lagler 1964; Koelz 1929

Blackfin Cisco

Coregonus nigripinnis · *Coregonus* is derived from the Greek for "angle eye"; *nigripinnis* means "black fins" in Latin.

Field Museum Specimen #13951

Description: The Blackfin Cisco has a fusiform body with its greatest depth at the nape. The coloration is silvery but is dulled by the intense spattering of black melanophores over the entire body. The dorsum is black, sometimes with a bluish or green sheen. The anterior maxillary seldom extends beyond the anterior edge of the pupil. The lower jaw does not have a symphyseal knob, and is thick and equal to the upper jaw. The gill rakers (41–52, usually 46–50) are long, the longest greater in length than the longest gill filaments. This species is one of the larger ciscoes, reaching 14 inches (350 mm) and 1.5 pounds (0.7 kg).

Natural History: The Lake Michigan Blackfin Cisco populations prefer water depths between 180 and 600 feet (55 and 182 m) but are uncommon above 300 feet (91 m). Mature individuals are reported to exclusively consume Opossum Shrimp. Exactly when and what substrates and depths are used for spawning is unknown; based on seasonal data, this fish likely spawns between November and February at depths between 350 and 600 feet (107 and 182 m).

Distribution and Status: The Blackfin Cisco is known in Lakes Michigan, Superior, Huron, Ontario,

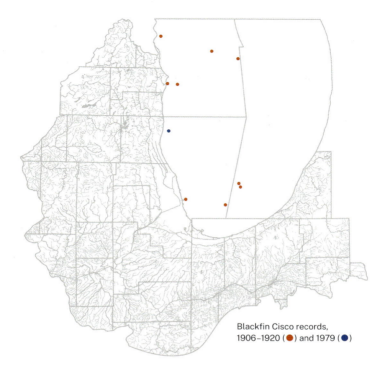

Blackfin Cisco records, 1906–1920 (●) and 1979 (●)

and Nipigon. In the Chicago Region, it is restricted to Lake Michigan, with only 10 total records. The most recent record is 85 feet (26 m), taken by the Illinois Natural History Survey in 1979, 4 miles northeast of Waukegan, Illinois. Since the Blackfin Cisco was an extremely important food commodity, it was most likely overfished by the early 1920s. This species is of critical status within the Chicago Region; further investigation is needed to determine distribution and natural history.

References: Hubbs and Lagler 1964; Koelz 1929

Field Museum Specimen #63400

Description: The Shortnose Cisco has a fusiform and slightly slab-sided body shape. The deepest portion of the fish is just anterior to the dorsal fin. The coloration is silvery with pinkish and bluish sheens, depending on light refraction. The snout is short. The premaxillaries are heavily pigmented and slanted down and forward. The anterior portion of the maxillary is pigmented and extends to about the middle of the eye. The lower jaw is robust, and the tip is heavily pigmented with black. The gill rakers number 30–41 and are short, with the longest shorter than the longest gill filaments. Several males taken off Port Washington, Wisconsin, had developed tubercles all over the body. Adults are usually smaller than 9 inches (240 mm).

Natural History: The Shortnose Cisco prefers the upper zones of deepwater areas, between 100 and 400 feet (30 and 120 m) in depth. In lower Lake Michigan, abundance has been noted to increase as samples approach 240 feet (73 m) and to decrease below that point. Based on Lake Ontario specimens, food items include primarily Opossum Shrimp and *Pontoporeia*, along with lesser numbers of copepods, aquatic insect larvae, and fingernail clams. Little is

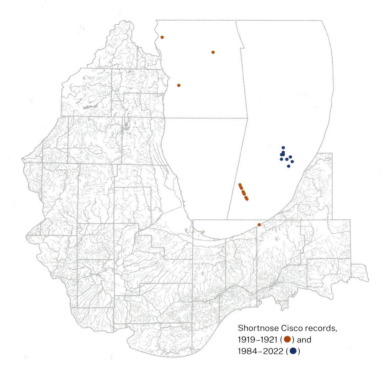

Shortnose Cisco records, 1919–1921 (●) and 1984–2022 (●)

known of their spawning habitat or behaviors.

Distribution and Status: The Shortnose Cisco is known from Lakes Huron, Michigan, Ontario, Superior, and Nipigon. In the Chicago Region, the Shortnose Cisco is restricted to Lake Michigan. Recent records include only the offshore waters (7–17 miles/11.3–27.4 km) near St. Joseph, Michigan. This species was described from the type specimen taken within the Chicago Region on April 1, 1921 (US National Museum #87351). A historic record from 1921 at Michigan City, LaPorte County, Indiana, is confirmed, with the specimen preserved at the Field Museum of Natural History. As an extremely important food commodity, it was overfished by 1922. Although the state of Michigan regards this species as extinct, relatively recent records near Berrien County, Michigan (MIFA 2001), indicate it may still be extant. Conservation status is considered critical within the Chicago Region, and further investigation is needed to determine if the species is still present in southern Lake Michigan.

References: Hubbs and Lagler 1964; Jobes 1943; Koelz 1929; Pritchard 1931

Shortjaw Cisco

Coregonus zenithicus · *Coregonus* is derived from the Greek for "angle eye"; *zenithicus* is named after Duluth, Minnesota, the Zenith City — Duluth is where David Starr Jordan and Barton Warren Evermann saw hundreds of specimens of this species in the deep-freeze plant of Booth and Company in 1909.

Field Museum Specimen #63397

Description: The Shortjaw Cisco has an elongated body, with its greatest depth just anterior to the dorsal fin. The color is silvery with a black base. The back varies from dark blue to pale green sheen. The dorsal fin margin and distal half of pectoral and caudal rays are often speckled with black melanophores. Older individuals may develop black melanophores on the pelvic and anal fins. The premaxillaries are angled down and forward, with black pigmentation. The anterior maxillary is lightly pigmented and reaches to the middle of eye. The lower jaw is heavy, lacks a symphyseal knob, and is usually shorter than the upper jaw. The gill rakers (35–44, usually 38–42) are typically short, with the longest equal in length to the longest gill filaments. Only Breeding males develop tubercles. Adults can reach 13 inches (330 mm) in length.

Natural History: The Lake Michigan Shortjaw Cisco populations prefer water depths between 70 and 550 feet (21 and 168 m). Specimens were not found in nearshore Lake Herring pound nets, suggesting a preference for deeper habitats. Like most ciscoes, this species is found primarily in schools. Mature individuals generally consume aquatic insects, copepods, crustaceans, small mollusks, and fish eggs. In Lake Michigan, spawning begins sometime

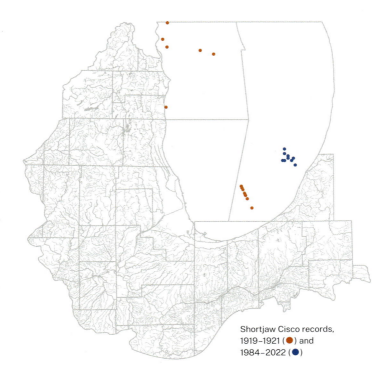

Shortjaw Cisco records, 1919–1921 (●) and 1984–2022 (●)

between October and November and continues for about 4 weeks. Spawning takes place over sand at depths of 60–180 feet (18–55 m).

Distribution and Status: The Shortjaw Cisco is known from Lakes Superior, Huron, Michigan, and Nipigon, and throughout Canada. In the Chicago Region, it is restricted to Lake Michigan. There are 23 records for this species between 1909 and 1998. Recent records include only the offshore waters (7–17 miles/11.3–27.4 km) near St. Joseph, Michigan (MIFA). The Shortjaw Cisco is listed as endangered in Michigan. It is of critical status within the Chicago Region. More information is needed on distribution and habits in Lake Michigan.

References: Dryer 1966; Eddy and Underhill 1974; Hubbs and Lagler 1964; Koelz 1929

Coho Salmon

Oncorhynchus kisutch · *Oncorhynchus* means "hook nose" in Latin, in reference to the upper and lower jaws of breeding males, also called a kype; *kisutch* is the Kamchatkan word for this species. For the common name, *Coho* is the Salish word for this species.

Description: The adult Coho Salmon is a fusiform fish, having a moderately forked tail and many sharp teeth set in white gums. It has 13–14 branchiostegal rays, 13–15 anal fin rays, and 45–85 pyloric caeca. The nonbreeding coloration is dark metallic above, silver on the sides, and whitish on belly. Irregular black spots are speckled along the back and upper two-thirds of the caudal fin. Breeding individuals become dark brown above and deep red on the sides. The breeding males form a kype, or extremely hooked mandible and maxilla. Post-spawning individuals become emaciated and covered with fungus, with eroded anal and lower caudal fins. In its native habitats, this species can reach up to 38 inches (965 mm) and 31 pounds (14 kg); an individual observed from Waukegan Harbor was 25.5 inches (651 mm) and 5 pounds (2.3 kg). See the Chinook Salmon account for differences.

Natural History: The Coho Salmon inhabits oceans, lakes, and confluent rivers and streams. Within the Chicago Region, it is propagated in hatcheries. It resides in feeder streams for up to 2 years. Following migration to Lake Michigan they typically spend 2 years here feeding. During the summer months, Coho occupies different areas than Chinook, preferring cooler water at depths of 50–260 feet (15–80 m), and migrate north where the water temperatures are in the range of 44–58° F. Coho feed on Opossum Shrimp, Sticklebacks, Alewives, Spottail Shiners, and Smelts. When water temperatures cool in the late fall, this species moves out of the thermals and migrates south. When it reaches 4 years of age, it ascends tributary streams in search of suitable spawning habitat in late fall; however, spawning habitat and conditions are not favorable for this species within the Chicago Region. Less than 1% of the Coho Salmon population is from natural reproduction, so they must be stocked annually to maintain the sport fishery. A thorough description of the Coho Salmon life history and habitat within its native range may be found in Wydoski and Whitney (2003).

Distribution and Status: The natural range of the Coho Salmon is the Pacific Ocean and tributary streams from Point Hope, Alaska, to Monterey Bay, California, in North America, and in Northeast Asia from the Anadyr River in Russia south to Hokkaido, Japan. Several stocks are listed as federally endangered. This species

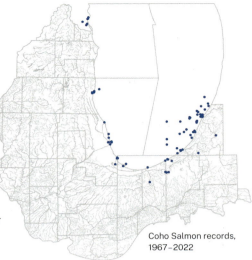

Coho Salmon records, 1967–2022

was first introduced to Lake Michigan in 1966. Within the Chicago Region, it is found primarily in Lake Michigan and tributary streams, where it is stocked annually to maintain the sport fishery population. This species is not native to Lake Michigan and may have adverse impacts to native fish species by consuming Opossum Shrimp and native minnows.

References: R. M. Bailey, Latta, and Smith 2004; Pollard et al. 1997; Stearley and Smith 1993; Wydoski and Whitney 2003

Rainbow Trout (Steelhead)

Oncorhynchus mykiss • *Oncorhynchus* means "hook nose" in Latin, referring to the upper and lower jaws of breeding males, also called a kype; *mykiss* is derived from the Kamchatkan word for this species, *mikizha*. Steelhead is the anadromous variety, which lives in the ocean and spawns in freshwater streams. The Rainbow Trout is the variety that lives its entire life in small fast-water streams.

Lake-run Steelhead, Skamania Strain

Description: Large Steelhead found in Lake Michigan are silver, with metallic blue along the back and faint spots along the upper surfaces and tail. Spawning Steelhead males form a hook on their lower jaw, whereas females do not. Breeding coloration is light pink to red, with horizontal bands separated by steel blue or gray running the length of the body. Speckles are darker on the upper third of the body and entire caudal fin. Stream-resident Rainbow Trout are pink with a bluish hue and speckled with dark spots, retaining their color throughout the year. Anal fin rays are 10–12. Both forms differ from the Chinook and the Coho by having 12 or fewer anal rays and from the Brown Trout by having small black dots on the tail. The Brown Trout lacks spots on the tail and can have several reddish-orange lateral dots. Adult lake-run Steelhead captured during US Army Corps harbor surveys (2002) measured up to 32 inches (822 mm) and 10 pounds (4.5 kg) for the Skamania stock, 30 inches (760 mm) and 13.5 pounds (6 kg) for the Chambers Creek stock, whereas stream-form Rainbow Trout encountered in the Chicago Region range from 6 to 12 inches (150 to 300 mm).

Natural History: The Rainbow Trout occurs naturally in oceans, lakes, and confluent rivers and streams. Within the Chicago Region, this species starts its life in fish hatcheries and is released in local lakes and streams in the spring and fall. It usually does not survive the summer months in smaller streams and lakes. It feeds on mayflies, caddisflies, terrestrial insects, and fish. In Lake Michigan tributaries it migrates downstream to spend 2 or 3 summer growing seasons in the lake. Steelhead are tolerant of wide-ranging temperatures (32–83°F/0–28.3°C), spending most of its time near the surface where it forages on Alewife and insects. Once water temperatures cool down sufficiently in September and October, 4- to 5-year-old fish will migrate to their originating stream and attempt to spawn. The 4-year-old fish will return to the lake after spawning and live another year, whereas most of the 5-year-old fish perish after spawning. Spawning habitat and conditions are not favorable for this species within the Chicago Region. Less than 1% of the Steelhead population is from natural reproduction, so they must be stocked annually to maintain the sport fishery.

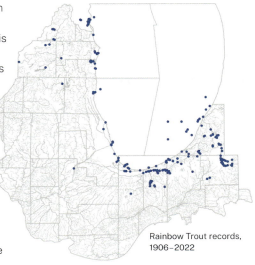

Rainbow Trout records, 1906–2022

Distribution and Status: The natural range of the anadromous Steelhead is the Pacific Ocean and tributary streams from the Kuskokwim River, Alaska, to Baja California in North America, and in Northeast Asia along the Kamchatka Peninsula. Non-anadromous Rainbow Trout occur naturally in Rocky Mountain streams on the Pacific slope within the same range. This species was first introduced to Lake Geneva, Walworth County, Wisconsin, in 1872, and then throughout the Great Lakes starting in 1885. It was even on exhibit at the 1893 World's Fair in Chicago, with the individuals released into Lake Michigan when the fair ended. Within the Chicago Region, it is found primarily in Lake Michigan and tributary streams and inland headwaters, where it is stocked annually to maintain the highly valued sport fishery population. There may be some persistence in inland populations. The Rainbow Trout is not native to the Chicago Region and may have adverse impacts through direct competition with native chars for food and habitat.

References: R. M. Bailey, Latta, and Smith 2004; Ricker, Mosbaugh, and Lung 1949; Stearley and Smith 1993; Woods 1960; Wydoski and Whitney 2003

Chinook Salmon

Oncorhynchus tshawytscha · *Oncorhynchus* means "hook nose" in Latin, in reference to the upper and lower jaws of breeding males, also called a kype; *tshawytscha* is the Kamchatkan word for this species. In the common name, the Salish word *Chinook* is a Native tribe that settled the north shore of the Columbia River mouth.

Chinook Salmon spawning female

Description: The adult Chinook Salmon is a fusiform fish with a moderately square tail and many sharp teeth set in black gums. Nonbreeding coloration is dark metallic above, silver on the sides, and a whitish belly. Breeding individuals become dark olive green with many black spots sprinkled over the upper body, dorsal fin, and entire caudal fin. Like those of other salmon species, Chinook breeding males develop an extremely hooked nose, known as a kype. Post-spawning individuals become emaciated and covered with fungus, with eroded anal and lower caudal fins. The Chinook Salmon has black gums and spots in the entire caudal fin, whereas the Coho has white gums and spots only in the upper lobe of the caudal fin. Juvenile Chinook may be distinguished from juvenile Coho by having parr marks wider than the spaces between. Also, the first 3 anal fin rays are shorter in the Chinook, and the edge of anal fin is not white. Other characteristics include 16–18 branchiostegal rays, 15–17 anal fin rays, and 135–185 pyloric caeca. In the Chicago Region, this species most closely resembles the Coho Salmon. In its native habitats, the Chinook can reach up to 5 feet (1,524 mm) and 130 pounds (59 kg).

An adult observed from Calumet Harbor in 2000 was 35 inches (885 mm) and 14 pounds (6.5 kg).

Natural History: The Chinook Salmon inhabits oceans, lakes, and confluent rivers and streams. Within the Chicago Region, this species starts its life in state hatcheries through artificial fertilization, where it is raised to 3-inch fingerlings. These parr are transported to the Lake Michigan coast or tributary streams, where they are released by the thousands. Those released in streams may reside there for up to a year, or they may simply migrate downstream and enter Lake Michigan where they feed and grow for 3–4 years. During the summer months, Chinook Salmon occupy the cold, deep thermal zones in 60–260 feet (18–80 m) depths, where they feed on Opossum Shrimp, Alewife, Cisco, Sculpin, and Smelt. Once water temperatures cool down in the late fall (54°F), they move out of the thermals and rove the nearshore waters for food. When the Chinook reaches 4 years of age, it ascends tributary streams in late fall in search of suitable spawning habitat; however, spawning habitat and conditions are not favorable within the Chicago Region. Natural recruitment is minimal, requiring annually stocking to maintain the fishery.

Distribution and Status: The natural range of the Chinook Salmon is the Pacific Ocean and tributary

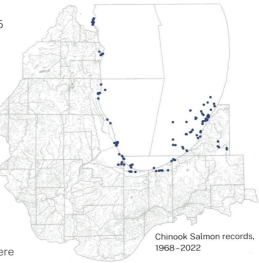

Chinook Salmon records, 1968–2022

streams from Point Hope Alaska to the Ventura River, California, in North America, and in Northeast Asia from the Anadyr River south to Hokkaido, Japan. There are about 108 different stocks of Chinook in its native range, and it is the least abundant of all the salmon species. Certain stocks are listed as federally endangered. This species was first introduced to Lake Michigan in 1966. Within the Chicago Region, it is found primarily in Lake Michigan and tributary streams. This nonnative species may have adverse predation impacts to Opossum Shrimp, small ciscoes, and sculpins in Lake Michigan.

References: R. M. Bailey, Latta, and Smith 2004; Pollard et al. 1997; Stearley and Smith 1993; Wydoski and Whitney 2003

(Menominee)

Prosopium cylindraceum · *Prosopium* means "mask," for the large bone in front of this fish's eyes; *cylindraceum* means "cylinder-like," referring to its body shape.

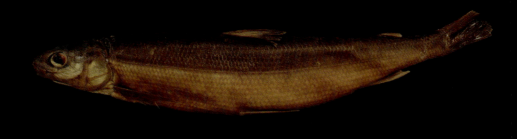

Field Museum Specimen #3106

Description: The Round Whitefish has a cylindrical body, completely round in circumference. The coloration is silvery along the sides and dark brown to bronze, shaded with green, along the dorsum. The scales of the dorsum are margined with black melanophores. The basal half of paired and anal fins are often fleshy orange. Juveniles under 7.5 inches (200 mm) are typically silvery, with horizontal rows of dark spots along the sides, merging with the dorsum pigmentation. The head is very small, with a proportionally large eye. The maxillary extends from the anterior edge of eye and overhangs the mandible, creating a subterminal mouth. Gill rakers (15–20, usually 16–18) are short. Teeth are absent except on the tongue. The Round Whitefish can be distinguished from other whitefishes and ciscoes by having a single skin flap between the nostrils; all other Chicago Region species have 2 flaps. Adults can reach 21.5 inches (550 mm) in length.

Natural History: The Round Whitefish inhabits coldwater lakes and rivers, seldom entering brackish water in marine drainages. Chicago Region populations of Lake Michigan prefer nearshore and littoral zones, likely not venturing into water deeper than 180 feet (55 m). Food items include insects, crayfish, bryozoans, fish eggs, and plant material. High

Round Whitefish records, 1920–1921 (●) and 1984–2022 (●)

quantities of sand found in specimen guts suggests foraging over sand flats and shoals. Based on seasonal data from anglers, this fish likely spawns between November and December in 24–32 feet (7–10 m) over honeycomb rock and gravel.

Distribution and Status: The Round Whitefish occurs naturally in the Arctic, Pacific, and Atlantic basins in Canada and Asia, and all the Great Lakes except Erie and Nipigon. In the Chicago Region, it is restricted to Lake Michigan, with only 12 records.

The most recent records are near Lake County, Illinois (INHS 1997), and Berrien County, Michigan (MIFA 2000). Round Whitefish were never a valuable commercial fishery, due to unfavorable food qualities and relative low abundance. This species is of special concern within the Chicago Region; further investigation is needed to determine natural history characteristics and distribution.

References: Eddy and Underhill 1974; Hubbs and Lagler 1964; Koelz 1929

Brown Trout

Salmo trutta · *Salmo* is derived from the word *salio*, which means "to leap" (*Salmo* is also the genus of Atlantic Salmon); *trutta* is Latin for "trout."

Brown Trout, lake-run form

Description: The Brown Trout within the Chicago Region has 2 distinct forms: lake-run trout and stream trout. Lake-run trout are typically silver, with dark spots on the body and dorsal fin; the pelvic, pectoral, anal and caudal fins remain mostly spot free. This variety achieves a larger size and is stockier. The stream variety is much more elaborate in coloration and dot patterns. Body color may vary from dark brown to tan to cream. The fins are usually cream colored, but during the breeding season may achieve deep reddish brown. Spots vary from brown to red and may be surrounded with an off-white or bluish halo. Both varieties have 9–10 anal fin rays. This species is different from the Chinook and the Coho by having 12 or fewer anal rays. It is distinguished from the Rainbow Trout by having large spots over a silver or brownish body, and no spots in the tail. It is distinguished from the chars by having 140 or fewer lateral line scales. Lake-run forms observed during US Army Corps harbor surveys measured up to 31 inches (787.4 mm) and 10.25 pounds (4.7 kg), whereas stream trout are 5–10 inches (127–224 mm).

Natural History: The Brown Trout prefers the cool to cold waters of lakes or small streams. The lake-run variety may be found along the coasts of Lake Michigan, seldom deeper than 50 feet (15 m). Here, they rove continuously in search of prey items, mainly Alewife, Smelt, minnows, and terrestrial insects. The lake form spawns along rock shoals or reefs within Lake Michigan; however, some groups do enter rivers and small streams to spawn. The stream variety prefers deeper pools with logs over sand and gravel. Prey items consist of small stream fish and aquatic and terrestrial insects. This form spawns from October to December in small streams. The female constructs a dish-shaped redd (nest) in sand or clay (not gravel) in moderate flow, which keeps eggs well oxygenated and free of fungus. Brown Trout do not die immediately after spawning and may live up to 10 years of age.

Distribution and Status: The native range of the Brown Trout includes Iceland, Europe, western Asia, and northwestern Africa. It has been spread worldwide for food and sport purposes. The first Brown Trout were introduced to the United States in 1883 in New York and Michigan via hatching fertilized eggs from Germany. The Chicago Region distribution includes Lake Michigan, its tributary streams, and some inland coldwater streams. It has also been stocked in the upper Fox River system, and transients may be found from time to time in the Kankakee River system. Because the Brown Trout is a nonnative species, naturalized populations may possibly pose the greatest threat to native Brook Trout in the northern portions of the region, where they outcompete them for habitat and food.

References: Becker 1979; Eddy and Underhill 1974; Ricker, Mosbaugh, and Lung 1949; Schwiebert 1983

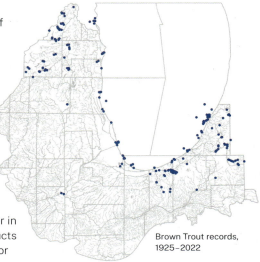

Brown Trout records, 1925–2022

SALMON, TROUT, CHARS, AND WHITEFISHES (SALMONIDAE)   303

(Brook Trout)

Salvelinus fontinalis · *Salvelinus* is derived from the word *salvelin*, an old, possibly Germanic name for the char. The word *char* is a derivative of the word *chare*, which is the root word meaning "blood" in Anglo-Saxon, Gaelic, and French, likely referring to the red-colored flesh; *fontinalis*, Latin, means "living in springs," referring to its spring-fed-stream habitats. This fish is in the char group but is commonly referred to as a trout.

Description: The Brook Char, or Brook Trout, has a streamlined body that is dark brown or olive to rusty red. The body is covered with many large cream-colored vermiculations and red spots, sometimes with bluish halos. The median fins have a leading edge of brilliant white paralleled by a black line. The dorsal and caudal fins have dark blotchy spots. Lake-run Brook Char, known as Coasters, are less heavily pigmented and have more of a silvery tinge. They have a terminal mouth, with the maxillary extending past the eye. The caudal fin is square to slightly forked. Other useful characteristics include 9–12 gill rakers, 7–8 mandibular pores, 9–13 branchiostegal rays, 10–14 dorsal fin rays, 9–13 anal fin rays, 8–10 pelvic fin rays, 11–14 pectoral fin rays, 210–244 lateral line scales, and 23–55 pyloric caeca. The Brook Char may be distinguished from the Lake Char (Lake Trout) by the square caudal fin and 7–8 mandibular pores, from *Oncorhynchus* species by lacking black spots, and from the Brown Trout by having more than 210 lateral line scales. Large Coasters can reach 28 inches (700 mm), but stream dwellers are usually 6–8 inches (152–203 mm).

Natural History: The Brook Char inhabits spring-fed, coldwater streams and lakes, with a preferred temperature of 68°F (20°C) or colder. It usually occupies runs and pools downstream from riffles near undercut banks and large woody debris. Current-swept aquatic and terrestrial invertebrates are its primary forage. Spawning takes place in late fall, with females constructing nests in gravel riffles and shoals with groundwater discharge. After spawning, the female covers the nest with gravel to protect the eggs from predatory suckers and minnows. The male guards the area, chasing other fish away. This upwelling of groundwater in the nest provides cold (37–50°F/2.8–10°C), oxygenated water while the eggs incubate. Coasters spawn in the shallows of lakes where spring upwelling occurs through the sand or gravel. Stream-form Brook Char exhibit home-range fidelity, rarely traveling more than a half mile (0.8 km) to find suitable habitat to forage or to spawn.

Brook Char records, 1920–1927 (●), 1941–1954 (●), and 1968–2022 (●)

Distribution and Status: The native range of the Brook Char includes the Hudson Bay drainage, the Great Lakes basin, the northern portion of the Mississippi River basin, and the high-elevation streams of the Appalachian Mountains from Maine to Georgia. The Brook Char has been successfully introduced to other portions of the United States and is established on all continents except Antarctica and Australia. Due to extensive stocking outside of the species' natural range, we don't know whether the Brook Char historically occurred within the Chicago Region. Most records are old (1920s) and from the Paw Paw and St. Joseph River systems in Berrien County,

Michigan (MIFA); however, these records were made after widespread stocking took place. It is also uncertain if Brook Char existed naturally elsewhere in Illinois. If so, this would likely have taken place in the Rock River system. The Brook Char probably did not occur in Indiana. It is clearer that southeastern Wisconsin was within the native range; however, current populations are the result of stocking programs. Coasters are observed from time to time along the coastline of Lake Michigan, likely traveling from northern waters. Its nativity and status are currently unknown within the Chicago Region and need study. The Brook Char is one of the more highly sought-after game fishes for its sport, fine flavor, and aesthetic appeal.

References: Eddy and Underhill 1974; MacKay 1963; Ricker, Mosbaugh, and Lung 1949

SALMON, TROUT, CHARS, AND WHITEFISHES (SALMONIDAE)   305

Lake Char (Lake Trout)

Salvelinus namaycush • *Salvelinus* is derived from the word *salvelin*, an old, possibly Germanic name for the char. The word *char* is a derivative of the word *chare*, which is the root word meaning "blood" in Anglo-Saxon, Gaelic, and French, likely referring to the red-colored flesh; *namaycush* is derived from the Cree word for Lake Char, *namekos*. This fish is in the char group, but commonly referred to as a trout.

Description: The Lake Char, or Lake Trout, has a fusiform body with a deeply forked tail fin. It has a bronze/copper to greenish-gray body with a white abdomen. Many cream-colored vermiculations cover the body laterally and dorsally, extending onto the dorsal and caudal fins. A white leading edge is prevalent on pectoral, pelvic, and anal fin spines. Males and females are not sexually dimorphic. Other useful characteristics include 12–24 gill rakers, 9–10 mandibular pores, 8–10 dorsal rays, 8–10 anal rays, 163–210 lateral line scales, 61–69 vertebrae, and 93–200 pyloric caeca. Juveniles, known as parr, have 7–12 narrow parr marks. This species may be distinguished from the Brook Char by the forked caudal fin, gill raker count, and mandibular pore count, the *Oncorhynchus* species by lacking black spots, and the Brown Trout by lacking dark brown and red spots. Old adults are known to reach 5 feet (1,524 mm) and 72 pounds (32.7 kg); however, the largest adults encountered during surveys (2001) of Burns Harbor, Porter County, Indiana, measured 34 inches (873 mm) and 14 pounds (6.4 kg).

Natural History: Lake Chars inhabit deep cold lakes and sometimes rivers. They occupy the coldwater thermals at depths around 300 feet

(90 m) during the warm months. In cooler months, some individuals move closer to shore, to depths as shallow as 15 feet (5 m). This species feeds primarily on deepwater sculpins and ciscoes. Due to non-native introductions in recent years, the forage base has shifted to the Alewife, Rainbow Smelt, and the Round Goby in southern Lake Michigan. In the fall, Lake Chars move out of deep water to shoals with bedrock, cobble, or gravel, at depths of 6–50 feet (2–15 m). Males typically arrive 5–10 days prior to the females, to claim preferred spawning territories, sweeping silt and sand from the rocky spawning substrates. Females are typically attended to by more than 1 male, but no aggression is displayed among the males. Lake Chars are communal broadcasters, scattering eggs and sperm over the substrate. Fry first appear in late winter and early spring and remain over the spawning sites to feed on zooplankton until late May.

Distribution and Status: The natural geographic range of the Lake Char includes the Pacific, Arctic, and Atlantic Ocean drainages and the Great Lake basin. It is restricted to the waters of Lake Michigan within the Chicago Region. Lake Michigan once supported the largest Lake Char fishery until about the 1940s, when the compounded effects of overexploitation and habitat degradation drove the native strains to extinction within Lake Michigan. Collection records were very limited from 1906 to 1945. Although restocking started in the 1960s, a concerted

Lake Char records, 1907–1945 (●) and 1960–2022 (●)

restoration effort in the Great Lakes did not begin until the 1990s. Agencies including natural resources departments in surrounding states, the US Fish and Wildlife Service, and the US Army Corps of Engineers implemented stocking programs, spawning-habitat creation, and harvest regulations to create self-sustaining populations in southern Lake Michigan. The Lake Char can currently be found throughout Lake Michigan and in Lake Geneva, Wisconsin. Although numbers are still below historic levels, its status is improving.

References: Brown et al. 1981; Crossman 1995; Dettmers 2000; Forbes and Richardson 1908; Goode 1887; Gunn 1995; Hile, Eschenmyer, and Lunger 1951; Khan 1971; Mardsen 1994; N. V. Martin 1960; N. V. Martin and Olver 1980; Morrow 1980; Ricker, Mosbaugh, and Lung 1949; Savitz 2000; Willink 2016

21

Smelts

Osmeridae

The nonnative Rainbow Smelt is the only smelt species in the Chicago Region, stocked in the Great Lakes ostensibly as food for salmon. Generally, smelts are relatively small, silvery fishes. They have a slender body and an adipose fin but differ from salmon by lacking a pelvic axillary process. Their mouths are rather large, reaching back to the eye, with a protruding lower jaw and teeth. The adipose fin sets them apart from the similar-looking herring and shad.

Many smelts are planktivorous; however, some, such as the Rainbow Smelt, are predatory. Most species are anadromous and spawn in freshwater. Smelts preferentially spawn in shallow water over gravel riffles but will utilize any available substrate. Some species spawn in the shallows of lakes. The males have breeding tubercles on their head, body, and fins.

Osmeridae contains 31 species distributed along the coasts of the North Atlantic, North Pacific, and Arctic Oceans.

Smelts can form large schools and are commercially important as a food fish for humans, predators (such as interesting birds like the Puffin [*Fratercula* spp.]), and large marine mammals.

Rainbow Smelt

Osmerus mordax · *Osmerus* is Greek, meaning "odorous"; the Latin *mordax* means "biting" or "caustic."

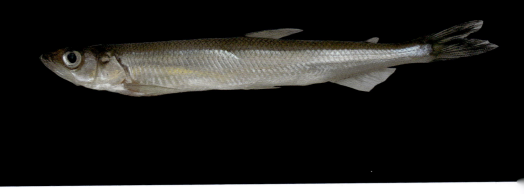

Description: The Rainbow Smelt is a relatively small, elongated fish with an adipose fin. Its proportionally larger mouth extends posterior to or past the middle of eye, and the lower anterior jaw protrudes in front of upper jaw. The pelvic axillary scale is absent, which differentiates this species from the whitefish subfamily Coregoninae. Other Rainbow Smelt characters include long canine teeth, a forked tail, and a silvery to transparent coloration with bluish to greenish back. It grows up to 13 inches (325 mm).

Natural History: The Rainbow Smelt lives in the cool waters of Lake Michigan, where young spend their time in the water column around 60–80 feet (18.3–24.4 m) deep; older fish stay near the bottom in 40–120 feet (12.2–36.6 m) of water but can be found much deeper. Rainbow Smelt are unusual in that they produce antifreeze proteins that prevent ice from forming in the body. Mature individuals will congregate nearshore when ready to spawn, but otherwise avoid shallow warm waters. In western Lake Superior, the Rainbow Smelt reaches maturity after 2–3 years and lives a total of 5–7 years. Food items include but are not limited to crustaceans, fishes, aquatic insects, and worms. Opossum Shrimp are particularly important to Great Lakes populations, adding pressure to an already impaired food source. Based on its diet, the Rainbow Smelt may be a competitor or predator on native fishes in the upper 4 Great Lakes. In turn, Rainbow Smelts are eaten by the Lake Char, the Yellow Perch, the

Walleye, the Burbot, and other non-native salmonids.

Distribution and Status: Rainbow Smelts are native along sections of the North American coasts adjacent to the North Atlantic, North Pacific, and Arctic Oceans. The state of Michigan started stocking Rainbow Smelt in Lake Michigan in 1906 as a food source for stocked salmon. Most attempts were unsuccessful. The first Chicago Region record was from 1931. Rainbow Smelt in Lakes Michigan and Huron experienced a massive die-off from 1942 to 1943. Only this species was affected; the cause was uncertain but was attributed to an infectious disease. The population recovered by 1951. In the Chicago Region, they are found in Lake Michigan for most of the year. During the late winter and early spring spawning season, they can be found in streams and rivers flowing into Lake Michigan. Stray individuals may enter the Chicago Area Waterway System and the Illinois River drainage, but this is the exception and not the rule. Rainbow Smelt are usually fished for during their spawning runs, when they are most concentrated and vulnerable. People drop large nets into the water and use small explosives or whatever else they can to harvest them. This scene is often depicted in old images of the Chicago shoreline. This tradition has mostly ended with the decline in Rainbow Smelt populations. For unknown reasons, the Rainbow Smelt is becoming very rare in the Chicago Region. The massive spring spawning runs appear to be a thing of the past, and the status of this nonnative species is uncertain.

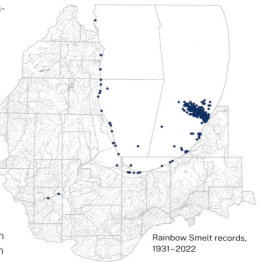

Rainbow Smelt records, 1931–2022

References: M. M. Bailey 1964; Becker 1983; Creaser 1925; Ewart and Fletcher 1990; Hankinson and Hubbs 1922; Laird and Page 1996; Lievense 1954; Rupp 1959; Wells 1968; Woods 1954

22

Trout-perches

Percopsidae

Trout-perches earned their common name by having smooth-edged (cycloid) scales and an adipose fin like a trout, and rough-edged (ctenoid scales) and fin spines like a perch. They have small, slender bodies that appear somewhat transparent. The head is large and lacks scales. The mouth is subterminal.

The trout-perch family Percopsidae consists of 2 species, restricted to northern North America: the Sand Roller (*Percopsis transmontana*) occurs in Washington, Oregon, and Idaho; the Trout-perch species can be found from New England to Alaska, including the Chicago Region.

Because of their bizarre combination of characteristics, with 2 types of scales and an adipose fin, they are sometimes thought to occupy an important link in the evolution of fishes. They are quite rare in the Chicago Region.

Trout-perch

Percopsis omiscomaycus · *Percopsis* means "perch-like"; *omiscomaycus* is an Algonkian word referring to trout.

Description: The Trout-perch has a fusiform body, looking somewhat like a small perch. This species is distinguished from perches and minnows by having an adipose fin and cycloid scales, and from small salmonids by having ctenoid scales, fin spines, and no teeth. The lower jaw contains a row of peculiar pearl organs. The head and eyes are proportionally large. The mouth is subterminal and horizontal. Body color ranges from tan and yellow to a slivery white, sometimes with an iridescent bluish-purple hue on the sides. A row of spots occurs along the lateral line, and another row of smaller spots above. Adults grow to 4 inches (100 mm).

Natural History: The Trout-perch inhabits the deep waters of lakes and large rivers. This species is usually associated with shifting sands and small gravel, where it lives along the bottom, foraging on aquatic insects. In Lake Michigan, it occupies deep waters but will enter shallow sandy beaches at night or seasonally; we have observed a gravid female in mid-April on a shifting sandspit along the shoreline in Michigan. The lower Kankakee River has optimal habitat, consisting of small island chains with sandy beaches that grade into deep sand-laden pools; the conditions here are almost lake-like. Trout-perches are most active at night, utilizing their sensory pearl organs to help find

Trout-perch records, 1895–2022

prey hiding in the sediment. This species spawns in the spring to early summer, usually in the shallows on sandbars and beaches.

Distribution and Status: Records for the Trout-perch within the Chicago Region are from only Lake Michigan, the upper Illinois River, and the lower Kankakee River. In Lake Michigan, the Michigan DNR transect records show this species is likely dispersed throughout deep waters, from the shoreline to about 90 feet. The Trout-perch is a species of special concern in Indiana, and we considered it the same within the Chicago Region.

References: Wells 1968; Woods 1957b

23

Pirate Perches

Aphredoderidae

The pirate perches are related to cavefishes. Their most distinguishing characteristic is the anal and urogenital pore location just behind the gills, or in the "throat." Fishes in this family are small, less than 6 inches (150 mm), with a large mouth. The body is rather deep and stout, covered by rough-edged (ctenoid) scales. These fish have only 1 dorsal fin with both stiff and soft rays. The tail fin is large and slightly forked, with a dark edge.

The family consists of only 1 species, restricted to the United States. This species occurs in the lower Mississippi River system,

Gulf and Atlantic slopes, and southern portions of the Great Lakes, including the Chicago Region.

This fish family was given the name "pirate perch" due to its propensity to eat all the other fish when kept in aquaria. Interestingly, the anal and urogenital pore starts out in the normal position on the belly in the juvenile and migrates forward as the fish develops into an adult.

Description: The Pirate Perch is a small, stout fish with a noticeably deeper body profile at the insertion of the pelvic fin. The mouth is proportionally large, with a protruding lower jaw. The body coloration is dark brown with a purple tinge and no distinctive pigmentation pattern. There is a dark vertical band just in front of the tail fin and a dark teardrop below the eye. The body and cheeks are covered with ctenoid scales. The dorsal fin has 2–3 spines and 10–11 rays. The anal fin has 2–3 spines and 6–7 rays. Fins have a dark band of pigment near their base. The anal pore is in the normal position in the young but migrates just posterior to the branchiostegal membranes as they mature. No other fish in the Chicago Region has a forward anal pore. Although adults can grow to 4 inches (100 mm), most are much smaller.

Natural History: The Pirate Perch primarily occupies low-gradient streams, riverine backwaters, and marshes. It is often associated with undercut banks, woody debris, rootwads, and herbaceous root mats. It can also be found in drainage ditches of former wetlands with abundant overhanging vegetation. Forage consists of a variety of aquatic

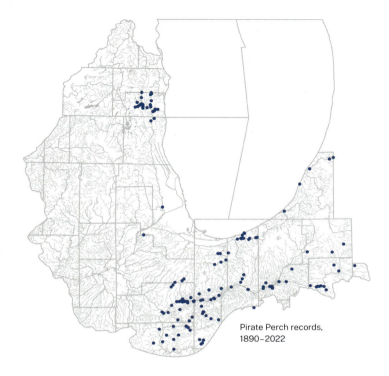

Pirate Perch records, 1890–2022

macroinvertebrates, primarily insects. Spawning takes place in spring in loosely constructed nests among dense rootwads or vegetation. Pirate Perches are not mouth brooders, as once believed; instead, both the male and female take the released sperm and eggs into their respective mouths and eject them into the nest cavity. The male guards the nest until after the young are hatched.

Distribution and Status: Distribution of the Pirate Perch is rather limited in most of the Chicago Region but is relatively widespread in the Kankakee Sands ecoregion. Usually, no more than a few individuals are found during any given collection. This species was first recorded within the region from the Yellow River, Marshall County, Indiana, taken by David Starr Jordan in 1890. Current distribution may reflect areas that previously had extensive wetlands. The largest threat to the Pirate Perch is the armoring of undercut banks, the removal of woody debris, and stream channelization. We consider the Pirate Perch a species of special concern within the Chicago Region.

References: Page and Burr 2011; Poly and Wetzel 2003; Tiemann 2004; Wetzel and Edwards 2014

24

Hakes, Lings, Rocklings, and Burbots

Lotidae

Burbots are found in Lake Michigan and have some curious common names, including Eelpout, Lawyer Fish, Lingcod, and Coney-fish. This family can be distinguished by having a single chin barbell, 1 very short and 1 very long dorsal fin, and a rounded caudal fin. These fishes have a large head with a small eye, and a long slender body that tapers and becomes narrow at the tail. Their scales are very small and embedded. They typically inhabit deep, cold waters, where their diets consist of invertebrates and small fishes. Another interesting characteristic is the presence of an oil globule in their eggs that serves as an energy source for the larval stage.

This group has about 22 species, with a northern circumpolar (Holarctic) distribution. All species are marine except the Burbot, which occurs in the northern latitudes of Eurasia and North America, including the Chicago Region. This is the only species in the genus *Lota*.

Burbots are often sought by anglers but are not very abundant in the Chicago Region. Their flesh is flavorful and somewhat sweet, often referred to as the "poor man's lobster." They are related to codfishes.

Burbot

Lota lota · *Lota* is derived from the French *la lotte*, which means "codfish."

Description: The Burbot is a freshwater cod that has a long, slender body quite slimy to the touch. Other distinctive characters include a single chin barbel, a rounded caudal fin, and a very long anal fin (52–76 soft rays). The 2 dorsal fins are spineless and not connected, the second one being quite long (61–81 soft rays). The coloration is dark brown, with mottling on the body and fins transitioning to a white belly. It appears to have no scales, but is covered with very small, embedded cycloid (smooth) scales. Adults can exceed 30 inches (750 mm).

Natural History: The Burbot is a coldwater fish, occupying the deep waters of lakes as well as coldwater rivers and streams. During colder months, particularly at low light, it moves from deeper habitats into shallower water and stream mouths among rocky cover. It is an ambush predator, hiding from prey in constructed trenches or under natural ledges and rocks. We have observed juvenile Burbots in riffle habitat of a Wisconsin coldwater stream. Communal spawning typically takes place in mid to late winter under the ice, where eggs and sperm are broadcast over rock, gravel, sand, or a mix of substrates. Burbot young are reared in riffles of coldwater streams, where they feed on macroinvertebrates and crustaceans.

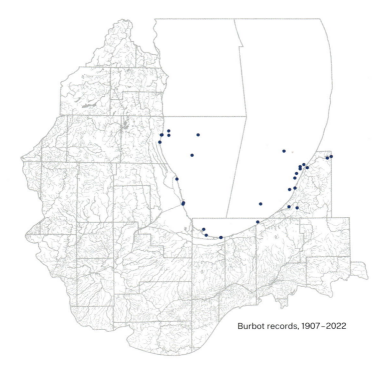

Burbot records, 1907–2022

Distribution and Status: The Burbot occurs in North America and Eurasia, with its North American distribution throughout all of Canada, its southern extent being the upper Mississippi River and Great Lakes basins. This species is restricted within the Chicago Region to Lake Michigan, confluent stream mouths, and the groundwater-fed streams of Berrien County, Michigan. One record for this species in the Chicago Region was taken by the authors in the mouth of Pettibone Creek, Lake County, Illinois (INHS 1999), from beneath a rubber tire. The status of this species is of special concern due to limited knowledge of its regional distribution and movements, habitat requirements, and its reliance on coldwater systems. The taste of Burbot is described as delicious, just like a Cod; however, due to its naturally low abundance, Burbot does not support a commercial fishery.

References: Becker 1983; Boyer et al. 1989; Forbes 1884; Forbes and Richardson 1920; Hubbs, Lagler, and Smith 2004; Madenjian et al. 2012; Woods 1957a, 1957b

25

Gobies

Gobiidae

Gobies arrived in the Great Lakes from the Black Sea in the ballast water of large cargo ships. They are small fishes, typically less than 4 inches (100 mm) long, with a large head and large protruding eyes. They can range from brown and mottled to brightly colored. The fused pelvic fins directly below the pectoral fins are a unique characteristic in many species. These fused fins form a suction disc, allowing gobies to attach to rocks and other substrates. The pectoral fins are quite large. There are 2 separated dorsal fins, the front one short with spiny rays, the back one long with only soft rays. The anal fin is also long, and the caudal fin is rounded. They do not have lateral lines.

Gobiidae is a large family, with 1,900 species globally, occupying both fresh-and saltwater habitats. There are 68 species of gobies native to the Atlantic and Pacific coasts of North America, with

5 freshwater species. The introduced Round Goby is the only species found in the Chicago Region. Since their release in the Great Lakes in the early 1990s, they have spread downriver to St. Louis.

The goby group includes unique fishes such as mud skippers (Oxudercidae) that live out of water, as well as one of the world's smallest vertebrates, the Midget Dwarfgoby (*Trimmatom nanus*), which is less than 0.5 inches (12 mm) in length. Some gobies live symbiotically with other organisms — for example, Randall's Prawn Goby (*Amblyeleotris randalli*) is a "seeing-eye dog" for Randall's Pistol Shrimp (*Alpheus randalli*), alerting the shrimp of danger when predators are nearby. Some can climb sheer rock walls using their fused pelvic fin. The Round Goby is now very abundant in Lake Michigan, possibly competing with native fishes.

Round Goby

Neogobius melanostomus • *Neogobius*, Greek, means "new small fish"; *melanostomus*, Latin, means "pigmented mouth."

Description: The Round Goby is a robust, ventrally compressed fish with a brown to gray body, dark mottling, and a white abdomen. The eyes are very high on the rounded head. The mouth is terminal and moderately sized. The short tubular nostrils do not reach past the lip. There are 2 separate dorsal fins: the front fin is shorter, with flexible spines, while the rear dorsal fin is long, containing 11 or more rays. The pelvic fins are fused, appearing as a single fin. A black oval spot is present on the rear of the first dorsal fin. Breeding males are black with a faint yellow fringe on median fins. The Round Goby is different than the similar-looking Mottled Sculpin by having 1 fused pelvic fin instead of 2 separate fins. Adult size is typically 3–6 inches (75–150 mm), but large males guarding nests have been noted to reach 11 inches (280 mm).

Natural History: The Round Goby inhabits lakes, rivers, and streams within the Chicago Region. This species is usually most abundant in areas with hard, rocky substrates, but can also be found over sand and silt, but typically not in detritus or woody debris. Specimens have been collected in cobble riffles and runs of smaller rivers and streams, and vegetated, sandy lakeshores. The species is both euryhaline and eurythermal, meaning they tolerate a wide range of salinity concentrations or temperatures and therefore are very resilient to degraded water quality. It is reported to be migratory in Lake Michigan, where it utilizes nearshore areas during warm seasons and deeper waters in winter. The Round Goby is a benthic feeder that preys on dreissenid mussels (Dreissenidae) and other mollusks, benthic invertebrates, fish eggs, and small fish. It uses a specific twisting technique to tear mussels and mollusks from their substrates. Recent observations indicate they do not prefer Yellow Perch eggs. Spawning takes place multiple times from April through September. Nests are constructed beneath stones, logs, and other debris or in cavities. The male will guard and clean the nest containing up to 10,000 eggs from multiple females and has been observed fending off Smallmouth Bass. Males usually die once the fry mature and leave the nest.

Distribution and Status: The Round Goby's native range is the Black and Caspian Seas in Eurasia. It was introduced to southern Lake Michigan in 1993 via ballast water release from oceangoing vessels; it is now found throughout the Great Lakes basin. The aggressive nature of the Round Goby has led to the displacement of the native Mottled Sculpin from many areas of Lake Michigan. This species is also reported to be affecting the Lake Char (Trout) recovery program by consuming eggs from spawning

Round Goby records, 1994–1999 (●), 2000–2009 (●), and 2010–2022 (●)

beds. The Round Goby has also become a nuisance to shoreline anglers, becoming the dominant catch. It has the potential to be spread via bait-bucket release, as indicated by the recent introduction into the East Branch DuPage River, DuPage County, Illinois. The Round Goby has entered the Des Plaines and Illinois River basins via the Chicago Area Waterway System, which now connects the Great Lakes to the Mississippi River basin.

References: Berg 1949; Charlebois et al. 1997; Dubs and Corkum 1996; Feldheim et al. 2009; French and Jude 2001; Janssen and Jude 2001; Jude, Reider, and Smith 1992; Kuhns and Berg 1999; Miller 1986; Moskal'kova 1996; J. S. Nelson 1994; Skora and Stolarski 1996; Willink 2016

26

New World Silversides

Atherinopsidae

Superficially resembling fishes from other small-bodied families, the presence of 2 dorsal fins distinguishes silversides from minnows, topminnows, and killifishes, all of which have only 1 dorsal fin. Silversides are small, very slender, and semitranslucent, with a bright silver lateral stripe. The dorsal surface is flattened, there is no lateral line, and the head is scaled. Silversides are also similar to smelts, which differ in having large teeth and an adipose fin between the dorsal and caudal fins.

Silversides are a very large family — more than 160 species worldwide, most of which live in marine habitats. There are only

3 species of freshwater silversides in North America, only one of which, the Brook Silverside, resides in the Chicago Region.

Silversides are known to swim in large schools, generally near the surface. The pointed snout and flattened head are well adapted for surface foraging. They are often seen jumping out of the water to capture prey or to avoid predators. In freshwater, silversides are found primarily in the quiet waters of larger rivers and in lakes and serve as an important forage food. They are intolerant of handling and are not typically used as live baitfish.

Brook Silverside

Labidesthes sicculus · *Labidesthes*, from the Greek *labidos*, "forceps," and *esthio*, "to eat," referring to the beak-like mouth; *sicculus*, Latin, meaning "dried," in reference to being found in isolated pools.

Description: The Brook Silverside has a very slender, elongated body with a pale, semitranslucent straw color and a bright silver lateral stripe. Scales are outlined with pigment on the upper surface, which has a pale green hue. The distinctive mouth is long and beak-like, turning slightly upward. The head area is scaled. It has 2 widely separated dorsal fins, the front one with 4–6 rays and the back fin with 10–11 rays. The anal fin is long and sickle shaped, with 22–25 rays. The eye is relatively large, and the pectoral fin is high on the body, situated in front of the lateral stripe. Spawning males exhibit a red snout and yellowish fins. Although it appears minnow-like, the beak-shaped mouth, 2 dorsal fins, and long anal fin distinguish it from minnows and other small fishes. Adult size is typically less than 5 inches (125 mm).

Natural History: The Brook Silverside inhabits larger rivers and lakes, and infrequently smaller streams and ponds. It prefers open-water areas lacking strong currents, primarily occupying the upper portion of the water column. The upturned mouth is well adapted for feeding at the surface, ingesting aquatic and terrestrial invertebrates. Commonly found in schools, it can often be seen jumping out of the water as a predator avoidance. Spawning takes place throughout

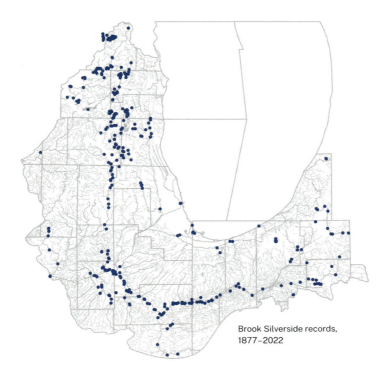

Brook Silverside records, 1877–2022

the summer season in shallow areas over vegetation and gravel. Eggs contain a filament to aid in attachment. Growth is relatively rapid for this short-lived (1.5–2 years) species.

Distribution and Status: The Brook Silverside occurs naturally in the Great Lakes, Mississippi River, and Ohio River basins, and in Gulf and southern Atlantic slope drainages. Records in the Chicago Region occur primarily in larger rivers, particularly the Kankakee River, the Fox River, and lakes throughout Wisconsin. This species is generally absent from smaller-and higher-gradient tributary streams. Its status is stable throughout the region, and sometimes abundant where it provides a forage base for larger game fishes.

References: Pflieger 1975; Smith 1979; Trautman 1957

27

Topminnows and Killifishes

Fundulidae

Fundulids are relatively easy to observe, as they swim in schools near the surface. They can be recognized by an upturned mouth and a flattened head. Other characteristics include a single dorsal fin located along the posterior section of the back over the anal fin, no lateral line, and no fin spines. These fishes are small bodied and rarely exceed 4 inches (100 mm). They are also sexually dimorphic, with males and females generally having different pigmentation patterns. The flattened head and upturned mouth facilitate feeding at the surface. These characteristics are shared with silversides; silversides can be distinguished by having 2 rather than 1 dorsal fin. Topminnows and killifishes have scaled heads, which distinguishes them from other small fishes, such as minnows.

The topminnow and killifish family has more than 40 species distributed throughout North America from Canada to Yucatan, including Bermuda and Cuba. They live in freshwater and saltwater, with some species being particularly abundant in brackish systems. There are 3 species of topminnows in the Chicago Region.

Some species are brightly colored and make popular aquarium pets. One of the major roles this group plays in a healthy ecosystem is the consumption of a large amount of mosquito larvae.

Banded Killifish

Fundulus diaphanus · *Fundulus*, Latin for "bottom"; *diaphanus*, Greek for "transparent."

Western Banded Killifish

Description: The Banded Killifish has a rather slender body with a flattened head. A single dorsal fin is set back on the body, originating just in front of the anal fin. The tail fin is rounded. Coloration is tan with a greenish hue. The lateral surface has fine vertical bars (10–13), evenly spaced from the gill cover to the tail. The mouth is small and upturned. Eyes are moderately sized, without a blotch of pigment below (that is, no teardrop). The Banded Killifish can be distinguished from other killifishes by the fine lateral bars and the lack of a teardrop below the eye. In the Chicago Region, there are 2 subspecies. The native subspecies Western Banded Killifish (*Fundulus diaphanus menona*) typically has 35–44 (usually 38–43) lateral scale rows, 10–14 dorsal rays, 9–12 anal rays, 13–17 pectoral rays, and fewer vertical bars. The invasive subspecies Eastern Banded Killifish (*Fundulus diaphanus diaphanus*) typically has 48–51 lateral scale rows, 12–15 dorsal rays, 10–13 anal rays, 15–19 pectoral rays, and more numerous vertical bars. Hybrid characteristics are usually intermediate. Typical adult size for the Banded Killifish is 3 inches (75 mm).

Natural History: The Banded Killifish prefers the nearshore areas of clear, glaciated lakes and connected streams. It is often associated with aquatic vegetation but is also found in unvegetated areas. Among the top-minnow species, it is the least surface oriented, often foraging along the bottom and in the midwater zone. Its diet consists of crustaceans, insects (both terrestrial and aquatic), amphipods, and a wide variety of other small invertebrates. Schooling behavior is common. The Banded Killifish spawns in late spring. Males will drive off rival males from loosely defined territories. The dominant male chases a female into a patch of vegetation, where spawning takes place with the release of a few eggs at time. The fertilized eggs have adhesive threads that attach to the vegetation. This behavior is repeated several times until all eggs are deposited.

Distribution and Status: The natural range of the Banded Killifish group includes the upper Mississippi River, Great Lakes, and northern Atlantic slope drainages. There are 2 subspecies and several intergrades currently recognized within this greater natural range; hybridization is very common. The Eastern Banded Killifish is found naturally in Atlantic slope drainages, whereas the Western Banded Killifish inhabits the Great Lakes and upper Mississippi River basins. Based on the examination of older preserved specimens, the Eastern Banded Killifish invaded the Chicago Region at some point around the year 2000 and began hybridizing with the Western Banded Killifish. The recent population expansion along the Lake Michigan

Western Banded Killifish records, 1879–2022 (●), and Eastern Banded Killifish and Hybrid records, 2000–2022 (●)

shoreline and into deeper waters, into the Chicago Area Waterway System, and into the upper Illinois River are the result of this invasion. Subsequent genetic analysis corroborates this progression. Apparently, only isolated populations not connected with Lake Michigan waters retain the genotype of Western Banded Killifish; the other interconnected areas of the Chicago Region appear to have both subspecies, with intensive interbreeding. The subspecies Western Banded Killifish is listed as threatened in Illinois.

References: Cahn 1927; Forbes and Richardson 1920; E. W. Nelson 1876; Pearse 1918; Richardson 1939; B. J. Smith and Harris 2020; Tiemann, Hartman, et al. 2021; Willink 2017; Willink, Tiemann, et al. 2019; Willink, Widloe, et al. 2018

TOPMINNOWS AND KILLIFISHES (FUNDULIDAE)   335

Starhead Topminnow

Fundulus dispar · *Fundulus*, Latin for "bottom"; *dispar*, Latin for "dissimilar."

Description: The Starhead Topminnow has a rather deep body that begins to narrow at the anal fin. The head is flattened, with an upturned mouth. The single dorsal fin is set back on the body, originating just in front of the anal fin. The tail fin is rounded. A dark triangular blotch is present below the moderately sized eye, forming a prominent teardrop. Small dark-red spots are arranged to form several fine horizontal stripes. On top of the head there is a shiny silver blotch, or the star. The top body surface is tan and green, fading to pale yellow on the belly. The dorsal fin, anal fin, and tail fin may have small red spots. These spots are more prominent in males, which also have 10–14 conspicuous fine vertical bars along the lateral surface. The lines are faint or absent on females. The combination of a dark teardrop and fine horizontal stripes helps distinguish the Starhead Topminnow from other killifish; further, the live-bearing Mosquitofish has a teardrop but lacks fine horizontal stripes and has a prominently narrowed posterior. Typical size for the Starhead Topminnow is in the 3-inch (75-mm) range.

Natural History: The Starhead Topminnow inhabits glacial lakes, ponds, backwaters, and the slower-moving sections of rivers. They are often found over finer-bottom substrates, but sometimes sand or gravel, and associated with aquatic vegetation. We have observed specimens in the discharge flow of a

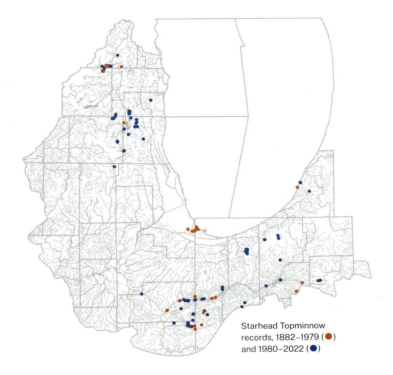

Starhead Topminnow records, 1882–1979 (●) and 1980–2022 (●)

Kankakee River backwater in Lake County, Indiana, schooling with Ironcolor Shiners. The Starhead Topminnow forages on terrestrial insects, aquatic insects, mollusks, crustaceans, and algae. The dietary occurrence of terrestrial insects is consistent with its upturned mouth and its habit of swimming near the surface. Spawning takes place from late spring until early summer, associated with thick vegetation.

Distribution and Status: The Starhead Topminnow's natural distribution is somewhat restricted and disjunct within the Mississippi River south of Wisconsin, the southern Lake Michigan drainage, and Gulf slope drainages in Mississippi and Alabama. Records within the Chicago Region are concentrated in the glacial lakes of the Valparaiso Moraine and the Kankakee Sands area. Although records are few, they have been consistent over time in these areas. This species is not often found in abundance; as a result, it is listed as endangered in Wisconsin, threatened in Illinois, of special concern in Michigan, and generally of special concern within the Chicago Region. Although the Starhead Topminnow is a beautiful aquarium fish, taking it for this purpose should be avoided due to its vulnerable status.

References: Becker 1983; Cahn 1927; Forbes and Richardson 1920; Gunning and Lewis 1955; Robinson and Buchanan 1988; Smith 1979; Taylor and Burr 1997

Blackstripe Topminnow

Fundulus notatus · *Fundulus*, Latin for "bottom"; *notatus*, Latin for "spotted."

Description: The Blackstripe Topminnow has a small, slender body with a prominent black stripe extending from the snout to the base of the tail. The head is flattened, with an upturned, terminal mouth. A single dorsal fin is set far back on the body and is even with the anal fin. The tail fin is rounded. The body coloration is greenish tan above the black stripe and pale below. Fine black spots are scattered on the tail, dorsal, and anal fins. In males, the black stripe has a sawtooth edge, whereas the edge of the stripe is smoother in females. Males can also have yellowish dorsal, anal, and pelvic fins. The single prominent black stripe distinguishes the Blackstripe Topminnow from the other topminnows and killifishes. Adult size is 3 inches (75 mm) or less.

Natural History: Blackstripe Topminnow inhabits slow-moving areas of rivers and large streams. Forage includes terrestrial insects, aquatic insects, and filamentous algae. The upturned mouth allows it to feed on terrestrial insects on the water's surface. It is often found in small schools. Spawning takes place in late spring to early summer. A single male and female pair up and establish a loosely defined territory along the shore, chasing away same-sex rivals. Eggs are released and fertilized one at a time. A flick of the tail sends the egg into the vegetation,

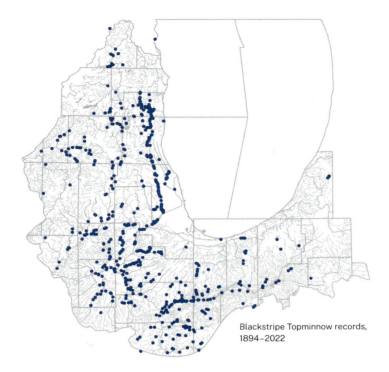

Blackstripe Topminnow records, 1894–2022

where it attaches by adhesive filaments. During a series of reproductive bouts, up to 24 eggs can be laid. A single female may mate with several males, although usually only one at a time. The Blackstripe Topminnow spends the winter months in deeper water, away from surface ice.

Distribution and Status: The Blackstripe Topminnow occurs naturally in southern portions of Lake Michigan and Lake Erie drainages, the Mississippi River basin south from Wisconsin, the Ohio River basin, and Gulf slope drainages from Texas to Alabama. This species is common, occurring throughout much of the Chicago Region. Its regional distribution follows lower-gradient streams like the Des Plaines River and the upper Fox and Kankakee Rivers. It is relatively tolerant of environmental degradation and pollution, with stable populations throughout the region. This species is both tolerant and abundant enough to make a great aquarium substitute for the more rare and sensitive killifish species.

References: Cahn 1927; Carranza and Winn 1954; Forbes and Richardson 1920; Pflieger 1975; Smith 1979; Thomerson and Wooldridge 1970; Trautman 1957

28

Livebearers

Poeciliidae

Livebearers generally have small and stout bodies with large dorsal and tail fins, and are often brightly colored and/or spotted. The males have modified anal fin rays that are elongated and hooked on the end. This structure is called a gonopodium, used to insert sperm packets directly into the female. As the common name implies, almost all species in this family give birth to live young. The female retains the fertilized eggs in her body releasing them as fry. This life-history strategy is unusual among fishes.

The livebearer family, Poeciliidae, has more than 300 species living in fresh, salt, and brackish waters. Their range includes the southern coastal regions of the eastern United States, the southern Mississippi basin, Mexico, Central America, some Caribbean islands, the coasts of northern and eastern South America, and Africa. The Western Mosquitofish is the only species of livebearer found in the Chicago Region.

Many species are popular aquarium fishes, like guppies, swordtails, mollies, and platies. Because of their popularity, they have been introduced around the world — especially the Western Mosquitofish, the Eastern Mosquitofish (*Gambusia holbrooki*), and the Guppy (*Poecilia reticulata*).

Western Mosquitofish

Gambusia affinis • *Gambusia* is derived from the Cuban word *gambusino*, for "nothing" — apparently a joke that if you go fishing and all you catch are gambusia, then you have caught nothing; *affinis*, Latin, means "related," probably referring to relation to *Gambusia holbrooki*.

Description: The Western Mosquitofish is a small, stout fish with an enlarged abdominal area. The most distinctive characteristics include a black triangular teardrop below the eye, 1–3 rows of black spots on the dorsal and tail fins, the absence of the lateral line, a rounded tail fin, and a dorsal fin set far back behind the anal fin origin. The mouth is terminal and oblique. The body color is yellowish to olive, becoming paler closer to the belly. Pregnant females develop a black spot anterior to the anus, and breeding males develop gonopodium. This species can be distinguished from the Starhead Topminnow by lacking a gold spot on top of the head, rows of horizontal lines, and spots along the side. Females are typically larger than males, but both are small, rarely exceeding 1.5 inches (38 mm).

Natural History: The Western Mosquitofish prefers the slow-flowing and still water of streams and rivers with abundant vegetation. It is quite hardy in marsh-like habitats and aquatic plant beds but is sensitive to extreme cold. It usually swims near the surface, often in small schools, foraging on algae, diatoms, mosquito larvae, crustaceans, small aquatic insect larvae, and terrestrial insects that fall into the water. Spawning takes place from midsummer to fall in small groups, often in association with vegetation. A female is chased by several males; she tilts her body, presenting her abdomen to a male, who inserts his gonopodium and internally fertilizes the eggs. Live young are born soon after. It is not unusual to find females with swollen bellies full of soon-to-be-born young. The Western Mosquitofish in the southern part of its range will spawn several times in a year, but spawning frequency in the Chicago Region is not well known.

Distribution and Status: The Western Mosquitofish occurs naturally in the lower Mississippi River, lower Ohio River, and Gulf basins. This species has a rather limited and sporadic distribution due to its more recent colonization of the Chicago Region. Although it was first discovered in 1936 (FMNH) from the Jackson Park Lagoon in Chicago, its presence was not established until the 1960s and '70s, when colonization from southern populations traversed through the upper Illinois Waterway

Western Mosquitofish records, 1936 (●) and 1964–2022 (●)

System. This species is considered native within the Illinois and Des Plaines Rivers, as there is natural connectivity with southern populations via the Illinois River. It is nonnative to the Great Lakes basin, where it was physically introduced for mosquito abatement and self-dispersal via the Chicago Area Waterway System. Mosquitofish were marketed as a natural mosquito-control method and have been widely introduced, even though these fishes have no specific dependence on mosquito larvae for survival; there are many native species within the Chicago Region that are effective at controlling mosquito larvae.

References: Clem and Whitaker 1995; Chipps and Wahl 2004; Forbes and Richardson 1920; Krumholz 1948; R. G. Martin 1975; Robison and Buchanan 1988; Wiegert and Rice 2006

LIVEBEARERS (POECILIIDAE)   343

29

Sunfishes

Centrarchidae

Sunfishes occur naturally only within the freshwaters of North America and are among the most familiar and recognized families of fishes. Their bodies are laterally compressed, with 3–8 anal spines, smooth-edged (cycloid) scales, and thoracic (chest) pectoral fins. The 2 dorsal fins are connected, appearing as one, the front fin with spines and the second with soft rays. They differ from the temperate basses by lacking an opercular spine on the edge of the gill cover and serrations at the margin of the cheek bone. Sunfishes in the genus *Lepomis* are typically small and display alluring colors. The crappies (*Pomoxis*) are slab sided, with deep bodies and posterior dorsal fins, pigmented with black instead of color. The black basses (*Micropterus*) are large, fusiform, and predatory fishes with large mouths. The rock basses (*Ambloplites*) have qualities of the sunfishes and black basses but are unique in having uniform black spots along the sides.

All Chicago Region species are ecologically similar in that they inhabit both flowing and still waters, build and guard nests, and exhibit home-range fidelity. Some are sedentary ambush predators and are rarely found away from submerged cover, while others actively forage, eating small insects, copepods, and plankton. A few species have modifications to the pharyngeal arches, allowing them to crush and eat small snails and fingernail clams.

There are 8 genera and about 37 species, with all but one, the Sacramento Perch (*Archoplites interruptus*), occurring east of the

Rocky Mountains. Centrarchids have been introduced outside of their native range across the world in Europe, Africa, and Asia, often with unfavorable effects on native species. The Chicago Region has 12 species within 4 genera, with 1 introduced species.

Centrarchids have long been of great importance to recreational fishing. The smaller, more colorful sunfishes are often used as native aquarium fish but can be very aggressive. Almost all sunfish species can be taken on hook and line. The Largemouth Bass is probably the most widely sought-after sport fish by both professional and amateur anglers. The Bluegill is very popular, especially among younger anglers. The charismatic and hard-fighting Smallmouth Bass also has a dedicated group of avid stream anglers, who in the Chicago Region fish primarily by wading. A relatively new group of anglers known as microfishers target many of the smaller-bodied sunfishes, including Green Sunfish.

Rock Bass

Ambloplites rupestris • *Ambloplites*, Greek, means "blunt armature"; *rupestris*, Latin, means "among the rocks."

Description: The Rock Bass is a very stout-bodied fish, thick in cross section. Its large mouth extends past the middle of the eye. It has small and inconspicuous ear flaps and rather large red eyes. The front dorsal fin has 12 spines, and the anal fin has 5–7 spines and 9–11 soft rays. Rock Bass coloration is typically golden with irregular blotches of black pigment and an overall dusky appearance. Rows of black dots run horizontally across the lateral surface. In turbid water it is lighter in color and the blotches are less distinct or absent. The pectoral fins are golden bronze close to the body and lighter toward the outer edge. All other fins are speckled and often have black margins. The belly area is usually white with a silver or dusky sheen. It is conspicuously scaled on the cheeks. The Rock Bass is the only sunfish in the Chicago Region to have 5 or more anal spines and spots running in a horizontal pattern. Most adults are 5–7 inches (125–175 mm), but it can reach 11 inches (280 mm) in length.

Natural History: The Rock Bass inhabits rivers, streams, and lakes of all sizes. This species is often associated with a wide variety of habitats,

Rock Bass records, 1890–2022

including aquatic vegetation, large woody debris, rocky reefs, large boulders, undercut banks, and deep pools. Juveniles are often found in beds of emergent plants, particularly Water Willow (*Justicia americana*) on the margins of riffles and cobble bars. In areas lacking instream cover, such as agricultural ditches, it may be associated with dense overhanging terrestrial vegetation. The Rock Bass generally avoids areas of high current, although it does well in higher-gradient streams. Although most abundant in streams with lower turbidity and clean substrates, it is also found in moderately degraded streams with higher turbidity and nutrients. In Lake Michigan, the Rock Bass is closely associated with shoreline rock structures such as revetments, breakwaters, and rubble mounds. It is a visual predator feeding on crayfish and smaller fishes, as well as aquatic and terrestrial macro-invertebrates. Spawning takes place from April to June. The male clears a nest in sand or gravel in moderate to slow-flowing pools in association with large boulders or brush. Nesting behavior is like that of other sunfishes.

Distribution and Status: The Rock Bass is native to the Hudson Bay, Great Lakes, Mississippi River, and Ohio River basins. This species was first observed from the Chicago Region in 1890 from the Yellow River, Marshall County, Indiana, by David Star Jordan. It is widely distributed throughout the St. Joseph, Kankakee, Fox, and lower Illinois Rivers. While once rare in the Des Plaines River, it is now common throughout the mainstem due to improved water quality. It is very abundant along the Lake Michigan shoreline, where it can be readily caught on hook and line with small spinners or minnows. Its status is secure.

References: Becker 1983; Forbes and Richardson 1920; Hubbs and Lagler 1964; W. B. Scott and Crossman 1973; Smith 1979; Trautman 1957

SUNFISHES (CENTRARCHIDAE) **347**

Green Sunfish

Lepomis cyanellus · *Lepomis*, Greek meaning "scaled gill cover"; *cyanellus*, Greek meaning "blue."

Description: The Green Sunfish has a somewhat laterally compressed and stout body. The mouth is comparatively large, with the rear edge extending to the middle of the eye. The gill rakers (11–14) are long and thin. The pectoral fin has a rounded margin and is relatively short, not reaching past the eye when bent forward. The lateral line is complete, with 41–53 lateral scales. The pectoral ray count is 13–14. The anal fin includes 3 smaller spines and 9 soft rays. The ear flap is short, with black pigment in the center and a lighter margin. The body coloration is sea green, speckled with yellow and light-blue spots on the back and sides, fading to gold on the belly. Faint vertical bars of pigment are variably present on the sides. The pelvic fin is golden yellow with a white margin at the leading edge. The front of the anal fin is also white, with a golden edge. The margins of the anal and dorsal fins are white. Large black spots are present at the rear of the dorsal and anal fins. Aqua-blue or cyan wavy lines crisscross the cheek and gill cover. The Green Sunfish can be distinguished from other sunfishes by its large mouth, black dorsal and anal

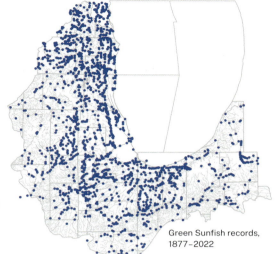

Green Sunfish records, 1877–2022

fin spots, and cyan lines on the cheeks and gill covers. Typical adult size is 3–5 inches (75–125 mm) but can exceed 10 inches (250 mm).

Natural History: The Green Sunfish lives in a wide variety of habitats. In lakes and ponds, it can be found in nearshore areas among woody debris, vegetation, large rock or cobble, and any artificial structures. In streams and rivers, it avoids faster currents, occupying deeper pools, sluggish backwaters, or areas of slow-moving current. It is attracted to woody debris, undercut banks, overhanging vegetation, and exposed roots, and can be abundant around rocky shoreline habitat. This species is quite tolerant of degraded conditions, often the dominant species in these locations. Its diet consists of aquatic and terrestrial insects as well as fish. Green Sunfish spawn from May through August. Males construct nests nearshore in slow water at variable depths. Males are very territorial and emit a grunting sound during courtship and spawning. This species is notorious for hybridizing with other *Lepomis* species, especially in degraded systems where species recognition may be difficult due to impaired visionary cues.

Distribution and Status: The natural range of the Green Sunfish is throughout most of the United States, with introductions to the Pacific coast. This species is one of the most common and widespread fish species in the Chicago Region, with 3,600 records, occurring in virtually every watershed and in Lake Michigan. It is considered tolerant to water quality and habitat degradation, and is usually more abundant in these degraded conditions compared to higher-quality streams. Its status is secure.

References: Eddy and Underhill 1974; Forbes and Richardson 1920; Gerald 1971; Hubbs and Lagler 1964; Hunter 1963; Jenkins and Burkhead 1994; Page and Burr 2011; Pflieger 1975; Smith 1979; Trautman 1957

Pumpkinseed

Lepomis gibbosus · *Lepomis*, Greek, means "scaled gill cover"; *gibbosus*, Latin, means "bulging outward," like the moon phase between half and full, in reference to its body profile.

Description: Pumpkinseed has a rather deep, laterally compressed, but slightly rounded body, with a small, upturned mouth not extending to the front of the eye. The pectoral fin is long and pointed, reaching past the eye when folded forward. The ear flap is short and stiff with a dark center, rimmed in white, and with a distinct red spot at the back margin. The anal fin has 3 spines and 11 soft rays. The gill rakers (9–12) are short and wide compared to those of similar species. Lateral line scales range from 35 to 43. The head color is tan with wavy blue lines. The body has faint green and tan vertical bars, alternating with paler bars. Small orange dots ringed with olive form loose vertical rows. Darker olive spots are scattered over the body. The belly is gold. The tail and lower fins have slim, white margins. The Pumpkinseed can be distinguished from other

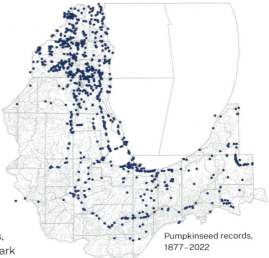

Pumpkinseed records, 1877–2022

sunfishes by the short gill rakers, long pectoral fin, small mouth, dark and stiff ear flap with a red dot, and patchwork of lateral orange blotches. Its maximum adult size is 10 inches (250 mm), but average length is 3–5 inches (75–125 mm).

Natural History: The Pumpkinseed primarily inhabits lakes and lower-current areas of larger rivers and streams. It is typically associated with dense aquatic vegetation, woody debris, rootwads, and undercut banks. It feeds on aquatic insect larvae, crustaceans, mollusks, amphipods, and small fishes. It is one of a few native fishes that eats mussels and snails, using its somewhat molar-like pharyngeal teeth. The Pumpkinseed spawns in the early summer, exhibiting behavior typical of other sunfishes, with males constructing nests in fine substrate in shallow nearshore areas. Males defend a small territory around the nest, guarding eggs and fry from predators, often of the same species.

Distribution and Status: The natural distribution of the Pumpkinseed includes the Atlantic slope drainages south to the Carolinas, the Great Lakes basin, and the upper Mississippi River basin. Chicago Region records are numerous in the upper Fox River system, but this species is common throughout the Chicago Region except in the Rock River drainage, where it is less abundant. It also occurs sporadically in the shallow, vegetated harbors and river mouths of Lake Michigan. The Pumpkinseed is considered common and abundant within the Chicago Region.

References: Andraso 2005; Becker 1983; Eddy and Underhill 1974; Forbes and Richardson 1920; Jenkins and Burkhead 1994; Parks 1949; Pearse 1921b; W. B. Scott and Crossman 1973

Warmouth

Lepomis gulosus · *Lepomis* is Greek, meaning "scaled gill cover"; *gulosus* is Latin, meaning "with a large mouth" or "gluttonous."

Description: The Warmouth has a slightly compressed body, thicker and more rounded than most other sunfishes. The mouth is quite large, extending to or beyond the middle of the eye. The tongue has a small patch of short teeth, which is difficult to see but feels like sandpaper to the touch. The gill rakers are moderately long and thin (9–12). The front dorsal fin has 10 spines; the rear dorsal fin has 9–10 rays. The anal fin has 3 spines and 8–10 rays. Lateral line scales range from 36 to 44. The pectoral fin is short and round, with 14 rays. The body is a deep olive brown with dense, dark mottling. The color is darker on the back, fading to bright yellow on the belly. The darker colors can appear purplish. Five or more bold, dark lines radiate out from the eye on the side of the head. The iris of the large eye is red. The ear flap is short and black, with a cream-colored margin and a small, often faint red spot. Large males have small red flecks along the lower sides and an orange-red spot at the rear base of the dorsal fin. The larger mouth distinguishes the Warmouth from all other *Lepomis* spp. except the Green Sunfish, which lacks the radiating

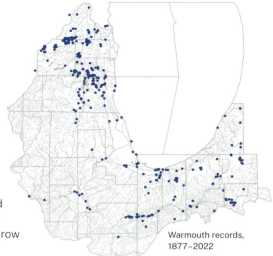

Warmouth records, 1877–2022

bands on the cheek, the mottled brown coloration, and the small red dot on the ear flap. Adults grow up to 10 inches (250 mm).

Natural History: The Warmouth lives in lakes, backwaters, and slow-moving areas of rivers and streams. It is most often associated with clear water, aquatic vegetation, and finer substrates of sand or mud. Warmouth juveniles feed on crustaceans and insect larvae, whereas adults incorporate small fishes and crayfishes into their diet. The Warmouth can withstand lower oxygen concentrations than many other regional fishes, allowing it to occupy swamps, marshes, and wetlands. It spawns in early summer, exhibiting typical sunfish behaviors of nest building and parental care. The circular nests are built by the males in shallow water near cover, typically in sand or gravel in groups with other Warmouths. Males defend the nest from fishes, crayfishes, or other Warmouth males.

Distribution and Status: The Warmouth occurs naturally throughout the Mississippi River, Ohio River, and Great Lakes basins, and in the Atlantic and Gulf slope drainages. Distribution in the Chicago Region is typically restricted to the glacial lakes of the high kettle moraine in Wisconsin and northern Illinois, and the Kankakee Marsh and glacial lakes natural areas of Indiana. It also occurs sporadically in shallow, vegetated harbor and river mouths of Lake Michigan. One interesting record of this species was taken by Victor Shelford in his 1909 study of diurnal pond succession in the once pristine Grand Calumet Lagoons, Lake County, Indiana. Typically, only a few individuals are captured at any given location; however, its persistence in collections over time indicates that its status is secure.

References: Forbes and Richardson 1920; Jenkins and Burkhead 1994; Larimore 1957; Pflieger 1975; Smith 1979; Trautman 1957

Orangespotted Sunfish

Lepomis humilis · *Lepomis*, Greek meaning "scaled gill cover"; *humilis*, Latin for "humble."

Description: The Orangespotted Sunfish is one of the smaller-bodied fishes of the *Lepomis* genus, as the species name suggests. Although it can grow to 6 inches (150 mm), it rarely exceeds 3 or 4 inches (75 or 100 mm) in length. The mouth is moderately large, extending to the pupil of the eye. The pectoral fin (14 rays) is short and rounded, not extending past the eye when folded forward. The anal fin has 3 spines and 8–9 rays. The gill rakers (10–15) on the first gill arch are long and thin. The spawning male is not as humble, displaying a brilliant combination of orange and blue, with the breast and entire bottom surface in a bright-orange color, extending onto the anal fin. The lateral surface and gill cover are varying shades of blue, covered with small orange spots outlined in black pigment. While the female and juvenile lack the brilliant colors, they retain the lateral orange spots. The ear flap is moderately long and black, with a broad white outline, which together with its lateral orange spots and diminutive size distinguish it from other sunfishes in the Chicago Region.

Natural History: The Orangespotted Sunfish is among the more tolerant

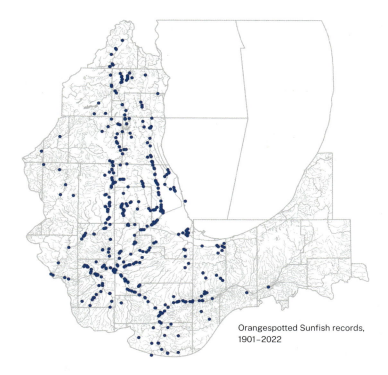

Orangespotted Sunfish records, 1901–2022

species of the genus, being naturally adapted to the warm, turbid Grand Prairie streams and rivers. It avoids fast currents like other sunfishes, preferring quiet pools of large rivers and low-gradient tributaries. Food habits are similar to those of other sunfishes, consuming a variety of insect larvae and other aquatic invertebrates. Spawning takes place from June to August over constructed nests, which are found in clusters along shallow areas with fine substrate. Orangespotted Sunfish mature early and are short lived (2–3 years) compared to other sunfishes.

Distribution and Status: The Orangespotted Sunfish occurs naturally in the Mississippi River, lower Ohio River, and southern Great Lakes basins, and some Gulf slope drainages. As such, its distribution within the Chicago Region reflects its prairie-stream preference, with many records located along the mainstems of the Fox, Kankakee, and Des Plaines Rivers. Its tolerance to degraded conditions also allows it to persist in the Chicago Area Waterway System in various reaches. The Orangespotted Sunfish is considered tolerant and stable within the Chicago Region. It is too small to be of interest to any but microanglers.

References: Eddy and Underhill 1974; Forbes and Richardson 1920; Gerald 1971; Pflieger 1975; Smith 1979; Trautman 1957

Bluegill

Lepomis macrochirus · *Lepomis*, Greek for "scaled gill cover"; *macrochirus*, Greek for "large hand," referring to the shape of the body.

Description: The Bluegill is one of the more recognizable species in the Chicago Region due to its widespread distribution and popularity as a sport fish. The body is hand shaped and laterally compressed. Distinguishing characteristics include: a small mouth, not reaching back to the front of the eye; a dark blotch on the back of the soft dorsal fin; 6–8 vertical bars on the sides (sometime faded in turbid waters); a short, stiff black ear flap; and pointed pectoral fins reaching beyond the eye when folded forward. The pectoral fins have 13 rays, and the anal fin has 11 rays. Gill rakers (13–16) on the first arch are long and thin. Juveniles and females are bluish green and yellow; adult males have an orange belly and blue gill covers. Colors of the male intensify during breeding season. It is most similar to the Redear Sunfish, which has a red-edged ear flap and lacks a dark spot on the dorsal fin. Bluegill can grow to lengths exceeding 10 inches (250 mm) but are typically in the 5–8 inch (125–200 mm) range.

Natural History: The Bluegill inhabits lakes, ponds, rivers, and streams of all sizes. It generally avoids fast

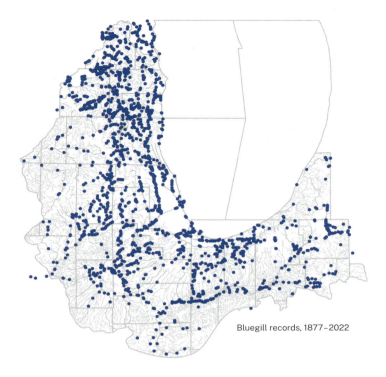

Bluegill records, 1877–2022

currents and is typically associated with aquatic vegetation or woody debris. The Bluegill is tolerant of wide range of water-quality and habitat conditions and can inhabit agricultural ditches, canals, and detention basins. Those found in stream habitats are typically smaller with few individuals larger than 3–5 inches. Consuming a variety of insect larvae and other aquatic invertebrates, it is like other sunfish, but may generally eat smaller prey items due to its small mouth size. Spawning takes place from late May to August over nests constructed in fine substrate, often found in colonies along shallow areas.

Distribution and Status: The natural distribution of the Bluegill is the United States from the eastern slope of the Rocky Mountains to the Atlantic slope drainages. It has been introduced worldwide. It is one of the most widely distributed and abundant fish in the Chicago Region, with over 3,250 records. Rarely is a collection made without finding this species. It is typically not found in higher-gradient upland and morainetop streams. It is considered tolerant and abundant, and is a popular sport fish within the Chicago Region.

References: Andraso 2005; Eddy and Underhill 1974; Forbes and Richardson 1920; Gerald 1971; Hubbs and Lagler 1964; Jenkins and Burkhead 1994; Pflieger 1975; W. B. Scott and Crossman 1973; Smith 1979; Trautman 1957

Longear Sunfish

Lepomis megalotis · *Lepomis*, Greek, meaning "scaled gill cover"; *megalotis*, Greek, meaning "longear."

Description: The Longear Sunfish has a laterally compressed, deep body. It's coloration and patterns make it one of the most visually stunning Chicago Region fishes. It can be distinguished from other Chicago Region sunfish by having short, rounded pectoral fins that do not reach beyond the eye when folded back, and an elongated ear flap. The Longear Sunfish is very similar to the Northern Sunfish. The best characteristics to distinguish these 2 species are the ear flap configuration and the pectoral ray count (13–14 for Longear versus 12 for Northern Sunfish). The Northern Sunfish's ear flap is slanted upward, with a white margin and a red dot at the tip, whereas the Longear Sunfish's ear flap is more horizontal and lacks a red spot at the tip. Coloration can be subtly different but not a reliable characteristic. Lateral line scale counts may also be used but can be overlapping: 33–46 (usually 39 or more) for the Longear versus 40 or fewer for the Northern Sunfish. Adult

Longear Sunfish are typically a bit larger, often exceeding 5 inches (125 mm) in length.

Natural History: The Longear Sunfish inhabits upland rivers and streams with higher gradients compared to most other sunfishes' preference for lower-gradient habitats. It is typically associated with moderate flows with large woody debris, rootwads, undercut banks, aquatic vegetation, and coarse substrates. This species is less tolerant of poor water quality and habitat degradation than many of the other sunfishes and does not do well in ponds and smaller lakes. The diet consists of insects, aquatic invertebrates, and small fish. Spawning takes place from June to August over close-knit colonies of nests constructed in clean sand or fine gravel. The male guards the eggs and newly hatched young until they disperse.

Distribution and Status: The Longear Sunfish occurs in the lower Mississippi River basin, Ohio River basin, and Gulf slope drainages. Chicago Region records are concentrated in the upper Illinois River, Iroquois River, and lower Kankakee River and tributaries. This subspecies

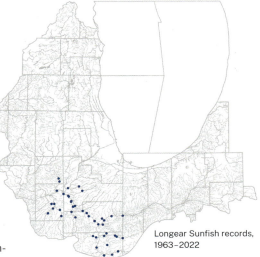

Longear Sunfish records, 1963–2022

has been recently elevated to a full species and separated from the Northern Sunfish, which poses an issue with some records only being identified to the species and not the subspecies level. Those collections with existing museum or collection specimens and accurate locality data for resampling can be rectified over time; however, some may never be parsed out. Records in which there is reliable confirmation of species differentiation were utilized here to the extent possible. The Longear Sunfish is listed as threatened in Wisconsin. We consider this species sensitive to water-quality and habitat degradation but stable where it occurs within the Chicago Region.

References: Forbes and Richardson 1920; Gerald 1971; Metzke, Taylor, and Caton 2023; Page and Burr 2011; Pflieger 1975; Smith 1979; Trautman 1957

Redear Sunfish

Lepomis microlophus · *Lepomis*, Greek, meaning "scaled gill cover"; *microlophus*, meaning "small nape."

Description: The Redear Sunfish has a deep, slightly compressed body profile. The snout is somewhat pointed, and the small mouth does not reach back to the front of the eye. The pectoral fin is long and pointed, with 13–14 rays, reaching beyond the eye when folded forward. There are 9 anal rays. Gill rakers on the first gill are short and wide. Its ear flap is moderate in length, with a dark center and a wide red rim. The sides are yellowish green with gray mottling, forming indistinct vertical bars. The belly and throat are yellow to off-white. Breeding males are golden in color, with darker pectoral fins. The small mouth and dark gill flap with a red margin distinguish the Redear Sunfish from all other Chicago Region sunfishes. Redear Sunfish can grow to 12 inches (300 mm) or larger in ponds and lakes but are typically smaller, especially in stream habitats.

Natural History: In its native southern range, the Redear Sunfish prefers lakes, ponds, swamps, backwaters, and slow-moving areas of streams, often associated with aquatic vegetation. In the Chicago Region, it is most common in clear lakes where it has

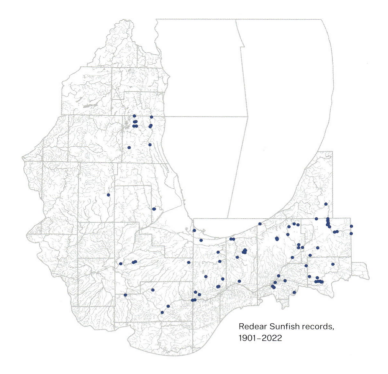

Redear Sunfish records, 1901–2022

been stocked for angling and snail control. Escapees are occasionally found in streams. Redear Sunfish forage along the bottom, feeding on snails, insect larvae, and crustaceans. The ability to eat snails and small mollusks using its stout pharyngeal teeth is reflected in its alternate common name, the Shellcracker. The Redear Sunfish spawns in the late spring to early summer in nests, exhibiting typical sunfish mating behavior, defending its nests, and guarding eggs and fry.

Distribution and Status: The Redear Sunfish's native range includes the lower Mississippi River up to southern Illinois, the Ohio River basin, and Gulf slope and southern Atlantic slope drainages. This species is widely introduced. Stocking throughout the Midwest is documented starting in the mid-1800s. It was intentionally introduced to the Chicago Region as early as the 1890s, especially within Indiana. The Redear Sunfish is not native to the Chicago Region; however, it is not considered problematic in natural water bodies, as it is rarely abundant, with only a few individuals present.

References: Etnier and Starnes 1993; Gerald 1971; Lauder 1983; Parks 1949; Robison and Buchanan 1988; Smith 1979

Northern Sunfish

Lepomis peltastes · *Lepomis*, Greek, meaning "scaled gill cover"; *peltastes*, Greek for "soldier armed with a shield."

Description: The Northern Sunfish has a laterally compressed and deep body. It can be distinguished from other Chicago Region sunfish by having short, rounded pectoral fins that do not reach beyond the eye when folded back, and an elongated ear flap. The Northern Sunfish ear flap is slanted upward with a white margin; quite often, it has a red dot at the tip. Its mouth is moderate in size, almost reaching back to the front edge of the eye. Gill rakers (9–11) on the first gill arch are short and thick. The Northern Sunfish is also one of the more colorful fishes in the Chicago Region, although highly variable. It has an aqua-blue and orange patchwork on the lateral surfaces, with aqua on the back and orange on the belly. The snout and cheek have radiating vermiculations of aqua and orange. Fins are typically translucent with some color bleeding into the dorsal and caudal fin bases. Females and juveniles are less brilliantly colored than the breeding males. See the Longear Sunfish for distinguishing characteristics. Northern Sunfish are small, typically less than 5 inches (125 mm) in length.

Natural History: The Northern Sunfish inhabits upland rivers and streams with higher gradients compared to most other sunfishes, which prefer lower-gradient habitats. It is typically associated with moderate flows with large woody debris, rootwads, undercut banks, aquatic vegetation, and coarse substrates. This species is less tolerant of poor water quality and habitat degradation than many of the other sunfishes and does not do well in ponds and smaller lakes. The Northern Sunfish diet consists of insects, aquatic invertebrates, and small fish. Spawning takes place from June to August over colonies of nests constructed in clean sand or fine gravel. The male guards the eggs and newly hatched young until they disperse.

Distribution and Status: Current literature indicates that the native distribution of Northern Sunfish is the Great Lakes basin and the upper Mississippi River in Illinois, Iowa, Wisconsin, and Minnesota. Populations of this species occur in

Northern Sunfish records, 1880–1945 (●), 1950–1979 (●), and 1980–2022 (●)

the higher-gradient reaches of the St. Joseph River, the Kankakee River, the upper Fox River in Wisconsin, and tributaries of the Illinois River. The first time the Northern Sunfish was recorded in the Chicago Region was in 1880 from South Chicago on the Calumet River, Cook County, Illinois (INHS); it was collected again a hundred years later at the same spot by the INHS. The Northern Sunfish is listed as threatened in Wisconsin, but appears stable in Illinois, Indiana, and Michigan. Although smaller than most sunfishes, this species can be caught by hook and line, as it readily takes bait. See the Longear Sunfish account for a comparative discussion.

References: Hubbs and Lagler 1964; Metzke, Taylor, and Caton 2023; Page and Burr 2011; W. B. Scott and Crossman 1973; Smith 1979; Trautman 1957

SUNFISHES (CENTRARCHIDAE) **363**

Smallmouth Bass

Micropterus dolomieu · *Micropterus* is Greek for "small fin"; *dolomieu* is after Dieudonné Dolomieu, a friend of Citoyen Lacepede.

Description: The Smallmouth Bass has a fusiform but somewhat laterally compressed body. The mouth is moderately large, extending back to the middle of the eye. The front dorsal fin has 9–11 spines and is rather low and gently curving. Eyes are typically red. Smallmouth Bass may display a variety of coloration, including green, olive, brown, or yellowish brown. Lateral pigmentation is mottled, often forming distinct vertical bars; cheeks may also display darker, radiating bands. The Smallmouth Bass can be distinguished from the Largemouth Bass by its shorter mouth and its bronze mottled body. Juvenile Smallmouth Bass have a distinctly tricolored tail fin with white, black, and orange bars and bronze vertical bars on the lateral surfaces. In contrast, Largemouth Bass juveniles have only white and black bands in the tail fin, with a distinct horizontal midlateral stripe. A large individual measuring 23 inches (584.2 mm) and 6.5 pounds (2.95 kg) was captured during US Army Corps harbor surveys from Lake Michigan's Buffington Harbor, Lake County, Indiana (2000), but these larger fish are rare in river and stream habitats, where most adults are in the 12–16-inch (304–406 mm) range.

Natural History: The Smallmouth Bass lives in rivers, streams, and clear lakes. It is typically associated with rocky habitats and large woody debris. It is usually found in higher-gradient reaches where velocities are moderate to fast. The Smallmouth Bass is considered an intolerant species, sensitive to pollution, low dissolved oxygen, and habitat degradation. However, it is somewhat tolerant of high temperatures and does well in some power plant cooling lakes. Food consists largely of fish and crayfish, but it will also feed on larger insect larvae and adults. Adults typically reach maturity at age 4, with spawning taking place in May and June with increased movement into tributary streams. Males construct nests in gravel shoals along banks with reduced current. In Lake Michigan, a nest was observed being guarded by a large male in 10 feet (3 m) of water; the nest was excavated in sand, exposing cobbles beneath. The males guard eggs and young larvae. In streams and rivers, reproductive success is higher in years with moderately high, stable water levels.

Distribution and Status: The Smallmouth Bass is native to Hudson Bay, Great Lakes, Mississippi River, and Ohio River basins. It is widely introduced elsewhere. Records for the Chicago Region are concentrated in the Fox, Kankakee, lower DuPage, and St. Joseph Rivers. Due to water-quality problems, it was once rare or

Smallmouth Bass records, 1877–2022

absent from the lower and upper Des Plaines River. In 2017, lower Des Plaines River populations increased markedly — likely in response to a reduction in combined sewer overflows resulting from expansion of the tunnel-and-reservoir system. It is quite common and abundant along the Lake Michigan shoreline revetments, breakwaters, and rubble mounds. It is uncommon in lowland rivers such as the Galien River in Michigan and in the Chicago Area Waterway System. This species has been widely studied due to its popularity among anglers. Its status is secure.

References: Eddy and Underhill 1974; Forbes and Richardson 1920; Hubbs and Lagler 1964; Jenkins and Burkhead 1994; Pflieger 1975; W. B. Scott and Crossman 1973; Smith 1979; Trautman 1957

SUNFISHES (CENTRARCHIDAE)   **365**

Largemouth Bass

Micropterus salmoides · *Micropterus*, Greek for "small fin"; *salmoides*, Latin for "troutlike."

Description: The Largemouth Bass is one of the more recognizable fishes due to its popularity among anglers and its ubiquitous distribution. The body is fusiform, robustly oval in cross-section, and somewhat laterally compressed. The mouth extends to the back of or beyond the eye. The dorsal fin has 9–11 spines and is quite curved, highest in the middle. The dark green or black lateral stripe consists of a series of pigment blotches, which can fade or even be absent in turbid water. Largemouth Bass have a much larger mouth and different pigmentation and coloration than the Smallmouth Bass. Most observed juvenile and smaller adults are less than 12 inches (300 mm), with some adults exceeding 20 inches (500 mm).

Natural History: The Largemouth Bass inhabits lakes, ponds, rivers, and streams of all sizes and types, including agricultural ditches. It is associated with a wide variety of habitats including aquatic vegetation, large woody debris, deep pools, and shoreline revetments. Although it can be found in faster-moving areas of streams, it typically prefers moderate to slow currents. It is very tolerant of turbidity, pollution, and low dissolved oxygen, unlike the more sensitive Smallmouth Bass. Primary prey is fish, but crayfish, macroinvertebrates, and even small mammals and water-

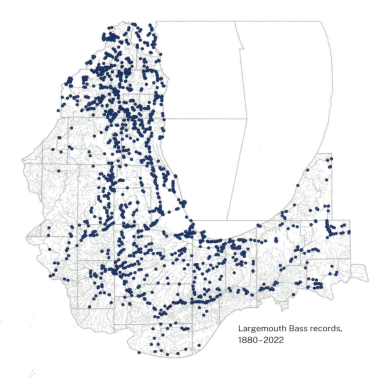

Largemouth Bass records, 1880–2022

fowl have been found in the stomach of this voracious predator. Adults reach maturity at age 3–4 and spawning typically occurs in May and June. Males build nest in any type of substrate, creating depressions using their tails. Eggs and young larvae are guarded by the male prior to dispersal from the nest.

Distribution and Status: The natural distribution of the Largemouth Bass includes the Mississippi River, Ohio River, and Great Lakes basins, and Atlantic and Gulf slope drainages. This species has been widely introduced throughout North America and globally. It is tolerant of a wide range of habitat and water-quality conditions and is relatively common in the degraded Chicago Area Waterway System. The Largemouth Bass is one of the more widespread species in the Chicago Region, where its common and abundant.

References: Eddy and Underhill 1974; Forbes and Richardson 1920; Hubbs and Lagler 1964; Jenkins and Burkhead 1994; Pflieger 1975; W. B. Scott and Crossman 1973; Smith 1979; Trautman 1957

Description: The White Crappie has a slab-sided, laterally compressed body with a narrow cross-section. Its mouth is large, extending well past the middle of the eye. The first dorsal fin has 6 hard spines; the second dorsal fin has 14–15 soft rays. The length of the dorsal fin base is much less than the distance between the front of the dorsal fin and the eye. It has long, pointed pectoral fins. The anal fin has 6 hard spines and 17–19 soft rays. The soft dorsal, anal, and tail fins are large and prominent, with dark bands and mottled pigmentation patterns. The top surface coloration is olive with a dark green hue, fading to silvery white on the sides and belly. The sides are lightly mottled, with black markings forming 6–9 vertical bars, which can range from faint to very dark, especially in breeding males. The White Crappie is different from the similar Black Crappie by having 6 rather than 7 or 8 dorsal spines and by having vertical bands of pigment on the lateral surfaces. Adult size can reach up to or exceeding 15 inches (375 mm).

Natural History: The White Crappie inhabits lakes, ponds, rivers, and occasionally smaller streams. In riverine habitats it avoids faster currents, pre-

ferring deeper, slow-flowing pools and off-channel areas. It is often associated with submerged cover, especially large woody debris, where it forms loose aggregations. In lakes, it can be found in deeper waters at the edge of weed beds and drop-offs. Juveniles feed on zooplankton, with insect larvae becoming more common as the fish gets larger. Adults are largely piscivorous. White Crappie move into shallower water in early spring, congregating around available structure. In later spring, spawning begins in typical sunfish fashion, building circular nests in loose colonies in sand or gravel substrate, most often in areas away from current or wave action. The male defends the nest and protects the eggs and the young fry until they leave the nest. After the spawning period in the late spring and early summer, White Crappie typically move into deeper water.

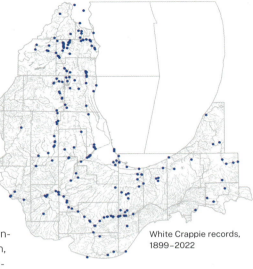

White Crappie records, 1899–2022

Distribution and Status: The natural range of the White Crappie includes the Great Lakes basin, Mississippi River basin, Ohio River basin, Gulf slope drainages, and northern Atlantic slope drainages. Records within the Chicago Region are concentrated in the lower Kankakee and upper Fox River; otherwise, it has a sporadic distribution. Abundance is low in streams and rivers, usually represented by only 1 or a few small individuals. It is more abundant in lakes, where they are commonly fished, sometimes supplemented by stocking. The White Crappie is a popular sport fish. Its is considered common but not abundant in Chicago Region.

References: Becker 1983; Cahn 1927; Etnier and Starnes 1993; Forbes and Richardson 1920; Hansen 1943, 1951, 1965; Smith 1979

SUNFISHES (CENTRARCHIDAE) **369**

Black Crappie

Pomoxis nigromaculatus · *Pomoxis*, Greek, means "sharp opercle"; *nigromaculatus*, Latin, means "black spotted."

Description: The Black Crappie has a slab-sided body with a thin cross-section. The mouth is large, extending well past the middle of the eye. Its front dorsal fin has 7–8 hard spines, broadly connected to the rear soft dorsal fin, which has 17–19 soft rays. The length of the dorsal fin base is about equal to the distance between the front dorsal fin and the eye. The soft dorsal, anal, and tail fins are large and prominent, appearing almost black with pigment, scattered with white spots. The pectoral fin is long and pointed. The anal fin has 6 hard spines and 17–19 soft rays.

Surface coloration is dark olive with a purple hue on top, fading to silvery white on the sides and belly. Mottled dark black markings are randomly spread throughout the side surfaces, not forming a distinct pattern. The Black Crappie differs from the similar White Crappie by having 7 or more dorsal spines and dark, mottled lateral pigmentation without distinct banding. Adult size can exceed 15 inches (375 mm).

Natural History: The Black Crappie inhabits rivers, streams, and lakes. Like most sunfishes, it prefers areas

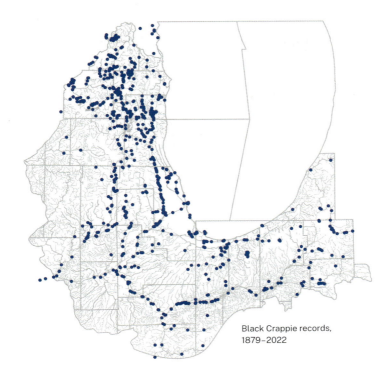

Black Crappie records, 1879–2022

of lower current, in deep pools or off-channel habitats. Foraging largely takes place in the middle of the water column. Juveniles feed on crustaceans (zooplankton), with insect larvae and amphipods becoming more common as the fish get larger. Fish are not typically a prominent component of the diet — adults continue to eat zooplankton. Black Crappie spawn in early to late spring. Nests are typically found at variable depths near vegetation or woody structures.

Distribution and Status: The natural range of the Black Crappie was probably the Great Lakes, Mississippi, Gulf, and Atlantic drainages, although this is difficult to ascertain, as the species has been stocked nationwide for many years. It is native to the Chicago Region, with records concentrated in upper Fox River streams and lakes, and along larger rivers such as the Kankakee and the Des Plaines. Black Crappie are targeted by anglers throughout their range including a population in Lake Calumet. The species is common and secure within the Chicago Region.

References: Becker 1983; Cahn 1927; Etnier and Starnes 1993; Forbes and Richardson 1920; Jenkins and Burkhead 1994; W. E. Johnson 1945; Page and Burr 2011; Pearse 1918, 1919, 1921a; Smith 1979

SUNFISHES (CENTRARCHIDAE)   **371**

30

Temperate Basses

Moronidae

The temperate basses have a fusiform body and a large mouth. The jaws, roof of the mouth, and the tongue have small teeth, but canines are absent. There are 2 pointed or rounded spines on the gill cover (opercle) and serrations along the rear edge of the cheekbone. The first dorsal fin is spiny; the second has soft rays with 1 anterior spine. These fish have a general silvery or yellow hue, most with horizontal stripes along their sides. Each species has a slightly different ecology. Naturally, the Striped Bass (*Morone saxatilis*) is marine and anadromous, living in the ocean and running up freshwater rivers to spawn; however, it can live entirely in freshwater. The White Perch can move back and forth between any given salinity gradient (amphidromous) living and spawning in estuaries. The White and Yellow Basses are both freshwater species. These fishes are pelagic spawners with no parental care. Striped Bass have been hybridized with the native White Bass, and the offspring are called Wipers. These hybrids can be difficult to identify but usually have 2 tooth patches very close together on the tongue, and the stripe immediately below the lateral line is complete all the way to the tail. Striped Bass differ from other Chicago Region species by having a different body shape, dorsal fins that are more separated, 1–2 tooth patches on the rear of the tongue, and the second anal spine is shorter than the third anal spine.

Moronidae is composed of 2 genera and 6 species in eastern North America, coastal Europe, and coastal northern Africa. In North America, there is only 1 genus, whose 4 species all have been found in the Chicago Region. The taxonomic history of these fishes has been complex and somewhat confusing. They were placed in the sea bass family Serranidae for some time and then moved to the family Percichthyidae, the temperate perches. Most recently, they have been given the family name Moronidae. Adding to the confusion, the genus *Roccus* was used for many years instead of the current *Morone*. You could find any of these names in older fish books and publications.

This family is important economically for recreational and food fisheries. The anadromous Striped Bass suffered a dramatic decline due to dams and pollution but has recently rebounded to some extent. The story of its comeback in Chesapeake Bay is widely cited. Due to its popularity as a sport fish, given their potential size (6 feet/1.8 m) and fighting ability, it is widely stocked across the country in large reservoirs and impoundments. Striped Bass stocking programs in the Chicago Region are no longer maintained; therefore, no species account is provided in this book. However, a chance encounter may be possible.

White Perch

Morone americana · The origin and meaning of *Morone* are uncertain; *americana* refers to America.

Description: The White Perch has a deep, laterally compressed body. The nape is sharply arched and deepest under the origin of the first dorsal fin. The 2 dorsal fins are slightly connected. The first dorsal fin is tall and triangular, with 8–11 hard pointy spines; the second dorsal fin has 1 hard spine and 10–13 soft rays. There are 3 strong anal spines, the second and third about equal in length; the anal fin usually has 9–10 rays. The lateral line is complete, usually with 46–49 scales. There is no tooth patch on the rear of the tongue. The body coloration is silver on the sides and greenish on top. Adults do not have horizontal stripes. Juveniles may have 6 faint stripes, with some of the stripes disjointed immediately above the anal fin. White Perch can be distinguished from the other 2 Moronidae species by the lack of lateral stripes. The White Perch is most like White Bass due to similar coloration. In addition to the difference in striping, White Bass have 12 anal rays, versus 9–10 on White Perch. Although White Perches can grow to over 20 inches (500 mm), most are smaller.

Natural History: The White Perch is present in canals and rivers in the Chicago Region but can also inhabit eutrophic lakes and ponds. It prefers still to slow-moving waters over finer substrates, sometimes forming schools. Juveniles forage on copepods and aquatic insect larvae, whereas adults eat more fish. The gut contents of White Perch found in Cedar Lake, Lake County, Indiana, were full of copepods, algae, and fine sediment. The White Perch spawns in late spring, swimming into shallow water in tributaries, a suitable shallow section of river mainstem, or bays of lakes. It does not appear to use any specific substrate type. Eggs are randomly scattered near the surface, fertilized, then sink to the bottom and stick to rocks, plants, and debris.

White Perch records, 1980–1988 (●), 1990–1999 (●), and 2000–2022 (●)

Distribution and Status: The White Perch is native to freshwater and estuarine systems along the East Coast of North America. This species used the Erie Canal to enter Lake Erie in the 1950s and spread throughout the rest of the Great Lakes. The first record in the Chicago Region was from 1980 in Wolf Lake, Cook County, Illinois (INHS), thereafter dispersing to the Illinois River by the early 1990s. White Perch is found in Lake Michigan, the Chicago Area Waterway System, the Illinois River, the lower Des Plaines River, the Kankakee River, and some Indiana lakes. In 2015, the WDNR discovered a White Perch in the Mukwonago River, Waukesha County, Wisconsin. Populations have slowly increased and may be spreading. The White Perch is a popular sport fish within its native range but is not yet highly targeted in the Chicago Region.

References: AuClair 1966; Burr, Eisenhour, et al. 1996; Holm, Mandrak, and Burridge 2009; Laird and Page 1996; Savitz, Aiello, and Bardygula 1989; Simon, Moy, and Barnes 1998

TEMPERATE BASSES (MORONIDAE)

White Bass

Morone chrysops • The origin and meaning of *Morone* is uncertain; *chrysops* is Greek, meaning "gold eye."

Description: The White Bass has a deep, laterally compressed body. The nape is rounded and deepest under the rear of the first dorsal fin. The 2 dorsal fins are slightly separate and not connected by membrane. The first dorsal fin is tall and triangular, with 9 hard pointy spines; the second dorsal fin has 1 hard spine and 12–14 soft rays. There are 3 stout anal spines, the second shorter than the third; the anal fin has 11–13 rays. There are 1–2 small tooth patches at the rear of tongue and the roof of mouth. The lateral line is complete, with 51–60 scales. The lateral surface is silvery, with 6–8 horizontal stripes, sometimes faint, but obvious. The stripes are usually continuous but can be slightly disjointed near the anal fin. The White Bass differs from the White Perch by having stripes and tooth patches on the tongue. The Yellow Bass lacks tooth patches but has distinctly broken lateral stripes, compared to the continuous stripes on the White Bass. In addition to the color difference, dorsal fins are separated on the White Bass and connected on the Yellow Bass, such that pulling forward on the spiny dorsal also moves the soft dorsal. The White Bass can grow up to 20 inches (500 mm) but most are smaller, in the 10–14 inch (250–350 mm) range.

Natural History: The White Bass is most common in large rivers but can

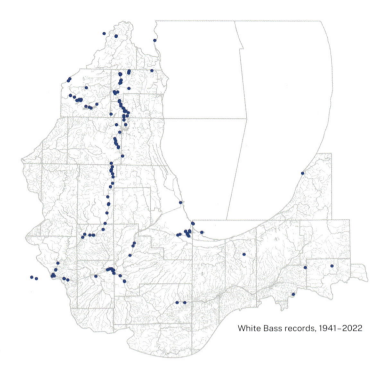

White Bass records, 1941–2022

also be found in larger lakes or lakes near large rivers. Its preferred substrate is gravel or cobble. Schooling behavior is common. Juveniles forage on crustaceans and aquatic insect larvae, whereas adults also eat fish. The White Bass spawn in late spring, congregating in shallow water over rocky substrates with fast water velocities in rivers or lakeshores with wind-induced current. Spawning may also take place in smaller tributaries. Eggs are randomly scattered near the surface, fertilized, sink to the bottom, and stick to rocks, plants, and debris.

Distribution and Status: The White Bass occurs in the Great Lakes, Mississippi River, and Ohio River basins, and in Gulf slope drainages from Texas to Alabama. Chicago Region records for this species are most common in the Fox and Illinois Rivers. We frequently observe them in Lake Calumet and the Calumet River. The White Bass can also be found very sporadically in Lake Michigan and other scattered locations in Illinois and Indiana. The status of this species is secure, and it is usually found in abundance only during spawning runs, especially on the Illinois River, where it is a popular sport fish.

References: Becker 1983; Robison and Buchanan 1988; Smith 1979; Tiemann, Taylor, et al. 2015; Voightlander and Wissing 1974

Description: The Yellow Bass has a moderately deep, laterally compressed body. The nape is arched and deepest under the origin of the first dorsal fin. The 2 dorsal fins are slightly connected. The first dorsal fin is tall and triangular, with 9 hard pointy spines; the second dorsal fin has 1 hard spine and 12–15 soft rays. There are 3 stout anal spines, the second and third about equal in length; the anal fin usually has 9 rays. There is no tooth patch on the rear of tongue. The lateral line is complete, with 49–51 scales. The body can have a yellow hue in turbid waters but can also be silvery with greenish hues. The lateral surface has 6–8 horizontal stripes that are disjointed above the anal fin. The yellow color and broken lateral stripes distinguish the Yellow Bass from the White Bass and the White Perch. It seldom exceeds 6 inches (150 mm) but can grow up to 18 inches (200 mm) in larger rivers and lakes.

Natural History: The Yellow Bass is most common in lakes, reservoirs, floodplain lakes, and some rivers. It is found over a wide range of substrate types and prefers still or slower-moving water and warmer temperatures, sometimes in very tur-

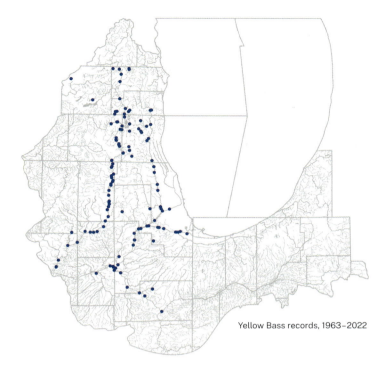

Yellow Bass records, 1963–2022

bid waters. It generally forms small schools. Juveniles forage on crustaceans and aquatic insect larvae, while adults are primarily piscivorous. The Yellow Bass spawns in late spring in the shallow water of tributaries, or in the main river over various types of substrates. Eggs are randomly scattered, floating a short distance before settling to the bottom where they attach to the bottom.

Distribution and Status: The Yellow Bass occurs in the Lake Michigan drainage, the lower Mississippi River basin, and some Gulf slope drainages. This species was not observed in the Chicago Region until 1963, when it was taken in Miltmore Lake, Lake County, Illinois (INHS). Records are most common in the Fox River, but occur also in the lower Des Plaines River, lower Kankakee River, and the Chicago Area Waterway System. Abundance can be quite variable, but its status is secure. The Yellow Bass is a sport fish, but due to its smaller size it is not as popular as the White Bass or the Striped Bass.

References: Becker 1983; Burnham 1909; Helm 1964; Pflieger 1975; Smith 1979

TEMPERATE BASSES (MORONIDAE) 379

31

Drums and Croakers

Sciaenidae

The common names *drum* and *croaker* refer to the sounds these fishes make using their air bladder. They are mostly large, deep-bodied fish, with an arched back and a relatively large terminal mouth. The dorsal fin has 2 distinct sections: a short spiny front fin and a very long rear fin with soft rays. Their heads have large, cavernous canals and pores that are part of the sensory system. Drums are largely bottom-dwelling fishes. Some have ridged gill arches, allowing them to eat mollusks and crabs. They also feed on invertebrates and smaller fishes. They spawn in open waters (pelagic spawners).

This family is widespread globally, having 210 species, most occupying temperate and tropical marine waters along coastlines and reefs. There are a few freshwater species, with the Freshwater Drum as the single representative in the Chicago Region.

Many drum species support important commercial and sport fisheries. They are an excellent food fish with flavorful flesh and few bones. The Red Drum (*Sciaenops ocellatus*) is popular among marine anglers and the Yellow Croaker (*Larimichthys polyactis*) supports a large commercial fishery. Freshwater Drums are not a popular food fish among anglers but, like their marine counterparts, are quite edible. Many anglers also know them as Sheepshead.

Description: The Freshwater Drum is a laterally compressed perch-like fish with a humped nape sloping sharply down to a proportionally smaller head. The most distinctive characteristics of this fish are the pelvic fins ending in a thin filament, a rounded to square caudal fin, and the unique croaking sound. The dorsal fin is in 2 parts: the first with about 10 spines, the second one elongated with 29–32 soft rays. It has ctenoid scales that are rough to the touch. Its mouth is subterminal and does not have teeth. The body is silver, becoming whitish on the belly and margins of paired fins. This species can exceed 30 inches (762 mm) in length, but most adults in the Chicago Region are in the 12–18-inch (305–457-mm) range. Specimens of up to 100 pounds (45.4 kg) were reported by Hubbs and Lagler (1947) and Trautman (1957); archaeological evidence indicates specimens up to 200 pounds (90.7 kg) based on pharyngeal teeth size.

Natural History: The Freshwater Drum occurs in large lakes and rivers, rarely occurring in smaller tributary streams or glacial lakes. It is typically associated with sluggish water over any kind of substrate. It resides mainly near the bottom, where it feeds on small mussels, fish, crayfish, and aquatic insects. It is well adapted for bottom feeding with its subtermi-

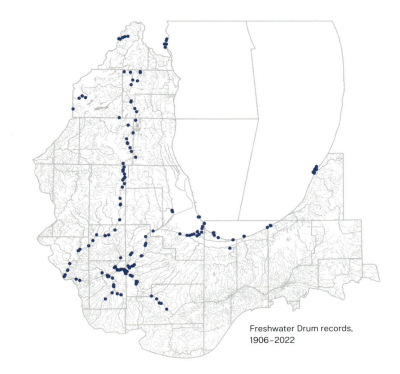

Freshwater Drum records, 1906–2022

nal mouth, sensory pores on the chin, and stout pharyngeal teeth. It is reasonably tolerant of habitat alteration and water-quality degradation and is often associated with revetments and breakwaters. Spawning within the Chicago Region has been observed in late June and July, when eggs were broadcast in shallow, quiet waters. The eggs are pelagic and float until hatched.

Distribution and Status: The Freshwater Drum occurs from the Hudson Bay in Canada to Guatemala — essentially, between the parallels confining the Mississippi and Ohio River basins. This species is found along the shoreline of Lake Michigan, typically associated with river mouths and navigation harbors. Riverine records are concentrated in the deep sluggish sections of the Fox and upper Illinois Rivers. It is abundant in some areas and is readily caught by hook and line using crayfish, worms, or small minnows as bait. There is archaeological evidence that Native Americans heavily spearfished this species. The Freshwater Drum is considered tolerant and stable within the Chicago Region.

References: Hubbs and Lagler 1964; Smith 1979; Trautman 1957

32

Darters and Perches

Percidae

Percidae is an interesting and diverse family, including very small, colorful species known as darters, as well as the large predatory Walleye. Characteristics of the perch family include a body that is oval in cross-section (fusiform), spiny fins, and rough-edged (ctenoid) scales. They also have 2 dorsal fins, a shorter front fin containing 6 or more spines and a longer back fin with 23 or fewer soft rays. They can be distinguished from the Sunfishes and Temperate Basses by the presence of 1–2 anal fin spines instead of 3 or more, and a fusiform body compared to a laterally com-pressed body. Darters are grouped into 3 genera. *Ammocrypta* has a very slender, translucent body with only 1 anal spine; *Etheostoma* and *Percina* have 2 anal spines. *Percina* has 1 or more modified breast scales between the pelvic fins, whereas *Etheostoma* lacks this character.

Darters and perches have 220 species in North America, all but 3 of which are darters. There are also 17 percids in Eurasia and 4 darters in Mexico. They inhabit only freshwater habitats except for a few that can tolerate brackish water. The Chicago Region has 16 percid species, including 13 darters.

The 3 larger perch species — Walleye, Sauger, and Yellow Perch — are all popular sport and commercial species. Large Yellow Perch were once quite abundant in Lake Michigan and a very highly sought-after food fish; however, numbers now are too low within Chicago Region waters to support a commercial fishery. Walleye and Sauger are both stocked in Illinois due to inconsistent natural reproduction.

Western Sand Darter

Ammocrypta clara · *Ammocrypta*, Greek, meaning "concealed by sand"; *clara*, Latin for "clear," referring to this fish's translucent appearance.

Description: The Western Sand Darter has a very thin and elongated body. This species can be distinguished from other Chicago Region darters by having 1 anal spine, a translucent body, and body patches without scales. The snout is pointed, with a proportionally small subterminal and horizontal mouth. The groove above the upper lip is continuous (no frenum). The gill cover has a prominent spine. There are small horizontal blotches along the lateral and dorsal midlines. Adults can reach 3 inches (75 mm).

Natural History: The Western Sand Darter inhabits medium to large streams and rivers. It requires shifting sandbars associated with the dynamic reaches of meandering channels. This species is adapted to living in and over the shifting-sand formations, often burrowing into the sand, leaving only its eyes and mouth exposed. It has been reported to eat aquatic insects and larvae. The natural history and behavior of the Western Sand Darter within the Chicago Region is largely unknown and considered an opportunity for study.

Distribution and Status: The Western Sand Darter occurs in the middle Mississippi River basin and Texas Gulf drainages, with sporadic populations and occurrences east to

Western Sand Darter records, 1988–1992 (●) and 2015–2022 (●)

the Appalachian Mountains. It is known from just a few Chicago Region localities in the lower Kankakee River. In 2020, we found a single specimen in the late fall from Horse Creek, Will County, Illinois. The Western Sand Darter is endangered in Illinois and Indiana. We consider this rare species vulnerable within the region due to its high dependence on natural riverine functions.

The specific localities where it is found are under threat by infrastructure projects (roads, bridges, etc.) that often prevent rivers from meandering, which is required to sequester and transport sand naturally.

References: Forbes and Richardson 1920; Kuehne and Barbour 1983; Lutterbie 1976; Page 1983; Smith 1979

Description: The Greenside Darter has a cylindrical body, a very blunt snout, and a rounded head. This species can be distinguished from all other darters by having the skin on the rear of the upper lip fused to the skin on the snout. Other characteristics include a complete lateral line, 6–7 green rectangular vertical bars, and distinct W-or V-shaped patterns along the sides. Body coloration can be light green, yellow, or tan, with rusty-orange spots above the lateral line. The breeding male becomes intense emerald green with a red-orange band near the base of each dorsal fin. It is the largest species within the genus *Etheostoma*, growing up to 7 inches (175 mm).

Natural History: The Greenside Darter lives in rivers and streams with swift to moderate currents. It was found among pondweed (*Potamogeton* spp.) beds in moderately swift current in the St. Joseph River, likely spawning. This species was also observed in Christiana Creek, Elkhart County, Indiana, inhabiting a very fast cobble riffle. Its diet is composed of aquatic insect larvae, particularly midge larvae. The Greenside Darter spawns during early spring in riffles, with the female attaching sticky fertilized eggs to filamentous algae or aquatic vegetation. This process is repeated multiple times with different partners. Males defend the territory

Greenside Darter records, 1979 (●) and 2003–2022 (●)

during spawning, but there is no parental care of eggs or young.

Distribution and Status: The Greenside Darter occurs in the southern Great Lakes, the Ohio River, disjunct populations on the Atlantic slope, and the Mississippi River in Missouri and Arkansas. There are 4 different subspecies described for the entire range, with *E. blennioides pholidotum* occurring in the Chicago Region. Regional records are restricted to the St. Joseph River system in Berrien County, Michigan, and St. Joseph County, Indiana. This species is naturally restricted within the Chicago Region, which is at the edge of its larger geographic range. It is considered sensitive to habitat and water-quality degradation.

References: Kuehne and Barbour 1983; Page 1983; Page and Burr 2011; Smith 1979; Trautman 1957; Turner 1921

Rainbow Darter

Etheostoma caeruleum · *Etheostoma* is Greek, meaning "a mouth that strains"; *caeruleum* is Latin, meaning "blue" referring to the fish's body and fin coloration.

Description: The Rainbow Darter has a robust body, deepest at the middle of the first dorsal fin; an incomplete lateral line; a premaxillary fleshy ridge (frenum); an uninterrupted indention around the eye (infraorbital canal); and 6–10 vertical bars evenly spaced along the side that are of uniform width from top to bottom. Coloration of females and nonbreeder males is typically brown to tan with dark markings. The breeding male, as the fish's common name implies, is among the most colorful and striking fishes in the Chicago Region. The anal fin is blue, with a distinct patch of red in the central portion. The throat becomes orange; the vertical bars, belly, and cheek are blue; and the dorsal fins are banded with red, white, and blue. This species can be distinguished from the similar Orangethroat Darter by having unscaled cheeks and red in the anal fin of adult fish. The uniform, evenly spaced lateral bands on Rainbow Darter differ from the irregular lateral bands of the similar Orangethroat Darter, which also has horizontal rows of small lateral spots, lacking on the Rainbow Darter. Although there are reported differences in pectoral ray count, 11–12 for the Orangethroat versus 13 for the Rainbow, we have found this characteristic to be somewhat unreliable within most of the Chicago Region. The adult Rainbow Darter rarely exceeds 3 inches (75 mm) in length.

Natural History: The Rainbow Darter lives in large rivers to small headwater creeks in swiftly flowing riffles over clean cobble and large gravel. Juveniles may be found in slower waters surrounding riffles, and in runs and glides. Food items include tiny aquatic insects, larval crayfish, and fish eggs. Spawning takes place in early spring, with the colorful males defending small, ill-defined territories in riffles. This is one of many darter species in which the males engage in sparring to defend their spawning territories. Eggs and sperm are deposited in gravel in short bursts. Seemingly unique to the Chicago Region, Rainbow Darters have been found in glacial lakes, although habitat specifics by the surveyors were not described.

Distribution and Status: The Rainbow Darter occurs in the Mississippi River, Ohio River, and Great Lakes basins. This species is relatively widespread throughout the Chicago Region, generally excluding lake plain and lowland areas. Chicago Region records are concentrated in the St. Joseph River, the lower Kankakee River, and tributaries to the Fox and Rock Rivers. Glacial-lake records of interest include Wolf Lake in Lake County, Indiana (FMNH 1900), and Lake Maxinkuckee in Marshall County, Indiana (DSJ 1890), and a handful of lakes in Walworth and Waukesha Counties, Wisconsin (USGSWI). Although considered sensitive to habitat and water-quality alterations, this species appears to be stable within the Chicago Region.

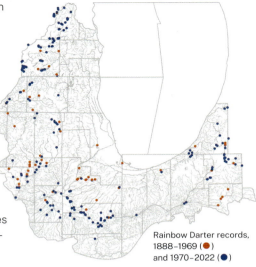

Rainbow Darter records, 1888–1969 (●) and 1970–2022 (●)

References: Kuehne and Barbour 1983; Page 1983; Page and Burr 2011; Smith 1979; Trautman 1957; Willink 2009

Bluntnose Darter

Etheostoma chlorosoma · *Etheostoma* is Greek, meaning "a mouth that strains"; *chlorosoma*, is also Greek, for "green bodied."

Description: The Bluntnose Darter is a slender fish with a very blunt snout extending slightly beyond the mouth. The lateral line is incomplete, not usually reaching the second dorsal fin. The anal fin contains 1 flexible spine. The body is opaque and very drab colored — mostly tan and yellow, with several dark saddles along the midline of the back. Irregular patches of dark pigment along the sides form X- and W-shaped marks. There is a dark line or bridle in front of the eyes that is connected above the lip. The most similar species is the Johnny Darter, which has a complete lateral line, an unconnected bridle above the mouth, a more pointed snout, and more distinct X and W markings on the side. Adults are 2 inches (50 mm) or less.

Natural History: The Bluntnose Darter inhabits backwaters, oxbows, and side channels of large rivers. This species has been observed in a backwater of the Kankakee River in dense aquatic vegetation over a silty bottom in about 3 feet (0.915 m) of water. Like other darters, it feeds on small aquatic invertebrates. Page, Retzer, and Stiles (1982) reported spawning on sunken twigs, leaves, and filamentous algae.

Distribution and Status: The Bluntnose Darter occurs in the Mississippi River basin from southern

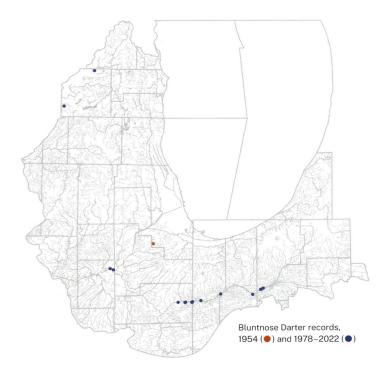

Bluntnose Darter records, 1954 (●) and 1978–2022 (●)

Wisconsin to Louisiana. Chicago Region records for this species are from a few localities in the upper Illinois and Kankakee Rivers. There is 1 old record from Marley Creek, Will County, Illinois (FMNH 1954), and 2 recent discoveries in Walworth County, Wisconsin: Mukwonago River (WDNR 2021) and Little Turtle Creek (WDNR 2017). It was likely once more widespread when backwaters and riverine wetlands were more abundantly connected, but now are at the limits of its larger North American distribution. It is considered uncommon and rare within Chicago Region, with only 20 total records. The Bluntnose Darter is listed as endangered in Wisconsin. Additional information on its distribution and habits within the region is needed.

References: Becker 1983; Forbes and Richardson 1920; Kuehne and Barbour 1983; Page 1983; Page and Burr 2011; Page, Retzer, and Stiles 1982; Smith 1979

Iowa Darter

Etheostoma exile · *Etheostoma*, Greek, meaning "a mouth that strains"; *exile* means "slim."

Description: The Iowa Darter has a slender body and a rounded snout. Distinguishing characteristics include an incomplete lateral line extending to the gap between the dorsal fins; 8–9 dorsal spines; a scaled cheek, gill cover, and nape; a groove in upper lip broken by a wide, fleshy frenum; and a distinct teardrop below the eye. Pigment markings include mottling on the body and 10–12 square-shaped orange blotches along the sides. The body color is olive to tan above and yellow below. Breeding males develop blue and red alternating blotches along the sides and a smattering of orange-red pigment along the edge of the belly. The first dorsal fin becomes banded with blue at the base and tip, with an orange band in the center; the second dorsal fin spots become orange. A typical adult's length is less than 3 inches (75 mm).

Natural History: The Iowa Darter lives in glacial lakes and connecting sloughs, and other small lowland streams. In glacial lakes and sloughs, it is associated with clear water and abundant native vegetation. In flowing streams, it has been observed among aquatic vegetation and woody debris. Forage includes midge larvae, amphipods, aquatic insect larvae, and crustaceans. Spawning takes place in spring months. Males establish breeding territories in shallow waters

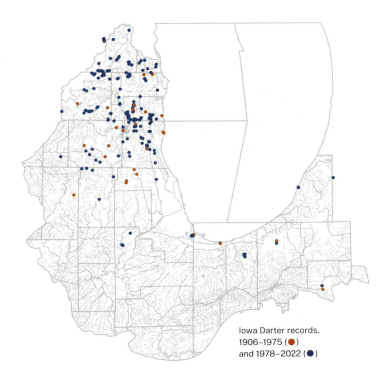

Iowa Darter records,
1906–1975 (●)
and 1978–2022 (●)

along the edges of lakes or streams, usually over root masses with aquatic vegetation. Typically, a few eggs at a time are deposited and fertilized simultaneously on vegetation by a single female accompanied by multiple males. This species does not exhibit territoriality or nest guarding.

Distribution and Status: The Iowa Darter occurs in the Great Lakes basin, upper Mississippi basin, Hudson Bay basin, and the Mackenzie River system in Canada. This is the most northern and western naturally occurring of all darter species. The Chicago Region is at the southern limits of this species' natural distribution, with most records from the high-moraine glacial lakes of northern Illinois and southern Wisconsin. It is uncommon elsewhere, but records are consistent over time. This species was formerly listed as endangered in Illinois but has since been removed.

References: Bland and Willink 2018; Cahn 1927; Hatch and Johnson 2014; Kuehne and Barbour 1983; Lutterbie 1976; Page 1983; Pearse 1918; Sherwood et al. 2018; Tiemann, Taylor, et al. 2015; Turner 1921

DARTERS AND PERCHES (PERCIDAE)

Description: The Fantail Darter has a long cylindrical body and a pointed snout. This species can be distinguished from all other Chicago Region darters by having egg-mimic structures, or gold knobs, on the spines of the first dorsal fin. Other distinguishing traits include the lower jaw being longer than the upper jaw, the first dorsal fin being lower than the second, an incomplete lateral line, a rounded tail, and small spots that form horizontal lines along the body. Body coloration is typically dark olive to brown, with light orange on the belly and fins. The tail fin is elaborately spotted in concentric rows, giving the visual of a rounded fan. Sometimes there can be 8–16 dusky vertical triangular bars along the sides. Breeding-male body coloration darkens, the orange pigment becoming more intense; the dorsal fin knobs become enlarged and turn orange. Adults rarely exceed 3 inches (70 mm).

Natural History: The Fantail Darter lives primarily in small upland streams and headwater creeks but can be found in rivers. It occupies shallow areas of slow to moderate current with cobble, flag, or bedrock stone. Its diet is like other darters, mostly small invertebrates. Spawning takes place in early to midspring. The male establishes his position underneath a rock with showy orange egg

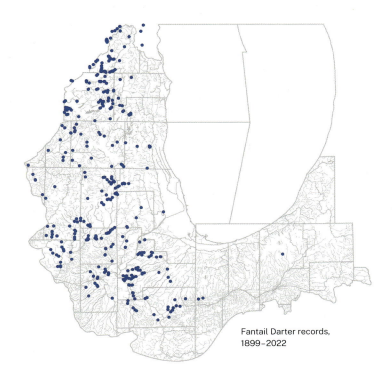

Fantail Darter records, 1899–2022

mimics, attracting the female to the nest. A single layer of eggs is deposited by the female upside down on the bottom side of the rock. The male simultaneously fertilizes the eggs and then guards them until hatching.

Distribution and Status: The Fantail Darter occurs in the middle Mississippi River, Ohio River, and southern Great Lakes basins. Chicago Region records are widespread in Illinois and Wisconsin, sparse in Indiana, and absent from Berrien County, Michigan. This species is considered stable and usually abundant where found.

References: Kuehne and Barbour 1983; Page 1983; Page and Burr 2011; Smith 1979; Trautman 1957

Description: The Least Darter is the smallest of all darter species, growing no larger than 1.5 inches (38 mm). It has a blunt, rounded head, a small mouth, and a very short lateral line (0–3 pores). Other characteristics include a premaxillary frenum, 5–6 soft anal rays, 5–7 dorsal spines, and 30–38 lateral scales. Normal body coloration is olive brown above and white below. The back and sides are mottled, and there is a prominent teardrop below each eye. The dorsal and tail fins have rows of spots. Breeding-male body coloration becomes more intense, with a red band on the first dorsal fin and a reddish hue to the lower fins. The male also develops long, pointed pectoral fins that reach to the anus.

Natural History: The Least Darter inhabits rivers, prairie sloughs, glacial lakes, and connecting channels. It is most often associated with dense aquatic vegetation such as Coontail (*Ceratophyllum demersum*) or Canadian Waterweed (*Elodea canadensis*) in sluggish to still waters. It also inhabits prairie sloughs and agriculture ditches where patches of aquatic vegetation grow on silt bars. This species was also observed bouncing on the bottom of a sandy shoreline of a glacial lake in Wisconsin. Food items are primarily

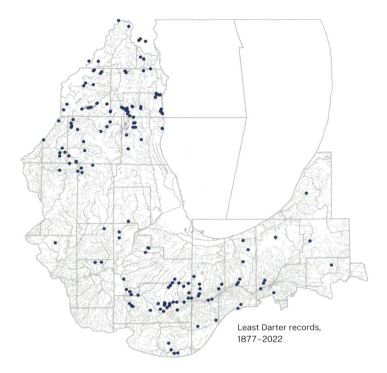

Least Darter records, 1877–2022

aquatic insect larvae and microcrustaceans. Spawning takes place in May, with individual eggs laid on vegetation in shallow water.

Distribution and Status: The Least Darter occurs primarily in the Great Lakes basin, with disjunct populations in the Hudson Bay, Ohio River, and Mississippi River. Records exist throughout the Chicago Region where habitat is favorable, especially in the glacial lakes of northern Illinois and Wisconsin and in the prairie streams of the Kankakee River. It is rarely found in abundance at any given location. Although considered stable, the Least Darter may be vulnerable to loss of aquatic vegetation due to stream channelization, herbicide use, and other shoreline-clearing activities.

References: Burr and Page 1979; Kuehne and Barbour 1983; Page 1983; Page and Burr 2011; Smith 1979; Tiemann, Taylor, et al. 2015; Trautman 1957

Johnny Darter

Etheostoma nigrum • *Etheostoma*, Greek, meaning "a mouth that strains"; *nigrum*, "black" in Latin, likely referring to breeding-male coloration.

Description: The Johnny Darter is a small, slender fish with distinctive black W- and X-shaped marks along the sides. The lateral line is complete. The body is pale, light brown or straw colored, scattered with small spots of pigment. There are 6–8 moderately dark bands of pigment along the back. Faint spots are also found on the dorsal, caudal, and pectoral fins. The anal fin has only 1 spine. The cheek is scaleless and with no teardrop marking below the eye. The snout is rounded, and the mouth is horizontal with an upper lip completely separated from the snout (no frenum). Breeding males are very dark in color, especially in the head region. The Johnny Darter can be distinguished from the similar Bluntnose and Iowa Darters by having a complete lateral line. Adults are typically less than 3 inches (75 mm) in length.

Natural History: The Johnny Darter inhabits rivers, streams, and lakes in the Chicago Region. This species has been observed along the bottom in slow- to moderately moving stream segments over finer substrates. It can also be found among rocks, woody debris, aquatic vegetation, and other objects. In lakes it can be observed along sandy beaches. It has been found as deep as 90 feet (27 m) of water in Lake Michigan. Food consists of midges and other small aquatic invertebrates. Spawning

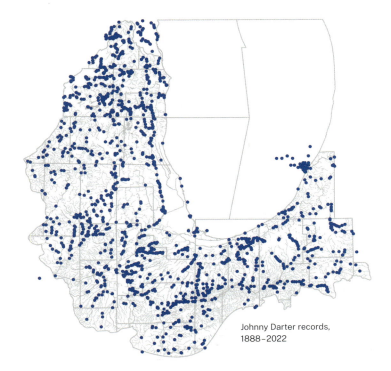

Johnny Darter records, 1888–2022

takes place in spring, with eggs deposited and fertilized on the undersides of rocks and stones.

Distribution and Status: The Johnny Darter occurs in the Hudson Bay, Great Lakes, Mississippi River, and Ohio River basins. Owing to its adaptability and tolerance to moderately degraded habitat and water-quality conditions, it has the widest distribution of any of the darters in the region. In general, it is absent only from highly degraded and manmade water bodies such as the Chicago Area Waterway System. This species is considered common and abundant, with more than 2,600 records.

References: Kuehne and Barbour 1983; Page 1983; Page and Burr 2011; Smith 1979; Trautman 1957

Orangethroat Darter

Etheostoma spectabile · *Etheostoma*, Greek, "a mouth that strains"; *spectabile*, Latin for "conspicuous."

Description: The Orangethroat Darter has a robust body, deepest at the nape before the first dorsal fin, and incomplete lateral line, a frenum, an interrupted infraorbital canal, and 6–9 irregular vertical bars crosscutting the side. Vertical bars are narrower than the spaces between and are not uniform in width, tapering at the bottom. Coloration of females and nonbreeder males is typically brown to tan with dark markings. The breeding male develops blue and orange alternating lateral bars, an orange throat and belly, blue and orange stripes in the dorsal fins, and a blue anal fin. This species can be distinguished from the similar Rainbow Darter by having partially scaled cheeks and a lack of red in the anal fin. The Orangethroat Darter also has horizontal rows of small dots along the lateral surface, which are lacking in the Rainbow Darter. Additionally, the vertical lateral bars of the Rainbow Darter are wider, evenly spaced, and of uniform width from top to bottom, in contrast to the irregular spike-shaped bars of the Orangethroat Darter. Adults rarely exceed 3 inches (75 mm) in length.

Natural History: The Orangethroat Darter lives in streams and headwater creeks. It has been observed in bedrock cascades with slow to moderate current, in rocky riffles with fast currents, and in a cold head-

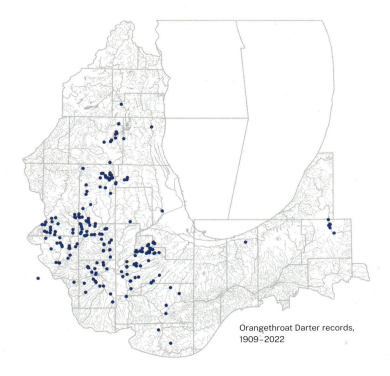

Orangethroat Darter records, 1909–2022

water stream over gravel with moderate current. Food consists of small stream organisms such as macroinvertebrates, copepods, and amphipods. Spawning within the Chicago Region occurs from February thru April, where males define small territories and display aggression toward other males. The female deposits her eggs in soft gravel by partially burrowing into it, while the male fertilizes simultaneously.

Distribution and Status: The Orangethroat Darter is a Grand Prairie species, occurring in the middle Mississippi and Ohio River basins, with disjunct populations in the Texas Gulf drainages and southwestern Lake Erie. Records within the Chicago Region are primarily from smaller tributaries to the Fox River, lower Kankakee River, lower Des Plaines River, Mazon River, and Aux Sable Creek. It is largely absent from lowland streams and degraded urban areas of Chicago. The Orangethroat Darter is listed as threatened in Michigan. This species is considered sensitive to habitat and water-quality degradation but currently stable within the region.

References: Kuehne and Barbour 1983; Page 1983; Page and Burr 2011; Smith 1979; Trautman 1957

Banded Darter

Etheostoma zonale • *Etheostoma*, Greek, meaning "a mouth that strains"; *zonale*, Latin, meaning "banded."

Description: The Banded Darter has a fusiform body that is dusky olive and mottled on the top and sides. The dorsal and lateral surface have 9–11 irregular green bands, which run the entire depth of the body. It has scales on the cheek and a weak suborbital teardrop. The mouth is nearly horizontal, with the upper lip connected to the tip of the blunt snout (frenum). The spiny dorsal fin has 1 dusky band close to the body surface, which in breeding males becomes bright red. Breeders become dark emerald green, the vertical green bars along the sides becoming darker. Banded Darters may be distinguished from the Orangethroat and Rainbow Darters by having green coloration, a fully scaled cheek, and a blunter snout. Greenside Darter has less than 9 lateral bars and has a fused upper lip. Adults are typically less than 2.5 inches (63 mm) in length.

Natural History: The Banded Darter lives in rivers and larger tributary streams. It is found in fast-moving riffle areas with boulders, cobble, and gravel, often associated with attached filamentous algae or aquatic vegetation. It has been observed in agricultural ditches with developed riffles. Food consists of midge larvae and other small invertebrate prey. Breeding is later than other darters, taking place in late spring, when eggs are laid and fertil-

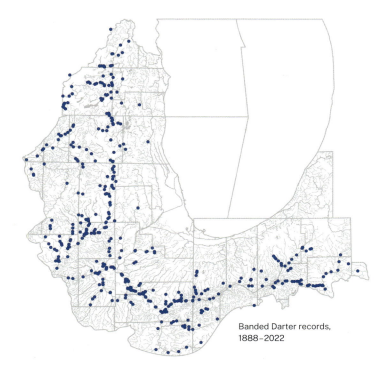

Banded Darter records, 1888–2022

ized on algae and aquatic vegetation. The Banded Darter can tolerate turbidity and some water-quality degradation but cannot tolerate habitat degradation, as it is a riverine obligate requiring fast water velocities in riffles.

Distribution and Status: The Banded Darter occurs in 3 disjunct populations: the upper Mississippi River basin, the Ozarks, and the Ohio River basin. This species is not native to the Great Lakes basin and does not occur in Lake Michigan drainages. Records for the Chicago Region are concentrated along the mainstems and larger tributaries of the Kankakee, Fox, Illinois, and Kishwaukee Rivers. The Banded Darter is relatively abundant where found.

References: Kuehne and Barbour 1983; Page 1983; Page and Burr 2011; Smith 1979; Trautman 1957

Yellow Perch

Perca flavescens · *Perca*, Greek, meaning "perch" or general nondescript fish; *flavescens*, Latin, "yellowish."

Description: The Yellow Perch has a fusiform body, with a mouth that extends to the middle of the eye. The nape is humped, which is more pronounced in older individuals. The soft dorsal fin has 12–14 rays and the anal fin has 6–8 rays. Yellow Perch coloration is dark olive above and green interspersed with yellow on the sides, broken by 6–7 dark triangular saddles over the back and sides. The belly is white. The lower fins are typically orange. Coloration can be muted depending on water turbidity. This species can be distinguished from the Walleye and the Sauger by the dorsal saddle count, the soft dorsal ray count, and the anal ray count, as well as having a more laterally compressed body and lacking canine teeth. Adults in Lake Michigan can exceed 14 inches (355 mm), while those found inland are typically much smaller, 3–8 inches (75–200 mm).

Natural History: The Yellow Perch can live in all types of water bodies, including lakes, ponds, rivers, streams, canals, and agricultural ditches. In most habitats it is associated with vegetation over fine-grained substrates. In Lake Michigan, it inhabits river mouths, rocky shorelines, weed beds, clay mounds, and

Yellow Perch records, 1877–2022

deep sandy flats up to 70 feet (22 m) deep. Spawning takes place in spring to early summer, usually at night, in shallow water less than 10 feet (3 m) deep with little or no current. A single female lays eggs in a strand with distinctive folds like an accordion, which are fertilized by multiple males. The fertilized strand comes to rest on vegetation, brush, or rocks, where it sticks in place. There is no parental care. Young fry feed on crustaceans, switching to insect larvae and amphipods as they grow. The adult Yellow Perch adds fish to its diet, although it continues to eat insect larvae, crayfishes, mollusks, and isopods. Foraging usually takes place during the day along or near the bottom.

Distribution and Status: The Yellow Perch occurs throughout Canada and the United States from the Rockies to the Atlantic slope and has been introduced widely inside and outside its native range. Records within the Chicago Region are concentrated in Lake Michigan and the high-moraine glacial lakes, especially in Wisconsin. The Yellow Perch is a popular sport fish and well known for its delicate flavor. The populations in Lake Michigan once supported a productive commercial and recreational fishery but have since declined due to overfishing and completion from introduced fishes. Reduced lake productivity and filter feeding by Zebra (*Dreissena polymorpha*) and Quagga (*Dreissena bugensis*) Mussels may also be a factor. Populations in rivers and streams do not support recreational or commercial fisheries, as their size and abundance are small. This species is considered stable. Lake Michigan populations are highly managed and research into limiting factors is ongoing.

References: Becker 1983; Breder and Rosen 1966; Forbes and Richardson 1920; Herman 1978; C. E. Johnson 1970; Parks 1949; Pearse 1918, 1921b; Pearse and Achtenberg 1920; Wells 1968; Wilberg et al. 2005; Woods 1957a

Logperch

Percina caprodes • *Percina*, Latin, diminutive for "perch"; *caprodes*, Greek for "pig-like," referring to the fish's snout.

Description: The Logperch has a long, cylindrical body and a protruding conical snout. Overall coloration is tan olive, fading to a pale white on the belly. A dusky, indistinct blotch is present below each eye. Dorsal and caudal fins have faint-brown bands, and there is a distinct small black spot at the base of the caudal fin. It can be distinguished from other Chicago Region darters by having 15–20 distinctive brown saddles over the back and down the sides, and a modified breast scale between the pelvic fins. The Logperch is the largest darter species within the Chicago Region, attaining a length of up to 7 inches (180 mm).

Natural History: The Logperch inhabits rivers and large glacial lakes. In rivers, it has been observed in fast-flowing rocky riffles, but it is more common in moderately flowing sandy runs with woody debris, and sluggish areas with some aquatic vegetation. In Lake Michigan, this species has been observed along sandy bars and beaches with limited wave action. The diet consists of insect larvae and other microcrustaceans; the Logperch forages by using its long snout to overturn rocks or dig into sandy substrate. Spawning takes place in the spring, when the male and female bury eggs and sperm in the sand, vibrating to

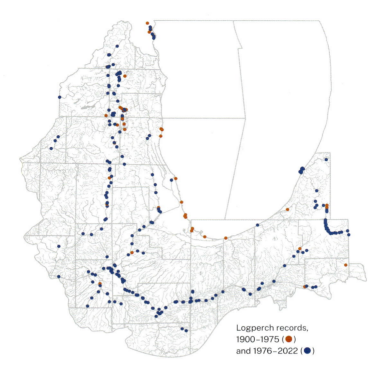

Logperch records, 1900–1975 (●) and 1976–2022 (●)

help stir up and cover the eggs with substrate.

Distribution and Status: The Logperch occurs throughout the Mississippi River, Great Lakes, and Hudson Bay basins. It is possible there are multiple species present throughout its North American range. Records within the Chicago Region are widespread, but concentrated along the mainstems of the Fox, Kankakee, and St. Joseph Rivers. In recent years, this species has expanded into the upper Des Plaines River in Illinois due to water-quality improvement and dam removals. We consider this species stable and expanding within the region.

References: Trautman 1957; Smith 1979; Page 1983; Kuehne and Barbour 1983; Page and Burr 2011

Blackside Darter

Percina maculata · *Percina*, Latin, diminutive for "perch"; *maculata*, Latin, meaning "spotted."

Description: The Blackside Darter has a cylindrical body and a rounded snout. Identifying characteristics include 13–15 dorsal spines, 2 anal spines, and a discontinuous groove (frenum) in the upper lip. The coloration is dusky olive on the back grading to a tan or cream belly. There are 8–9 dark dorsal saddles interspersed by pigmented wavy lines. The dorsal and caudal fins are dusky, and there is a well-developed teardrop below the eye. There is a distinct black spot at the base of the tail fin. This species can be distinguished from other Chicago Region darters by having 6–9 large and interconnected black blotches along the lateral line, and a modified breast scale between the pelvic fins. Adults can reach up to 4 inches (100 mm).

Natural History: The Blackside Darter primarily inhabits large streams and rivers but is sometimes found in smaller streams. It has been observed mostly in areas of lower water velocities — usually over sand and silt associated with woody debris and leaf litter. It has been reported to swim up to midwater and feed on immature aquatic insects and small crustaceans. Spawning takes place in the spring in pools or slow runs, where eggs are deposited in gravel

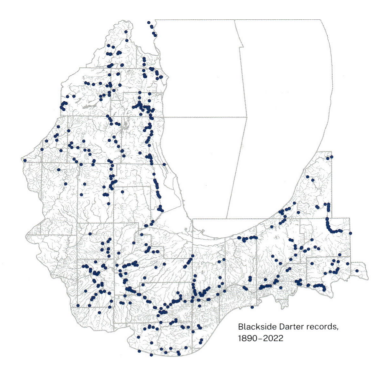

Blackside Darter records, 1890–2022

or sand. No parental care has been reported.

Distribution and Status: The Blackside Darter occurs in the Mississippi River, Ohio River, Hudson Bay, and Great Lakes basins. Records are widespread throughout the Chicago Region, with one of the first records taken by the Field Museum's O. P. Hay in 1896 from the Kankakee River, Lake County, Indiana. This species is considered regionally stable.

References: Trautman 1957; Page 1983; Kuehne and Barbour 1983; Page and Burr 2011

Description: The Slenderhead Darter has a long cylindrical body with a slender head and pointed snout. Identifying characteristics include 12–13 dorsal spines, 2 anal spines, a partially scaled breast, and a discontinuous grove (frenum) in the upper lip. Body coloration is light olive brown to tan, with a distinct caudal spot. The back is mottled with pigment. The snout has a dark bridle in front of the eye, whereas the teardrop marking is faint to absent. This species can be distinguished from other Chicago Region darters by having 10–16 distinctive brown blotches along the sides, a slender orange line near the outer margin of the first dorsal fin, and a modified breast scale between the pelvic fins. Typical adult size is 3–4 inches (75–100 mm).

Natural History: The Slenderhead Darter inhabits rivers in slack eddies of fast, rocky riffles where sand and small gravel settles out in bars. This species, similar to other darters, consumes immature aquatic insects and small crustaceans. Spawning takes place primarily in late spring over course gravel substrates in areas with faster currents.

Distribution and Status: The Slenderhead Darter occurs in the Mississippi and Ohio River basins, and in select rivers from the Lake Michigan drainage. Records within

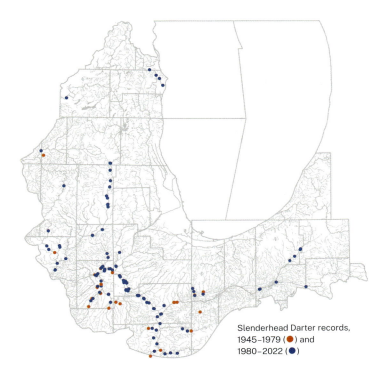

Slenderhead Darter records, 1945–1979 (●) and 1980–2022 (●)

the Chicago Region are primarily in the Mazon, Fox, and Kankakee Rivers. The records for the Root River system of Lake Michigan are recent in Racine County, Wisconsin (USGSWI 2002), and Kenosha County, Wisconsin (USGSWI 2001). This species is rarely abundant where it occurs, likely due to its habitat specificity; however, persistent records indicate stability throughout the region. The Slenderhead Darter is more intolerant than the other *Percina* species, being found only where natural fluvial processes are unimpeded.

References: Trautman 1957; Smith 1979; Page 1983; Kuehne and Barbour 1983; Page and Burr 2011

Sauger

Sander canadensis · *Sander*, after the European relative the Zander; *canadensis*, "from Canada"

Description: The Sauger has a cylindrical body with a large, canine-toothed mouth that extends past the middle of a glassy eye. The soft dorsal fin has 17–19 rays, and the anal fin has 11–12 rays. The body coloration is dark above, olive interspersed with tan and bronze flecks on the sides, and bright white on the belly. Coloration can be muted, depending on water turbidity. This species can be distinguished from the Walleye by having the first dorsal fin with distinct black half-moon-like blotches, 3–4 dark irregular saddles over the back and sides, a mottled pattern along the sides, and a fine white line (sometimes absent) along the lower tail fin. Body length can reach 18–22 inches (450–550 mm). The Saugeye is a hybrid between the Sauger and the Walleye and is difficult to distinguish.

Natural History: The Sauger lives in large-river and lake habitats throughout its natural range. Within the Chicago Region it is found only in riverine habitats, utilizing submerged structures such as large woody debris, bridge abutments, and large rocks. The Sauger is more tolerant of turbidity than the Walleye and less dependent on fast-flowing water for foraging and spawning. In the Des Plaines River it is often found in deeper runs, not directly associated with riffles or strong currents. Its

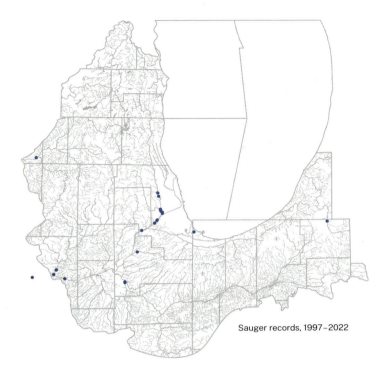

Sauger records, 1997–2022

food habits are very similar to the Walleye's. The Sauger is typically less dependent than the Walleye on strong, stable flows for spawning.

Distribution and Status: The Sauger occurs in the Mississippi River, Ohio River, Great Lakes, and Hudson Bay basins. Although the Chicago Region is within the native range of this species, no historic records exist for it, due to the lack of large-river habitats. The first records for the region are from state of Illinois stocking programs initiated in 1997 in the Des Plaines River. Although the Sauger is naturally limited by habitat availability within the Chicago Region, populations are maintained through annual stocking in both the Des Plaines and Illinois Rivers. This species is listed as endangered in Michigan.

References: Trautman 1957; Eddy and Underhill 974; Smith 1979; Page and Burr 2011

Walleye

Sander vitreus · *Sander*, after the European relative the Zander; *vitreus*, Latin for "glassy," referring to the reflective eye.

Description: The Walleye has a cylindrical body, with a large, canine-toothed mouth that extends past the middle of the eye. This perch is named for its large glassy eye, which has a retina coated by a reflective crystalline matter called the tapetum lucidum. The soft dorsal fin has 19–23 rays; the anal fin has 12–14 rays. Body coloration is dark green above, green interspersed with gold on the sides, and bright white on the belly. Coloration can be muted, depending on water turbidity. This species can be distinguished from the Sauger by having a distinct blotch on the last 2–3 membranes of the first dorsal fin, 5–12 diffuse saddles over the back, much less mottling along the sides, and a distinctive white patch on the lower tail fin. Adults can reach 28 inches (700 mm) or larger in favorable habitats. The hybrid Saugeye is intermediate in appearance between Walleye and Sauger, making identification difficult.

Natural History: The Walleye inhabits large to medium rivers and lakes. In rivers, it prefers deep areas with moderate current. Structure such as woody debris, bridge abutments, and large rocks provides cover. In lakes, it is found along deep rocky shores and weed beds. The Walleye will travel long distances in search of forage and spawning habitat. Dams often hamper its movement and reproductive success. Its diet consists primarily of fish; however, it will feed on crayfish, worms, and large invertebrates throughout its life. The reflective eye is adapted to low-light conditions, allowing this fish to be crepuscular — that is, actively feeding at dawn and twilight. The Walleye typically seeks out rocky riffles and runs of rivers to spawn. Recruitment is limited within the Chicago Region, most likely due to dams and highly variable flows during spring spawning season, as they are dependent on stable higher flows for successful recruitment. Young fish grow rapidly, reaching 6–8 inches (150–200 mm) in the first year.

Distribution and Status: The Walleye occurs throughout Canada and the United States from the Rockies to the Atlantic slope. It has been introduced widely inside and outside its native range. Records for this species within the Chicago Region are concentrated along the mainstem of the Fox, Kankakee, and St. Joseph Rivers, and

Walleye records, 1895–2022

along the shoreline of Lake Michigan. Due to low natural reproduction of this species, some rivers and lakes within the Chicago Region receive supplemental hatchery stocking to enhance angling opportunities — notably, the Fox Chain O' Lakes, the Fox River, and the Kankakee River. In the Kankakee River, hatchery fish made up 70% of the population (Illinois DNR). The Walleye is a highly sought species for its flavorful flesh and the sport it provides to anglers. We consider this species stable within the region. Saugeye are hybrids between the Walleye and the Sauger that can occur naturally or are bred in hatcheries and then stocked, which can occasionally be found.

References: Trautman 1957; Eddy and Underhill 1974; Page and Burr 2011

DARTERS AND PERCHES (PERCIDAE)   417

33

Sticklebacks

Gasterosteidae

Sticklebacks are known for their complex courtship and territorial defensive behaviors, which are often studied in the laboratory. True to their name, these fishes have 3–16 individual dorsal spines, in front of a rear dorsal fin of 14–16 soft rays. They have a pointed snout with large eyes. Their bodies are deep in the front, tapering to a very narrow region just in front of the tail, giving them a very distinctive shape. The body is scaleless, although some have large bony plates on the sides. Stickleback feeding habits are varied, including benthic invertebrates or plankton. The male builds nests of sticks and vegetation held together by adhesive excretions; they then guard the nest and tend to the young. Sticklebacks can be very aggressive, attacking and driving off much larger fishes.

The stickleback family includes 5 genera and 12 species, although their taxonomy is rather complicated. They inhabit freshwater and marine habitats in the Northern Hemisphere (Holarctic), with 3 species in the Chicago Region, where they inhabit a range of habitats from small streams to the open waters of Lake Michigan. They tend to prefer cool to coldwater streams like Lake Michigan and the northern areas of the region. Two of the three species are native.

Brook Stickleback

Culaea inconstans • *Culaea* is a partial anagram from its former generic name *Eucalia*; *inconstans* means "variable" in Latin.

Description: The Brook Stickleback is a small, delicate-looking fish with a row of 4–6 spines (modally 5) along the back, constituting the first dorsal fin. The second dorsal fin lacks spines, and the anal fin has only 1 spine. Each pelvic fin has 1 spiny ray and 1 soft ray. Its body is tall and laterally compressed, tapering considerably near the tail, lacking a lateral keel. It has an upturned mouth; below the neck, the membrane between the gill covers has a deep furrow and is not attached to the breast. No scales are present on the body. The tail fin is moderately round or sometimes more angular. The body coloration is green with small pale blotches. Its belly is white with no distinct pattern. Breeding males are much darker, with pale fins. The Brook Stickleback can be distinguished from the other 2 Chicago Region sticklebacks by the dorsal spine count and the lack of a lateral keel in the tail area. Adult size is typically 3 inches (75 mm) long.

Natural History: The Brook Stickleback is most common in smaller streams with cool, clear water and abundant vegetation. It can also be found in wetlands and along the calmer margins of lakes. In cooler water habitats it is often very abundant and may be the dominant species. Food consists of aquatic insect larvae, crustaceans, and algae. Spawning takes place in the late spring to early summer. The male

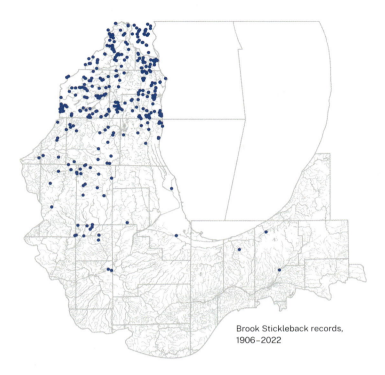

Brook Stickleback records, 1906–2022

builds a spherical nest of plant material attached to a stalk of vegetation. The entry to the nest is a small single hole. The male guards the nest and nearby territory. When a female approaches the nest, a very complicated courtship ensues. If the female is courted, she enters the nest and lays eggs. She will either exit out the original entrance or may make a second hole. The male repairs the second hole and remains to guard the nest and eggs until the young swim away. The mating ritual itself is quite complex and has been the topic of numerous research studies.

Distribution and Status: The Brook Stickleback occurs in the Arctic and Atlantic drainages, and in the Great Lakes, upper Mississippi River, and upper Ohio River basins. Records for this species are most common in cold and cool headwater streams of Wisconsin and the upper Fox River in Illinois. This species was first recorded from the Chicago Region in 1906 from Nippersink Creek, Walworth County, Wisconsin (USGSWI). There are scattered records in the south and east of the Chicago Region. We have observed this species in bait buckets. Its status is secure.

References: Pearse 1918; Forbes and Richardson 1920; Smith 1979; Becker 1983

Threespine Stickleback

Gasterosteus aculeatus • *Gasterosteus* means "bony belly" in Greek; *aculeatus* means "with spines" in Greek.

Field Museum Specimen #144766

Description: The Threespine Stickleback, true to its name, typically has 3 spines along the back, constituting the first dorsal fin. The second dorsal fin lacks spines. This species has many of the same features as the Brook Stickleback: having 1 anal fin spine and 1 pelvic fin spine, with a tall, laterally compressed body tapering considerably at the tail area. However, unlike the Brook Stickleback's tail area, the Threespine Stickleback's has a lateral keel. Its tail fin is slightly rounded to square, with a small indentation at the center. The mouth is upturned, and the gill membranes are attached to the breast. It also lacks scales but may have a series of bony plates along the lateral surface. The Threespine Stickleback is brownish green in color, with dark mottling that can coalesce to form diffuse bands or saddles. The breeding male is blue with a red belly. The Threespine Stickleback is the only stickleback with a gill membrane connected to the breast. The 3 dorsal spines also distinguish it from the other species. It grows to 3 inches (75 mm).

Natural History: Threespine Sticklebacks live in marine oceans and bays and freshwater lakes and sometimes rivers. This species inhab-

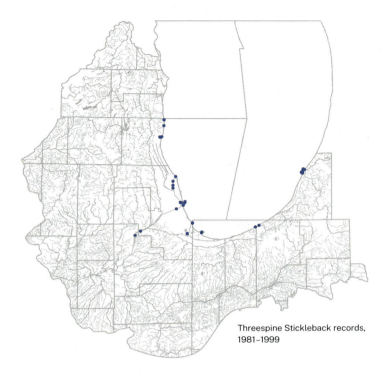

Threespine Stickleback records, 1981–1999

its the near shore of Lake Michigan and infrequently uses confluent tributaries. Forage consists of crustaceans and aquatic insects. Spawning takes place during the summer; typical stickleback behavior is displayed, including nest building, complex courtship, and parental care by the males.

Distribution and Status: The Threespine Stickleback is widespread, occurring naturally in Pacific, Arctic, and Atlantic drainages, and in the Hudson Bay and Lake Ontario. This species is considered to have been introduced to the Lake Michigan drainage, where it is most abundant along the shoreline, particularly along rocky breakwaters and revetments. It can also be found in tributaries such as the Chicago Area Waterway System. Native to Lake Ontario, it is believed to have entered the upper Great Lakes via ballast water. The first records from the Chicago Region were taken in 1981 from the Calumet River (INHS). Its status is introduced but not invasive, and we last recorded it in 1999 (INHS).

References: Laird and Page 1996; Hubbs, Lagler, and Smith 2004; Holm, Mandrak, and Burridge 2009; Madenjian et al. 2012

Ninespine Stickleback

Pungitius pungitius • *Pungitius*, Latin, means "pricking."

Description: The Ninespine Stickleback is very similar to the other sticklebacks except for the greater number of dorsal spines, ranging from 8 to 11, modally 9. The other fins are typical of the sticklebacks: 1 spine in each of the pelvic fins and 1 spine in the anal fin. The tail fin is also rounded, with a small indentation at the center. The body is tall and laterally compressed; a very narrow tail region contains lateral keels. Neither scales nor armoring plates are present. The mouth is upturned, and the gill membranes are not attached to the breast, below the neck. The body is greenish in color, with roughly 6 dark blotches along the back forming wavy saddles. The belly is white. Breeding males are very dark colored, with white pelvic fins. The Ninespine Stickleback can be distinguished from the other 2 sticklebacks by the number of dorsal spines (9 versus 3 and 5). Adult size is 3 inches (76.2 mm).

Natural History: The Ninespine Stickleback lives in the cold waters of marine oceans and bays, and freshwater streams, lakes, and ponds. It occupies shallow vegetated areas, as well as deeper water over sand. In Lake Michigan it has been found in waters more than 265 feet (80 m) deep. Its forage includes aquatic insects, especially midge larvae and crustaceans. Spawning takes place

Ninespine Stickleback records, 1936–2022

in late spring in deep or shallow water. In deeper water with finer substrates, the male may build a burrow. In shallower water with rocks and vegetation, the male uses plant material to build a nest between or under rocks. Spawning behaviors are typical of the other sticklebacks, including nest building, complex courtship displays, and parental care by the males. Marine populations are anadromous.

Distribution and Status: The Ninespine Stickleback occurs in the Arctic, Atlantic, and Pacific drainages of North America and Eurasia, the Hudson Bay, and the Great Lakes except for Lake Erie. Records within the Chicago Region are restricted to Lake Michigan. It is rarely found in tributaries. Records are few (81) but were consistent from the 1970s to the 2000s. The status of the Ninespine Stickleback is seemingly stable, but as a coldwater species it is under threat from warming temperatures due to climate change.

References: Forbes and Richardson 1920; Woods 1957b; Anderson and Smith 1971; Smith 1979; Becker 1983; Madenjian et al. 2012

STICKLEBACKS (GASTEROSTEIDAE)   425

34

Sculpins

Cottidae

Sculpins have a unique body shape with a large, flat head, a large mouth, and large pectoral fins. Unlike most fishes, sculpin eyes sit high on the head rather than on the sides. The body is usually scaleless but can have some modified scales, and/or prickles. The first dorsal fin is supported by soft spinous rays; the rear dorsal fin has soft rays. Stiff spines are present on the face and cheek. Some of these spines tend to be relatively short, and some are covered by skin. In general, sculpins have a mottled body pattern, usually with browns, oranges, reds, white, or black, which helps camouflage them from prey and predator alike. The reduced swim bladder and large pectoral fins aid in exploiting bottom habitats, especially in fast-moving water. As such, sculpins live along a range of substrate types, typically using rocks, woody debris, and vegetation for cover. They are ambush predators, capturing their prey with a short, swift burst. Inland species prefer cooler, groundwater-fed streams.

The sculpin family includes about 74 genera, with 280 species worldwide. Most of these are marine, living in northern oceans, including the Pacific, the Atlantic, and the Arctic, with a few species in New Zealand. These fishes appeared in the fossil record during the middle Oligocene epoch of the Tertiary period, or about 25 million years ago. The sculpins are represented in the Chicago Region by 4 native freshwater species within 2 genera.

Sculpins also have a rather unique distribution pattern in the Chicago Region, due in part to their preference for cooler water habitats. The Mottled Sculpin is the only true stream species, occurring primarily in the northern part of the region in Wisconsin, the lower Fox River in Illinois, and the areas south of Lake Michigan in Indiana and Michigan where cooler streams with groundwater inputs are found. The other 3 species inhabit Lake Michigan, where they were once quite abundant. Their numbers have seemingly decreased since the 1990s, when the Round Goby was introduced.

Mottled Sculpin

Cottus bairdii · *Cottus* is Greek for "bull's head"; *bairdii* is in honor of Spencer F. Baird, a famous fish biologist and the first US Fish Commissioner.

Description: The Mottled Sculpin has a flattened, large head and a robust body that tapers toward the tail. There is 1 short opercular spine pointing back, with 1–2 small spines below pointing down. The body is without scales except for a few prickles below the lateral line. The lateral line is incomplete, ending under the second dorsal fin, and having 14–27 pores. The dorsal fins are interconnected, with the second being long and low. The pelvic fins usually have 4 rays. Coloration is mottled brown, often with 2–4 distinct saddles and widely scattered light spots. There are rows of orange-red blotches on the second dorsal fin and tail. The first dorsal fin of breeding males is darker along the base and orange along the margin. The Mottled Sculpin is more mottled than the Slimy Sculpin and has 4 versus 3 pelvic fin rays. Adults can reach 5 inches (127 mm) in length, but their usual size is between 3 and 4 inches (76 and 100 mm).

Natural History: The Mottled Sculpin lives in cold glacial lakes and groundwater-rich streams. In Lake Michigan it primarily inhabits rocky shorelines; it has been infrequently found as deep as 150 feet (45 m). It is associated with stream reaches that have high groundwater inputs, which maintain cool to cold temperatures. The Mottled Sculpin can utilize various habitats free of fine substrates and siltation. For instance, in Fox River valley streams, it is found in fast-flowing cobble riffles. In the upper Kankakee River, it is found in sand streams with aquatic vegetation. Again, the direct or indirect influence of cold groundwater discharge is the key feature for both habitats. The Mottled Sculpin swims in short bursts and is rarely far from cover. It eats aquatic insect larvae, amphipods, crustaceans, and occasionally small fish. Spawning takes place in the spring, using cavities between or below rocks as nests. Sometimes the male digs a short tunnel. After brief courting, the female lays eggs on the roof of the nest. The male will continue to guard the nest while fry are present.

Mottled Sculpin records, 1890–2022

Distribution and Status: The Mottled Sculpin's natural distribution is widespread throughout central and eastern Canada, and in the Great Lakes and upper Mississippi River basins; there is a disjunct population along the eastern slope of the Rocky Mountains. Records within the Chicago Region are concentrated in the St. Joseph, upper Kankakee, Fox, and Rock River systems. The distribution largely coincides with streams that are in geologic position to receive groundwater discharge, either at the headwaters or along valley walls. The species also occurs in Lake Michigan, where cold waters are maintained year-round. Mottled Sculpin numbers have dropped precipitously in streams due to groundwater impacts, and in Lake Michigan due to the Round Goby invasion. The Round Goby appears to outcompete the Mottled Sculpin for nesting sites. It is now difficult to find the Mottled Sculpin in the nearshore zone of Lake Michigan. Due to the species' declining and vulnerable status, it is now listed as threatened in Illinois.

References: Pearse 1918; Cahn 1927; Ludwig and Norten 1969; Becker 1983; Dubs and Corkum 1996; Janssen and Jude 2001; Hubbs, Lagler, and Smith 2004; Arciszewski et al. 2015; Willink 2017

SCULPINS (COTTIDAE)   **429**

Field Museum Specimen #63406

Description: The Slimy Sculpin has a flattened, large head and a robust body that tapers toward the tail. There is 1 large opercular spine pointing back, with 1–2 small spines below pointing down. The body is naked, with small protuberances on the side of the head. The lateral line is incomplete, ending under the second dorsal fin, and has 12–26 pores. The dorsal fins are touching, with the second being long and low. The pelvic fins usually have 3 rays. Coloration is mottled brown, often with 2 indistinct saddles and widely scattered spots. There are rows of orange-red blotches in the second dorsal fin and tail. The first dorsal fin of breeding males is darker along the base and orange along the margin. The Slimy Sculpin has less mottling than the Mottled Sculpin and has only 3 versus 4 pelvic fin rays. Adults can reach 4.5 inches (127 mm).

Natural History: The Slimy Sculpin inhabits cold lakes and rivers. Little is known about their natural history within large glacial lakes, with most documentation coming from smaller streams. In southern Lake Michigan, it is found from the shoreline to more than 375 feet deep (115 m). Although the Slimy Sculpin overlaps with the 3 three sculpin species in Lake Michigan, studies indicate there is no direct competition, likely due to partitioning by unique niches and utilize various habitats free of fine substrates and siltation. For instance, in Fox River valley streams, it is found in fast-flowing cobble riffles. In the upper Kankakee River, it is found in sand streams with aquatic vegetation. Again, the direct or indirect influence of cold groundwater discharge is the key feature for both habitats. The Mottled Sculpin swims in short bursts and is rarely far from cover. It eats aquatic insect larvae, amphipods, crustaceans, and occasionally small fish. Spawning takes place in the spring, using cavities between or below rocks as nests. Sometimes the male digs a short tunnel. After brief courting, the female lays eggs on the roof of the nest. The male will continue to guard the nest while fry are present.

Distribution and Status: The Mottled Sculpin's natural distribution is widespread throughout central and eastern Canada, and in the Great Lakes and upper Mississippi River basins; there is a disjunct population along the eastern slope of the Rocky Mountains. Records within the Chicago Region are concentrated in the St. Joseph, upper Kankakee, Fox, and Rock River systems. The distribution largely coincides with streams

Mottled Sculpin records, 1890–2022

that are in geologic position to receive groundwater discharge, either at the headwaters or along valley walls. The species also occurs in Lake Michigan, where cold waters are maintained year-round. Mottled Sculpin numbers have dropped precipitously in streams due to groundwater impacts, and in Lake Michigan due to the Round Goby invasion. The Round Goby appears to outcompete the Mottled Sculpin for nesting sites. It is now difficult to find the Mottled Sculpin in the nearshore zone of Lake Michigan. Due to the species' declining and vulnerable status, it is now listed as threatened in Illinois.

References: Pearse 1918; Cahn 1927; Ludwig and Norten 1969; Becker 1983; Dubs and Corkum 1996; Janssen and Jude 2001; Hubbs, Lagler, and Smith 2004; Arciszewski et al. 2015; Willink 2017

Slimy Sculpin

Cottus cognatus • *Cottus* is Greek, meaning "bull's head"; *cognatus* is Latin, meaning "related," presumably to a European species of sculpin.

Field Museum Specimen #63406

Description: The Slimy Sculpin has a flattened, large head and a robust body that tapers toward the tail. There is 1 large opercular spine pointing back, with 1–2 small spines below pointing down. The body is naked, with small protuberances on the side of the head. The lateral line is incomplete, ending under the second dorsal fin, and has 12–26 pores. The dorsal fins are touching, with the second being long and low. The pelvic fins usually have 3 rays. Coloration is mottled brown, often with 2 indistinct saddles and widely scattered spots. There are rows of orange-red blotches in the second dorsal fin and tail. The first dorsal fin of breeding males is darker along the base and orange along the margin. The Slimy Sculpin has less mottling than the Mottled Sculpin and has only 3 versus 4 pelvic fin rays. Adults can reach 4.5 inches (127 mm).

Natural History: The Slimy Sculpin inhabits cold lakes and rivers. Little is known about their natural history within large glacial lakes, with most documentation coming from smaller streams. In southern Lake Michigan, it is found from the shoreline to more than 375 feet deep (115 m). Although the Slimy Sculpin overlaps with the 3 three sculpin species in Lake Michigan, studies indicate there is no direct competition, likely due to partitioning by unique niches and

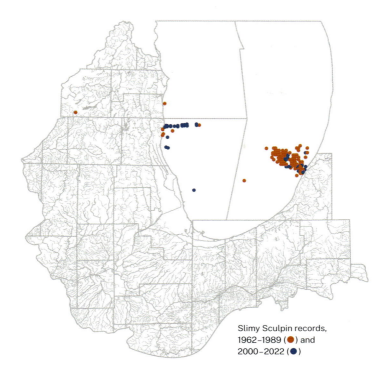

Slimy Sculpin records, 1962–1989 (●) and 2000–2022 (●)

behaviors. Food items of the Slimy Sculpin consists of Opossum Shrimp, amphipods, and to a lesser extent chironomids. Slimy Sculpins are reported to excavate holes beneath large stones to create nests. Eggs are then deposited on the top inside surface, which are guarded by the male until fry are hatched and leave the nest.

Distribution and Status: The natural distribution of the Slimy Sculpin includes Arctic, Pacific, Atlantic, Great Lakes, and upper Mississippi River basins. The Chicago Region is at the southern extent of its distribution, with all records for this species except 1 taken from Lake Michigan. There is 1 riverine specimen taken from a small headwater creek in Walworth County, Wisconsin (MPM 1975). Its status within the Chicago Region is considered stable; however, further study is needed for a better characterization of distribution and habitat. It is listed as a species of special concern in Indiana, and is considered the same throughout the Chicago Region.

References: Becker 1983; Hubbs, Lagler, and Smith 2004; Madenjian et al. 2012; Arciszewski et al. 2015; Willink 2017

Spoonhead Sculpin

Cottus ricei • *Cottus*, Greek, means "bull's head"; *ricei* honors the Northwestern University student F. L. Rice, who discovered the type specimen while walking on a beach in Evanston, Illinois, in 1876.

Field Museum Specimen #42905

Description: The Spoonhead Sculpin has a wide, spoon-like head and a slender body that tapers sharply toward the tail. This species can be distinguished from other Chicago Region sculpins by the opercular spines and extremely flattened head. There is 1 long crescent-shaped opercular spine pointing up, with 2–3 small spines below pointing down. The body is naked except for many prickles all over the head and body, giving it a sandpaper-like feel. The lateral line is complete, with 33–36 pores. The dorsal fins are touching; the second is long and low. The pelvic fins usually have 4 rays. Coloration is mottled brown, with 3–4 dark pigment saddles. Adults can reach 5 inches (127 mm), but their usual size is between 3 and 4 inches (76 and 100 mm).

Natural History: The Spoonhead Sculpin inhabits cold glacial lakes and rivers. Little is known about the biology of the Spoonhead Sculpin within the Chicago Region, except that it inhabits only Lake Michigan. Individuals were found primarily along the shoreline; however, 1 specimen was taken at 165 feet (50 m) deep. In northern ecoregions where average temperatures are much lower, this species moves out of glacial-lake habitats and can utilize

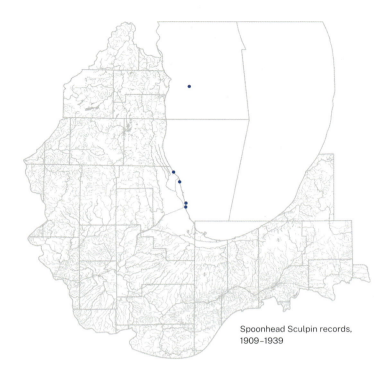

Spoonhead Sculpin records, 1909–1939

fast-flowing river habitats. It forages on amphipods, crustaceans, midge larvae, worms, and isopods. In rivers, the Spoonhead Sculpin attach and fertilize adhesive eggs on the underside of rocks in riffles, where males guard the egg masses. In lakes, they likely do the same, except using rocky, wave-driven shores.

Distribution and Status: The Spoonhead Sculpin occurs naturally throughout Canada and the Great Lakes in the United States. It is restricted to Lake Michigan within the Chicago Region. There are only 5 old records from the Chicago Region, the most recent record from 1939 (University of Michigan). It reportedly disappeared throughout Lake Michigan in the 1960s, with recent reappearance in more northern waters. The Spoonhead Sculpin is not listed by any of the Chicago Region states but is currently considered extirpated from the Chicago Region, hopefully recolonizing in the future from northern waters.

References: Deason 1939; Anderson and Smith 1971; Wells and McLain 1973; Eck and Wells 1987; Potter and Fleischer 1992; Hubbs, Lagler, and Smith 2004; Arciszewski et al. 2015; Willink 2017

Deepwater Sculpin

Myoxocephalus thompsonii · *Myoxocephalus*, Greek, means "dormouse head"; *thompsonii* is in honor of Rev. Zadock Thompson, a famous Vermont naturalist.

Field Museum Specimen #63408

Description: The Deepwater Sculpin has a wide, flattened, large head and a slender body that tapers sharply toward the tail. Like other sculpins, its eyes sit on top of the head. This species can be distinguished from other Chicago Region sculpins by having 4 opercular spines (2 up and 2 down), 2 widely separated dorsal fins, an elongated second dorsal fin, and a narrow gill membrane isthmus. The body is naked except for bony plates along the lateral line and a few prickles above the lateral line. The color is dark brown, grayish, or green, with 4–7 dark pigment saddles. Additional characters used to separate this species from the Spoonhead Sculpin are palatine teeth (on the palatine bone inside the upper jaw) and 3 pelvic fin rays. The reported maximum size for adults is 9 inches (225 mm).

Natural History: The Deepwater Sculpin, true to its name, lives only in the very deep waters of glacial lakes. This preference for deepwater habitats is driven primarily by its need for cold water. When water temperatures drop, it can be found closer to shore. As such, this species is documented from the shallow shoreline habitats to depths of up to 395 feet (120 m) in southern Lake Michigan. In Lake Superior, it has been found in depths exceeding 1,350 feet (450 m). It forages primarily on Opossum Shrimp and amphipods, but it will also eat midge larvae and fish eggs. Since there are few other species of fish at these depths, the Deepwater Sculpin is primary prey for top-level predators such as the Lake Char and the Burbot. Jude, Van Sumeren, and Lutchko (2022) documented the first observation of nest guarding from Grand Traverse Bay, Lake Michigan. Video footage clearly shows an individual Deepwater Sculpin guarding an egg ball within a circular depression created in the silty sandy substrate near woody debris. The nest was observed in mid-March and located in 650 feet (190 m) of water.

Deepwater Sculpin records, 1920–1984 (●) and 1998–2022 (●)

Distribution and Status: The Deepwater Sculpin is considered a glacial relict species from Arctic marine forms that were pushed south by the last glaciation. This species occurs naturally throughout Canada and the Great Lakes basin in the United States. It is restricted to Lake Michigan within the Chicago Region. The most recent records are from deepwater trawls off Lake County, Illinois (USGS 2016). Although populations are reported to be declining, records for this species consistently appear from 1920 to 2016. This species is considered highly vulnerable to water-temperature increases, eutrophication, Round Goby invasion, and the lack of natural connectivity between populations. Although the Deepwater Sculpin is not listed by any of the Chicago Region states, we consider it locally imperiled.

References: Woods 1957b; Dryer 1966; Wells 1968; McPhail and Lindsey 1970; Anderson and Smith 1971; Wells and McLain 1973; Hubbs, Lagler, and Smith 2004; Madenjian et al. 2012; Arciszewski et al. 2015; Willink 2017; Jude, Van Sumeren, and Lutchko 2022

Acknowledgments

The culmination of this book required input from many institutions and individuals throughout the four-state Chicago Region. We are indebted to them and grateful for their cooperation and contributions. Hopefully, we have listed all those people and entities for which we are so grateful.

Special Thanks

Dr. Larry M. Page, University of Florida/University of Illinois, our lead author's fish mentor, whose suggestion and encouragement spawned this publication; we all look up to him as the godfather of North American fishes and Chicago pizza. Dr. Thomas J. Near, University of Yale, our lead author's drill sergeant-major and inspiration to keep studying fishes — a true Chicago boy. Dr. John Lyons, University of Wisconsin–Madison, for sheer inspiration in the joy he brings to studying fishes. Steve is indebted to many fisheries professionals for his inspiration and knowledge. First and foremost, the late Dr. Weldon (Larry) Larimore, as well as others at the Illinois Natural History Survey; the late Michael Sule; Dr. Michael Wiley; and Thomas Skelly. Steve's late colleague at the DNR, Robert Rung, shared his vast knowledge of the Chicago Region and its fishes and collected specimens from countless sites across northeastern Illinois. His tireless dedication and energy were pivotal to Steve's career. And to Joel Greenburg, the Bilbo Baggins of the Chicago Region . . .

Reviewers

We would like to express our sincere gratitude to Larry Page, Chris Taylor, Jeremy Tiemann, Brant Fischer, Eric Hilton, and Len

Kring, whose input helped improve the quality and content of this manuscript.

Mapping Support

The US Army Corps of Engineers, Chicago District. Special thanks and credit to John D. Ennis for critical geospatial analysis and mapping support.

Ichthyological Aid and Data

The Field Museum of Natural History fish collection records and fish identification, with support from Kevin Swagel, Barry Chernof, Mary Anne Rogers, Chris Jones, Tom Anton, Michael Littmann, Susan Mochel, and Jamie Ladonski. The Illinois Natural History Survey fish collection records and fish identification, with support from Jeremy Tiemann, Christopher Taylor, Kevin Cummings, and Chris Phillips. The US Army Corps of Engineers, Chicago District, with support from Nick Barkowski, John Belcik, Sam Belcik, Shawna Herleth-King, Matt Shanks, Brook Herman, Robbie Sliwinski, Alex Catalano, Kathleen Chernich, Eugene Fleming, Susanne Davis, Adam Karr, and Mark Cornish; and in memoriam of Melvin MacLaurin, who collected many Lake Michigan and Calumet River fishes for this book and gave his life in service of our country. The Illinois Department of Natural Resources fish collection records, with support from Tristan Widloe, Frank Jakubicek, Scott Bartel, Vic Santucci, Rob Miller, and the late Robert Rung, who was a true "fish head" and worked tirelessly for 30 years sampling fishes around the Chicago Region. The Indiana Department of Environmental Management fish database, with support from Stacey Sobat, Kayla Werbianskyj, and Ali Meils. The Indiana Department of Natural Resources fish collection records, with support from Brant Fischer, Nathan Brindza, and Bob Robertson. Illinois EPA fish collection records, with support from Roy Smoger. The Wisconsin Department of Natural Resources fish collection records, with support from Craig Helker, Bradley Eggold, Matt Caffaro, and Brent Peterson. The University of Michigan for providing online Michigan Fish Atlas Records. The Southeastern Wisconsin Regional Planning Commission fish collection, with support from Tom Slawski. The Auburn University fish collection records, with support from Jon Armbruster. The Southern Illinois University fish collection records, with support from Brooks M. Burr. The Milwaukee Public Museum for fish collection records, with support from Randy Moi. The City of Elkhart, Indiana, fish collection records, with support from Len Kring, Daragh Deegan, and Joe Foy. The McHenry County Conservation District fish collection records, with support from Ed Collins and Brad Woodson. The Lake County Forest Preserve fish collection records, with support from Nick Huber, Jim Anderson, and Ken Klick.

We would also like to thank Dave Jude, Pat Charlebois, Joe Exl, Michael Boos, Charlie Morris, Phil Moy, John Janssen, Shawn Cirton, Elizabeth McCloskey, Jim Smith, Kirs Krouse, the late John Mendelsohn, Jean Sellar, Gary Kaspar, John Rogner, Greg Siegert, Jim Bland, Dave Giordano, Gina Lettiere, Mark Sabaj, Mike Hardman, Jason Knouft, Ed Hammer, Jennifer Hammer, Stephen McCracken, Mike Hari, Steven Markulin, Matt Vujic, Michael Veraldi, and Tom Perkovic.

Funding Support

We would like to thank the Association for the Wolf Lake Initiative and board member Marianne Kozlowski; the Illinois Chapter of the American Fisheries Society; and the Illinois River Biological Station, directed by Dr. James Lamar, for their generous financial support. Also, in gracious memoriam, we would like to thank the late Ann Marie Starr for her financial support.

Friends and Family

Frank Veraldi: The most special person in my life, my wife, Cathy Starr, for ensuring I finished this book, not to mention providing some graphic design, much data management, and our son Huxley Francis. Rafal Steinberg, for teaching me how to identify and collect fishes, and to have a reasonably good time while doing it. My aunt Nancy Chereso, for encouraging me to write and letting me use her computer for hours to peck away at early-stage species accounts. My mom and dad, Linda and Rosario Veraldi, for sending me to the University of Illinois, where I met fish friends of a lifetime. And in memory of my grandpa Michael J. Chereso, who showed me my first fish . . .

Steve Pescitelli: Like all other things in my life, I must first thank my wife, Pam, for her support, encouragement, and patience. I am also very grateful to my girls, Stephani, Audrey, and Jeanette, for their inspiration and tolerance, especially on the long vacation road trips when my nose was in the computer working on species accounts. My parents, Maurice Sr. and Betty, inculcated a love of nature, rivers, and fish on our many camping and fishing trips. For my inspiration in biology, I always looked up to my big brother, Maurice Jr. Thanks to him for being a great scientist and helping me plant my feet firmly on that ground — he was an OK fisherman, too. I have been very lucky to have had so many amazing colleague friends who have helped me in countless ways throughout my career. Maybe too numerous to mention, but to name a few: Diana Day, Doug Austin, Kevin Cummins, Tristan Widloe, and Dan Sallee. One of my dearest friends as well as one of the best fisheries scientists I knew was Tom Kwak. He was an unbelievably generous and humble person who sadly passed away far too young, leaving a huge hole in many lives.

Philip Willink: First and foremost, a huge thanks to my wife, Jolynn, and our son, Tolkien, for their endless patience as this book was written. This project would not have been completed without their continual support and willingness to go on crazy adventures throughout the Great Lakes region and beyond. And special thanks to my parents, Wesley and Mary, and brother Jonathan for instilling in me and nurturing an appreciation for the natural world around us. From canoeing for days down the Allagash River to lobstering in Casco Bay off Maine's rugged coast, we were never far from the outdoors!

Appendix: Fish Identification

What is a fish? Most people would say an animal with scales and fins that lives in the water. This is true under most circumstances; however, out of the 30,000-plus species of fishes that live on this planet, many lack scales and/or fins. Some fishes can even live out of the water for short periods of time.

So, what is a fish? Surprisingly, the definition is arbitrary and a matter of opinion because of the vast diversity of living organisms in the past and present. For the purposes of this book on the Chicago Region, a fish is an aquatic animal with gills and vertebrae that lacks limbs (i.e., arms or legs).

Anatomy

Body Shapes and Scales

Fish come in a wide variety of shapes: streamlined like trout, laterally compressed like Bluegill and other sunfishes, flattened like Flathead Catfish, and elongated or eel-like. The body can be scaleless (catfishes), partially scaled (sculpins), or fully scaled (sunfishes) in rows along the length of the fish.

There are typically 3 types of scales. Cycloid scales are thin, smooth edged, and overlapping — trout or carps have these. Ctenoid scales are like cycloid scales but have comb-like teeth on their outer edge, found on sunfishes and perches. Ganoid scales are the thick, bony, and non-overlapping scales found on more primitive fishes like gars.

On some fishes, the central row of scales along the lateral surface is perforated with small pores that connect to a channel in the skin. This is called the lateral line system, which enables a fish to sense changes in pressure in its surrounding environment. The pored lateral line scales can be complete, running the entire body length; partial; or totally absent.

Fins

A fin is a thin layer of skin that is supported by small pieces of bone or cartilage. The small pieces of bone are called spines if they are stiff and in 1 solid piece or rays if they are soft and divided into multiple segments. Rays are either branched if they are split at their far (distal) end or unbranched if they are not split along their length.

Typical fin placements are shown in figure 35.1. The fin on the back is called the dorsal fin and may have 1 or 2 separate sections. For fishes with 2 dorsal fins, the front fin usually contains spines, while the back fin has soft rays. The 2 dorsal fins may be either

35.1. Features of the typical fish

connected or separated by a small space. The fin at the far back end (posterior) of the fish is called the caudal fin or tail fin. The fin under the body immediately in front of the caudal fin is the anal fin, so called because its origin is immediately behind the anus. The fins immediately in front of the anus are the pelvic fins — 1 on the left side of the fish, 1 on the right. Behind the head are the pectoral fins, also with 1 on each side. The pectoral and pelvic fins are often called paired fins. The dorsal, caudal, and anal fins are often called the median or unpaired fins. Fins can be in a variety of shapes. For example, the caudal fin can be rounded, squared, or forked. Other fins are typically straight, concave, convex, or sickle shaped (falcate).

Some fishes have an extra fin between the dorsal fin and the caudal fin (figure 35.2). This fin, called the adipose fin, is anatomically different than the other fins. Instead of using spines and rays for internal structural support, it is simply made up of fatty (adipose) tissue surrounded by skin. The purpose of this fin is unknown.

35.2. Features of a catfish showing barbels and adipose fin

Body Regions

The very top of the fish in front of the dorsal fin is called the nape (figure 35.1). The abdomen, or belly, of the fish is immediately behind the head and in front of the anus. The stomach, intestines, liver, kidney, and other internal organs of the fish may be found here. The heart is further forward, near the back of the head; the rest of the body behind the head is muscle. The region between the anal fin and the caudal fin is called the caudal peduncle. This is an area of greater flexibility that is important for the swimming dynamics of a fish.

Head and Mouth

Fish heads are incredibly complex and dynamic structures. For example, there are 29 bones in the human head; fish heads can have more than 100 bones. Most of this complexity is internal, but here we will focus on some of the more obvious external bones and structures.

The mouth can be in various positions, and usually indicates a fish's feeding ecology. A mouth positioned below the tip of the snout is called inferior or ventral, adapted for bottom feeding (e.g., suckers). A mouth positioned at the tip of the snout is called terminal — think bass or perches, which typically feed on organisms directly in front of them. Finally, a mouth above the tip of the snout as found in killifishes, are called superior for foraging at the water surface.

The mouth is composed of the upper and lower jaws, which may be equal in length or have the upper or lower portion protruding. The lower jaw is known as the mandible or dentary (figure 35.3). The upper jaw is composed of 2 bones: the premaxilla and the maxilla. The premaxilla is more anterior and often slides forward when the fish opens its mouth. In some species, the premaxilla and the maxilla are fused together, making it very difficult to tell them apart. There may be teeth on the mandible, premaxilla, or maxilla, although many fishes are toothless. Teeth can be large or small, in 1 row or many rows, sharp or blunt.

Some fishes have barbels near the mouth (figure 35.2). Barbels are whisker-like structures that are often covered with taste buds and help the fish find food. They can be long, as in some catfishes, or short, as in some minnows. Barbels can be found just inside lips near the corners of the mouth, near the nares (nasal barbels), extending from the corners of the mouth (maxillary barbels), or under the head (mental barbels).

The nares are holes, sometimes paired, found on each side of the head between the mouth and the eye, enabling the fish to sense chemical signals in the water.

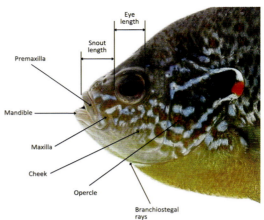

35.3. Mouth and head structures

A fish's eyes are functionally and structurally similar to other vertebrate eyes, although the lens is more spherical than in most other vertebrates. Immediately surrounding the eye and helping to hold it in place is the orbital rim. The orbital rim can be flesh, thin bone, or a combination of the two. In some fishes, a clear tissue called an adipose eyelid covers all or part of the eye and orbital rim. Eyes can be a variety of shapes (round, oval, spherical) and sizes. Sometimes eye length (figure 35.3) is useful in distinguishing similar species.

The operculum is a relatively large and rounded set of bones on the side of the head (figure 35.3). Some fishes have spines on the operculum, while others have soft flaps of tissue attached, referred to as ears (e.g., Longear Sunfish). Underneath the operculum is a slit that opens into the branchial cavity. A series of long thin bones called branchiostegal bones can be found ventral to the operculum and forming a continuous border with it along the edge of the gill cover slit. The branchiostegal bones and the skin covering them are often referred to as the branchiostegal membrane. On the opposite side of the opercular slit from the branchiostegal membrane is a V-or U-shaped piece of muscle and skin called the isthmus. The operculum and branchiostegal membrane can be contracted, closing off the opercular slit and preventing the backward flow of water and other unwanted debris from entering the mouth.

Inside the opercular slit is the branchial cavity containing the branchial arches. On the posterior side of the branchial arches are the gills. Water flows in through the mouth, past the gills, then out the opercular slit. This is how the fish obtains oxygen from the water. On the anterior side of the branchial arches are small bumps or rods of bone and flesh called gill rakers. Gill rakers help retain prey items sucked into the fish's mouth. Sometimes gill rakers have small teeth-like structures called denticles that help subdue struggling prey.

Fishes typically have 4 branchial arches. The fifth or rear branchial arch has been modified into a second set of jaws. These pharyngeal jaws can have a wide variety of teeth. Molars are used to crush prey. Canines are used to serrate prey. Spoon- or comb-shaped teeth are used to move prey down the fish's throat. It is not uncommon for a fish to have teeth on the pharyngeal jaws, but no teeth on the dentary, premaxilla, and maxilla.

Lamprey Oral Disc

The adult lamprey is unique from all other Chicago Region fishes by having a large circular mouth with different kinds and patterns of teeth among species (figure 35.4). The adult lamprey mouth is usually referred to as an oral disc or oral hood, where the larvae or ammocoete has a diminutive puckered oblong version of a disc with no teeth. There is a 2-part tongue in the esophageal cavity, or buccal funnel, with the longitudinal lingual lamina on top and the transverse lingual lamina on the bottom. These can either be smooth or have small, jagged teeth-like serrations for rasping flesh. The top longitudinal lingual lamina can be singular

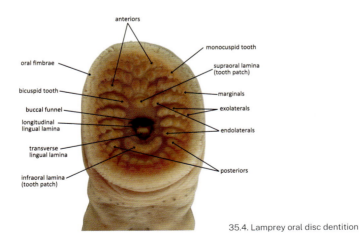

35.4. Lamprey oral disc dentition

or bilobed to varying degrees. Teeth can either be monocuspid or bicuspid, meaning they have 1–2 sharp points or cusps. Directly above the buccal funnel is a tooth patch called the supraoral lamina, which can have 1–3 teeth. Teeth above the supraoral lamina are called anteriors. Directly below the buccal funnel is the infraoral lamina, which varies greatly in teeth number among species. Teeth below the infraoral lamina are called posteriors. Teeth directly below the anteriors and above the posteriors are called lateral teeth. The lateral teeth directly next to the buccal funnel are called endolaterals. The lateral teeth rows outside of the endolaterals are called the exolaterals. The first circular row of teeth surrounding the buccal funnel include the endolaterals, the teeth directly above the supraoral lamina, and the teeth below the infraoral lamina; this collective group of teeth are called the circumorals. There are smaller teeth that circle the inside rim of the oral disc called marginals. The frills on the outside rim of the oral disc are called oral fimbrae.

Meristics

Meristics are the countable or measurable external characteristics of the fish that are used to identify species. While many are observable to the naked eye, others may require a dissecting scope, especially for smaller individuals.

Lengths

Total body length is the distance from the very front of the snout to the end point on the caudal fin, compressed or "pinched" together. This is the most common length measurement among biologists and anglers. Other body length measurements you may encounter are fork length (from the tip of the head to the fork of the caudal fin) or standard length (from the tip of the head to the caudal peduncle).

Head length is the distance from the front of the snout to the back of the operculum or gill flap, excluding soft tissue such as excessively thick lips, barbels, or opercular flaps.

Snout length is the distance from the front of the snout to the front of the eye (figure 35.3).

Postorbital length is the distance from the back of the eye to the posterior-most point on the operculum but excluding the soft tissue of the opercular flaps.

Eye diameter or length is the maximum inner diameter of the eye (figure 35.3).

Interorbital width is the minimum distance between the eyes, measured in a straight line (i.e., not including the curvature of the head). To obtain a more accurate measurement, it is often necessary to push gently against the rim of the orbit to compress the soft flesh and find the harder bone.

Body depth or *body height* is the maximum distance from the top of the fish to the bottom as measured along a line perpendicular to the long axis of the body (excluding fins).

Caudal peduncle length is the straight-line distance from the end of the anal fin base to the middle point of the caudal fin base. The caudal fin base is also the posterior border of the hypural plate. The hypural plate is an internal bone where the backbone stops and the tail begins. To determine its posterior border, hold the body of the fish steady, then bend the tail at an angle to the body. A wrinkle or fold will appear above the posterior border of the hypural plate.

Caudal peduncle depth is the shortest straight-line distance between the dorsal and ventral edges of the caudal peduncle.

Scale Counts

The most common scale counts are shown in figure 35.5. The number of scales along the *lateral line* are counted from immediately posterior to the gill cover slit to the posterior border of the hypural plate (see description above). The lateral line may shift from scale row to scale row, in which case, simply follow where the lateral line goes. The lateral line may end before reaching the hypural plate, in which case, continue counting along the row of scales that would bear the lateral line if it were complete. If pored lateral line scales are specified, then only those scales with pores are counted. Other counts include above or below the lateral line;

predorsal (between the head and the dorsal fin); circumbody (around the circumference of body immediately anterior of the dorsal fin); and the caudal peduncle (the number of scales or scale rows around the part of the caudal peduncle just behind the anal fin; figure 35.6).

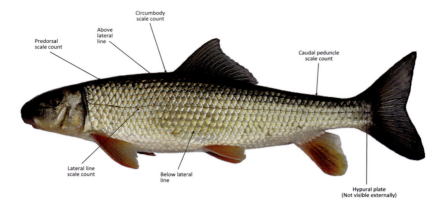

35.5. Typical scale counts used in fish identification

Fin Ray and Spine Counts

Fin ray counts include the total number of unbranched and branched fin rays. However, in some cases — for example, minnows — the anterior or front fin rays are very short, difficult to see, and may even be buried under skin and scales. These are called rudimentary rays (figure 35.6), and because they can be difficult to find, they are ignored when counting. Counts start with the first full-length anterior fin ray that is substantially longer than the preceding fin ray and end with the rear fin ray. These full-length fin rays are called principal rays, regardless of whether or not they are branched. In other fishes (e.g., catfishes), the fin rays gradually increase in length; therefore, it is not possible to distinguish between rudimentary and principal rays. In these instances, every visible fin ray is counted. Note that the 2 posterior-most fin rays are usually counted as 1 because even though they look separate, they are connected beneath the skin and flesh at the base of the fin. Fin rays are segmented and usually flexible. For spiny ray counts, all visible spines in the fin are counted, regardless of size. Spines are unsegmented and usually stiff.

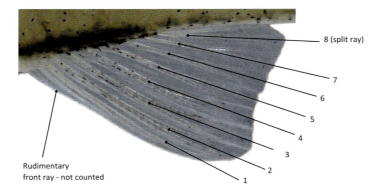

35.6. Fin ray configuration and counting guide

Gill Rakers and Pharyngeal Teeth

Gill rakers and pharyngeal teeth are internal structures found under the gill cover and within the throat of the fish. Gill rakers are usually on the anterior and posterior sides of most gill (branchial) arches. Those on the front of the first gill arch are typically used for identification, either by their length and thickness or by their number. The front arch can sometimes be viewed by lifting the gill cover. Pharyngeal or throat teeth are behind the gill arches and are difficult to observe without dissecting the fish. The teeth are modified in some species to aid in processing food items — for example, in River Redhorse, the teeth are hardened, with broad surfaces to crush mollusk shells; Grass Carp have a series of small grinding teeth to macerate aquatic vegetation. In a few instances, the throat teeth can be used for identification, by either their structure or number. In this book we have avoided using these internal structures in our species descriptions and primarily refer to them as part of the descriptions of food habits.

Glossary

adipose eyelid. Translucent fatty tissue that partially covers eyeball in some fishes.

adipose fin. Small, fleshy fin, usually without spines or rays, on the back between the dorsal and caudal fins.

ammocoete. Blind larva of lamprey.

anadromous. Migrating from the ocean to spawn in freshwater (e.g., sturgeons).

anal fin. Median fin located on the undersurface, usually just behind the anus.

axillary process. Bony splint, usually narrow and projecting to the rear, just above the pectoral or pelvic fin.

backwater. Quiet pool over an expanse of still water on the side of a stream channel, caused by the river changing course.

band. Bar or stripe of pigment on the body or fin.

barbel. Fleshy projection around the mouth region, used for smell and taste.

basin. Land area draining to a body of water. Also referred to as a watershed.

belly. Lower surface of the body between the pelvic fins and the anus. Also referred to as the abdomen.

benthic. Dwelling, eating, or spawning near the substrate of the bottom of a water body.

body depth. Distance in a straight line at the deepest point, from top to bottom of a fish.

branchiostegal membrane. Skin layer covering branchiostegal rays or bones.

branchiostegal ray. Series of long, thin bones under the gill covers.

breast. The lower area between the gill openings and pelvic fins. Also referred to as the chest.

bridle. A band of pigment across the snout.

canal. *Anatomy* Narrow, elongated indentation, usually around the eye. *Hydrogeophysical* Manmade ditch carrying water; may be lined with concrete.

canines. Larger teeth at the tip of the mouth.

cartilage. Flexible connective tissue, turning to bone in older fish, or it can remain soft through adulthood.

caudal fin. Tail fin of the fish.

caudal peduncle. Area of the body just in front of the caudal fin.

caudal spot. Pigment forming a spot at the base of the caudal fin.

channel. Deepest part of a river or a connection.

ctenoid. Fish scale with a rough or toothed rear edge.

cycloid. Fish scale with a smooth rear edge.

disc. Usually referring to the circular-shaped mouth of a lamprey; *oral disc.*

distal. Point or area furthest from the body — for example, the tip of a fin.

dorsal. Very top of the upper area of the body.

dorsal fin. Fin located on the back or upper part of the fish.

ear flap. Extension on the rear edge of the gill cover; can be soft or bony.

electrofishing. Method for collecting fish using an electrical current to stun and net specimens.

embedded. Covered by skin; typically refers to scales.

forked. Indentation near the middle; typically refers to the tail fin.

frenum. Fleshy ridge between the snout and the upper lip.

fusiform. Spindle shaped, tapering at both ends.

ganoid. Describes hard, non-overlapping scales; found on more primitive fishes, like gars.

gas bladder. Interior sac-like structure enabling the fish to suspend itself in the water column.

genital papillae. Small conical tube used to expel spawn and milt, just anterior of the anal fin; visible right before and during spawning.

gill. Structures in the throat area, used for absorbing oxygen from the water.

gill arch. Bony or cartilaginous structure supporting gill filaments; rakers are attached.

gill cover. Bony, flap-like structure covering the gill chamber.

gill filament. Red, feathery portion of the gill for respiratory gases and excretion.

gill opening. Opening to the gill chamber.

gill raker. Projections on the front of the gill arch; often used to sift food items.

gonopodium. Modified front rays of the anal fin of the male livebearer to transfer sperm to the female.

gular plate. Thin, bony plate between the lower jaws.

heterocercal. Caudal fin with the upper lobe (containing the vertebral column) longer than the bottom lobes.

Holarctic. Northern Hemispheres of the Old and New Worlds.

hypural plate. Bone where the backbone stops and the tail begins.

ichthyologist. Person who studies fishes.

infraorbital. Located below the eye.

infraorbital canal. A branch of the lateral line system located beneath the eye and is evident by surface pores.

interorbital. Located between the eyes.

invertebrate. Animal without a backbone (e.g., insect, crayfish, worm).

isthmus. V-or U-shaped piece of muscle and skin between the bottom of the gills.

juvenile. Young, fully developed individual like an adult but not sexually mature.

keel. Shelflike fleshy or bony ridge.

keratinous. Made of keratin, a fibrous protein.

larva (larvae pl). Newly hatched fish, typically with a remaining egg sac.

lateral. Side of the body.

lateral line. Pores along the side of the fish involved in sensory function; may be complete or partial.

lateral scale count. Number of scales along the lateral line, or where the lateral line would be if absent.

median fin(s). Dorsal, caudal, and anal fins, unpaired and located on median plane of body.

melanophore. Cell containing dark brown or black pigment.

midwater. In or near the middle of the water column; not at the surface or on the bottom.

milt. Sperm fluid produced by male fishes.

myomere. Segment of the body, usually referring to lampreys or eels.

ocellus. Spot resembling an eye; dark, bordered by ring of light pigment.

opercle (opercular adj.). Bones forming the gill cover.

opercular flap. Bony flap that covers the gills.

operculum. Group of bones that provides structure to the head and covers the gill.

oral disc. Fleshy circular structure surrounding the mouth of a lamprey.

orbital. Referring to or related to the eye.

Palatine teeth. Teeth on the Palatine bones, found on the roof of the mouth.

papilla (papillae pl). Small nipple-like protuberance.

papillose. Having papillae.

parr. Juvenile Salmonid between the fry and smolt stages.

pectoral fin. Pair of fins just behind the head.

peduncle. See *caudal peduncle*.

pelagic. Living in open water, away from the bottom or shoreline.

pelvic fin. Paired fins behind or below the pelvis.

peritoneum. Tissue lining of the abdominal cavity.

pharyngeal. Of or near the throat.

plankton. Free-floating single-cell plants (phytoplankton) or animals (zooplankton).

plicate. Having folds of skin; ridged.

predorsal scales. Row of scales along the middle of the back, between the head and the dorsal fin.

premaxilla. Bones at the front of the upper jaw.

preopercle. Bone in front of the gill cover, often separated from the gill cover by a groove.

preorbital. Area in front of the eye.

prickle. Very small spine (for example, in sculpins).

protrusible. Describes an upper lip not attached to the snout.

punctate lateral line. Black spots above and below the pores of the lateral line.

pyloric caeca. Small intestine pockets that increase the surface area.

ray. Soft segmented structure supporting fin membranes.

riffle. Area of a stream that is shallower, with fast-flowing water.

rudiment. Small, incompletely developed body part (eye, fin ray, or gill raker).

run. Area of a stream between riffle and pool habitats, with moderate current and depth.

saddle. Pigment on the back that forms rectangular or triangular bars.

scute. Enlarged scale, often with 1 or more bony projections.

serrate. With sawtooth-like notches along the outer edge.

spine. Stiff, sharp, bony part of a fin or a bony projection on the head; can be serrated.

spiracle. Opening behind the eye of primitive fishes; not a gill opening.

subopercle. Lowermost bone of the operculum, below the opercle.

subspecies. Populations that live in different areas and vary in size or shape but still can interbreed.

subterminal. Mouth position below the snout.

supraoral cusps. Lamprey teeth located above the mouth opening.

terete. Cylindrical and slightly tapering at the ends.

terminal. Describes a mouth located at the tip of the snout.

thoracic. Located on the breast.

tooth patch. A small area of teeth on roof of mouth or tongue.

truncated. Not pointed or forked.

tubercle. Hard bump on the skin or head, usually on breeding males.

vent. Anal opening.

ventral. Lower or bottom area of the body.

vermiculation. Wavy, wormlike color pattern.

References

Anderson, E. D., and L. L. Smith Jr. 1971. *A Synoptic Study of Food Habits of 30 Fish Species from Western Lake Superior.* University of Minnesota Agricultural Experimental Station Technical Bulletin 279.

Andraso, G. M. 2005. "Summer Food Habits of Pumpkinseeds (*Lepomis gibbosus*) and Bluegills (*Lepomis macrochirus*) in Presque Isle Bay, Lake Erie." *Journal of Great Lakes Research* 31:397–404.

Applegate, V. C. 1950. *Natural History of the Sea Lamprey (Petromyzon marinus) in Michigan.* US Fish and Wildlife Service, Special Scientific Report: Fisheries 55.

Arciszewski, T., M. A. Gray, C. Hrenchuk, P. A. Cott, N. J. Mochnacz, and J. D. Reist. 2015. *Fish Life History, Diets, and Habitat Use in the Northwest Territories: Freshwater Sculpin Species.* Canadian Manuscript Report of Fisheries and Aquatic Sciences 3066.

AuClair, R. P. 1966. "White Perch." In *Fishes of Maine*, by W. H. Everhart, 74–76. Augusta: Maine Department of Inland Fisheries and Game.

Bailey, M. M. 1964. "Age, Growth, Maturity, and Sex Composition of the American Smelt, *Osmerus mordax* (Mitchill), of Western Lake Superior." *Transactions of the American Fisheries Society* 93:382–95.

Bailey, R. M. 1954. "Distribution of the American Cyprinid Fish *Hybognathus hankinsoni* with Comments on Its Original Description." *Copeia*, no. 4: 289–91.

———. 1959. "Distribution of the American Cyprinid Fish *Notropis anogenus*." *Copeia*, no. 2: 119–23.

Bailey, R. M., W. C. Latta, and G. R. Smith. 2004. *An Atlas of Michigan Fishes with Keys and Illustrations for Their Identification.* Miscellaneous Publications Museum of Zoology University of Michigan 192.

Bailey, R. M., and G. R. Smith. 1981. "Origin and Geography of the Fish Fauna of the Laurentian Great Lakes Basin." *Canadian Journal of Fisheries and Aquatic Sciences* 38:1539–61.

Balon, E. K. 1995. "The Common Carp, *Cyprinus carpio*: Its Wild Origin, Domestication in Aquaculture, and Selection as Colored Nishikigoi." *Guelph Ichthyology Reviews* 3:1–55.

Becker, G. C. 1983. *The Fishes of Wisconsin.* Madison: University of Wisconsin Press.

Belcik, J. T. 2017. "Population Genetics and Distribution of the Oriental Weatherfish, *Misgurnus anguillicaudatus*, in Chicago Area Waterways." Master's thesis, Loyola University, Chicago.

Bemis, W. E., E. K. Findeis, and L. Grande. 1997. "An Overview of Acipenseriformes." *Environmental Biology of Fishes* 48:25–71.

Berg, L. S. 1949. "Freshwater Fishes of the USSR and Adjacent Countries." *Israel Program for Scientific Translations, Jerusalem* 2:496.

Bersamin, S. V. 1958. "A Preliminary Study of the Nutritional Ecology and Food Habits of the Chubs (*Leucichthys* spp.) and Their Relation to the Ecology of Lake Michigan." *Papers of the Michigan Academy of Science, Arts, and Letters* 43:107–18.

Black, J. D. 1945. "Natural History of the Northern Mimic Shiner *Notropis volucellus volucellus* Cope." *Investigations of Indiana Lakes and Streams* 2:449–69.

Bland, J. K., and P. W. Willink. 2018. *Conservation Guidance for Iowa Darter* Etheostoma exile. Illinois Department of Natural Resources, Division of Natural Heritage.

Blatchley, W. S., and G. H. Ashley. 1901. *The Lakes of Northern Indiana and Their Associated Marl Deposits.* 25th Annual Report, Department of Geology and Natural Resources, Indiana, 1900:31–321.

Bosanko, D. 2021. *Fish of Michigan: Field Guide.* 2nd ed. Cambridge, MN: Adventure Publications.

Boyer, L. F., R. A. Cooper, D. T. Long, and T. M. Askew. 1989. "Burbot (*Lota lota*) Biogenic Sedimentary Structures in Lake Superior." *Journal of Great Lakes Research* 15:174–85.

Breder, C. M. Jr., and D. E. Rosen. 1966. *Modes of Reproduction in Fishes.* New York: American Museum of Natural History.

Brown, E. H. Jr., G. W. Eck, N. R. Foster, R. M. Horrall, and C. E. Coberly. 1981. "Historical Evidence for Discrete Stocks of Lake Trout (*Salvelinus namaycush*) in Lake Michigan." *Canadian Journal of Fisheries and Aquatic Sciences* 38:1747–58.

Brownstein, C. D., D. Kim, O. D. Orr, G. M. Hogue, B. H. Tracy, M. W. Pugh, R. Singer, et al. 2022. "Hidden Species Diversity in an Iconic Living Fossil Vertebrate." *Biology Letters* 18:20220395.

Brussard, P. F., M. Collings Hall, and J. Wright. 1981. "Structure and Affinities of Freshwater Sea Lamprey (*Petromyzon marinus*)." *Canadian Journal of Fisheries and Aquatic Sciences* 38:1708–14.

Bryan, M. B., D. Zalinski, K. B. Filcek, S. Libants, W. Li, and K. T. Scribner. 2005. "Patterns of Invasion and Colonization of the Sea Lamprey (*Petromyzon marinus*) in North America as Revealed by Microsatellite Genotypes." *Molecular Ecology* 14, no. 12 (2005): 3757–73.

Burkhead, N. M, and J. D. Williams. 1991. "An Intergeneric Hybrid of a Native Minnow, the Golden Shiner, and an Exotic Minnow, the Rudd." *Transactions of the American Fisheries Society* 120:781–95.

Burnham, C. W. 1909. "Notes on the Yellow Bass." *Transactions of the American Fisheries Society* 39:103–8.

Burr, B. M., D. J. Eisenhour, K. M. Cook, C. A. Taylor, G. L. Seegert, R. W. Sauer, and E. R. Atwood. 1996. "Non-native Fishes in Illinois Waters: What Do the Records Reveal?" *Transactions of the Illinois State Academy of Science* 89:73–91.

Burr, B. M., and L. M. Page. 1979. "The Life History of the Least Darter, *Etheostoma microperca*, in the Iroquois River, Illinois." *Illinois Natural History Survey Biological Notes* 112:1–15.

Burr, B. M., V. J. Santucci, M. E. Roberts, A. M. Davis, and M. R. Whiles. 2005. *Conservation Status and Life History Characteristics of the Blacknose Shiner,* Notropis heterolepis *(Cyprinidae), and Blackchin Shiner,* Notropis heterodon *(Cyprinidae), with Conservation Evaluations of the Pugnose Shiner,* Notropis anogenus *(Cyprinidae), and Banded Killifish,* Fundulus diaphanus *(Fundulidae), in Illinois.* Dundee, IL: Max McGraw Wildlife Foundation.

Butler, S. E., and D. H. Wahl. 2017. "Movement and Habitat Use of River Redhorse (*Moxostoma carinatum*) in the Kankakee River, Illinois." *Copeia* 105, no. 4: 734–42.

Cahn, A. R. 1927. "An Ecological Study of the Southern Wisconsin Fishes: The Brook Silverside (*Labidesthes sicculus*) and the Cisco (*Leucichthys artedi*) in Their Relations to the Region." *Illinois Biological Monographs* 11:1–151.

Carranza, J., and H. E. Winn. 1954. "Reproductive Behavior of the Blackstripe Topminnow, *Fundulus notatus*." *Copeia* 1954 no. 4: 273–78.

Casselman, J. M., and C. A. Lewis. 1996. "Habitat Requirements of Northern Pike (*Esox lucius*)." *Canadian Journal of Fisheries and Aquatic Sciences* 53(S1): S161–74.

Charlebois, P. M., R. G. Mardsen, R. G. Goettel, R. K. Wolfe, D. J. Jude, and S. Rudinka. 1997. *The Round Goby,* Neogobius melanostomus *(Pallas): A Review of European and North American Literature, Illinois–Indiana Sea Grant Program and Illinois Natural History Survey.* Illinois Natural History Survey Special Publication 20.

Chicago Wilderness. 2011. *An Atlas of Biodiversity.* 2nd ed. Chicago: Chicago Wilderness Corporate Council.

Chipps, S. R., and D. H. Wahl. 2004. "Development and Evaluation of a Western Mosquitofish Bioenergetics Model." *Transactions of the American Fisheries Society* 133:1150–62.

Christie, G. C. 2000. *Protecting Mudpuppies, Protecting Stream Ecosystems.* Great Lakes Fishery Commission Forum, vol. 7.

Clem, P. D., and J. O. Whitaker Jr. 1995. "Distribution of the Mosquitofish, *Gambusia affinis* (Baird and Girard), in Indiana, with Comments on Resource Competition." *Proceedings of the Indiana Academy of Science* 104:249–58.

Cochran, P. A. 2014. "Observations on Spawning by Captive Sand Shiners (*Notropis stramineus*) from Minnesota." *American Currents* 39, no. 2:13–14.

Cochran, P. A., S. E. Malotka, and D. Deegan. 2015. "Lampreys of the St. Joseph River Drainage in Northern Indiana, with Emphasis on the Chestnut Lamprey (*Ichthyomyzon castaneus*)." *Proceedings of the Indiana Academy of Science* 124:26–31.

Cole, L. J. 1905. "The German Carp in the United States." Appendix to *Report of the Commissioner of Fisheries to the Secretary of Commerce and Labor for the Year Ending June 30, 1904,* 523–641.

Cook, S. J., and C. M. Bunt. 1999. "Spawning and Reproductive Biology of the Greater Redhorse, *Moxostoma valenciennesi*, in the Grand River, Ontario." *Canadian Field-Naturalist* 113:497–502.

Creaser, C. W. 1925. "The Establishment of the Atlantic Smelt in the Upper Waters of the Great Lakes." *Papers of the Michigan Academy of Science, Arts and Letters* 5:405–23.

Crossman, E. J. 1995. "Introduction of Lake Trout (*Salvelinus namaycush*) in Areas Outside Its Native Distribution." *Journal of Great Lakes Research* 21 (S1): S17–29.

Deason, H. J. 1939. "The Distribution of Cottid Fishes in Lake Michigan." *Papers of the Michigan Academy of Science, Arts, and Letters* 24:105–15.

Deegan, D. 2022. *Elkhart–South Bend Aquatic Community Monitoring*. Annual report. City of Elkhart Public Works & Utilities.

Dettmers, J. 2000. Pers. comm. Letter regarding lake trout environmental window for Burns Harbor Indiana.

Dombeck, M. P., B. W. Menzel, and P. N. Hinz. 1984. "Muskellunge Spawning Habitat and Reproductive Success." *Transactions of the American Fisheries Society* 113, no. 2: 205–16.

Dowling, T. E., R. E. Broughton, and B. D. DeMarais. 1997. "Significant Role for Historical Effects in the Evolution of Reproductive Isolation: Evidence from Patterns of Introgression between the Cyprinid Fishes, *Luxilus cornutus* and *Luxilus chrysocephalus*." *Evolution* 51:1574–83.

Dryer, W. R. 1966. "Bathymetric Distribution of Fish in the Apostle Islands Region, Lake Superior." *Transactions of the American Fisheries Society* 95:248–59.

Dryer, W. R., and J. Beil. 1964. "Life History of the Lake Herring in Lake Superior." *Fisheries Bulletin* 63:493–530.

Dubs, D. O. L., and L. D. Corkum. 1996. "Behavioral Interactions between Round Gobies (*Neogobius melanostomus*) and Mottled Sculpins (*Cottus bairdi*)." *Journal of Great Lakes Research* 22:838–44.

Eck, G. W., and L. Wells. 1987. "Recent Changes in Lake Michigan's Fish Community and Their Probable Causes, with Emphasis on the Role of the Alewife *Alosa pseudoharengus*." *Canadian Journal of Fisheries and Aquatic Science* 44 (S2): S53–60.

Eddy, S., and J. C. Underhill. 1974. *Northern Fishes: With Special Reference to the Upper Mississippi Valley*. Minneapolis: University of Minnesota Press.

Edwards, E. A. 1983. *Habitat Suitability Index Models: Longnose Sucker*. US Department of the Interior, Fish and Wildlife Service, FWS/OBS-82/10.35.

Eigenmann, C. H., and C. H. Beeson. 1894. "The Fishes of Indiana." *Proceedings of the Indiana Academy of Science, 1893* 9:76–108.

Etnier, D. A., and W. C. Starnes. 1993. *The Fishes of Tennessee*. Knoxville: University of Tennessee Press.

Evermann, B. W., and O. P. Jenkins. 1888. "Notes on Indiana Fishes." *Proceedings of the United States National Museum*, 43–57.

Ewart, K. V., and G. L. Fletcher. 1990. "Isolation and Characterization of Antifreeze Proteins from Smelt (*Osmerus mordax*) and Atlantic Herring (*Clupea harengus harengus*)." *Canadian Journal of Zoology* 68:1652–58.

Feldheim, K. A., P. Willink, J. E. Brown, D. J. Murphy, M. E. Neilson, and C. A. Stepien. 2009. "Microsatellite Loci for Ponto-Caspian Gobies: Markers for Assessing Exotic Invasions." *Molecular Ecology Resources* 9:639–44.

Fey, D. G. 1955. "Distributional Ecology of the Cisco (*Coregonus artedii*) in Indiana." *Investigation of Indiana Lakes and Streams* 4:177–228.

Forbes, S. A. 1884. "A Catalogue of the Native Fishes of Illinois." In *Report of the Illinois State Fish Commissioner for 1884*, 60–89.

——. 1885. "Description of New Illinois Fishes." *Illinois State Laboratory of Natural History Bulletin* 2:135–39.

Forbes, S. A., and R. E. Richardson. 1908. *The Fishes of Illinois*. Illinois State Laboratory of Natural History. Danville: Illinois Printing Company.

——. 1920. *The Fishes of Illinois*. 2nd ed. Champaign: Illinois Natural History Survey.

Ford, E. R. 1956. *Birds of the Chicago Region*. Chicago: Chicago Academy of Sciences.

French, J. R. P., and D. J. Jude. 2001. "Diets and Diet Overlap of Nonindigenous Gobies and Small Benthic Native Fishes Co-inhabiting the St. Clair River, Michigan." *Journal of Great Lakes Research* 27:300–311.

Gerald, J. W. 1971. "Sound Production during Courtship in Six Species of Sunfish (Centrarchidae)." *Evolution* 25:75–87.

Gerking, S. D. 1945. *The Distribution of the Fishes of Indiana.* Investigations of Indiana Lakes and Streams 3.

Gilbert, C. R., and R. M. Bailey. 1972. *Systematics and Zoogeography of the American Cyprinid Fish* Notropis (Opsopoeodus) emiliae. Occasional Papers of the Museum of Zoology University of Michigan 664.

Goode, G. B. 1887. *The Fisheries and Fishery Industries of the United States.* US Government Printing Office.

Graham, J. B. 1997. *Air-Breathing Fishes: Evolution, Diversity, and Adaptation.* San Diego: Academic Press.

Grande, L. 2010. "An Empirical Synthetic Pattern Study of Gars (Lepisosteiformes) and Closely Related Species, Based Mostly on Skeletal Anatomy. The Resurrection of Holostei." *Ichthyology & Herpetology* 10, no. 2A (2010): 1.

Grande, L., and W. E. Bemis. 1991. "Osteology and Phylogenetic Relationships of Fossil and Recent Paddlefishes (Polyodontidae) with Comments on the Interrelationships of Acipenseriformes." *Journal of Vertebrate Paleontology* 11, S1:S1–121.

———. 1998. "A Comprehensive Phylogenetic Study of Amid Fishes (Amiidae) Based on Comparative Skeletal Anatomy: An Empirical Search for Interconnected Patterns of Natural History." Memoir (Society of Vertebrate Paleontology) 4 (supplement).

Greenberg, J. R. 2002. *A Natural History of the Chicago Region.* Chicago: University of Chicago Press.

Greene, C. W. 1935. *The Distribution of Wisconsin Fishes.* State of Wisconsin Conservation Commission.

Gunn, J. M. 1995. "Spawning Behavior of Lake Trout: Effects on Colonization Ability." *Journal of Great Lakes Research* 21 (S1): S323–29.

Gunning, G. E., and W. M. Lewis. 1955. "The Fish Population of a Spring-Fed Swamp in the Mississippi Bottoms of Southern Illinois." *Ecology* 36:552–58.

Hackney, P. A., W. M. Tatum, and S. L. Spencer. 1967. "Life History Study of the River Redhorse, *Moxostoma carinatum* (Cope), in the Cahaba River, Alabama, with Notes on the Management of the Species as a Sport Fish." *Proceedings of the Southeastern Association of Game and Fish Commissioners* 21:324–332.

Hankinson, T. L. 1919. "Notes of Life Histories of Illinois Fish." *Illinois Academy of Science* 12:132–50.

———. 1920. *Report on Investigations of the Fish of the Galien River, Berrien County, Michigan.* Occasional Papers of the Museum of Zoology no. 89. Ann Arbor: University of Michigan.

———. 1932. "Observations on the Breeding Behavior and Habitats of Fishes in Southern Michigan." *Papers of the Michigan Academy of Science, Arts, and Letters* 15, no. 1931: 411–25.

Hankinson, T. L., and C. L. Hubbs. 1922. "The Establishment of the Smelt in Great Lakes Waters." *Copeia,* no. 109: 57–59.

Hansen, D. F. 1943. "On Nesting of the White Crappie, *Pomoxis annularis.*" *Copeia,* no. 4: 259–60.

———. 1951. "Biology of the White Crappie in Illinois." *Illinois Natural History Survey Bulletin* 25:211–65.

———. 1965. "Further Observations on Nesting of the White Crappie, *Pomoxis annularis.*" *Transactions of the American Fisheries Society* 94:182–84.

Hatch, J. T., and J. D. Johnson. 2014. "A Life History Study of Minnesota's Great Northerner: The Iowa Darter." *American Currents* 39, no. 3: 9–16.

Hay, O. P. 1896. "On Some Collections of Fishes Made in the Kankakee and Illinois Rivers." *Field Columbian Museum, Zoological Series* 1:85–97.

Herald, E. S. 1962. *Living Fishes of the World.* Garden City, NY: Doubleday.

———. 1978. *The Yellow Perch: Its Life History, Ecology, and Management.* Vol. 3600, no. 21-1978. Department of Natural Resources.

Herrington, S. J., K. N. Hettiger, E. J. Heist, and D. B. Keeney. 2008. "Hybridization between Longnose and Alligator Gars in Captivity, with Comments on Possible Gar Hybridization in Nature." *Transactions of the American Fisheries Society* 137:158–64.

Hile, R., P. H. Eschenmyer, and G. F. Lunger. 1951. "Decline of the Lake Trout Fishery in Lake Michigan." *Fishery Bulletin of the US Fish and Wildlife Service* 52, no. 60: 77–95.

Holm, E., N. E. Mandrak, and M. E. Burridge. 2009. *The Royal Ontario Museum Field Guide to Freshwater Fishes of Ontario.* Toronto: Royal Ontario Museum.

Hoxmeier, R. H., and D. R. Devries. 1997. "Habitat Use, Diet, and Population Structure of Adult and Juvenile Paddlefish in the Lower Alabama River." *Transactions of the American Fisheries Society* 126:288–301.

Hubbs, C. L. 1936. "An Older Name for the Black-Nosed Dace." *Copeia,* no. 2: 124–25.

Hubbs, C. L., and G. P. Cooper. 1936. *Minnows of Michigan.* Bulletin 3. Bloomfield Hills, MI: Cranbrook Institute of Science.

Hubbs, C. L., and K. F. Lagler. 1958. *Fishes of the Great Lakes Region.* Bulletin 26. Cranbrook Institute of Science.

Hubbs, C. L., and K. F. Lagler. 1964. *Fishes of the Great Lakes Region.* Ann Arbor: University of Michigan Press.

Hubbs, C. L., K. F. Lagler, and G. R. Smith. 2004. *Fishes of the Great Lakes Region.* Rev. ed. Ann Arbor: University of Michigan Press.

Hubbs, C. L., and M. B. Trautman. 1937. *A Revision of the Lamprey Genus* Ichthyomyzon. Miscellaneous Publications 35. Museum of Zoology, University of Michigan.

Hunter, J. R. 1963. "The Reproductive Behavior of the Green Sunfish, *Lepomis cyanellus.*" *Zoologica* (New York) 48:13–24.

Janssen, J., and D. J. Jude. 2001. "Recruitment Failure of Mottled Sculpin *Cottus bairdi* in Calumet Harbor, Southern Lake Michigan, Induced by the Newly Introduced Round Goby *Neogobius melanostomus.*" *Journal of Great Lakes Research* 27:319–28.

Jenkins, R. E., and N. M. Burkhead. 1994. *Freshwater Fishes of Virginia.* Bethesda, MD: American Fisheries Society.

Jobes, F. W. 1943. "The Age, Growth, and Bathymetric Distribution of Reighard's Chub, *Leucichthys reighardi* Koelz, in Lake Michigan." *Transactions of the American Fisheries Society* 72:108–35.

John, D. R., and A. D. Hasler. 1956. "Observations of Some Factors Affecting the Hatching of Eggs and the Survival of Young Shallow-Water Cisco (*Leucichthys artedi* LeSueur) in Lake Mendota, Wisconsin." *Limnology and Oceanography* 1:176–93.

Johnson, C. E. 1970. "Factors Affecting Fish Spawning." *Wisconsin Conservation Bulletin* 36:16–17.

Johnson, W. L. 1945. "Age and Growth of the Black and White Crappies of Greenwood Lake." *Investigations of Indiana Lakes and Streams* 2:297–324.

Jordan, D. S. 1877. "On the Fishes of Northern Indiana." *Proceedings of the Academy of Natural Sciences of Philadelphia* 29:42–82.

———. 1878. "A Catalogue of the Fishes of Illinois." *Bulletin of the Illinois State Laboratory of Natural History* 2:37–70.

Jude, D. J., R. H. Reider, and G. R Smith. 1992. "Establishment of Gobiidae in the Great Lakes Basin." *Canadian Journal of Fisheries and Aquatic Science* 49:416–21.

Jude, D. J., H. W. Van Sumeren, and J. Lutchko. 2022. "First Documentation of Spawning by Deepwater Sculpins in the Great Lakes and Potential Impacts of Round Gobies." *Journal of Great Lakes Research* 48:614–19.

Koelz, W. 1929. "Coregonid Fishes of the Great Lakes." *Bulletin of the US Bureau of Fisheries* 43, no. 2: 297–643.

Kolar, C. S., D. C. Chapman, W. R. Courtenay Jr., C. M. Housel, J. D. Williams, and D. P. Jennings. 2007. *Bigheaded Carps: A Biological Synopsis and Environmental Risk Assessment.* Bethesda, MD: American Fisheries Society Special Publication 33.

Kottelat, M., and J. Freyhof. 2007. *Handbook of European Freshwater Fishes.* Cornol, Switzerland: Publications Kottelat.

Krebs, J. E. 2020. "Movements and Spawning Habitat of Muskellunge *Esox masquinongy* in Green Bay, Lake Michigan." Master's thesis, University of Wisconsin–Stevens Point.

Krumholz, L. A. 1948. "Reproduction in the Western Mosquitofish, *Gambusia affinis* (Baird and Girard), and Its Use in Mosquito Control." *Ecological Monographs* 18:1–43.

Kuehne, R. A., and R. W. Barbour. 1983. *The American Darters.* Lexington: University Press of Kentucky.

Kuhns, L. A., and M. B. Berg. 1999. "Benthic Invertebrate Community Responses to Round Goby (*Neogobius melanostomus*) and Zebra Mussel (*Dreissena polymorpha*) Invasion in Southern Lake Michigan." *Journal of Great Lakes Research* 25:910–17.

Kwak, T. J. 1991. "Ecological Characteristics of a Northern Population of the Pallid Shiner." *Transactions of the American Fisheries Society* 120:106–15.

Kwak, T. J., and T. M. Skelly. 1992. "Spawning Habitat, Behavior, and Morphology as Isolating Mechanisms of the Golden Redhorse, *Moxostoma erythrurum,* and the Black Redhorse, *M. duquesnei,* Two Syntopic Fishes." *Environmental Biology of Fishes* 34:127–37.

Laird, C. A., and L. M. Page. 1996. "Non-native Fishes Inhabiting the Streams and Lakes of Illinois." *Illinois Natural History Survey Bulletin* 35:1–51.

Lane, J. A., C. B. Portt, and C. K. Minns. 1996. *Nursery Habitat Characteristics of Great Lakes Fishes* (p. 44). Department of Fisheries and Oceans. Ottawa, Ontario: Fisheries and Oceans Canada.

Lane, J. A., C. K. Minns, and C. B. Portt. 1996. *Spawning Habitat Characteristics of Great Lakes Fishes* (p. 47). Port Hardy, BC: Fisheries and Oceans Canada.

Larimore, R. W. 1957. "Ecological Life History of the Warmouth (Centrarchidae)." *Illinois Natural History Survey Bulletin* 27:1–83.

Lauder, G. V. 1983. "Functional and Morphological Bases of Trophic Specialization in Sunfishes (Teleostei, Centrarchidae)." *Journal of Morphology* 178:1–21.

Lawrie, A. H. 1970. "The Sea Lamprey in the Great Lake." *Transactions of the American Fisheries Society* 99:766–75.

Lievense, S. J. 1954. "Spawning of American Smelt, *Osmerus mordax,* in Crystal Lake, Benzie County, Michigan." *Copeia,* no. 3: 232–33.

Ludwig, G. M., and C. R. Norten. 1969. *Age, Growth and Reproduction of the Northern Mottled Sculpin (Cottus bairdi bairdi) in Mt. Vernon Creek, Wisconsin.* Occasional Papers of Natural History from the Milwaukee Public Museum 2.

Lutterbie, G. W. 1976. "The Darters (Pisces: Percidae: Etheostomatinae) of Wisconsin." Master's thesis, University of Wisconsin–Stevens Point.

Lyons, J., and K. Schmidt. 2022. "An Updated Annotated List of Wisconsin's Fishes." *American Currents* 47, no. 4: 1–56.

MacKay, H. H. 1963. *Fishes of Ontario.* Ontario Department of Lands and Forests.

Madenjian, C. P., D. B. Bunnell, T. J. Desorcie, M. A. Chriscinske, M. J. Kostich, and J. V. Adams. 2012. "Status and Trends of Prey Fish Populations in Lake Michigan, 2011." Lake Michigan Committee Meeting.

Mardsen, J. E. 1994. "Spawning by Stocked Lake Trout on Shallow, Near-Shore Reefs in Southwestern Lake Michigan." *Journal of Great Lakes Research* 20:377–84.

Martin, N. V. 1960. "Homing Behaviour in Spawning Lake Trout." Department of Fisheries of Canada.

Martin, N. V., and Olver, C. H. 1980. "The Lake Charr, *Salvelinus namaycush*." In *Charrs: Salmonid Fishes of the Genus Salvelinus*, 205–77. Edited by E. K. Balon. The Hague, The Netherlands: Junk Publishers.

Martin, R. G. 1975. "Sexual and Aggressive Behavior, Density and Social Structure in a Natural Population of Mosquitofish, *Gambusia affinis holbrooki*." *Copeia*, no. 3: 445–54.

McPhail, J. D., and C. C. Lindsey. 1970. *Freshwater Fishes of Northwestern Canada and Alaska*. Fisheries Research Board of Canada Bulletin 173.

Meek, S. E., and S. F. Hildebrand. 1910. *A Synoptic List of the Fishes Known to Occur within Fifty Miles of Chicago*. Field Museum of Natural History, Zoological Series, Publication 142, 7:223–338.

Metzke, B. A., B. M. Burr, L. C. Hinz Jr., L. M. Page, and C. A. Taylor. 2022. *An Atlas of Illinois Fishes: 150 Years of Change*. Urbana: University of Illinois Press.

Metzke, B. A., C. A. Taylor, and C. P. Caton. 2023. "Northern Sunfish (*Lepomis peltastes*) Distribution in Illinois." *Northeastern Naturalist* 30:99–113.

Miller. P. J. 1986. "Gobiidae." In *Fishes of the Northeast Atlantic and Mediterranean*, edited by P. J. P. Whitehead, M. L. Bauchot, J. C. Hureau, J. Nielswn, and E. Tortonese, 1019–95. Paris: UNESCO.

Morrow, J. E. 1980. *The Freshwater Fishes of Alaska*. Anchorage: Alaska Northwest Publishing.

Moskal'kova, K. I. 1996. "Ecological and Morphophysiological Prerequisites to Range Extension in the Round Goby *Neogobius melanostomus* under Conditions of Anthropogenic Pollution." *Journal of Ichthyology* 36:584–90.

Nelson, E. W. 1876. "A Partial Catalogue of the Fishes of Illinois." *Illinois Natural History Survey Bulletin* 1:33–52.

———. 1878. "Fisheries of Chicago and Vicinity." In *United States Commission of Fish and Fisheries: Report of the Commissioner for 1875–1876*, 783–800.

Nelson, J. S. 1994. *Fishes of the World*. 3rd ed. New York: Wiley and Sons.

———. 2006. *Fishes of the World*. Hoboken, NJ: John Wiley and Sons.

Nico, L. G., J. D. Williams, and H. L. Jelks. 2005. *Black Carp: Biological Synopsis and Risk Assessment of an Introduced Fish*. Bethesda, MD: American Fisheries Society Special Publication 32.

Norris, K. E. 2015. "Growth, Fecundity, and Diet of Oriental Weatherloach *Misgurnus anguillicaudatus* in the Chicago Area Waterways." Master's thesis, Western Illinois University.

Okada, Y. 1960. Studies on the Freshwater Fishes of Japan. II. Special Part. *Journal of the Faculty of Fisheries*, Prefectural University of Mie 4:267–588.

Page, L. M. 1983. *Handbook of Darters*. Neptune City, NJ: T. F. H. Publications.

Page, L. M., and B. M. Burr. 2011. *Peterson Field Guide to Freshwater Fishes of North America North of Mexico*. 2nd ed. New York: Houghton Mifflin Harcourt.

Page, L. M., and C. E. Johnston. 1990a. "The Breeding Behavior of *Opsopoeodus emiliae* (Cyprinidae) and Its Phylogenetic Implications." *Copeia*, no. 4: 1176–80.

———. 1990b. "Spawning in the Creek Chubsucker, *Erimyzon oblongus*, with a Review of Spawning Behavior in Suckers (Catostomidae)." *Environmental Biology of Fishes* 27:265–72.

Page, L. M., and C. A. Laird. 1993. *The Identification of the Nonnative Fishes Inhabiting Illinois Waters*. Center for Biodiversity Technical Report 4.

Page, L. M., M. E. Retzer, and R. A. Stiles. 1982. "Spawning Behavior in Seven Species of Darters (Pisces: Percidae)." *Brimleyana* 8:135–43.

Parks, C. E. 1949. "The Summer Food of Some Game Fishes of Winona Lake." *Investigations of Indiana Lakes and Streams* 3:235–45.

Pearse, A. S. 1918. "The Food of the Shore Fishes of Certain Wisconsin Lakes." *Bulletin of the United States Bureau of Fisheries* 35:245–92.

——. 1919. "Habits of the Black Crappie in Inland Lakes of Wisconsin." Appendix 3 of *Report of the US Commissioner of Fisheries for 1918*, 5–16.

——. 1921a. "The Distribution and Food of the Fishes of Three Wisconsin Lakes in Summer." *University of Wisconsin Studies in Science* 3:5–61.

——. 1921b. "Fishing in Lake Michigan." *Scientific Monthly*, July, 81–91.

Pearse, A. S., and H. Achtenberg. 1920. "Habits of Yellow Perch in Wisconsin Lakes." *Bulletin of the Bureau of Fisheries* 36:297–366.

Pescitelli, S. M. 2018. "Reconnecting Illinois Waterways: Review of Dam Removal Projects and Benefits to Fish and River Ecosystems." Annual Meeting of the American Fisheries Society, Southern Division, San Juan, Puerto Rico, March 2018.

Pescitelli, S. M., and T. Widloe. 2018. *Current Status of Fish Assemblages and Sport Fishery in the Des Plaines River Watershed: Changes over 44 Years of Basin Surveys.* Plano: Illinois Department of Natural Resources Region II Streams Program.

Peterson, D. L., P. Vecsei, and C. A. Jennings. 2007. "Ecology and Biology of the Lake Sturgeon: A Synthesis of Current Knowledge of a Threatened North American Acipenseridae." *Reviews in Fish Biology and Fisheries* 17:59–76.

Pflieger, W. L. 1975. *The Fishes of Missouri.* Columbia: Missouri Department of Conservation.

——. 1997. *The Fishes of Missouri.* Rev. ed. Jefferson City: Missouri Department of Conservation.

Pollard, W. R., G. F. Hartman, P. Edgell, and C. Groot. 1997. *Field Identification of Coastal Juvenile Salmonids.* Madeira Park, BC: Harbour Publishing.

Poly, W. J., and J. E. Wetzel. 2003. "Transbranchioral Spawning: Novel Reproductive Strategy Observed for the Pirate Perch *Aphredoderus sayanus* (Aphredoderidae)." *Ichthyological Exploration of Freshwaters* 14:151–58.

Potter, I. C., and F. W. H. Beamish. 1977. "The Freshwater Biology of Anadromous Seal Lampreys *Petromyzon marinus.*" *Journal of Zoology* (London) 181:113–30.

Potter, R. L., and G. W. Fleischer. 1992. "Reappearance of Spoonhead Sculpins (*Cottus ricei*) in Lake Michigan." *Journal of Great Lakes Research* 18:755–58.

Pritchard, A. L. 1931. *Taxonomic and Life History Studies of the Ciscoes of Lake Ontario.* University of Toronto Studies in Biology Series 35. Publication of the Ontario Fisheries Research Laboratory 41.

Purkett, C. A. Jr. 1961. "Reproduction and Early Development in the Paddlefish." *Transactions of the American Fisheries Society* 90:125–29.

Radforth, Isobel. 1944. *Some Considerations on the Distribution of Fishes in Ontario.* Contributions of the Royal Ontario Museum of Zoology 25. Toronto: University of Toronto Press.

Richardson, L. R. 1939. "The Spawning Behavior of *Fundulus diaphanus* (LeSueur)." *Copeia*, no. 3: 165–67.

Ricker, W. E., and J. Gottschalk. 1941. "An Experiment in Removing Coarse Fish from a Lake." *Transactions of the American Fisheries Society* 70:382–90.

Ricker, W. E., H. F. Mosbaugh, and M. Lung. 1949. "Utilization and Survival of Trout in Indiana." *Investigation of Indiana Lakes and Streams* 3:271–81.

Roberts, M. E., B. M. Burr, and M. R. Whiles. 2006. "Reproductive Ecology and Food Habits of the Blacknose Shiner, *Notropis heterolepis*, in Northern Illinois." *American Midland Naturalist* 155:70–83.

Robison, H. W., and T. M. Buchanan. 1988. *Fishes of Arkansas.* Fayetteville: University of Arkansas Press.

Rupp, R. S. 1959. "Variation in the Life History of the American Smelt in Inland Waters of Maine." *Transactions of the American Fisheries Society* 88:241–52.

Savitz, J. 2000. Pers. comm. Lake trout primarily feed on alewife (*Alosa pseudoharengus*). Loyola University, Chicago, IL.

Savitz, J., C. Aiello, and C. L. Bardygula. 1989. "The First Record of the White Perch (*Morone americana*) in Illinois Waters of Lake Michigan." *Transactions of the Illinois Academy of Science* 82:57–58.

Schofield, P. J., J. D. Williams, L. G. Nico, P. Fuller, and M. R. Thomas. 2005. *Foreign Non-indigenous Carps and Minnows (Cyprinidae) in the United States — a Guide to Their Identification, Distribution, and Biology*. Reston, VA: US Geological Survey Scientific Investigations Report 2005-5041.

Schultze, H. P., and E. O. Wiley. 1984. "Neopterygian *Amia* as a Living Fossil." In *Living Fossils*, edited by N. Elderage and S. M. Stanley, 153–59. Springer-Verlag, New York.

Schwiebert, E. 1983. *Trout Strategies*. New York: E. P. Dutton.

Scott, W. B., and E. J. Crossman. 1973. *Freshwater Fishes of Canada*. Ottawa, Ontario: Fisheries Research Board of Canada Bulletin 184.

Scott, R. J., P. W. Willink, and B. M. Norton. 2018. "Biogeography and Distribution of the Cryptic Species Rosyface Shiner *Notropis rubellus* and Carmine Shiner *Notropis percobromus* in Illinois." *Copeia* 106, no. 3: 524–31.

Sherwood, J. L., A. J. Stites, M. J. Dreslik, and J. S. Tiemann. 2018. "Predicting the Range of a Regionally Threatened, Benthic Fish Using Species Distribution Models and Field Surveys." *Journal of Fish Biology* 93:972–77.

Simon, T. P. 2011. *Fishes of Indiana: A Field Guide*. Bloomington: Indiana University Press.

Simon, T. P., G. Bright, F. Veraldi, J. R. Smith, and J. R. Stahl. 2006. "New Records for the Alien Oriental Weatherfish, *Misgurnus anguillicaudatus*, in the Lake Michigan Basin, Indiana (Cypriniformes, Cobitidae)." In *Proceedings of the Indiana Academy of Science* 115, no. 1: 32–36.

Simon, T. P., P. B. Moy, and D. K. Barnes. 1998. "New Distribution Records for Exotic and Non-indigenous Fish Species in the Lake Michigan Drainage, Indiana." *Proceedings of the Indiana Academy of Science* 107:61–70.

Skora, K. E., and J. Stolarski. 1996. "*Neogobius melanostomus* (Pallas, 1811), a New Immigrant Species in the Baltic Sea." *Proceedings of the 2nd International Estuary Symposium, Gdynia*.

Smiley, C. W. 1882. "Changes in the Fisheries of the Great Lakes during the Decade 1870–1880." Bulletin of the US Fish Commission, vol. 1 for 1881.

Smith, B. J., and B. S. Harris. 2020. "Expansion of a Banded Killifish *Fundulus diaphanus* Population into Benthic Nearshore Waters of Lake Michigan around Calumet Harbor." *American Midland Naturalist* 183:260–67.

Smith, S. H. 1956. "Life History of Lake Herring of Green Bay, Lake Michigan." *Fishery Bulletin* 109:87–138.

———. 1964. "Status of the Deepwater Cisco Populations of Lake Michigan." *Transactions of the American Fisheries Society* 93:155–63.

Smith, P. W. 1979. *Fishes of Illinois*. Urbana: University of Illinois Press.

Stearley, R. F., and G. R. Smith. 1993. "Phylogeny of the Pacific Trouts and Salmon (*Oncorhynchus*) and Genera of the Family Salmonidae." *Transactions of the American Fisheries Society* 122:1–33.

Swink, F., and G. Wilhelm. 1994. *Plants of the Chicago Region*. 4th ed. Indianapolis: Indiana Academy of Science.

Tan, M., and J. W. Armbruster. 2018. "Phylogenetic Classification of Extant Genera of Fishes of the Order Cypriniformes (Teleostei: Ostariophysi)." *Zootaxa* 4476:6–39.

Taylor, C. A., and B. M. Burr. 1997. "Reproductive Biology of the Northern Starhead Topminnow, *Fundulus dispar* (Osteichthyes: Fundulidae), with a Review of Data for Freshwater Members of the Genus." *American Midland Naturalist* 137:151–64.

Thomerson, J. E., and D. P. Wooldridge. 1970. "Food Habits of Allotropic and Syntopic Populations of the Topminnows *Fundulus olivaceus* and *Fundulus notatus*." *American Midland Naturalist* 84:573–76.

Tiemann, J. S. 2004. "Observations of the Pirate Perch, *Aphredoderus sayanus* (Gilliams), with Comments on Sexual Dimorphism, Reproduction, and Unique Defecation Behavior." *Journal of Freshwater Ecology* 19:115–21.

Tiemann, J., J. Hartman, J. Sherwood, P. Willink, and E. Larson. 2021. *Genetic Analysis of the Rapid Expansion of the Banded Killifish (Fundulus diaphanus) in Illinois*. Illinois Natural History Survey Technical Report 8.

Tiemann, J. S., J. L. Sherwood, and A. J. Stites. 2022. "Status Assessment of the State-Threatened Gravel Chub (*Erimystax x-punctatus*) in Illinois." *Transactions of the Illinois State Academy of Science* 115:1–5.

Tiemann, J. S., C. A. Taylor, D. Wylie, J. Lamer, P. W. Willink, F. M. Veraldi, S. M. Pescitelli, B. Lubinski, T. Thomas, R. Sauer, and B. Cantrell. 2015. "Range Expansions and New Drainage Records for Select Illinois Fishes." *Transactions of the Illinois State Academy of Science* 108:47–52.

Trautman, M. B. 1957. *The Fishes of Ohio*. Baltimore: Waverly Press.

Turner, C. L. 1921. "Food of the Common Ohio Darters." *Ohio Journal of Science* 22:41–62.

Vladykov, V. D., and E. Kott. 1978. *A New Nonparasitic Species of the Holarctic Lamprey Genus* Lethenteron *Creaser and Hubbs, 1922, (Petromyzonidae) from Northwestern North America with Notes on other Species of the Same Genus*. Biological Papers of the University of Alaska 19, Institute of Arctic Biology.

———. 1980. "Description and Key to Metamorphosed Specimens and Ammocoetes of Petromyzonidae Found in the Great Lakes Region." *Canadian Journal of Fisheries and Aquatic Sciences* 37:1616–25.

Voightlander, C. W., and T. E. Wissing. 1974. "Food Habits of Young and Yearling White Bass." *Transactions of the American Fisheries Society* 103:25–31.

Waldman, J. R., C. Grunwald, N. K. Roy, and I. I. Wirgin. 2004. "Mitochondrial DNA Analysis Indicates Sea Lampreys Are Indigenous to Lake Ontario." *Transactions of the American Fisheries Society* 133:950–60.

Weed, A. C. 1927. *Pike, Pickerel and Muskalonge*. Field Museum of Natural History, Zoology Leaflet 9.

Wells, L. 1968. "Seasonal Depth Distribution of Fish in Southeastern Lake Michigan." *Fishery Bulletin of the US Fish and Wildlife Service* 67:1–15.

Wells, L., and A. L. McLain. 1973. *Lake Michigan — Man's Effects on Native Fish Stocks and Other Biota*. Great Lakes Fisheries Commission Technical Report 20.

Werbianskyj, Kayla. 2023. Pers. comm. Located at: Indiana Department of Environmental Management (IDEM), Assessment Information Management System (AIMS) Database, Indianapolis, Indiana.

Wetzel, J., and J. T. Edwards. 2014. "Artificial Spawning Site for Pirate Perch." *American Currents* 39, no. 3:7.

Wiegert, J., and R. Rice. 2006. "Mosquitofish to the Rescue? The Impact of Two *Gambusia* Species in and out of the Aquarium." *Freshwater and Marine Aquarium*, October, 82–88.

Wigley, R. L. 1959. "Life History of the Sea Lamprey of Cayuga Lake, New York." *Fishery Bulletin of the US Fish and Wildlife Service* 59:561–617.

Wilberg, M. J., J. R. Bence, B. T. Eggold, D. Makauskas, and D. F. Clapp. 2005. "Yellow Perch Dynamics in Southwestern Lake Michigan during 1986–2002." *North American Journal of Fisheries Management* 25:1130–52.

Wilhelm, G., and L. Rericha. 2017. *Flora of the Chicago Region: A Floristic and Ecological Synthesis.* Indiana Academy of Sciences.

Willink, P. W. 2002. "Function and Variation of Gill Rakers in the Fish Family Catostomidae, with Comments on Phylogenetic Tests of Natural Selection." PhD diss., University of Michigan, Ann Arbor.

——. 2009. "A Century of Shifting Fish Assemblages in Wolf Lake, Illinois–Indiana." *Proceedings of the Indiana Academy of Science* 118:187–95.

——. 2016. *Biological Survey of Morgan Shoal, Chicago.* National Oceanic and Atmospheric Administration. Office of Ocean and Coastal Resource Management. US Department of Commerce and Illinois Department of Natural Resources — Illinois Coastal Management Program.

——. 2017. *Assessing the Status of Potential Illinois Endangered and Threatened Fish Species.* United States Fish and Wildlife Service, Department of the Interior, and Illinois Department of Natural Resources.

Willink, P. W., and M. J. Dreslik. 2023a. *Conservation Guidance for: Northern Brook Lamprey* Ichthyomyzon fossor *(Reghard and Cummins, 1916).* Illinois Natural History Survey Technical Report 22.

——. 2023b. *Conservation Guidance for: Gravel Chub* Erimystax x-punctatus *(Hubbs and Crowe, 1956).* Illinois Natural History Survey Technical Report 25.

——. 2023c. *Conservation Plan for: Greater Redhorse* Moxostoma valenciennesi *Jordan, 1885.* Illinois Natural History Survey Technical Report 30.

——. 2023d. *Conservation Plan for: River Redhorse* Moxostoma carinatum *(Cope, 1870).* Illinois Natural History Survey Technical Report 31.

Willink, P. W., J. S. Tiemann, J. L. Sherwood, E. R. Larson, A. Otten, and B. Zimmerman. 2019. "The Mystery of the Banded Killifish *Fundulus diaphanus* Population Explosion: Where Did They All Come From?" *American Currents* 44, no. 4: 3–6.

Willink, P. W., and F. M. Veraldi. 2009. *The Fishes of Will County, Illinois.* Fieldiana, Zoology, n.s. 155.

Willink, P. W., F. M. Veraldi, and J. B. Ladonski. 2006. "Rediscovery of the Freckled Madtom *Noturus nocturnus* Jordan and Gilbert in the Des Plaines River, Illinois." *Transactions of the Illinois State Academy of Science* 99:169–73.

Willink, P. W., T. A. Widloe, V. J. Santucci Jr., D. Makauskas, J. S. Tiemann, S. D. Hertel, J. T. Lamer, and J. L. Sherwood. 2018. "Rapid Expansion of Banded Killifish *Fundulus diaphanus* across Northern Illinois: Dramatic Recovery or Invasive Species?" *American Midland Naturalist* 179:179–90.

Woods, L. P. 1954. "The Smelt, an Ocean Fish That Lives in the Great Lakes." *Chicago Natural History Museum Bulletin*, March, 4–6.

——. 1957a. "Seasonal Changes and Activities of Lake Fishes." *Chicago Natural History Museum Bulletin*, May, 3–4.

——. 1957b. "Some Little-Known Fishes of Lake Michigan." *Chicago Natural History Museum Bulletin*, August, 4–5.

——. 1960. "The Alewife." *Chicago Natural History Museum Bulletin* 31:6–8.

Wright, J. J., S. A. Bruce, D. A. Sinopoli, J. R. Palumbo, and D. J. Stewart. 2022. "Phylogenomic Analysis of the Bowfin (*Amia calva*) Reveals Unrecognized Species Diversity in a Living Fossil Lineage." *Scientific Reports* 12 (article 16514): 1–10.

Wuepper, J. 2001. "Old Record of Paddlefish (*Polyodon spathula*) from Berrien County." *Michigan Birds and Natural History* 8:77–78.

Wydoski, R. S., and R. W. Whitney. 2003. *Inland Fishes of Washington.* 2nd ed. University of Washington Press and American Fisheries Society.

Photo Credits

All photographs of fishes were taken by Philip Willink, except:

Jason DeBoer, Illinois River Biological Station, Illinois Natural History Survey: Paddlefish (full body) and Mooneye

Mike Hari, Fadeout Media: Paddlefish (closeups), Somonauk Creek habitat photo

M. W. Littmann, Field Museum of Natural History: Sea Lamprey adult

Seth Love, Illinois Department of Natural Resources: Largemouth Bass

Kristopher Maxson, Illinois River Biological Station, Illinois Natural History Survey: Shortnose Gar, Goldeye, Shoal Chub, and Silver Chub

Stephen Pescitelli: Spotted Gar

Francis Veraldi: Alewife, Smallmouth Buffalo, Bigmouth Buffalo, Grass Carp, Brown Bullhead, Lake Whitefish, Rainbow Trout (Steelhead), Chinook Salmon, Brown Trout, Trout-perch, and White Perch

Illinois Natural History Survey photo specimens include Northern Brook Lamprey (#90911).

The Field Museum photo specimens include Blackfin Cisco (#13951), Deepwater Cisco (#2089), Deepwater Sculpin (#63408), Kiyi (#9689), Lake Herring (#63396), Longjaw Cisco (#13939), Round Whitefish (#3106), Shortjaw Cisco (#63397), Shortnose Cisco (#63400), Silver Lamprey (#73646), Slimy Sculpin (#63406), Spoonhead Sculpin (#42905), Threespine Stickleback (#144766).

Photos of Black Bullhead, Blackstripe Topminnow, Central Mudminnow, Johnny Darter, Pirate Perch, Walleye, and Western Mosquitofish (female) also used in Willink and Veraldi 2009.

Photo of Freckled Madtom also used in Willink, Veraldi, and Ladonski 2006.

Taxonomic Index

Page numbers in italics refer to figures.

Acipenser fulvescens, 59–61
Acipenseridae, 58–59; *Acipenser fulvescens*, 59–61
Alosa chrysochloris, 89–91
Alosa pseudoharengus, 88, 90, 92–93, 275, 295, 297, 299, 303, 307
Alpheus randalli, 325
Ambloplites rupestris, 8, 344, 346–47
Amblyeleotris randalli, 325
Ameiurus melas, 244–45
Ameiurus natalis, 246–47, 249
Ameiurus nebulosus, 248–49
Amia calva, 74
Amia ocellicauda, 74, 76–77
Amiidae, 74–75; *Amia calva*, 74; *Amia ocellicauda*, 74, 76–77
Ammocrypta clara, 386–87
Anguilla rostrata, 78, 80–81
Anguillidae, 78–79; *Anguilla rostrata*, 78, 80–81
Aphredoderidae, 316–17; *Aphredoderus sayanus*, *11*, 32, 318–19
Aphredoderus sayanus, *11*, 32, 318–19
Aplodinotus grunniens, 381–83
Archoplites interruptus, 344–45
Atherinopsidae, 328–29; *Labidesthes sicculus*, 330–31
Atractosteus spatula, 66–67

Campostoma anomalum, 111, 152–55
Campostoma oligolepis, 152, 154–55
Carassius auratus, 136, 138–40

Carex spp., 12
Carpiodes carpio, 100–102, 104
Carpiodes cyprinus, 100–104
Carpiodes velifer, *17*, 100, 104–5
Catostomidae, 98–99; *Carpiodes carpio*, 100–102, 104; *Carpiodes cyprinus*, 100–104; *Carpiodes velifer*, *17*, 100, 104–5; *Catostomus catostomus*, 19, 98, 106–8; *Catostomus commersonii*, 106, 108–9; *Erimyzon claviformis*, *14*, 110–12; *Erimyzon sucetta*, 8, 110–13; *Hypentelium nigricans*, 114–15; *Ictiobus bubalus*, 116–17, 120; *Ictiobus cyprinellus*, 118–19; *Ictiobus niger*, *12*, 116, 120–21; *Minytrema melanops*, 122–23; *Moxostoma anisurum*, *12*, 124–25, 130, 132, 134; *Moxostoma carinatum*, 18, 126–27, 132, 134, 449; *Moxostoma duquesnei*, 128–30; *Moxostoma erythrurum*, 126, 128, 130–31, 133, 135; *Moxostoma macrolepidotum*, *17*, 103, 126, 130, 132–34; *Moxostoma valenciennesi*, 18, 126, 134–35; *Myxocyprinus asiaticus*, 98
Catostomus catostomus, 19, 98, 106–8
Catostomus commersonii, 106, 108–9
Centrarchidae, 344–45; *Ambloplites rupestris*, 8, 344, 346–47; *Archoplites interruptus*, 344–45; *Lepomis cyanellus*, 345, 348–49, 352; *Lepomis gibbosus*, 350–51; *Lepomis gulosus*, 8, 352–53; *Lepomis humilis*, 354–55; *Lepomis macrochirus*, 345, 356–57, 440; *Lepomis*

megalotis, 358–59, 362–63, 444; *Lepomis microlophus*, 356, 360–61; *Lepomis peltastes*, 358–59, 362–63; *Micropterus dolomieu*, 8, 18, 327, 345, 364–66; *Micropterus salmoides*, 345, 364, 366–67; *Pomoxis annularis*, 368–70; *Pomoxis nigromaculatus*, *10*, 368, 370–71

Cephalanthus occidentalis, 12

Ceratophyllum demersum, 398

Chrosomus eos, 156–58

Chrosomus erythrogaster, 14, 156–59

Clupeidae, 88–89; *Alosa chrysochloris*, 89–91; *Alosa pseudoharengus*, 88, 90, 92–93, 275, 295, 297, 299, 303, 307; *Dorosoma cepedianum*, 89–90, 94–96, 146; *Dorosoma petenense*, 90, 94, 96–97

Cobitidae, 238–39; *Misgurnus anguillicaudatus*, 240–41

Coregonus alpenae, 276

Coregonus artedi, 278–79, 292

Coregonus clupeaformis, 280–81

Coregonus hoyi, 278, 282–83

Coregonus johannae, 276, 284–85

Coregonus kiyi, 286–87

Coregonus nigripinnis, 288–89

Coregonus reighardi, 290–91

Coregonus zenithicus, 292–93

Cottidae, 426–27; *Cottus bairdii*, 14–15, *19*, 326–27, 427–30; *Cottus cognatus*, 428, 430–31; *Cottus ricei*, 432–34; *Myoxocephalus thompsonii*, 307, 434–35

Cottus bairdii, 14–15, *19*, 326–27, 427–30

Cottus cognatus, 428, 430–31

Cottus ricei, 432–34

Couesius plumbeus, 160–61, 236

Ctenopharyngodon idella, 142, 144–45, 148, 449

Culaea inconstans, 12, 14, 420–22

Cyprinella lutrensis, 162–64

Cyprinella spiloptera, 162, 164–65

Cyprinidae, 136–37; *Carassius auratus*, 136, 138–40; *Cyprinus carpio*, 136–38, 140–43; *Cyprinus rubrofuscus*, 140

Cyprinus carpio, 136–38, 140–43

Cyprinus rubrofuscus, 140

Dallia pectoralis, 270–71

Dorosoma cepedianum, 89–90, 94–96, 146

Dorosoma petenense, 90, 94, 96–97

Dreissena bugensis, 407

Dreissena polymorpha, 407

Dreissenidae, 327; *Dreissena bugensis*, 407; *Dreissena polymorpha*, 407

Elodea canadensis, 398

Erimystax x-punctatus, 166–67

Erimyzon claviformis, *14*, 110–12

Erimyzon sucetta, 8, 110–13

Esocidae, 262–63; *Esox americanus*, 12, 262–65; *Esox lucius*, 11, *12*, 262–63, 266–69; *Esox masquinongy*, 109, 262–63, 268–69

Esox americanus, 12, 262–65

Esox lucius, 11, *12*, 262–63, 266–69

Esox masquinongy, 109, 262–63, 268–69

Etheostoma blennioides, 15, 388–89, 404

Etheostoma caeruleum, 390–91, 402, 404

TAXONOMIC INDEX 469

Etheostoma chlorosoma, 11, 18, 392–93
Etheostoma exile, 8, *10*, 394–95, 400
Etheostoma flabellare, 396–97
Etheostoma microperca, 8, 398–99
Etheostoma nigrum, 392, 400–401
Etheostoma spectabile, 390, 402–3
Etheostoma zonale, 404–5

Fratercula spp., 309
Fundulidae, 332–33; *Fundulus diaphanus*, 8, 334–35; *Fundulus dispar*, 8, *11*, 336–37, 342; *Fundulus notatus*, 338–39
Fundulus diaphanus, 8, 334–35
Fundulus dispar, 8, *11*, 336–37, 342
Fundulus notatus, 338–39

Gambusia affinis, 341–43
Gambusia holbrooki, 341
Gasterosteidae, 295, 418–19; *Culaea inconstans*, 12, 14, 420–22; *Gasterosteus aculeatus*, 422–23; *Pungitius pungitius*, 424–25
Gasterosteus aculeatus, 422–23
Gnathonemus petersii, 83
Gobiidae, 324–25; *Amblyeleotris randalli*, 325; *Neogobius melanostomus*, 307, 325–27, 427, 429, 435; *Oxudercidae*, 325; *Trimmatom nanus*, 325

Hiodon alosoides, 84–85
Hiodon tergisus, 86–87
Hiodontidae, 82–83; *Hiodon alosoides*, 84–85; *Hiodon tergisus*, 86–87
Hybognathus hankinsoni, 168–70
Hybognathus nuchalis, 170–71
Hybopsis amblops, 151
Hybopsis amnis, 18, 172–73
Hypentelium nigricans, 114–15
Hypophthalmichthys molitrix, 142, 146–49
Hypophthalmichthys nobilis, 136, 142, 146, 148–49

Ichthyomyzon castaneus, 14, 48–49
Ichthyomyzon fossor, *19*, 50–51
Ichthyomyzon unicuspis, 52–53
Ictaluridae, 242–43; *Ameiurus melas*, 244–45; *Ameiurus natalis*, 246–47, 249; *Ameiurus nebulosus*, 248–49; *Ictalurus punctatus*, 242–43, 250–51; *Noturus*

exilis, 252–53, 258; *Noturus flavus*, 19, 254–55, 258; *Noturus gyrinus*, *10*, 256–58; *Noturus nocturnus*, 18, 258–59; *Pylodictis olivaris*, *17*, 242–43, 250, 260–61, 440
Ictalurus punctatus, 242–43, 250–51
Ictiobus bubalus, 116–17, 120
Ictiobus cyprinellus, 118–19
Ictiobus niger, *12*, 116, 120–21

Labidesthes sicculus, 330–31
Larimichthys polyactis, 381
Lepisosteidae, 66–67; *Atractosteus spatula*, 66–67; *Lepisosteus oculatus*, 68–69; *Lepisosteus osseus*, 70–71; *Lepisosteus platostomus*, 72–73
Lepisosteus oculatus, 68–69
Lepisosteus osseus, 70–71
Lepisosteus platostomus, 72–73
Lepomis cyanellus, 345, 348–49, 352
Lepomis gibbosus, 350–51
Lepomis gulosus, 8, 352–53
Lepomis humilis, 354–55
Lepomis macrochirus, 345, 356–57, 440
Lepomis megalotis, 358–59, 362–63, 444
Lepomis microlophus, 356, 360–61
Lepomis peltastes, 358–59, 362–63
Lethenteron appendix, 14, 48, 50, 52, 54–56
Leuciscidae, 150–52; *Campostoma anomalum*, 111, 152–55; *Campostoma oligolepis*, 152, 154–55; *Chrosomus eos*, 156–57; *Chrosomus erythrogaster*, 14, 156–59; *Couesius plumbeus*, 160–61, 236; *Cyprinella lutrensis*, 162–64; *Cyprinella spiloptera*, 162, 164–65; *Erimystax x-punctatus*, 166–67; *Hybognathus hankinsoni*, 168–70; *Hybognathus nuchalis*, 170–71; *Hybopsis amblops*, 151; *Hybopsis amnis*, 18, 172–73; *Luxilus chrysocephalus*, 174–77; *Luxilus cornutus*, 15, 175–77, 187; *Lythrurus umbratilis*, 178–79; *Macrhybopsis hyostoma*, 180–82; *Macrhybopsis storeriana*, 182–83; *Margariscus nachtriebi*, 184–85; *Nocomis biguttatus*, 159, 175, 186–87, 211, 234, 236; *Notemigonus crysoleucas*, 151, 188–89; *Notropis anogenus*, 8,

190–91; *Notropis atherinoides*, 192–93, 214; *Notropis blennius*, 194–95; *Notropis buccatus*, 19, 196–97, 202; *Notropis buchanani*, 198–99; *Notropis chalybaeus*, 11, 200–201, 218, 337; *Notropis dorsalis*, 19, 195, 202–3; *Notropis heterodon*, 8, 204–5; *Notropis heterolepis*, 8, 206–7; *Notropis hudsonius*, 208–9, 295; *Notropis nubilus*, 15, 210–11; *Notropis percobromus*, 192, 212–13; *Notropis rubellus*, 192, 212–15; *Notropis stramineus*, 194–95, 202, 216–17, 220; *Notropis texanus*, 200, 218–19; *Notropis volucellus*, 8, 195, 220–21; *Opsopoeodus emiliae*, 222–23; *Phenacobius mirabilis*, 224–25; *Pimephales notatus*, 8, 226–28, 230; *Pimephales promelas*, 12, 151, 228–30; *Pimephales vigilax*, 226, 228, 230–31; *Ptychocheilus lucius*, 150; *Rhinichthys cataractae*, 232–34; *Rhinichthys obtusus*, 12, 14, 232, 234–35; *Semotilus atromaculatus*, 14, 160, 184, 186, 236–37
Lota lota, 32, 277, 311, 320–23, 435
Lotidae, 320–21; *Lota lota*, 32, 277, 311, 320–23, 435
Luxilus chrysocephalus, 174–77
Luxilus cornutus, 15, 175–77, 187
Lythrurus umbratilis, 178–79

Macrhybopsis hyostoma, 180–82
Macrhybopsis storeriana, 182–83
Margariscus nachtriebi, 184–85
Micropterus dolomieu, 8, 18, 327, 345, 364–66
Micropterus salmoides, 345, 364, 366–67
Minytrema melanops, 122–23
Misgurnus anguillicaudatus, 240–41
Morone americana, 372, 374–76, 378
Morone chrysops, 43, 372, 374, 376–79
Morone mississippiensis, 372, 376, 378–79
Morone saxatilis, 372–73, 379
Moronidae, 372–73; *Morone americana*, 372, 374–76, 378; *Morone chrysops*, 43, 372, 374, 376–79; *Morone mississippiensis*, 372, 376, 378–79; *Morone saxatilis*, 372–73, 379
Moxostoma anisurum, 12, 124–25, 130, 132, 134

Moxostoma carinatum, 18, 126–27, 132, 134, 449
Moxostoma duquesnei, 128–30
Moxostoma erythrurum, 126, 128, 130–31, 133, 135
Moxostoma macrolepidotum, 17, 103, 126, 130, 132–34
Moxostoma valenciennesi, 18, 126, 134–35
Myoxocephalus thompsonii, 307, 434–35
Mysis relicta, 277, 279, 284, 286, 288, 290, 295, 299, 310, 431, 434
Myxocyprinus asiaticus, 98

Neogobius melanostomus, 307, 325–27, 427, 429, 435
Nocomis biguttatus, 159, 175, 186–87, 211, 234, 236
Notemigonus crysoleucas, 151, 188–89
Notropis anogenus, 8, 190–91
Notropis atherinoides, 192–93, 214
Notropis blennius, 194–95
Notropis buccatus, 19, 196–97, 202
Notropis buchanani, 198–99
Notropis chalybaeus, 11, 200–201, 218, 337
Notropis dorsalis, 19, 195, 202–3
Notropis heterodon, 8, 204–5
Notropis heterolepis, 8, 206–7
Notropis hudsonius, 208–9, 295
Notropis nubilus, 15, 210–11
Notropis percobromus, 192, 212–13
Notropis rubellus, 192, 212–15
Notropis stramineus, 194–95, 202, 216–17, 220
Notropis texanus, 200, 218–19
Notropis volucellus, 8, 195, 220–21
Noturus exilis, 252–53, 258
Noturus flavus, 19, 254–55, 258
Noturus gyrinus, 10, 256–58
Noturus nocturnus, 18, 258–59
Novumbra hubbsi, 271

Oncorhynchus gorbuscha, 275
Oncorhynchus kisutch, 294–96, 298, 302
Oncorhynchus mykiss, 296–97, 302
Oncorhynchus tshawytscha, 294, 296, 298–99, 302
Opsopoeodus emiliae, 222–23
Osmeridae, 308–9; *Osmerus mordax*, 307–8, 310–11

TAXONOMIC INDEX   471

Osmerus mordax, 307–8, 310–11
Osteoglossum bicirrhosum, 83

Perca flavescens, 161, 311, 327, 385, 406–7
Percidae, 384–85; *Ammocrypta clara*, 386–87; *Etheostoma blennioides*, 15, 388–89, 404; *Etheostoma caeruleum*, 390–91, 402, 404; *Etheostoma chlorosoma*, 11, 18, 392–93; *Etheostoma exile*, 8, *10*, 394–95, 400; *Etheostoma flabellare*, 396–97; *Etheostoma microperca*, 8, 398–99; *Etheostoma nigrum*, 392, 400–401; *Etheostoma spectabile*, 390, 402–3; *Etheostoma zonale*, 404–5; *Perca flavescens*, 161, 311, 327, 385, 406–7; *Percina caprodes*, 408–9; *Percina maculata*, 410–11; *Percina phoxocephala*, 17, 412–13; *Sander canadensis*, 385, 406, 414–17; *Sander vitreus*, 311, 384–85, 406, 414–17
Percina caprodes, 408–9
Percina maculata, 410–11
Percina phoxocephala, 17, 412–13
Percopsidae, 312–13; *Percopsis omiscomaycus*, 314–15; *Percopsis transmontana*, 312–13
Percopsis omiscomaycus, 314–15
Percopsis transmontana, 312–13
Petromyzon marinus, 48–53, 56–57
Petromyzontidae, 46–47; *Ichthyomyzon castaneus*, *14*, 48–49; *Ichthyomyzon fossor*, *19*, 50–51; *Ichthyomyzon unicuspis*, 52–53; *Lethenteron appendix*, 14, 48, 50, 52, 54–56; *Petromyzon marinus*, 48–53, 56–57
Phalaris arundinacea, 13
Phenacobius mirabilis, 224–25
Pimephales notatus, 8, 226–28, 230
Pimephales promelas, 12, 151, 228–30
Pimephales vigilax, 226, 228, 230–31
Poecilia reticulata, 341
Poeciliidae, 340–41; *Gambusia affinis*, 341–43; *Gambusia holbrooki*, 341; *Poecilia reticulata*, 341
Polyodon spathula, 29, 64–65
Polyodontidae, 62–63; *Polyodon spathula*, 29, 64–65; *Psephurus gladius*, 62
Pomoxis annularis, 368–70
Pomoxis nigromaculatus, *10*, 368, 370–71

Pontederia cordata, 12
Potamogeton spp., 12, 388
Prosopium cylindraceum, 300–301
Psephurus gladius, 62
Pseudoscaphirhynchus fedtschenkoi, 58
Pungitius pungitius, 424–25
Pylodictis olivaris, *17*, 242–43, 250, 260–61, 440

Rhinichthys cataractae, 232–34
Rhinichthys obtusus, 12, *14*, 232, 234–35

Salmonidae, 274–75; Coregoninae, 274–75; *Coregonus alpenae*, 276–77; *Coregonus artedi*, 275, 278–79, 292; *Coregonus clupeaformis*, 280–81; *Coregonus hoyi*, 278, 282–83; *Coregonus johannae*, 276, 284–85; *Coregonus kiyi*, 286–87; *Coregonus nigripinnis*, 288–89; *Coregonus reighardi*, 290–91; *Coregonus zenithicus*, 292–93; *Oncorhynchus gorbuscha*, 275; *Oncorhynchus kisutch*, 294–96, 298, 302; *Oncorhynchus mykiss*, 296–97, 302; *Oncorhynchus tshawytscha*, 294, 296, 298–99, 302; *Prosopium cylindraceum*, 300–301; Salmoninae, 275; *Salmo trutta*, 14, 275, 296, 302–4, 306; *Salvelinus fontinalis*, 14, 304–6; *Salvelinus namaycush*, 8, 277, 304, 306–7, 310, 327, 435; Thymallinae, 275
Salmo trutta, 14, 275, 296, 302–4, 306
Salvelinus fontinalis, 14, 304–6
Salvelinus namaycush, 8, 277, 304, 306–7, 310, 327, 435
Sander canadensis, 385, 406, 414–17
Sander vitreus, 311, 384–85, 406, 414–17
Sciaenidae, 380–81; *Aplodinotus grunniens*, 381, 382–83; *Larimichthys polyactis*, 381; *Sciaenops ocellatus*, 381
Sciaenops ocellatus, 381
Scombridae, 89
Semotilus atromaculatus, 14, 160, 184, 186, 236–37

Trimmatom nanus, 325

Umbra krameria, 271
Umbra limi, 11, 271–73

Umbra pygmaea, 271

Umbridae, 270–71; *Dallia pectoralis*, 270–71; *Novumbra hubbsi*, 271; *Umbra krameria*, 271; *Umbra limi*, 11, 271–73; *Umbra pygmaea*, 271

Xenocyprididae, 94, 142–43; *Ctenopharyngodon idella*, 142, 144–45, 148, 449; *Hypophthalmichthys molitrix*, 142, 146–49; *Hypophthalmichthys nobilis*, 136, 142, 146, 148–49

Subject Index

Page numbers in italics refer to figures.

adipose eyelids, *35*, 88, 444
adipose fins, *30*; anatomical difference,
442; catfishes (*Ictaluridae*), 242,
250, 252, 254, 256, 258, 260;
loaches (*Cobitidae*), 238; mooneyes
(*Hiodontidae*), 82; salmon, trout, chars,
and whitefishes (*Salmonidae*), 274;
silversides (*Atherinopsidae*), 328;
smelts (*Osmeridae*), 308, 310; suckers
(*Catostomidae*), 98; trout-perches
(*Percopsidae*), 312–14; true minnows
(*Leuciscidae*), 196
African Elephant Fish (*Gnathonemus
petersii*), 83
agriculture: and darters and perches
(*Percidae*), 398, 404, 406; impact of, 3,
9–10, 13–14; and pikes (*Esocidae*), 264;
and suckers (*Catostomidae*), 111; and
sunfishes (*Centrarchidae*), 347, 357, 366;
and true minnows (*Leuciscidae*), 153,
158, 178, 196; wetlands, 9
Alaska Blackfish (*Dallia pectoralis*),
270–71
Alewife (*Alosa pseudoharengus*), 92–93;
population control, 93, 275, 297, 299,
303, 307; and salmon, trout, chars, and
whitefishes (*Salmonidae*), 295, 299, 307;
and shads and herrings (*Clupeidae*),
90, 92
Alligator Gar (*Atractosteus spatula*), 66–67
American Brook Lamprey (*Lethenteron
appendix*), 14, 48, 50, 52, 54–56
American Eel (*Anguilla rostrata*), 78, 80–81

ammocoete, lampreys (*Petromyzontidae*),
46–50, 52, 54, 56, 445
Amur Carp (*Cyprinus rubrofuscus*), 140
anadromous migration: lampreys
(*Petromyzontidae*), 47; mudminnows
(*Umbridae*), 274; salmon, trout,
chars, and whitefishes (*Salmonidae*),
296–97; smelts (*Osmeridae*), 308–9;
sticklebacks (*Gasterosteidae*), 425;
sturgeons (*Acipenseridae*), 58; true
minnows (*Leuciscidae*), 372–73
Anadyr River, Russia, 295
anal fins: barbs and carps (*Cyprinidae*),
138, 140; catfishes (*Ictaluridae*),
244–54, 260; darters and perches
(*Percidae*), 384, 390, 392, 400, 402,
406, 414, 416; eels (*Anguillidae*), 80;
fish identification, 442–43, 447–
48; gobies (*Gobiidae*), 324; hakes
(*Lotidae*), 322; livebearers (*Poeciliidae*),
340, 342; mooneyes (*Hiodontidae*),
82, 84, 86; pictorial keys, *32, 35–41*;
pirate perches (*Aphredoderidae*), 318;
salmon, trout, chars, and whitefishes
(*Salmonidae*), 280, 292–306; shads and
herrings (*Clupeidae*), 94; sharpbellies
(*Xenocyprididae*), 146, 148; silversides
(*Atherinopsidae*), 330; sticklebacks
(*Gasterosteidae*), 420, 422, 424; suckers
(*Catostomidae*), 98, 100, 110, 112, 122,
126–32; sunfishes (*Centrarchidae*),
346–56, 368, 370; temperate basses
(*Moronidae*), 374–78; topminnows and

killifishes (*Fundulidae*), 332–38; true minnows (*Leuciscidae*), 152, 154, 160, 164, 178–82, 188, 190, 198–210, 214–20, 224–30, 234, 236

animal waste, 4

Atlas of Illinois Fishes, An (Metzke et al.), viii, xi

Aux Sable Creek, Illinois, 18, 131, 135, 259, 403

axillary process: mooneyes (*Hiodontidae*), 82; pictorial keys, *31*; salmon, trout, chars, and whitefishes (*Salmonidae*), 274; shads and herrings (*Clupeidae*), 88–92; smelts (*Osmeridae*), 308

backwaters: bowfins (*Amiidae*), 76–77; catfishes (*Ictaluridae*), 248; connected lakes, 62, 66, 85, 118, 393; darters and perches (*Percidae*), 392–93; gars (*Lepisosteidae*), 66, 70; migration, 11, 64; mooneyes (*Hiodontidae*), 85; mudminnows (*Umbridae*), 272; paddlefishes (*Polyodontidae*), 62, 64; pikes (*Esocidae*), 262, 264, 268; pirate perches (*Aphredoderidae*), 318; sharpbellies (*Xenocyprididae*), 146, 148; suckers (*Catostomidae*), 117–19; sunfishes (*Centrarchidae*), 349, 353, 360; topminnows and killifishes (*Fundulidae*), 336–37; true minnows (*Leuciscidae*), 164, 170, 198, 200, 218, 222, 228; vegetation, 18, 66, 76, 200, 222, 228, 248, 262, 264, 268, 318, 336–37, 349, 353, 360, 392; wetlands, 6, 10–12, 318, 393

Bailey, Reeve M., viii

bait: bowfins (*Amiidae*), catching with, 75; catfishes (*Ictaluridae*), catching with, 245; drums and croakers (*Sciaenidae*), catching with, 383; eels (*Anguillidae*), catching with, 81; gobies (*Gobiidae*) as, 327; lampreys (*Petromyzontidae*) as, 47; mudminnows (*Umbridae*) as, 271; silversides (*Atherinopsidae*) as poor live baitfish, 329; sticklebacks (*Gasterosteidae*) as, 421; suckers (*Catostomidae*), catching with, 99, 109; sunfishes (*Centrarchidae*), catching with, 363; true minnows (*Leuciscidae*) as, 151, 159, 163, 171, 175, 177, 179, 189, 228–29, 231, 237

Banded Darter (*Etheostoma zonale*), 404–5

Banded Killifish (*Fundulus diaphanus*), 8, 334–35

bands: darters and perches (*Percidae*), 388, 390, 394, 398, 400, 404, 408; loaches (*Cobitidae*), 240; pirate perches (*Aphredoderidae*), 318; salmon, trout, chars, and whitefishes (*Salmonidae*), 296; sticklebacks (*Gasterosteidae*), 422; suckers (*Catostomidae*), 106, 114; sunfishes (*Centrarchidae*), 353, 364, 368; true minnows (*Leuciscidae*), 152, 156, 158, 172, 190, 200, 204, 206, 210, 214, 218, 222, 224, 234, 236

barbels: barbs and carps (*Cyprinidae*), 136–40; bowfins (*Amiidae*), 76; catfishes (*Ictaluridae*), 242–48; fish identification, *442*, *443*, *446*; hakes (*Lotidae*), 320, 322; loaches (*Cobitidae*), 238, 240;

SUBJECT INDEX   475

barbels (*continued*)
  pictorial keys, *27, 29–30, 32*; sculpins
  (*Cottidae*), 442–43, 446; sturgeons
  (*Acipenseridae*), 58, 60; suckers
  (*Catostomidae*), 98; true minnows
  (*Leuciscidae*), 151, 160, 166, 172, 180–86,
  208, 232, 234, 236
barbs and carps (*Cyprinidae*): anal fins, 138,
  140; barbels, 136–40; caudal fins, 140;
  characteristics of, 136–37; Common
  Carp (*Cyprinus carpi*), 136–38, 140–43;
  in the Des Plaines River, 137, 139; dorsal
  fins, 136, 140; gills, 138, 141; Goldfish
  (*Carassius auratus*), 136, 138–40; in the
  Illinois River, 139; in Lake Michigan, 139;
  and larvae, 139, 141; lateral line, 138–40;
  pictorial keys, *34*; protrusible lips, 140;
  serration, 136, 138, 140; spines, 136–40;
  as sport fishes, 136–37, 141; terminal
  mouth, 138, 140; tubercles, 136; and
  water quality, 136, 139
basses. *See* temperate basses (*Moronidae*)
Beaver Creek, Illinois/Indiana, 219
Beaver Lake (drained), Indiana, 6
Becker, George C., viii
belly: catfishes (*Ictaluridae*), 244–48,
  252, 254, 260; darters and perches
  (*Percidae*), 390, 394, 396, 402, 406–
  10, 414, 416; drums and croakers
  (*Sciaenidae*), 382; fish identification,
  442; hakes (*Lotidae*), 322; lampreys
  (*Petromyzontidae*), 50, 54; livebearers
  (*Poeciliidae*), 342; mooneyes
  (*Hiodontidae*), 82, 84, 86; mudminnows
  (*Umbridae*), 276, 294, 298; pirate
  perches (*Aphredoderidae*), 317; shads
  and herrings (*Clupeidae*), 92, 94;
  sharpbellies (*Xenocyprididae*), 142,
  146, 148; sticklebacks (*Gasterosteidae*),
  420, 422, 424; suckers (*Catostomidae*),
  108, 124–34; sunfishes (*Centrarchidae*),
  346–52, 356, 360, 362, 368, 370;
  topminnows and killifishes (*Fundulidae*),
  336; true minnows (*Leuciscidae*), 156–
  59, 168, 170, 174–78, 186, 196, 214,
  232–34
benthic dwellers: catfishes (*Ictaluridae*) as,
  242; gobies (*Gobiidae*) as, 327; loaches
  (*Cobitidae*) as, 240; paddlefishes
  (*Polyodontidae*) as, 60; and sticklebacks

(*Gasterosteidae*), 418; and suckers
  (*Catostomidae*), 111, 117; and true
  minnows (*Leuciscidae*), 202
Bigeye Chub (*Hybopsis amblops*), 151
Bighead Carp (*Hypophthalmichthys nobilis*),
  136, 142, 146, 148–49
Bigmouth Buffalo (*Ictiobus cyprinellus*),
  118–19
Bigmouth Shiner (*Notropis dorsalis*), *19*, 195,
  202–3
Big Rock Creek, Illinois, 15, 103
Birds of the Chicago Region (Ford), xi
Black Buffalo (*Ictiobus niger*), *12*, 116,
  120–21
Black Bullhead (*Ameiurus melas*), 244–45
Blackchin Shiner (*Notropis heterodon*), 8,
  204–5
Black Crappie (*Pomoxis nigromaculatus*), *10*,
  368, 370–71
Blackfin Cisco (*Coregonus nigripinnis*),
  288–89
Blacknose Shiner (*Notropis heterolepis*), 8,
  206–7
Black Redhorse (*Moxostoma duquesnei*),
  128–30
Blackside Darter (*Percina maculata*),
  410–11
Blackstripe Topminnow (*Fundulus notatus*),
  338–39
Bloater (*Coregonus hoyi*), 278, 282–83
Bluegill (*Lepomis macrochirus*), 345, 356–
  57, 440
Bluntnose Darter (*Etheostoma chlorosoma*),
  11, 18, 392–93
Bluntnose Minnow (*Pimephales notatus*), 8,
  226–28, 230
body depth, 110, 112, 447
bogs, 3, 10, 156, 168, 272
bowfins (*Amiidae*): *Amia calva*, 74; in
  backwaters, 76–77; bait, catching with,
  75; barbels, 76; caudal fins, 76; caudal
  peduncle, 76; characteristics of, 74–75;
  cycloid scales, 76; dorsal fins, 76; and
  drainage, 74, 77; extinct, 74; Eyetail
  Bowfin (*Amia ocellicauda*), 74, 76–77;
  in the Fox River, 77; gas bladder, 74,
  76; gular plate, *28*, 74, 76; heterocercal
  fins, 74, 76; in the Kankakee River, 77; in
  marshes, 76; in the Mississippi River, 77;
  ocellus, *76*; in oxbows, 76; pictorial keys,

28; protrusible lips, 76; as sport fishes, 77; terminal mouth, 74

Braidwood Cooling Lake, Illinois, 173

branchiostegal membrane: fish identification, 444; pikes (*Esocidae*), 266; pirate perches (*Aphredoderidae*), 318

branchiostegal ray: pikes (*Esocidae*), 264, 266, 268; salmon, trout, chars, and whitefishes (*Salmonidae*), 294, 298, 304

Brassy Minnow (*Hybognathus hankinsoni*), 168–70

breast: darters and perches (*Percidae*), 384, 408–12; sticklebacks (*Gasterosteidae*), 420–24; sunfishes (*Centrarchidae*), 354

bridle: darters and perches (*Percidae*), 392, 412; true minnows (*Leuciscidae*), 172, 218

Brook Char (Brook Trout) (*Salvelinus fontinalis*), 14, 304–6

Brook Silverside (*Labidesthes sicculus*), 330–31

Brook Stickleback (*Culaea inconstans*), 12, 14, 420–22

Brown Bullhead (*Ameiurus nebulosus*), 248–49

Brown Trout (*Salmo trutta*), 14, 275, 296, 302–4, 306

Bullhead Minnow (*Pimephales vigilax*), 226, 228, 230–31

Burbot (*Lota lota*), *32*, 277, 311, 320–23, 435

burbots (*Lotidae*): anal fins, 322; barbels, 320, 322; belly, 322; Burbot (*Lota lota*), *32*, 277, 311, 320–23, 435; caudal fins, 320, 322; characteristics of, 320–21; in coldwater habitat, 322–23; cycloid scales, 322; description of, 320–23; dorsal fins, 88–94, 320, 322; juveniles, 322; in Lake Michigan, 320, 323; larvae, 320; in the Mississippi River, 323; pictorial keys, *32*; riffles, 322; and salmon, trout, chars, and whitefishes (*Salmonidae*), 277; and smelts (*Osmeridae*), 311; spines, 322

Buttonbush (*Cephalanthus occidentalis*), 12

Cal–Sag (Calumet–Saganashkee) Channel, Illinois, 117, 198–99, 257

Calumet Beach, Illinois, 217

Calumet River system, Illinois/Indiana: catfishes (*Ictaluridae*) in, 249, 255; Chicago Region, 3–4, 6, 10, *14*, 17; lampreys (*Petromyzontidae*) in, 49; loaches (*Cobitidae*) in, 241; as marsh, 10; paddlefishes (*Polyodontidae*) in, 65; sticklebacks (*Gasterosteidae*) in, 423; suckers (*Catostomidae*) in, 111, 117, 121, 131, 133; sunfishes (*Centrarchidae*) in, 363; temperate basses (*Moronidae*) in, 377; true minnows (*Leuciscidae*) in, 171, 187, 199

Camp Lake, Wisconsin, 8

Canadian Waterweed (*Elodea canadensis*), 398

canals, hydrogeophysical: fish habitats, 6, 13; Michigan Canal, 65; Welland Canal, 57, 93

canines: darters and perches (*Percidae*), 406, 414, 416; fish identification, 445; pictorial keys, *37–38*; smelts (*Osmeridae*), 310; temperate basses (*Moronidae*), 372

Carmine Shiner (*Notropis percobromus*), 192, 212–13

carps. *See* barbs and carps (*Cyprinidae*)

cartilage, 58, 441

catfishes (*Ictaluridae*): adipose fins, 242, 250, 252, *254*, *256*, *258*, 260; anal fins, 244–54, 260; in backwaters, 248; bait, catching with, 245; barbels, 242–48; belly, 244–48, 252, 254, 260; as benthic dwellers, 242; Black Bullhead (*Ameiurus melas*), 244–45; Brown Bullhead (*Ameiurus nebulosus*), 248–49; in the Calumet River system, 249, 255; caudal fins, 260; Channel Catfish (*Ictalurus punctatus*), 242–43, 250–51; characteristics of, 242–43; in the Des Plaines River, 259; dorsal fins, 246, 252, 254; and drainage, 247–48, 257–58, 261; Flathead Catfish (*Pylodictis olivaris*), 17, 242–43, 250, 260–61, 440; forked fins, 242–50; in the Fox River, 253, 260–61; Freckled Madtom (*Noturus nocturnus*), 18, 258–59; in Hudson Bay, 245; in the Illinois River, 253, 258–59, 261; juveniles, 250, 260–61; in the Kankakee River, 248, 261; in Lake Erie, 254; in Lake Michigan, 251, 261; and

SUBJECT INDEX   477

catfishes (*continued*)
larvae, 251, 254, 256, 258; madtoms, *10*, 18, 242, 252–60; in marshes, 256; melanophores, 258; migration of, 251; in the Mississippi River, 245–48, 253–58, 261; in the Ohio River, 245, 254, 256, 261; pictorial keys, *30*; in pools, 251; premaxilla, 252, 254, 256, 258; riffles, 242, 252, 254, 261; in the Rock River, 253; Slender Madtom (*Noturus exilis*), 252–53, 258; spines, 242–58; in the St. Joseph River, 249; Stonecat (*Noturus flavus*), *19*, 254–55, 258; Tadpole Madtom (*Noturus gyrinus*), *10*, 256–58; terminal mouth, 252–58; tooth patch, 252–60; and water quality, 257; Yellow Bullhead (*Ameiurus natalis*), 246–47, 249

caudal fins: barbs and carps (*Cyprinidae*), 140; bowfins (*Amiidae*), 76; catfishes (*Ictaluridae*), 260; darters and perches (*Percidae*), *396*, 408, 410; drums and croakers (*Sciaenidae*), 382; eels (*Anguillidae*), 80; fish identification, 442–43, 446–47; gars (*Lepisosteidae*), 68, 70; gobies (*Gobiidae*), 324; hakes (*Lotidae*), 320, 322; loaches (*Cobitidae*), 240; mudminnows (*Umbridae*), 273; pictorial keys, *28*, *36*, *41–42*; salmon, trout, chars, and whitefishes (*Salmonidae*), 280–84, 294–98, 302–6; silversides (*Atherinopsidae*), 328; suckers (*Catostomidae*), *124*; sunfishes (*Centrarchidae*), 362; true minnows (*Leuciscidae*), 175–76, 188, 216

caudal peduncle: bowfins (*Amiidae*), *76*; fish identification, 443, 446–48; loaches (*Cobitidae*), 240; sharpbellies (*Xenocyprididae*), 144; sturgeons (*Acipenseridae*), 60; suckers (*Catostomidae*), 124–34, 138; true minnows (*Leuciscidae*), 174, 186

caudal spot: darters and perches (*Percidae*), 412; true minnows (*Leuciscidae*), 186, 226, 228, 230

caviar, 62

Central Mudminnow (*Umbra limi*), 11, 271–73

Central Stoneroller (*Campostoma anomalum*), 111, 152–55

Channel Catfish (*Ictalurus punctatus*), 242–43, 250–51

chars. *See* salmon, trout, chars, and whitefishes (*Salmonidae*)

Chestnut Lamprey (*Ichthyomyzon castaneus*), *14*, 48–49

Chicago Area Waterway System, 4; darters and perches (*Percidae*) in, 401; gobies (*Gobiidae*) in, 327; livebearers (*Poeciliidae*) in, 343; loaches (*Cobitidae*) in, 241; sharpbellies (*Xenocyprididae*) in, 145, 147, 149; smelts (*Osmeridae*) in, 311; sticklebacks (*Gasterosteidae*) in, 423; suckers (*Catostomidae*) in, 101, 115; sunfishes (*Centrarchidae*) in, 355, 365, 367; temperate basses (*Moronidae*) in, 375, 379; topminnows and killifishes (*Fundulidae*) in, 335; true minnows (*Leuciscidae*) in, 199

Chicago Lake Plain, 3, 131, 133

Chicago Region: agricultural impacts in, 3, 9–10, 13–14; Calumet River, 3–4, 6, 10, *14*, 17; Chicago River, 3–4; climate, 2–3; defined, viii, 2; Des Plaines River, 3, 7, 10; fish collections, 24–25; fish habitats, 6–10; Fox River, 3, 6–8, 10, 13, 15, 17–18; Galien River, 3; Illinois River, 3–5, 10, 17; Kankakee River, 3, 7, *11*, 13, 15; Lake Michigan, 2–3, 6–8, *9*, 11; major watersheds, 3; Pike River, 3; Rock River, 3; Root River, 3, 6, 18, *19*; setting, 2–6; species distribution in, viii–xi; St. Joseph River, 3, 15, 17, *18*; vegetation, 2–3; wetlands, 10–18, *19–21*

Chicago River, Illinois, 3–4, 241, 269

Chicago Sanitary and Ship Canal, 96–97, 149, 256

Chicago Wilderness Alliance, 2

Chinese Sucker (*Myxocyprinus asiaticus*), 98

Chinook Salmon (*Oncorhynchus tshawytscha*), 294, 296, 298–99, 302

Christiana Creek, Indiana, 15, 388

Clean Water Act, x, 5, 139

Coho Salmon (*Oncorhynchus kisutch*), 294–96, 298, 302

coldwater: Berrien County, streams in, 13; fish habitats, 6, 13–14; hakes (*Lotidae*) and, 322–23; headwater streams,

478 SUBJECT INDEX

13–14; salmon, trout, chars, and whitefishes (*Salmonidae*) and, 300, 303–6; sticklebacks (*Gasterosteidae*) and, 419, 425; suckers (*Catostomidae*) and, 106; true minnows (*Leuciscidae*) and, 184–85

Colorado Pikeminnow (*Ptychocheilus lucius*), 150

Common Carp (*Cyprinus carpio*), 136–38, 140–43

Common Shiner (*Luxilus cornutus*), 15, 175–77, 187

connected lakes: backwaters, 62, 66, 85, 118, 393; lampreys (*Petromyzontidae*) in, 47, 52; migration and, 7–8; mooneyes (*Hiodontidae*) in, 84–85; paddlefishes (*Polyodontidae*) in, 62; shads and herrings (*Clupeidae*) in, 90; suckers (*Catostomidae*) in, 118

Coontail (*Ceratophyllum demersum*), 398

Cowles, Henry, 8

Creek Chub (*Semotilus atromaculatus*), 14, 160, 184, 186, 236–37

croakers. *See* drums and croakers (*Sciaenidae*)

Cross Lake, Illinois, 8, 190

ctenoid scales: darters and perches (*Percidae*), 384; drums and croakers (*Sciaenidae*), 382; pictorial keys, 29, 31; pirate perches (*Aphredoderidae*), 316, 318; trout-perches (*Percopsidae*), 312, 314

cycloid scales: bowfins (*Amiidae*), 76; hakes (*Lotidae*), 322; mudminnows (*Umbridae*), 272; pictorial keys, 29, 31; salmon, trout, chars, and whitefishes (*Salmonidae*), 274; shads and herrings (*Clupeidae*), 88; suckers (*Catostomidae*), 98; sunfishes (*Centrarchidae*), 344; trout-perches (*Percopsidae*), 312

dams: darters and perches (*Percidae*) and, 417; eels (*Anguillidae*) and, 81; and habitat, 5–6; lampreys (*Petromyzontidae*), 49, 53, 57; loaches (*Cobitidae*), 239; paddlefishes (*Polyodontidae*) and, 63–64; pools, 6, 147; salmon, trout, chars, and whitefishes (*Salmonidae*) and, 275;

suckers (*Catostomidae*) and, 99, 105, 115, 119, 125; temperate basses (*Moronidae*) and, 373; true minnows (*Leuciscidae*) and, 167, 173, 181, 183, 215

darters and perches (*Percidae*): agriculture and, 398, 404, 406; anal fins, 384, 390, 392, 400, 402, 406, 414, 416; in backwaters, 392–93; Banded Darter (*Etheostoma zonale*), 404–5; bands, 388, 390, 394, 398, 400, 404, 408; belly, 390, 394, 396, 402, 406–10, 414, 416; Blackside Darter (*Percina maculata*), 410–11; Bluntnose Darter (*Etheostoma chlorosoma*), 11, 18, 392–93; breast, 384, 408–12; bridle, 392, 412; canines, 406, 414, 416; caudal fins, 396, 408, 410; characteristics of, 384–85; Chicago Area Waterway System, absence in, 401; ctenoid scales, 384; and dams, 417; in the Des Plaines River, 403, 409, 414–15; dorsal fins, 384–416; and drainage, 386, 403, 405, 412; Fantail Darter (*Etheostoma flabellare*), 396–97; in the Fox River, 391, 403, 405, 409, 413, 417; frenum, 386, 390, 394, 398–404, 410–12; fusiform body, 384, 404, 406; gill cover, 386, 394; Greenside Darter (*Etheostoma blennioides*), 15, 388–89, 404; in Hudson Bay, 395, 399, 401, 409, 411, 415; in the Illinois River, 415; Iowa Darter (*Etheostoma exile*), 8, 10, 394–95, 400; Johnny Darter (*Etheostoma nigrum*), 392, 400–401; juveniles, 391; in the Kankakee River, 387, 391–93, 399, 403, 405, 409, 411, 413, 417; in Lake Erie, 403; in Lake Michigan, 385, 400, 405–8, 412–13, 417; and larvae, 386, 388, 391, 394, 399, 404, 407–8; lateral line, 388–402, 410; lateral scales, 398; Least Darter (*Etheostoma microperca*), 8, 398–99; Logperch (*Percina caprodes*), 408–9; in the Mississippi River, 386, 389, 391–92, 397, 399, 401, 405, 409, 411, 415, 421; in the Ohio River, 389, 391, 397–405, 411–12, 415; Orangethroat Darter (*Etheostoma spectabile*), 390, 402–3; overfishing of, 407; in oxbows, 392; pectoral fins, 398, 400; pelvic fins, 384, 408, 410, 412; pictorial keys,

SUBJECT INDEX   479

darters and perches (*continued*)
42; in pools, 410; premaxilla, 390, 398;
Rainbow Darter (*Etheostoma caeruleum*),
390–91, 402, 404; riffles, 388, 391,
402, 404–5, 408, 412, 414, 417; in the
Rock River, 391; in the Root River, 413;
saddles, 392, 406–16; and sandbars,
386, 408; Sauger (*Sander canadensis*),
385, 406, 414–17; Slenderhead Darter
(*Percina phoxocephala*), *17*, 412–13;
spines, 384, 386, 392–400, 410, 412; as
sport fishes, 407; in the St. Joseph River,
388–89, 391, 409, 417; subspecies of,
389; subterminal mouth, 386; Walleye
(*Sander vitreus*), 311, 384–85, 406, 414–
17; and water quality, 389, 391, 401–5,
409; Western Sand Darter (*Ammocrypta
clara*), 386–87; Yellow Perch (*Perca
flavescens*), 161, 311, 327, 385, 406–7
Deepwater Cisco (*Coregonus johannae*),
276, 284–85
Deepwater Sculpin (*Myoxocephalus
thompsonii*), 307, 434–35
Des Plaines River, Illinois: barbs and
carps (*Cyprinidae*) in, 137, 139;
catfishes (*Ictaluridae*) in, 259; Chicago
Region, 3, 7, 10; darters and perches
(*Percidae*) in, 403, 409, 414–15; glacial
lakes, 7; livebearers (*Poeciliidae*) in,
343; perennial streams, 17; shads
and herrings (*Clupeidae*) in, 91, 96;
sharpbellies (*Xenocyprididae*) in,
147, 149; suckers (*Catostomidae*) in,
101, 103, 119, 123, 125, 135; sunfishes
(*Centrarchidae*) in, 347, 355, 365;
temperate basses (*Moronidae*) in,
375, 379; topminnows and killifishes
(*Fundulidae*) in, 339; true minnows
(*Leuciscidae*) in, 173, 179, 201, 205, 215,
219, 231
discs: eels (*Anguillidae*), 80; fish
identification, 445–46; gars
(*Lepisosteidae*), 66, 324; lampreys
(*Petromyzontidae*), 46–56, 445–46;
oral, 46–56, 445–46; pictorial keys, *39*;
suction, *39*, 46, 324
distal areas, 175–76, 292, 441
Distribution of the Fishes of Indiana, The
(Gerking), xi

dorsal fins: barbs and carps (*Cyprinidae*),
136, 140; bowfins (*Amiidae*), 76;
catfishes (*Ictaluridae*), 246, 252, 254;
darters and perches (*Percidae*), 384–
416; drums and croakers (*Sciaenidae*),
380, 382; eels (*Anguillidae*), 80;
fish identification, 441–42, 447–
48; gars (*Lepisosteidae*), 324, 326;
hakes (*Lotidae*), 320, 322; lampreys
(*Petromyzontidae*), 48–56; livebearers
(*Poeciliidae*), 340, 342; loaches
(*Cobitidae*), 240; mudminnows
(*Umbridae*), 270, 272; paddlefishes
(*Polyodontidae*), 64; pictorial keys,
29, 32–43; pikes (*Esocidae*), 262;
pirate perches (*Aphredoderidae*),
316, 318; salmon, trout, chars, and
whitefishes (*Salmonidae*), 274, 280,
282, 284, 290, 292, 298, 302, 304,
306; sculpins (*Cottidae*), 426–34;
shads and herrings (*Clupeidae*), 88–94;
sharpbellies (*Xenocyprididae*), 144–
48; silversides (*Atherinopsidae*), 328,
330; sticklebacks (*Gasterosteidae*),
418–24; sturgeons (*Acipenseridae*),
60; suckers (*Catostomidae*), 98–104,
110–34; sunfishes (*Centrarchidae*), 344,
346, 348, 352, 356, 362, 366, 368,
370; temperate basses (*Moronidae*),
372, 374, 376, 378; topminnows and
killifishes (*Fundulidae*), 332, 334, 336,
338; true minnows (*Leuciscidae*), 150,
152, 156–64, 168–94, 198–210, 214–30,
234, 236
drainage: bowfins (*Amiidae*) and, 74, 77;
catfishes (*Ictaluridae*) and, 247–48,
257–58, 261; darters and perches
(*Percidae*) and, 386, 403, 405, 412;
gars (*Lepisosteidae*) and, 68, 70;
glacial lakes, 205; habitat, 7–13; Lake
Michigan, 7–8, 13, 49, 53, 105, 134,
155, 197, 199, 205, 209, 221, 300, 311,
337, 339, 351, 377, 379, 403, 405, 412;
lampreys (*Petromyzontidae*) and, 49,
53, 55; mudminnows (*Umbridae*) and,
272; paddlefishes (*Polyodontidae*) and,
62, 65; pikes (*Esocidae*) and, 265; pirate
perches (*Aphredoderidae*) and, 318;
salmon, trout, chars, and whitefishes

(*Salmonidae*) and, 300, 305, 307; shads and herrings (*Clupeidae*) and, 91, 95, 97; silversides (*Atherinopsidae*) and, 331; smelts (*Osmeridae*) and, 311; sticklebacks (*Gasterosteidae*) and, 421–25; suckers (*Catostomidae*) and, 101, 103, 105, 111–17, 123, 134; sunfishes (*Centrarchidae*) and, 351–61, 367–71; temperate basses (*Moronidae*) and, 377, 379; topminnows and killifishes (*Fundulidae*) and, 335, 337, 339; true minnows (*Leuciscidae*) and, 155, 165, 169, 171, 181, 185, 197–205, 209, 211, 221, 227, 231, 237

dreissenid mussels (*Dreissenidae*), 327

drums and croakers (*Sciaenidae*): bait, catching with, 383; belly, 382; caudal fins, 382; characteristics of, 380–81; ctenoid scales, 382; dorsal fins, 380, 382; in the Fox River, 383; Freshwater Drum (*Aplodinotus grunniens*), 381–83; gills, 380; in Hudson Bay, 383; in the Illinois River, 383; in Lake Michigan, 383; in Ohio River, 383; pelagic habitat, 380, 383; pelvic fins, 382; pharyngeal area, 382–83; pictorial keys, *41*; spines, 382; as sport fishes, 381; subterminal mouth, 382; terminal mouth, 380; and water quality, 383

DuPage River, Illinois, 18

ear flaps, sunfishes (*Centrarchidae*), 346–62

eels (*Anguillidae*): American Eel (*Anguilla rostrata*), 78, 80–81; anal fins, 80; bait, catching with, 81; caudal fins, 80; characteristics of, 78–79; and dams, 81; discs, 80; dorsal fins, 80; gas bladder, 80; in the Illinois River, 81; in the Kankakee River, 81; in Lake Michigan, 81; larvae, 78–79; and marshes, 81; migration of, 78, 81; in the Mississippi River, 81, 85, 87; pectoral fins, 80; pelvic fins, 78; pictorial keys, *27*

electrofishing, 127, 135, 190

embedded scales, 80, 320, 322

Emerald Shiner (*Notropis atherinoides*), 192–93, 214

Eocene Green River Formation, 88

ephemeral streams, 12–13

Erie Canal, New York, 375

etymology, 22

European Brown Trout (*Salmo trutta*), 14, 275

European Mudminnow (*Umbra krameria*), 271

eutrophic lakes, 8–9, 279, 374, 435

Eyetail Bowfin (*Amia ocellicauda*), 74, 76–77

Fantail Darter (*Etheostoma flabellare*), 396–97

Fathead Minnow (*Pimephales promelas*), 12, 151, 228–30

Ferson Creek, Illinois, 103

Field Museum of Natural History, 24; barbs and carps (*Cyprinidae*), 137; bowfins (*Amiidae*), 74; darters and perches (*Percidae*), 411; Oliver Perry Hay, 74, 411; lampreys (*Petromyzontidae*), 52; salmon, trout, chars, and whitefishes (*Salmonidae*), *276, 278, 284, 286, 288, 290,* 291, *292, 300*; sculpins (*Cottidae*), *430, 432, 434*; sticklebacks (*Gasterosteidae*), *422*

Fishes of Illinois (P. W. Smith), viii, xi

Fishes of Illinois, The (Forbes and Richardson), viii

Fishes of Indiana (Simon), xi

Fishes of the Great Lakes Region (Hubbs, Lagler, and Smith), xi

Fishes of Wisconsin, The (Becker), viii, xi

fish habitat: coldwater, 6, 13–14; drainage, 7–13; glacial lakes, 6–8; littoral zones, 6, 8, 164, 206, 280, 300; and migration, 4–6, 11–13, 24; oxbows, 6; port fishes, 9, 23; and urban development, 3, 10, 14

fish identification: anal fins, 442–43, 447–48; barbels, *442*, 443, 446; belly, 442; body regions, 442–43; body shape, 440–41; canines, 445; caudal fins, 442–43, 446–47; caudal peduncle, 443, 446–48; discs, 445–46; dorsal fins, 441–42, 447–48; ganoid scales, 440; gill cover, 444, 447, 449; gill rakers, 445, 449; head, 443–45, 446; interorbital width, 447; keels, *35*; larvae, 445; lateral line, *36–37, 39, 41–42*, 441,

fish identification (*continued*)
447; lengths, 446–47; maxilla, 443;
mouth, 443–45; operculum, 444–47;
oral disc, 445–46; pectoral fins, 442;
pelvic fins, 442; pharyngeal area, 445,
449; premaxilla, 443–45; scales, 440–
41, 447–48; serration, 445; spines,
441–42, 444, 448; supraoral cusps,
446; terminal mouth, 443; tooth patch,
446; ventral area, 443–44, 447
Fish of Michigan (Bosanko), xi
Flathead Catfish (*Pylodictis olivaris*), 17,
242–43, 250, 260–61, 440
Flora of the Chicago Region (Wilhelm and
Rericha), xi
Forbes, Stephen A., viii
Ford, Edward R., xi
forests: boreal, 161; habitat and, 6–9, 24;
northern, 157, 169, 191, 207; vegetation, 2
forked fins: catfishes (*Ictaluridae*), 242–
50; pictorial keys, *28*; pirate perches
(*Aphredoderidae*), 316; salmon, trout,
chars, and whitefishes (*Salmonidae*),
294, 304, 306, 310
Fox Chain O' Lakes, Illinois, 417
Fox River, Illinois/Wisconsin: bowfins
(*Amiidae*) in, 77; catfishes (*Ictaluridae*)
in, 253, 260–61; Chicago Region, 3, 6–8,
10, 13, 15, 17–18; darters and perches
(*Percidae*) in, 391, 403, 405, 409, 413,
417; drums and croakers (*Sciaenidae*) in,
383; gars (*Lepisosteidae*) in, 73; glacial
lakes, 7; mooneyes (*Hiodontidae*) in,
87; paddlefishes (*Polyodontidae*) in,
65, 73; perennial streams, 15; pikes
(*Esocidae*) in, 265, 269; salmon, trout,
chars, and whitefishes (*Salmonidae*)
in, 303; sculpins (*Cottidae*) in, 427,
429; silversides (*Atherinopsidae*) in,
331; sticklebacks (*Gasterosteidae*) in,
421; suckers (*Catostomidae*) in, 103,
105, 119, 125, 127, 133, 135; sunfishes
(*Centrarchidae*) in, 347, 351, 355, 363,
365, 369, 371; temperate basses
(*Moronidae*) in, 377, 379; topminnows
and killifishes (*Fundulidae*) in, 339; true
minnows (*Leuciscidae*) in, 153, 155, 169,
175, 203, 205, 209, 221, 223, 233, 235
Freckled Madtom (*Noturus nocturnus*), 18,
258–59

frenum: darters and perches (*Percidae*),
386, 390, 394, 398–404, 410–12;
mudminnows (*Umbridae*), 272; true
minnows (*Leuciscidae*), 232, 234
Freshwater Drum (*Aplodinotus grunniens*),
381–83
freshwater eels. *See* eels (*Anguillidae*)
fusiform body: darters and perches
(*Percidae*), 384, 404, 406; loaches
(*Cobitidae*), 238; salmon, trout,
chars, and whitefishes (*Salmonidae*),
280, 284, 288, 290, 294, 298, 306;
sharpbellies (*Xenocyprididae*), 146, 148;
suckers (*Catostomidae*), 130; sunfishes
(*Centrarchidae*), 344, 364, 366;
temperate basses (*Moronidae*), 372;
trout-perches (*Percopsidae*), 314; true
minnows (*Leuciscidae*), 156, 158, 168–
72, 178, 190, 192, 196–204, 208, 216–18,
222, 232, 234

Galien River, Michigan: Chicago Region,
3; lampreys (*Petromyzontidae*) in,
51; suckers (*Catostomidae*) in, 129;
sunfishes (*Centrarchidae*) in, 365
ganoid scales, *29*, 440
gars (*Lepisosteidae*): Alligator Gar
(*Atractosteus spatula*), 66–67; in
backwaters, 66, 70; caudal fins, 68, 70,
324; characteristics of, 66–67; discs, 66,
324; dorsal fins, 324, 326; and drainage,
68, 70; in the Fox River, 73; ganoid
scales, 66, 68; gas bladder, 66; in the
Illinois River, 67, 70, 72; juveniles, 7–10,
66–67; in the Kankakee River, 70, 72;
larvae, 70; lateral line, 72; Longnose Gar
(*Lepisosteus osseus*), 70–71; migration
of, 69; in the Mississippi River, 68, 70;
in the Ohio River, 70, 72; in oxbows,
70; pelvic fins, 72; pictorial key, *29*; in
pools, 68; Shortnose Gar (*Lepisosteus
platostomus*), 72–73; as sport fishes, 67;
Spotted Gar (*Lepisosteus oculatus*), 68–
69; in the St. Joseph River, 68, 70; and
water quality, 70
gas bladder, 66, 74, 76, 80
genital papillae, 46
Gerking, Shelby D., viii
Ghost Shiner (*Notropis buchanani*), 198–99
gill arch, 354, 362, 380, 449

gill cover: darters and perches (*Percidae*), 386, 394; fish identification, 444, 447, 449; paddlefishes (*Polyodontidae*), 64; pictorial keys, *43*; pikes (*Esocidae*), 264, 266, 268; sticklebacks (*Gasterosteidae*), 420; sturgeons (*Acipenseridae*), 58; suckers (*Catostomidae*), 102, 117; sunfishes (*Centrarchidae*), 344, 348–53; temperate basses (*Moronidae*), 372; topminnows and killifishes (*Fundulidae*), 334; true minnows (*Leuciscidae*), 162, 188

gill filament, 276, 280, 282, 288, 290, 292

gill opening, *26*, 46, 94, 148

gill rakers: barbs and carps (*Cyprinidae*), 138; fish identification, 445, 449; paddlefishes (*Polyodontidae*), 62, 64; salmon, trout, chars, and whitefishes (*Salmonidae*), 276–92, 300, 304, 306; sharpbellies (*Xenocyprididae*), 147; sunfishes (*Centrarchidae*), 348–56, 360, 362

gills: barbs and carps (*Cyprinidae*), 138, 141; darters and perches (*Percidae*), 386, 394; drums and croakers (*Sciaenidae*), 380; fish identification, 440, 444–45; lampreys (*Petromyzontidae*), 46; paddlefishes (*Polyodontidae*), 62, 64; pictorial keys, *26*, *43*; pikes (*Esocidae*), 264, 266, 268; pirate perches (*Aphredoderidae*), 316; preopercle, 453; salmon, trout, chars, and whitefishes (*Salmonidae*), 276–92, 300, 304, 306; sculpins (*Cottidae*), 434; shads and herrings (*Clupeidae*), 94; sharpbellies (*Xenocyprididae*), 146–49; sticklebacks (*Gasterosteidae*), 420–24; sturgeons (*Acipenseridae*), 58, 60; suckers (*Catostomidae*), 102, 117; sunfishes (*Centrarchidae*), 344–45, 348–53; temperate basses (*Moronidae*), 374; topminnows and killifishes (*Fundulidae*), 334; true minnows (*Leuciscidae*), 160, 162, 188, 198

Gizzard Shad (*Dorosoma cepedianum*), 89–90, 94–96, 146

glacial deposition, 15, 18

glacial lakes: Des Plaines River, 7; drainage, 205; fish habitats, 6–8; Fox River, 7; Lake Michigan, 7, 161, 165, 207,

279, 353, 407, 428, 430, 432, 435; meltwater, 8; perennial streams, 15; Pleistocene, viii; vegetated, 112

gobies (*Gobiidae*): anal fins, 324; as benthic dwellers, 327; as bait, 327; and the Chicago Area Waterway System, 327; in the Illinois River, 327; in Lake Michigan, 325, 327; lateral line, 324; median fins, 326; Midget Dwarfgoby (*Trimmatom nanus*), 325; migration of, 327; in the Mississippi River, 327; mud skippers (*Oxudercidae*), 325; pectoral fins, 324; pelvic fins, 324–26; pictorial keys, *39*; and Randall's Pistol Shrimp (*Alpheus randalli*), 325; Randall's Prawn Goby (*Amblyeleotris randalli*), 325; riffles, 326; Round Goby (*Neogobius melanostomus*), 307, 325–27, 427, 429, 435; and salmon, trout, chars, and whitefishes (*Salmonidae*), 307, 327; and sculpins (*Cottidae*), 327; spines, 326; terminal mouth, 326; and water quality, 327

Golden Redhorse (*Moxostoma erythrurum*), 126, 128, 130–31, 133, 135

Golden Shiner (*Notemigonus crysoleucas*), 151, 188–89

Goldeye (*Hiodon alosoides*), 84–85

Goldfish (*Carassius auratus*), 136, 138–40

gonopodium, 340–43

Grand Calumet River, Indiana/Illinois, 6

Grand Kankakee Marsh, Indiana, 6, 10

Grand Mere Lakes, Michigan, 3, 8

Grass Carp (*Ctenopharyngodon idella*), 142, 144–45, 148, 449

Grass Pickerel (*Esox americanus*), 12, 262–65

gravel bars, 6, 166, 196

Gravel Chub (*Erimystax x-punctatus*), 166–67

Greater Redhorse (*Moxostoma valenciennesi*), 18, 126, 134–35

Greenburg, Joel, xi

Greenside Darter (*Etheostoma blennioides*), 15, 388–89, 404

Green Sunfish (*Lepomis cyanellus*), 345, 348–49, 352

gular plate, *28*, 74, 76

hakes. *See* burbots (*Lotidae*)

Hay, Oliver Perry, 74, 411

herrings. *See* shads and herrings (*Clupeidae*)

heterocercal fins: bowfins (*Amiidae*), 74, 76; paddlefishes (*Polyodontidae*), 62; sturgeons (*Acipenseridae*), 58, 60

Highfin Carpsucker (*Carpiodes velifer*), *17*, 100, 104–5

Hildebrand, Samuel F., xi

Hofmann Dam, Illinois, 215

Holarctic hemispheres, 107, 262, 267, 321, 419

Hornyhead Chub (*Nocomis biguttatus*), 159, 175, 186–87, 211, 234, 236

Horse Creek, Illinois, 169, 387

Hudson Bay: catfishes (*Ictaluridae*) in, 245; darters and perches (*Percidae*) in, 395, 399, 401, 409, 411, 415; drums and croakers (*Sciaenidae*) in, 383; lampreys (*Petromyzontidae*) in, 51–52; mooneyes (*Hiodontidae*) in, 87; salmon, trout, chars, and whitefishes (*Salmonidae*) in, 305; sticklebacks (*Gasterosteidae*) in, 423, 425; suckers (*Catostomidae*) in, 103, 115, 125, 133; sunfishes (*Centrarchidae*) in, 347, 365; true minnows (*Leuciscidae*) in, 179, 185, 209, 229

Hudson River, New York, 136

hypereutrophic lakes, 9

hypural plate, 447

ichthyologists, 78, *168*, *182*, *282*, *290*

Illinois Department of Natural Resources, 6, 143

Illinois River: barbs and carps (*Cyprinidae*) in, 139; catfishes (*Ictaluridae*) in, 253, 258–59, 261; Chicago Region, 3–5, 10, 17; darters and perches (*Percidae*) in, 415; drums and croakers (*Sciaenidae*) in, 383; eels (*Anguillidae*) in, 81; gars (*Lepisosteidae*) in, 67, 70, 72; gobies (*Gobiidae*) in, 327; lampreys (*Petromyzontidae*) in, 49; livebearers (*Poeciliidae*) in, 343; and migration, 4; mooneyes (*Hiodontidae*) in, 85, 87; paddlefishes (*Polyodontidae*) in, 64–65; shads and herrings (*Clupeidae*) in, 91, 97; sharpbellies (*Xenocyprididae*) in, 142, 144–45, 147, 149; smelts (*Osmeridae*) in, 311; suckers (*Catostomidae*) in, 99, 101, 103, 105, 117, 119, 121, 129, 133, 135;

sunfishes (*Centrarchidae*) in, 347, 359, 363; temperate basses (*Moronidae*) in, 375, 377; topminnows and killifishes (*Fundulidae*) in, 335; trout-perches (*Percopsidae*) in, 315; true minnows (*Leuciscidae*) in, 151, 155, 163, 169, 173, 179, 181, 183, 194, 197, 199, 209, 215, 220, 235; wetland connections, 4

Indiana Harbor Canal, 241

infraorbital canal, 390, 402

interorbital width, 447

Iowa Darter (*Etheostoma exile*), 8, *10*, 394–95, 400

Ironcolor Shiner (*Notropis chalybaeus*), *11*, 200–201, 218, 337

isthmus, 434, 444

Jenkins, R. E., 135

Johnny Darter (*Etheostoma nigrum*), 392, 400–401

Jordan, David Starr, 175, 177, 209, 227, 255, 292, 319

juveniles: catfishes (*Ictaluridae*), 250, 260–61; darters and perches (*Percidae*), 391; gars (*Lepisosteidae*), 7–10, 66–67; habitat, 11; hakes (*Lotidae*), 322; parr, 298–99, 306; pikes (*Esocidae*), 266–67; pirate perches (*Aphredoderidae*), 317; salmon, trout, chars, and whitefishes (*Salmonidae*), 278, *282*, 298, 300, 306; shads and herrings (*Clupeidae*), 94; sharpbellies (*Xenocyprididae*), 145; sturgeons (*Acipenseridae*), 60; suckers (*Catostomidae*), 98, 102, 108, 112, 116, 120–21, 127–30, 133, 135; sunfishes (*Centrarchidae*), 347, 353–54, 356, 362–67, 369, 371; temperate basses (*Moronidae*), 374–79; true minnows (*Leuciscidae*), 161–62, 174–75, 184, 186, 188, 234

Kamchatka Peninsula, Russia, 297

Kankakee River, Illinois/Indiana: bowfins (*Amiidae*) in, 77; catfishes (*Ictaluridae*) in, 248, 261; Chicago Region, 3, 7, *11*, 13, 15; darters and perches (*Percidae*) in, 387, 391–93, 399, 403, 405, 409, 411, 413, 417; eels (*Anguillidae*) in, 81; gars (*Lepisosteidae*) in, 70, 72; lampreys (*Petromyzontidae*) in, 53, 55; mooneyes

(*Hiodontidae*) in, 87; perennial streams, 15; pikes (*Esocidae*) in, 265; pirate perches (*Aphredoderidae*) in, 319; salmon, trout, chars, and whitefishes (*Salmonidae*) in, 303; sculpins (*Cottidae*) in, 429; shads and herrings (*Clupeidae*) in, 91; sharpbellies (*Xenocyprididae*) in, 149; silversides (*Atherinopsidae*) in, 331; suckers (*Catostomidae*) in, 105, 117, 121, 127; sunfishes (*Centrarchidae*) in, 347, 353, 355, 359, 363, 365, 369, 371; temperate basses (*Moronidae*) in, 375, 379; topminnows and killifishes (*Fundulidae*) in, 337, 339; trout-perches (*Percopsidae*) in, 314–15; true minnows (*Leuciscidae*) in, 151, 169, 172–73, 179, 195, 197, 200–205, 215–23, 231, 235

keels: mooneyes (*Hiodontidae*), 82, 84, 86; pictorial keys, 35; shads and herrings (*Clupeidae*), 88, 94; sharpbellies (*Xenocyprididae*), 142, 146, 148; sticklebacks (*Gasterosteidae*), 420, 422, 424; suckers (*Catostomidae*), 116, 126; true minnows (*Leuciscidae*), 188, 190–220

keratin, 46

killifishes. *See* topminnows and killifishes (*Fundulidae*)

Kishwaukee River, Illinois, 167, 169, 171

Kiyi (*Coregonus kiyi*), 286–87

Koi, 140

Lake Beulah, Wisconsin, 279

Lake Char (Lake Trout) (*Salvelinus namaycush*), 8, 277, 304, 306–7, 310, 327, 435

Lake Chub (*Couesius plumbeus*), 160–61, 236

Lake Chubsucker (*Erimyzon sucetta*), 8, 110–13

Lake Erie: catfishes (*Ictaluridae*) in, 254; darters and perches (*Percidae*) in, 403; lampreys (*Petromyzontidae*) in, 57; sticklebacks (*Gasterosteidae*) in, 425; suckers (*Catostomidae*) in, 119; temperate basses (*Moronidae*) in, 375; topminnows and killifishes (*Fundulidae*) in, 339; true minnows (*Leuciscidae*) in, 183

Lake Geneva, Wisconsin, 8, 220–21, 279, 297, 307

Lake Herring (Cisco) (*Coregonus artedi*), 278–79, 292

Lake Huron: salmon, trout, chars, and whitefishes (*Salmonidae*) in, 277, 283, 285, 287–88, 291, 293; smelts (*Osmeridae*) in, 311; true minnows (*Leuciscidae*) in, 199

Lake Maxinkuckee, Indiana, 279

Lake Michigan: barbs and carps (*Cyprinidae*) in, 139; catfishes (*Ictaluridae*) in, 251, 261; Chicago Region, 2–3, 6–8, 9, 11; darters and perches (*Percidae*) in, 385, 400, 405–8, 412–13, 417; drainage, 7–8, 13, 49, 53, 105, 134, 155, 197, 199, 205, 209, 221, 300, 311, 337, 339, 351, 377, 379, 403, 405, 412; drums and croakers (*Sciaenidae*) in, 383; eels (*Anguillidae*) in, 81; fish habitats in, 6; and glaciers, 7, 161, 165, 207, 279, 353, 407, 428, 430, 432, 435; gobies (*Gobiidae*) in, 325, 327; Grand Mere, 3, 8; hakes (*Lotidae*) in, 320, 323; lampreys (*Petromyzontidae*) in, 49, 52–53, 56–57; and migration, 56–57, 69, 81, 294, 299; North Shore, 3, 68, 169, 241; as oligotrophic, 8; paddlefishes (*Polyodontidae*) in, 65, 69; pikes (*Esocidae*) in, 267, 269; salmon, trout, chars, and whitefishes (*Salmonidae*) in, 275–307; sculpins (*Cottidae*) in, 427–35; shads and herrings (*Clupeidae*) in, 92–94; sharpbellies (*Xenocyprididae*) in, 147, 149; size, viii; smelts (*Osmeridae*) in, 310–11; sticklebacks (*Gasterosteidae*) in, 419, 423–25; sturgeons (*Acipenseridae*) in, 61; suckers (*Catostomidae*) in, 103–7, 120–21, 124–25, 131–34; sunfishes (*Centrarchidae*) in, 347, 349, 351, 353, 364–65; temperate basses (*Moronidae*) in, 375, 377, 379; topminnows and killifishes (*Fundulidae*) in, 335, 337, 339; Trail Creek, 3; tributaries, 49, 52, 56, 81, 125, 261, 269, 295, 297, 299, 303, 365, 403, 423, 425; trout-perches (*Percopsidae*) in, 314–15; true minnows (*Leuciscidae*) in, 150, 155, 161, 165, 183, 193, 197, 199, 205, 208–9, 217, 220–21, 233; wetlands, 6, 11

Lake Nipigon, Canada, 283, 289, 291, 293, 301

SUBJECT INDEX   485

Lake Ontario: salmon, trout, chars, and whitefishes (*Salmonidae*) in, 287–91, 382; shads and herrings (*Clupeidae*) in, 93; sticklebacks (*Gasterosteidae*) in, 423

Lake Sturgeon (*Acipenser fulvescens*), 59–61

Lake Superior: salmon, trout, chars, and whitefishes (*Salmonidae*) in, 283, 287–88, 291, 293; sculpins (*Cottidae*) in, 434; smelts (*Osmeridae*) in, 310; suckers (*Catostomidae*) in, 106

Lake Whitefish (*Coregonus clupeaformis*), 280–81

lampreys (*Petromyzontidae*): American Brook Lamprey (*Lethenteron appendix*), 14, 48, 50, 52, 54–56; ammocoete, 46–50, 52, 54, 56, 445; anadromous migration of, 47; antitropical distribution of, 47; as bait, 47; belly, 50, 54; in the Calumet River, 49; in canals, hydrogeophysical, 57; characteristics of, 46–47; Chestnut Lamprey (*Ichthyomyzon castaneus*), *14*, 48–49; and connected lakes, 47, 52; and dams, 49, 53, 57; dorsal fins, 48–56; and drainage, 49, 53, 55; ecological importance of, 47; in the Galien River, 51; gills, 46, 334; in Hudson Bay, 51–52; in the Illinois River, 49; in the Kankakee River, 53, 55; lack of jaws, 46–47; in Lake Erie, 57; in Lake Michigan, 49, 52–53, 56–57; larvae, 46, 48, 54, 56; lateral line, 48, 52, 54; median fins, 46; migration of, 54–57; in the Mississippi River, 48, 51–52; Northern Brook Lamprey (*Ichthyomyzon fossor*), *19*, 50–51; in the Ohio River, 51–52, 55; oral disc, 46–56; papillae, 46, *54*; and phytoplankton, 46, 48; pictorial keys, *26*; and plankton, 46, 48, 54; in the Red River, 48; riffles, 48, 51, 57; and sandbars, 48, 50; Sea Lamprey (*Petromyzon marinus*), 48–53, 56–57; Silver Lamprey (*Ichthyomyzon unicuspis*), 52–53; in the St. Joseph River, 49, 53; supraoral cusps, 48, 50, 52, 54, 56; ventral area, 56; vents, 47; and water quality, 47, 55; and zooplankton, 46

Largemouth Bass (*Micropterus salmoides*), 345, 364, 366–67

Largescale Stoneroller (*Campostoma oligolepis*), 152, 154–55

larvae: and barbs and carps (*Cyprinidae*), 139, 141; and catfishes (*Ictaluridae*), 251, 254, 256, 258; and darters and perches (*Percidae*), 386, 388, 391, 394, 399, 404, 407–8; eels (*Anguillidae*), 78–79; fish identification, 445; gars (*Lepisosteidae*), 70; hakes (*Lotidae*), 320; lampreys (*Petromyzontidae*), 46, 48, 54, 56; and livebearers (*Poeciliidae*), 343; and loaches (*Cobitidae*), 241; mooneyes (*Hiodontidae*), 86; and pikes (*Esocidae*), 264; and salmon, trout, chars, and whitefishes (*Salmonidae*), 277, 290; and sculpins (*Cottidae*), 429, 433, 435; shads and herrings (*Clupeidae*), 93; and sticklebacks (*Gasterosteidae*), 420, 424; and suckers (*Catostomidae*), 100, 109, 113, 118, 124, 131, 133, 135; and sunfishes (*Centrarchidae*), 351, 353, 355, 357, 361, 365, 367, 369, 371; and temperate basses (*Moronidae*), 375, 377, 379; and topminnows and killifishes (*Fundulidae*), 333; and true minnows (*Leuciscidae*), 178, 180, 182, 186, 194, 196, 204, 220, 222, 224, 232, 235

lateral line: barbs and carps (*Cyprinidae*), 138–40; darters and perches (*Percidae*), 388–402, 410; fish identification, 441, 447; gars (*Lepisosteidae*), 72; gobies (*Gobiidae*), 324; lampreys (*Petromyzontidae*), 48, 52, 54; livebearers (*Poeciliidae*), 342; mooneyes (*Hiodontidae*), 82; pictorial keys, *36–37, 39, 41–42*; punctate, 194; salmon, trout, chars, and whitefishes (*Salmonidae*), 274, 276, 286, 302, 304, 306; sculpins (*Cottidae*), 428–34; shads and herrings (*Clupeidae*), 88, 94, 96; silversides (*Atherinopsidae*), 328; suckers (*Catostomidae*), 100–112, 116, *122*, 124–34; sunfishes (*Centrarchidae*), 348, 350, 352, 358; temperate basses (*Moronidae*), 372, 374, 376, 378; topminnows and killifishes (*Fundulidae*), 332; trout-perches (*Percopsidae*), 314; true minnows (*Leuciscidae*), 156, 158,

160, 164, 168, 170, 174, 176, 178, 184–88, 194, 198, 202, 206, 214, 216, 220, 224, 228, 234, 236

lateral scales: darters and perches (*Percidae*), 398; suckers (*Catostomidae*), 110, 112; sunfishes (*Centrarchidae*), 348; topminnows and killifishes (*Fundulidae*), 334

Latta, William C., viii

Least Darter (*Etheostoma microperca*), 8, 398–99

Leather Carp, 140

Little Rock Creek, Illinois, *13*, 259

Little Turtle Creek, Wisconsin, 393

littoral zone, 6, 8, 164, 206, 280, 300

livebearers (*Poeciliidae*): anal fins, 340, 342; belly, 342; characteristics of, 340–41; and the Chicago Area Waterway System, 343; in the Des Plaines River, 343; dorsal fins, 340, 342; gonopodium, 340–43; in the Illinois River, 343; and larvae, 343; lateral line, 342; in marshes, 342; in the Mississippi River, 343; in the Ohio River, 343; pictorial keys, *39*; terminal mouth, 342; Western Mosquitofish (*Gambusia affinis*), 341–43

loaches (*Cobitidae*): adipose fins, 238; bands, 240; barbels, 238, 240; as benthic dwellers, 240; in the Calumet River, 241; caudal fins, 240; caudal peduncle, 240; characteristics of, 238–39; and the Chicago Area Waterway System, 241; in the Chicago River, 241; and dams, 239; dorsal fins, 240; fusiform body, 238; and larvae, 241; in marshes, 240–41; migration of, 239; Oriental Weatherfish (*Misgurnus anguillicaudatus*), 240–41; pelvic fins, 240; pharyngeal area, 238; pictorial keys, *27*; pools, 240; spines, 240; subterminal mouth, 238; ventral area, 240

Logperch (*Percina caprodes*), 408–9

Longear Sunfish (*Lepomis megalotis*), 358–59, 362–63, 444

Longjaw Cisco (*Coregonus alpenae*), 276

Longnose Dace (*Rhinichthys cataractae*), 232–34

Longnose Gar (*Lepisosteus osseus*), 70–71

Longnose Sucker (*Catostomus catostomus*), *19*, 98, 106–8

Mackenzie River system, Canada, 109, 395

madtoms (*Ictaluridae*), 10, 18, 242, 252–60

marshes: bowfins (*Amiidae*) in, 76; catfishes (*Ictaluridae*) in, 256; eels (*Anguillidae*) and, 81; habitat, 3, 6, 10–12; livebearers (*Poeciliidae*) in, 342; loaches (*Cobitidae*) in, 240–41; pikes (*Esocidae*) in, 264–69; pirate perches (*Aphredoderidae*) in, 318; suckers (*Catostomidae*) in, 112; sunfishes (*Centrarchidae*) in, 353; true minnows (*Leuciscidae*) in, 184, 222–23

Mazon River, Illinois, 18, 81, 125, 131, 259, 403

median fins: gobies (*Gobiidae*), 326; lampreys (*Petromyzontidae*), 46; salmon, trout, chars, and whitefishes (*Salmonidae*), 282, 284, 304; true minnows (*Leuciscidae*), 152

Meek, Seth E., xi

melanophores: catfishes (*Ictaluridae*), 258; salmon, trout, chars, and whitefishes (*Salmonidae*), 288, 292, 300

meltwater, 8

Michigan Canal, 65

Midget Dwarfgoby (*Trimmatom nanus*), 325

migration: anadromous, 47, 58, 274, *296*, 297, 308, 372–74, 425; and backwaters, 11, 64; of catfishes (*Ictaluridae*), 251; and connected lakes, 7–8; of eels (*Anguillidae*), 78, 81; and ephemeral streams, 12–13; of gars (*Lepisosteidae*), 69; of gobies (*Gobiidae*), 327; and habitat, 4–6, 11–13, 24; Illinois River, 4; Lake Michigan, 56–57, 69, 81, 294, 299; of lampreys (*Petromyzontidae*), 54–57; of loaches (*Cobitidae*), 239; of paddlefishes (*Polyodontidae*), 64; of pikes (*Esocidae*), 267; of pirate perches (*Aphredoderidae*), 317–18; of salmon, trout, chars, and whitefishes (*Salmonidae*), 274, 294–99; of shads and herrings (*Clupeidae*), 88–92; of sturgeons (*Acipenseridae*), 58; of suckers (*Catostomidae*), 103, 107, 109, 133; of true minnows (*Leuciscidae*), 173

Miltmore Lake, Illinois, 379

Milwaukee River, Wisconsin, 53, 135, 185

Mimic Shiner (*Notropis volucellus*), 8, 195, 220–21

Mirror Carp, 140

SUBJECT INDEX   487

Mississippi River: bowfins (*Amiidae*) in, 77; catfishes (*Ictaluridae*) in, 245–48, 253–58, 261; Chicago Region, 4–5; darters and perches (*Percidae*) in, 386, 389, 391–92, 397, 399, 401, 405, 409, 411, 415, 421; eels (*Anguillidae*) in, 81, 85, 87; gars (*Lepisosteidae*) in, 68, 70; gobies (*Gobiidae*) in, 327; hakes (*Lotidae*) in, 323; lampreys (*Petromyzontidae*) in, 48, 51–52; livebearers (*Poeciliidae*) in, 343; paddlefishes (*Polyodontidae*) in, 65; pikes (*Esocidae*) in, 265, 269; pirate perches (*Aphredoderidae*) in, 316; salmon, trout, chars, and whitefishes (*Salmonidae*) in, 279, 305, 381; shads and herrings (*Clupeidae*) in, 90–91, 96–97; sharpbellies (*Xenocyprididae*) in, 142; silversides (*Atherinopsidae*) in, 331; sturgeons (*Acipenseridae*) in, 61; suckers (*Catostomidae*) in, 103, 105, 111–29, 133, 135; sunfishes (*Centrarchidae*) in, 347, 351, 353, 355, 359, 361–69; temperate basses (*Moronidae*) in, 377, 379; topminnows and killifishes (*Fundulidae*) in, 335, 337, 339; true minnows (*Leuciscidae*) in, 153, 157, 159, 165–66, 172, 175, 177, 183–87, 191–92, 202, 205, 209–12, 217, 221, 227, 231, 235, 237; and waste, 4–5

Mississippi Silvery Minnow (*Hybognathus nuchalis*), 170–71

Mobile River basin, Alabama, 65, 127, 129, 131, 155, 245

Monterey Bay, California, 295

mooneyes (*Hiodontidae*): adipose fins, 82; and African Elephant Fish (*Gnathonemus petersii*), 83; anal fins, 82, 84, 86; axillary process, 82; in backwaters, 85; belly, 82, 84, 86; characteristics of, 82–83; and connected lakes, 84–85; dorsal fins, 82, 84, 86; in the Fox River, 87; Goldeye (*Hiodon alosoides*), 84–85; in Hudson Bay, 87; in the Illinois River, 85, 87; in the Kankakee River, 87; keels, 82, 84, 86; larvae, 86; lateral line, 82; Mooneye (*Hiodon tergisus*), 86–87; pectoral fins, 84; pelvic fins, 82, 84, 86; pictorial keys, 35; in pools, 84; and South American Arawana (*Osteoglossum bicirrhosum*), 83; spines, 82; vents, 84, 86

Mottled Sculpin (*Cottus bairdii*), 14–15, *19*, 326–27, 427–30

muddy areas, 168, 171

Mud Lake (historic), Illinois, 6

mudminnows (*Umbridae*): Alaska Blackfish (*Dallia pectoralis*), 270–71; anadromous migration of, 274; in backwaters, 272; as bait, 271; belly, 276, 294, 298; caudal fins, 273; Central Mudminnow (*Umbra limi*), 11, 271–73; characteristics of, 270–71; cycloid scales, 272; dorsal fins, 270, 272; and drainage, 272; European Mudminnow (*Umbra pygmaea*), 271; frenum, 272; Olympic Mudminnow (*Novumbra hubbsi*), 271; pictorial keys, *38*; terminal mouth, 272; and water quality, 273

Mukwonago River, Wisconsin, 135, 393

Muskellunge (*Esox masquinongy*), 109, 262–63, 268–69

natural basins, 4

Natural History of the Chicago Region, A (Greenburg), xi

New World silversides. *See* silversides (*Atherinopsidae*)

Ninespine Stickleback (*Pungitius pungitius*), 424–25

Nippersink Creek, Wisconsin, 421

North American catfishes. *See* catfishes (*Ictaluridae*)

Northern Brook Lamprey (*Ichthyomyzon fossor*), *19*, 50–51

Northern Hog Sucker (*Hypentelium nigricans*), 114–15

Northern Pearl Dace (*Margariscus nachtriebi*), 184–85

Northern Pike (*Esox lucius*), 11, *12*, 262–63, 266–69

Northern Redbelly Dace (*Chrosomus eos*), 156–58

Northern Sunfish (*Lepomis peltastes*), 358–59, 362–63

North Shore Channel, Illinois, 68, 169, 241

ocellus, *76*

Ohio River: catfishes (*Ictaluridae*) in, 245, 254, 256, 261; darters and perches (*Percidae*) in, 389, 391, 397–405, 411–12, 415; drums and croakers (*Sciaenidae*) in, 383; gars (*Lepisosteidae*) in, 70, 72; lampreys (*Petromyzontidae*) in, 51–52, 55; livebearers (*Poeciliidae*) in, 343; pikes (*Esocidae*) in, 265, 269; shads and herrings (*Clupeidae*) in, 96; silversides (*Atherinopsidae*) in, 331; sticklebacks (*Gasterosteidae*) in, 421; suckers (*Catostomidae*) in, 101, 103, 105, 115–33; sunfishes (*Centrarchidae*) in, 347, 353, 355, 359, 361, 365, 367, 369; temperate basses (*Moronidae*) in, 377; topminnows and killifishes (*Fundulidae*) in, 339; true minnows (*Leuciscidae*) in, 153, 159, 165, 167, 175, 180, 187, 192, 197–98, 215, 217, 221, 225, 227, 231, 235, 237

Oligocene epoch, 427

oligotrophic lakes, 8, 192, 220

Olympic Mudminnow (*Novumbra hubbsi*), 271

opercle: suckers (*Catostomidae*), 102, 116–20; sunfishes (*Centrarchidae*), 368, 370; temperate basses (*Moronidae*), 372

operculum, 444–47

Opossum Shrimp (*Mysis relicta*): and salmon, trout, chars, and whitefishes (*Salmonidae*), 277, 279, 284, 286, 288, 290, 295, 299; and smelts (*Osmeridae*), 310

oral discs, lampreys (*Petromyzontidae*), 46–56, 445–46

Orangespotted Sunfish (*Lepomis humilis*), 354–55

Orangethroat Darter (*Etheostoma spectabile*), 390, 402–3

Oriental Weatherfish (*Misgurnus anguillicaudatus*), 240–41

overfishing: for caviar, 62–63; of darters and perches (*Percidae*), 407; of paddlefishes (*Polyodontidae*), 62–63; of salmon, trout, chars, and whitefishes (*Salmonidae*), 275, 279, 283, 285, 289, 291; of sharpbellies (*Xenocyprididae*), 142

oxbows: bowfins (*Amiidae*) in, 76; darters and perches (*Percidae*) in, 392; gars (*Lepisosteidae*) in, 70; habitat, 6; paddlefishes (*Polyodontidae*) in, 64; pikes (*Esocidae*) in, 266; suckers (*Catostomidae*) in, 117–18

Ozark Minnow (*Notropis nubilus*), 15, 210–11

paddlefishes (*Polyodontidae*): in backwaters, 62, 64; as benthic dwellers, 60; in the Calumet River, 65; caviar, 62–63; characteristics of, 62–63; and connected lakes, 62; and dams, 63–64; dorsal fins, 64; and drainage, 62, 65; in the Fox River, 65, 73; gill cover, 64; gill rakers, 62, 64; heterocercal fins, 62; in the Illinois River, 64–65; in Lake Michigan, 65, 69; migration of, 64; in the Mississippi River, 65; overfishing of, 62–63; in oxbows, 64; Paddlefish (*Polyodon spathula*), 64–65; pictorial keys, *29*; and plankton, 62, 64; riffles, 64; in the St. Joseph River, 65; and zooplankton, 62

Page, Larry M., viii–ix

Pallid Shiner (*Hybopsis amnis*), 18, 172–73

papillae: lampreys (*Petromyzontidae*), 46, *54*; pictorial keys, *36*; suckers (*Catostomidae*), 106, 108, 114, 124, 126, 132

parr, 298–99, 306

pectoral fins: darters and perches (*Percidae*), 398, 400; eels (*Anguillidae*), 80; fish identification, 442; gobies (*Gobiidae*), 324; mooneyes (*Hiodontidae*), 84; pictorial keys, *26, 30, 36–37, 40*; salmon, trout, chars, and whitefishes (*Salmonidae*), 304; sculpins (*Cottidae*), 426; sharpbellies (*Xenocyprididae*), 148; silversides (*Atherinopsidae*), 330; suckers (*Catostomidae*), 98, 114; sunfishes (*Centrarchidae*), 344–62, 368, 370; true minnows (*Leuciscidae*), 166, 180, 184, 186

pelagic habitat: of drums and croakers (*Sciaenidae*), 380, 383; of salmon, trout, chars, and whitefishes (*Salmonidae*), 277–79; of temperate basses (*Moronidae*), 372; of true minnows (*Leuciscidae*), 182, 192, 208

pelvic fins: darters and perches (*Percidae*), 384, 408, 410, 412; drums and croakers (*Sciaenidae*), 382; eels (*Anguillidae*), 78; fish identification, 442; gars (*Lepisosteidae*), 72; gobies (*Gobiidae*), 324–26; loaches (*Cobitidae*), 240; mooneyes (*Hiodontidae*), 82, 84, 86; pictorial keys, *26–27, 31, 36–37, 39–40*; pirate perches (*Aphredoderidae*), 318;

SUBJECT INDEX   **489**

pelvic fins (*continued*)
salmon, trout, chars, and whitefishes (*Salmonidae*), 274, 282, 304; sculpins (*Cottidae*), 428, 430, 432, 434; shads and herrings (*Clupeidae*), 88; sharpbellies (*Xenocyprididae*), 146, 148; sticklebacks (*Gasterosteidae*), 420, 422, 424; suckers (*Catostomidae*), 98, 102, 134; sunfishes (*Centrarchidae*), 348; topminnows and killifishes (*Fundulidae*), 338; true minnows (*Leuciscidae*), 150, 178, 180, 182, 188, 192, 198, 214

perches. *See* darters and perches (*Percidae*)

perennial streams, 15–17

peritoneum, true minnows (*Leuciscidae*), 151, 156, 158, 168, 170, 223, 230

Peterson Field Guide to Freshwater Fishes of North America (Page and Burr), xi

pharyngeal area: drums and croakers (*Sciaenidae*), 382–83; fish identification, 445, 449; loaches (*Cobitidae*), 238; sharpbellies (*Xenocyprididae*), 144, *146*; suckers (*Catostomidae*), 126–27, 135; sunfishes (*Centrarchidae*), 344, 351, 361

phytoplankton, 46, 48, 96

Pickerelweed (*Pontederia cordata*), 12

pictorial keys: anal fins, *32, 35–41*; axillary process, *31*; barbels, *27, 29–30, 32*; barbs and carps (*Cyprinidae*), *34*; bowfins (*Amiidae*), *28*; burbots (*Lotidae*), *32*; canines, *37–38*; catfishes (*Ictaluridae*), *30*; caudal fins, *28, 36, 41–42*; ctenoid scales, *29, 31*; cycloid scales, *29, 31*; darters and perches (*Percidae*), *42*; discs, *39*; dorsal fins, *28, 32–43*; drums and croakers (*Sciaenidae*), *41*; eels (*Anguillidae*), *27*; forked fins, *28*; ganoid scales, *29*; gars (*Lepisosteidae*), *29*; gills, *26, 43*; gobies (*Gobiidae*), *39*; lampreys (*Petromyzontidae*), *26*; livebearers (*Poeciliidae*), *39*; loaches (*Cobitidae*), *27*; mooneyes (*Hiodontidae*), *35*; mudminnows (*Umbridae*), *38*; paddlefishes (*Polyodontidae*), *29*; papillae, *36*; pectoral fins, *26, 30, 36–37, 40*; pelvic fins, *26–27, 31, 36–37, 39–40*; pikes (*Esocidae*), *37*; pirate perches (*Aphredoderidae*), *32*; plicate skin, *36*; salmon, trout, chars, and whitefishes (*Salmonidae*), *31*;

sculpins (*Cottidae*), *40*; serration, *34, 43*; shads and herrings (*Clupeidae*), *35*; sharpbellies (*Xenocyprididae*), *36–37*; silversides (*Atherinopsidae*), *41*; smelts (*Osmeridae*), *31*; spines, *30, 33–34, 41–43*; sticklebacks (*Gasterosteidae*), *33*; sturgeons (*Acipenseridae*), *29*; subterminal mouth, *29*; suckers (*Catostomidae*), *36*; sunfishes (*Centrarchidae*), *43*; terminal mouth, *38*; topminnows and killifishes (*Fundulidae*), *39*; trout-perches (*Percopsidae*), *31*; true minnows (*Leuciscidae*), *37*; ventral area, *29, 32, 35*; White Bass (*Morone chrysops*), *43*

Pike River, Wisconsin, 3

pikes (*Esocidae*): and agriculture, 264; in backwaters, 262, 264, 268; branchiostegal membrane, 266; branchiostegal ray, 264; characteristics of, 262–63; in the Chicago River, 269; dorsal fins, 262; and drainage, 265; in the Fox River, 265, 269; gill cover, 264, 266, 268; Grass Pickerel (*Esox americanus*), 12, 262–65; juveniles, 266–67; in the Kankakee River, 265; in Lake Michigan, 267, 269; and larvae, 264; in marshes, 264–69; migration of, 267; in the Mississippi River, 265, 269; Muskellunge (*Esox masquinongy*), 109, 262–63, 268–69; Northern Pike (*Esox lucius*), 11, *12*, 262–63, 266–69; in the Ohio River, 265, 269; in oxbows, 266; pictorial keys, 37; in the Red River, 269; in sidestreams, 266; subspecies of, 265; ventral area, 266

Pink Salmon (*Oncorhynchus gorbuscha*), 275

Pirate Perch (*Aphredoderus sayanus*), 11, *32*, 318–19

pirate perches (*Aphredoderidae*): anal fins, 318; in backwaters, 318; bands, 318; belly, 317; branchiostegal membrane, 318; characteristics of, 316–17; ctenoid scales, 316, 318; dorsal fins, 316, 318; and drainage, 318; embedded scales, 320, 322; forked fins, 316; gills, 316; juveniles, 317; in the Kankakee River, 319; in marshes, 318; migration of, 317–18; in the Mississippi River, 316; pelvic fins, 318; pictorial keys, *32*; Pirate Perch

(*Aphredoderus sayanus*), 11, *32*, 318–19; spines, 318

plankton: and lampreys (*Petromyzontidae*), 46, 48, 54; and paddlefishes (*Polyodontidae*), 62, 64; and salmon, trout, chars, and whitefishes (*Salmonidae*), 279, 307; and shads and herrings (*Clupeidae*), 90, 92, 95–96; and sharpbellies (*Xenocyprididae*), 147, 149; and sticklebacks (*Gasterosteidae*), 418; and suckers (*Catostomidae*), 111, 113, 118; and sunfishes (*Centrarchidae*), 344, 369, 371; and true minnows (*Leuciscidae*), 156, 184, 192, 220

Plants of the Chicago Region (Swink and Wilhelm), xi

Pleistocene age, viii, 74

plicate skin: pictorial keys, *36*; sticklebacks (*Gasterosteidae*), 419, 421; suckers (*Catostomidae*), 122, 126, 128, 130, 132, 134

pondweed (*Potamogeton* spp.), 12, 388

pools: catfishes (*Ictaluridae*) in, 251; dam, 6, 147; darters and perches (*Percidae*) in, 410; gars (*Lepisosteidae*) in, 68; isolated, 12–13, 237, 240, 330; loaches (*Cobitidae*) in, 240; mooneyes (*Hiodontidae*) in, 84; riffles, 6, 18, 108, 126, 162, 164, 175, 205, 347; runs, 17, 68, 126–27, 132, 162, 164, 175, 208, 305, 410; salmon, trout, chars, and whitefishes (*Salmonidae*) in, 303, 305; sharpbellies (*Xenocyprididae*) in, 147, 149; silt, 15, 18, 84, 100, 108, 130, 220; silversides (*Atherinopsidae*) in, *330*; suckers (*Catostomidae*) in, 100, 102, 108, 124, 126–32, 135; sunfishes (*Centrarchidae*) in, 347–49, 355, 366, 369, 371; trout-perches (*Percopsidae*) in, 314; true minnows (*Leuciscidae*) in, 162, 164, 175, 182, 198, 208, 220, 228, 237; vegetated, 68

predorsal scales, 110, 112, 174, 176

premaxilla: catfishes (*Ictaluridae*), 252, 254, 256, 258; darters and perches (*Percidae*), 390, 398; fish identification, 443–45; salmon, trout, chars, and whitefishes (*Salmonidae*), 276–84, 290, 292

prickels, 426, 428, 432, 434

protrusible lips, 76, 140

Puffin (*Fratercula* spp.), 309

Pugnose Minnow (*Opsopoeodus emiliae*), 222–23

Pugnose Shiner (*Notropis anogenus*), 8, 190–91

Pumpkinseed (*Lepomis gibbosus*), 350–51

punctate lateral line, 194

pyloric caeca, 294, 298, 304, 306

Quagga Mussel (*Dreissena bugensis*), 407

Quillback (*Carpiodes cyprinus*), 100–104

Rainbow Darter (*Etheostoma caeruleum*), 390–91, 402, 404

Rainbow Smelt (*Osmerus mordax*), 307–8, 310–11

Rainbow Trout (Steelhead) (*Oncorhynchus mykiss*), 296–97, 302

Randall's Pistol Shrimp (*Alpheus randalli*), 325

Randall's Prawn Goby (*Amblyeleotris randalli*), 325

Redear Sunfish (*Lepomis microlophus*), 356, 360–61

Redfin Shiner (*Lythrurus umbratilis*), 178–79

Red River of the North: lampreys (*Petromyzontidae*) in, 48; pikes (*Esocidae*) in, 269; shads and herrings (*Clupeidae*) in, 91; suckers (*Catostomidae*) in, 119, 126; true minnows (*Leuciscidae*) in, 183, 191, 212

Red Shiner (*Cyprinella lutrensis*), 162–64

Reed Canary Grass (*Phalaris arundinacea*), 13

Rericha, Laura, xi

Richardson, Robert E., viii

riffles: boulder, 18; catfishes (*Ictaluridae*), 242, 252, 254, 261; cobble, 18; darters and perches (*Percidae*), 388, 391, 402, 404–5, 408, 412, 414, 417; gobies (*Gobiidae*), 326; gravel, 48; hakes (*Lotidae*), 322; lampreys (*Petromyzontidae*), 48, 51, 57; paddlefishes (*Polyodontidae*), 64; pools, 6, 18, 108, 126, 162, 164, 175, 205, 347; runs, 126, 162, 164, 172, 175, 187, 196, 216, 234, 305, 326, 391, 408, 414, 417; salmon, trout, chars, and whitefishes (*Salmonidae*), 305; sculpins (*Cottidae*), 429, 433; smelts (*Osmeridae*), 309;

SUBJECT INDEX   491

riffles (*continued*)

    sturgeons (*Acipenseridae*), 60; suckers (*Catostomidae*), 107–8, 114–15, 122, 125–29; sunfishes (*Centrarchidae*), 347; true minnows (*Leuciscidae*), 162, 164, 166, 172–75, 187, 196–97, 216, 224, 232, 234

River Carpsucker (*Carpiodes carpio*), 100–102, 104

River Redhorse (*Moxostoma carinatum*), 18, 126–27, 132, 134, 449

River Shiner (*Notropis blennius*), 194–95

Rock Bass (*Ambloplites rupestris*), 8, 344, 346–47

Rock River, Wisconsin/Illinois: catfishes (*Ictaluridae*) in, 253; Chicago Region, 3; darters and perches (*Percidae*) in, 391; salmon, trout, chars, and whitefishes (*Salmonidae*) in, 305; suckers (*Catostomidae*) in, 119; sunfishes (*Centrarchidae*) in, 351; true minnows (*Leuciscidae*) in, 155, 167, 175, 185, 209, 211, 213, 225, 235

Root River, Wisconsin: Chicago Region, 3, 6, 18, *19*; darters and perches (*Percidae*) in, 413; sturgeons (*Acipenseridae*) in, 61; suckers (*Catostomidae*) in, 107

Rosyface Shiner (*Notropis rubellus*), 192, 212–15

Round Goby (*Neogobius melanostomus*), 307, 325–27, 427, 429, 435

Round Whitefish (Menominee) (*Prosopium cylindraceum*), 300–301

rudiment, 228, 448

runs: pools, 17, 68, 126–27, 132, 162, 164, 175, 208, 305, 410; riffles, 126, 162, 164, 172, 175, 187, 196, 216, 234, 305, 326, 391, 408, 414, 417

Sacremento Perch (*Archoplites interruptus*), 344–45

saddles: darters and perches (*Percidae*), 392, 406–16; sculpins (*Cottidae*), 428, 430, 432, 434; sticklebacks (*Gasterosteidae*), 422, 424; suckers (*Catostomidae*), 98, 114

Saganashkee Slough, Illinois, 6

salmon, trout, chars, and whitefishes (*Salmonidae*): adipose fins, 274; anadromous migration of, *296*, 297; anal fins, 280, 292–306; axillary

process, 274; bands, 296; Blackfin Cisco (*Coregonus nigripinnis*), 288–89; Bloater (*Coregonus hoyi*), 278, 282–83; branchiostegal ray, 294, 298, 304; Brook Char (*Salvelinus fontinalis*), 14, 304–6; Brown Trout (*Salmo trutta*), 14, 275, 296, 302–4, 306; and burbots (*Lotidae*), 277; caudal fins, 280–84, 294–98, 302–6; characteristics of, 274–75; Chinook Salmon (*Oncorhynchus tshawytscha*), 294, 296, 298–99, 302; Coho Salmon (*Oncorhynchus kisutch*), 294–96, 298, 302; in coldwater habitat, 300, 303–6; *Coregoninae*, 274–75; cycloid scales, 274; and dams, 275; Deepwater Cisco (*Coregonus johannae*), 276, 284–85; dorsal fins, 274, 280, 282, 284, 290, 292, 298, 302, 304, 306; and drainage, 300, 305, 307; European Brown Trout (*Salmo trutta*), 14, 275; and Field Museum of Natural History, *276, 278, 284, 286, 288, 290, 291, 292, 300*; forked fins, 294, 304, 306, 310; in the Fox River, 303; fusiform body, 280, 284, 288, 290, 294, 298, 306; gill rakers, 276–92, 300, 304, 306; in Hudson Bay, 305; juveniles, 278, *282*, 298, 300, 306; in the Kankakee River, 303; Kiyi (*Coregonus kiyi*), 286–87; Lake Char (*Salvelinus namaycush*), 8, 277, 304, 306–7, 310, 327, 435; Lake Herring (*Coregonus artedi*), 278–79, 292; in Lake Michigan, 275–307; in Lake Ontario, 287–91, 382; in Lake Superior, 283, 287–88, 291, 293; Lake Whitefish (*Coregonus clupeaformis*), 280–81; and larvae, 277, 290; lateral line, 274, 276, 286, 302, 304, 306; Longjaw Cisco (*Coregonus alpenae*), 276; median fins, 282, 284, 304; melanophores, 288, 292, 300; migration of, 274, 294–99; in the Mississippi River, 279, 305, 381; and Opossum Shrimp (*Mysis relicta*), 277, 279, 284, 286, 288, 290, 295, 299; overfishing of, 275, 279, 283, 285, 289, 291; parr, 298–99, 306; pectoral fins, 304; pelagic habitat of, 277–79; pelvic fins, 274, 282, 304; pictorial keys, *31*; Pink Salmon (*Oncorhynchus gorbuscha*), 275; and plankton, 279, 307; in pools, 303, 305; premaxilla, 276–84, 290,

292; Rainbow Trout (*Oncorhynchus mykiss*), 296–97, 302; riffles, 305; in the Rock River, 305; Round Whitefish (*Prosopium cylindraceum*), 300–301; Salmoninae, 275; Shortjaw Cisco (*Coregonus zenithicus*), 292–93; Shortnose Cisco (*Coregonus reighardi*), 290–91; spines, 306; as sport fishes, 275, 295, 297; in the St. Joseph River, 305; subterminal mouth, 280, 300; terminal mouth, 280, 304; *Thymallinae*, 275; tubercles, 276–84, 290, 292; and zooplankton, 279, 307

Salt Creek, Illinois, 91, 135

sandbars: and darters and perches (*Percidae*), 386, 408; and lampreys (*Petromyzontidae*), 48, 50; and trout-perches (*Percopsidae*), 315; and true minnows (*Leuciscidae*), 208

Sand Roller (*Percopsis transmontana*), 312–13

Sand Shiner (*Notropis stramineus*), 194–95, 202, 216–17, 220

Sauger (*Sander canadensis*), 385, 406, 414–17

sculpins (*Cottidae*): barbels, 442–43, 446; characteristics of, 426–27; Deepwater Sculpin (*Myoxocephalus thompsonii*), 307, 434–35; dorsal fins, 426–34; in the Fox River, 427, 429; gills, 434; and gobies (*Gobiidae*), 327; in the Kankakee River, 429; in Lake Michigan, 427–35; in Lake Superior, 434; and larvae, 429, 433, 435; lateral line, 428–34; in the Mississippi River, 4–5; Mottled Sculpin (*Cottus bairdii*), 14–15, *19*, 326–27, 427–30; and Opossum Shrimp (*Mysis relicta*), 431, 434; pectoral fins, 426; pelvic fins, 428, 430, 432, 434; pictorial keys, *40*; prickels, 426, 428, 432, 434; riffles, 429, 433; saddles, 428, 430, 432, 434; and salmons, trout, chars, and whitefishes (*Salmonidae*), 299; Slimy Sculpin (*Cottus cognatus*), 428, 430–31; spines, 426–34; Spoonhead Sculpin (*Cottus ricei*), 423–24

scutes, 58–60, 88

Sea Lamprey (*Petromyzon marinus*), 48–53, 56–57

sedges (*Carex* spp.), 12

serration: barbs and carps (*Cyprinidae*), 136, 138, 140; fish identification, 445; pictorial keys, *34*, *43*; spines, 34, 43, 136, 138, 140, 273; sunfishes (*Centrarchidae*), 344; temperate basses (*Moronidae*), 372

sewage, 4

shads and herrings (*Clupeidae*): Alewife (*Alosa pseudoharengus*), 90, 92–93, 275, 297, 299, 303, 307; anal fins, 94; axillary process, 88–92; belly, 92, 94; characteristics of, 88–89; and connected lakes, 90; cycloid scales, 88; in the Des Plaines River, 91, 96; and drainage, 91, 95, 97; gills, 94; Gizzard Shad (*Dorosoma cepedianum*), 89–90, 94–96, 146; in the Illinois River, 91, 97; juveniles, 94; in the Kankakee River, 91; keels, 88, 94; in Lake Michigan, 92–94; in Lake Ontario, 93; and larvae, 93; lateral line, 88, 94, 96; migration of, 88–92; in the Mississippi River, 90–91, 96–97; in the Ohio River, 96; pelvic fins, 88; and phytoplankton, 96; pictorial keys, *35*; and plankton, 90, 92, 95–96; in the Red River, 91; scutes, 88; Skipjack Herring (*Alosa chrysochloris*), 89–91; spines, 88; terminal mouth, 90; Threadfin Shad (*Dorosoma petenense*), 90, 94, 96–97; and water quality, 91, 94; and zooplankton, 96

sharpbellies (*Xenocyprididae*), *36–37*; anal fins, 146, 148; in backwaters, 146, 148; belly, 142, 146, 148; Bighead Carp (*Hypophthalmichthys nobilis*), 136, 142, 146, 148–49; caudal peduncle, 144; characteristics of, 142–43; and the Chicago Area Waterway System, 145, 147, 149; in the Des Plaines River, 147, 149; dorsal fins, 144–48; fusiform body, 146, 148; gills, 146–49; Grass Carp (*Ctenopharyngodon idella*), 142, 144–45, 148, 449; in the Illinois River, 142, 144–45, 147, 149; juveniles, 145; in the Kankakee River, 149; keels, 142, 146, 148; in Lake Michigan, 147, 149; in the Mississippi River, 142; overfishing of, 142; pectoral fins, 148; pelvic fins, 146, 148; pharyngeal area, 144, *146*; pictorial keys, *36*; and plankton, 147, 149; in pools, 147,

sharpbellies (*continued*)
149; and shads and herrings (*Clupeidae*), 94; Silver Carp (*Hypophthalmichthys molitrix*), 142, 146–49; terminal mouth, 148; ventral area, 142
Shelford, Victor, 8, 353
Shoal Chub (*Macrhybopsis hyostoma*), 180–82
Shorthead Redhorse (*Moxostoma macrolepidotum*), *17*, 103, 126, 130, 132–34
Shortjaw Cisco (*Coregonus zenithicus*), 292–93
Shortnose Cisco (*Coregonus reighardi*), 290–91
Shortnose Gar (*Lepisosteus platostomus*), 72–73
sidestreams, 6, 10, 266
Silver Carp (*Hypophthalmichthys molitrix*), 142, 146–49
Silver Chub (*Macrhybopsis storeriana*), 182–83
Silverjaw Minnow (*Notropis buccatus*), *19*, 196–97, 202
Silver Lamprey (*Ichthyomyzon unicuspis*), 52–53
Silver Redhorse (*Moxostoma anisurum*), *12*, 124–25, 130, 132, 134
silversides (*Atherinopsidae*): adipose fins, 328; anal fins, 330; bait, as poor live, 329; Brook Silverside (*Labidesthes sicculus*), 330–31; caudal fins, 328; characteristics of, 328–29; dorsal fins, 328, 330; and drainage, 331; in the Fox River, 331; in the Kankakee River, 331; lateral line, 328; in the Mississippi River, 331; in the Ohio River, 331; pectoral fins, 330; pictorial keys, *41*; in pools, 330
Skipjack Herring (*Alosa chrysochloris*), 89–91
Slenderhead Darter (*Percina phoxocephala*), *17*, 412–13
Slender Madtom (*Noturus exilis*), 252–53, 258
Slimy Sculpin (*Cottus cognatus*), 428, 430–31
sloughs, 66, 207; Saganashkee, 6; vegetation, 66, 76, 113, 190, 264, 270, 394, 398; wetlands, 6, 113, 270
Smallmouth Bass (*Micropterus dolomieu*), 8, 18, 327, 345, 364–66
Smallmouth Buffalo (*Ictiobus bubalus*), 116–17, 120

smelts (*Osmeridae*): adipose fins, 308, 310; anadromous migration of, 308–9; axillary process, 308; and burbots (*Lotidae*), 311; canines, 310; characteristics of, 308–9; and the Chicago Area Waterway System, 311; and drainage, 311; in the Illinois River, 311; in Lake Michigan, 310–11; in Lake Superior, 310; and Opossum Shrimp (*Mysis relicta*), 310; pictorial keys, *31*; and Puffins, 309; Rainbow Smelt (*Osmerus mordax*), 307–8, 310–11; riffles, 309; and salmon, trout, chars, and whitefishes (*Salmonidae*), 295, 299, 307
Smith, Gerald R., viii
Smith, Philip W., viii, xi
Somonauk Creek, Illinois, 210
South American Arawana (*Osteoglossum bicirrhosum*), 83
Southern Redbelly Dace (*Chrosomus erythrogaster*), 14, 156–59
spines: barbs and carps (*Cyprinidae*), 136–40; catfishes (*Ictaluridae*), 242–58; darters and perches (*Percidae*), 384, 386, 392–400, 410, 412; drums and croakers (*Sciaenidae*), 382; fish identification, 441–42, 444, 448; gobies (*Gobiidae*), 326; hakes (*Lotidae*), 322; loaches (*Cobitidae*), 240; mooneyes (*Hiodontidae*), 82; pictorial keys, *30*, *33–34*, *41–43*; pirate perches (*Aphredoderidae*), 318; salmon, trout, chars, and whitefishes (*Salmonidae*), 306; sculpins (*Cottidae*), 426–34; serrated, 34, 43, 136, 138, 140, 273; shads and herrings (*Clupeidae*), 88; sticklebacks (*Gasterosteidae*), 418, 420, 422–25; sunfishes (*Centrarchidae*), 344–54, 364–70; temperate basses (*Moronidae*), 372–78; topminnows and killifishes (*Fundulidae*), 332; trout-perches (*Percopsidae*), 312, 314; true minnows (*Leuciscidae*), 150
spiracles, 58, 60
Spoonhead Sculpin (*Cottus ricei*), 423–24
sport fishes: barbs and carps (*Cyprinidae*), 136–37, 141; bowfins (*Amiidae*), 77; darters and perches (*Percidae*), 407; drums and croakers (*Sciaenidae*), 381; gars (*Lepisosteidae*), 67; habitat, 9, 23;

salmon, trout, chars, and whitefishes (*Salmonidae*), 275, 295, 297; sunfishes (*Centrarchidae*), 345, 356–57, 369; temperate basses (*Moronidae*), 373–79

Spotfin Shiner (*Cyprinella spiloptera*), 162, 164–65

Spottail Shiner (*Notropis hudsonius*), 208–9, 295

Spotted Gar (*Lepisosteus oculatus*), 68–69

Spotted Sucker (*Minytrema melanops*), 122–23

Starhead Topminnow (*Fundulus dispar*), 8, *11*, 336–37, 342

Starved Rock Dam, Illinois, 147, 149

sticklebacks (*Gasterosteidae*): anadromous migration of, 425; anal fins, 420, 422, 424; as bait, 421; bands, 422; belly, 420, 422, 424; and benthic dwellers, 418; breast, 420–24; Brook Stickleback (*Culaea inconstans*), 12, 14, 420–22; in the Calumet River, 423; characteristics of, 418–19; and the Chicago Area Waterway System, 423; in coldwater habitat, 419, 425; dorsal fins, 418–24; and drainage, 421–25; in the Fox River, 421; gills, 420–24; in Hudson Bay, 423, 425; keels, 420, 422, 424; in Lake Erie, 425; in Lake Michigan, 419, 423–25; in Lake Ontario, 423; and larvae, 420, 424; Ninespine Stickleback (*Pungitius pungitius*), 424–25; in the Ohio River, 421; pelvic fins, 420, 422, 424; pictorial keys, *33*; and plankton, 418; plicate skin, 419, 421; saddles, 422, 424; and salmon, trout, chars, and whitefishes (*Salmonidae*), 295; spines, 418, 420, 422–25; Threespine Stickleback (*Gasterosteus aculeatus*), 422–23

St. Joseph River, Michigan/Indiana: catfishes (*Ictaluridae*) in, 249; Chicago Region, 3, 15, 17, *18*; darters and perches (*Percidae*) in, 388–89, 391, 409, 417; gars (*Lepisosteidae*) in, 68, 70; lampreys (*Petromyzontidae*) in, 49, 53; paddlefishes (*Polyodontidae*) in, 65; perennial streams, 15; salmon, trout, chars, and whitefishes (*Salmonidae*) in, 305; sturgeons (*Acipenseridae*) in, 61; suckers (*Catostomidae*) in, 107, 115, 123, 129, 131, 133, 135; sunfishes

(*Centrarchidae*) in, 363, 365; true minnows (*Leuciscidae*) in, 209, 220–21, 233

Stonecat (*Noturus flavus*), *19*, 254–55, 258

Striped Bass (*Morone saxatilis*), 372–73, 379

Striped Shiner (*Luxilus chrysocephalus*), 174–77

sturgeons (*Acipenseridae*): anadromous migration of, 58; barbels, 58, 60; caudal peduncle, 60; characteristics of, 58–59; dorsal fins, 60; gills, 58, 60; heterocercal fins, 58, 60; juveniles, 60; in Lake Michigan, 61; Lake Sturgeon (*Acipenser fulvescens*), 59–61; migration of, 58; in the Mississippi River, 61; pictorial keys, *29*; riffles, 60; in the Root River, 61; scutes, 58–60; spiracles, 58, 60; in the St. Joseph River, 61; subterminal mouth, 60; Syr Darya Sturgeon (*Pseudoscaphirhynchus fedtschenkoi*), 58

subopercle, 102, 116–20

subspecies: of darters and perches (*Percidae*), 389; of pikes (*Esocidae*), 265; of sunfishes (*Centrarchidae*), 359; of topminnows and killifishes (*Fundulidae*), 334–35

subterminal mouth: darters and perches (*Percidae*), 386; drums and croakers (*Sciaenidae*), 382; loaches (*Cobitidae*), 238; pictorial keys, *29*; salmon, trout, chars, and whitefishes (*Salmonidae*), 280, 300; sturgeons (*Acipenseridae*), 60; suckers (*Catostomidae*), 98, 116, 122; trout-perches (*Percopsidae*), 312, 314; true minnows (*Leuciscidae*), 152, 166, 172, *180*, 186, 196, 198, 202, 206, 220, 224, 226, 232

Suckermouth Minnow (*Phenacobius mirabilis*), 224–25

suckers (*Catostomidae*): adipose fins, 98; and agriculture, 111; anal fins, 98, 100, 110, 112, 122, 126–32; in backwaters, 117–19; bait, catching with, 99, 109; bands, 106, 114; barbels, 98; belly, 108, 124–34; and benthic dwellers, 111, 117; Bigmouth Buffalo (*Ictiobus cyprinellus*), 118–19; Black Buffalo (*Ictiobus niger*), 12, 116, 120–21; Black Redhorse (*Moxostoma*

SUBJECT INDEX 495

suckers (*continued*)
duquesnei), 128–30; body depth, 110, 112; in the Calumet River, 111, 117, 121, 131, 133; caudal fins, *124*; caudal peduncle, 124–34, 138; and the Chicago Area Waterway System, 101, 115; and the Chicago Lake Plain, 131, 133; Chinese Sucker (*Myxocyprinus asiaticus*), 98; in coldwater habitat, 106; and connected lakes, 118; cycloid scales, 98; and dams, 99, 105, 115, 119, 125; in the Des Plaines River, 101, 103, 119, 123, 125, 135; dorsal fins, 98–104, 110–34; and drainage, 101, 103, 105, 111–17, 123, 134; in the Fox River, 101, 103, 105, 115, 119, 125, 127, 129, 131, 133, 135; fusiform body, 130; in the Galien River, 129; gill cover, 102, 117; Golden Redhorse (*Moxostoma erythrurum*), 126, 128, 130–31, 133, 135; Greater Redhorse (*Moxostoma valenciennesi*), 18, 126, 134–35; Highfin Carpsucker (*Carpiodes velifer*), *17*, 100, 104–5; in Hudson Bay, 103, 115, 125, 133; in the Illinois River, 99, 101, 103, 105, 117, 119, 121, 129, 133, 135; juveniles, 98, 102, 108, 112, 116, 120–21, 127–30, 133, 135; in the Kankakee River, 105, 117, 121, 127; keels, 116, *126*; Lake Chubsucker (*Erimyzon sucetta*), 8, 110–13; in Lake Erie, 119; in Lake Michigan, 103–7, 120–21, 124–25, 131–34; in Lake Superior, 106; and larvae, 100, 109, 113, 118, 124, 131, 133, 135; lateral line, 100–112, 116, *122*, 124–34; lateral scales, 110, 112; Longnose Sucker (*Catostomus catostomus*), *19*, 98, 106–8; in marshes, 112; migration of, 103, 107, 109, 133; in the Mississippi River, 103, 105, 111–29, 133, 135; Northern Hog Sucker (*Hypentelium nigricans*), 114–15; in the Ohio River, 101, 103, 105, 115–33; opercle, 102, 116–20; oxbows, 117–18; papillae, 106, 108, 114, 124, 126, 132; pectoral fins, 98, 114; pelvic fins, 98, 102, 134; pharyngeal area, 126–27, 135; pictorial keys, *36*; and plankton, 111, 113, 118; plicate skin, 122, 126, 128, 130, 132, 134; in pools, 100, 102, 108, 124, 126–32, 135; predorsal scales, 110, 112; Quillback (*Carpiodes cyprinus*), 100–104; in the Red River, 119, 126; riffles, 107–8, 114–15, 122, 125–29; River Carpsucker (*Carpiodes carpio*), 100–102, 104; River Redhorse (*Moxostoma carinatum*), 18, 126–27, 132, 134, 449; in the Rock River, 119; in the Root River, 107; saddles, 98, 114; Shorthead Redhorse (*Moxostoma macrolepidotum*), *17*, 103, 126, 130, 132–34; Silver Redhorse (*Moxostoma anisurum*), *12*, 124–25, 130, 132, 134; Smallmouth Buffalo (*Ictiobus bubalus*), 116–17, 120; as sport fishes, 99; Spotted Sucker (*Minytrema melanops*), 122–23; in the St. Joseph River, 107, 115, 123, 129, 131, 133, 135; subopercle, 102, 116–20; subterminal mouth, 98, 116, 122; terminal mouth, 110–12, 118, 122; tubercles, 98, 102, 106–12, 116, 122–34; ventral area, 114; and water quality, 99–105, 115, 129–30; Western Creek Chubsucker (*Erimyzon claviformis*), *14*, 110–12; White Sucker (*Catostomus commersonii*), 106, 108–9

Sugar Creek, Wisconsin, 219

sunfishes (*Centrarchidae*): and agriculture, 347, 357, 366; anal fins, 346–56, 368, 370; in backwaters, 349, 353, 360; bait, 363; bands, 353, 364, 368; belly, 346–52, 356, 360, 362, 368, 370; Black Crappie (*Pomoxis nigromaculatus*), *10*, 368, 370–71; Bluegill (*Lepomis macrochirus*), 345, 356–57, 440; breast, 354; in the Calumet River, 363; caudal fins, 362; characteristics of, 98–99; and the Chicago Area Waterway System, 355, 365, 367; cycloid scales, 344; in the Des Plaines River, 347, 355, 365; dorsal fins, 344, 346, 348, 352, 356, 362, 366, 368, 370; and drainage, 351–61, 367–71; ear flaps, 346–62; in the Fox River, 347, 351, 355, 363, 365, 369, 371; fusiform body, 344, 364, 366; in the Galien River, 365; gill cover, 344, 348–53; gill rakers, 348–56, 360, 362; Green Sunfish (*Lepomis cyanellus*), 345, 348–49, 352; in Hudson Bay, 347, 365; in the Illinois River, 347, 359, 363; juveniles, 347, 353–54, 356, 362–67, 369, 371; in the Kankakee River, 347, 353, 355, 359, 363, 365, 369, 371; in Lake Michigan, 347, 349, 351, 353, 364–65; Largemouth

Bass (*Micropterus salmoides*), 345, 364, 366–67; and larvae, 351, 353, 355, 357, 361, 365, 367, 369, 371; lateral line, 348, 350, 352, 358; lateral scales, 348; *Lepomis*, 344; Longear Sunfish (*Lepomis megalotis*), 358–59, 362–63, 444; in marshes, 353; *Micropterus*, 344; in the Mississippi River, 347, 351, 353, 355, 359, 361–69; Northern Sunfish (*Lepomis peltastes*), 358–59, 362–63; in the Ohio River, 347, 353, 355, 359, 361, 365, 367, 369; opercle, *368, 370*; Orangespotted Sunfish (*Lepomis humilis*), 354–55; pectoral fins, 344–62, 368, 370; pelvic fins, 348; pharyngeal area, 344, 351, 361; pictorial keys, *43*; and plankton, 344, 369, 371; *Pomoxis*, 344; in pools, 347–49, 355, 366, 369, 371; Pumpkinseed (*Lepomis gibbosus*), 350–51; Redear Sunfish (*Lepomis microlophus*), 356, 360–61; riffles, 347; Rock Bass (*Ambloplites rupestris*), 8, 344, 346–47; in the Rock River, 351; Sacramento Perch (*Archoplites interruptus*), 344–45; serration, 344; Smallmouth Bass (*Micropterus dolomieu*), 8, 18, 327, 345, 364–66; spines, 344–54, 364–70; as sport fishes, 345, 356–57, 369; in the St. Joseph River, 363, 365; subspecies of, 359; thoracic fins, 344; vermiculation, 362; Warmouth (*Lepomis gulosus*), 8, 352–53; and water quality, 347, 349, 357, 359, 363–67; White Crappie (*Pomoxis annularis*), 368–70; and zooplankton, 369, 371

supraoral cusps: fish identification, 446; lampreys (*Petromyzontidae*), 48, 50, 52, 54, 56

swamps, 6, 10, 72, 120, 238, 353, 360, 458

Swink, Floyd, xi

"Synoptic List of the Fishes Known to Occur within 50 Miles of Chicago, A" (Meek and Hildebrand), xi

Syr Darya Sturgeon (*Pseudoscaphirhynchus fedtschenkoi*), 58

Tadpole Madtom (*Noturus gyrinus*), *10*, 256–58

temperate basses (*Moronidae*): anal fins, 374–78; in the Calumet River, 377; characteristics of, 324–25, 372–73; and the Chicago Area Waterway System, 375, 379; and dams, 373; in the Des Plaines River, 375, 379; dorsal fins, 372, 374, 376, 378; and drainage, 377, 379; in the Fox River, 377, 379; fusiform body, 372; gills, 372, 374; in the Illinois River, 375, 377; juveniles, 374–79; in the Kankakee River, 375, 379; in Lake Erie, 375; in Lake Michigan, 375, 377, 379; and larvae, 375, 377, 379; lateral line, 372, 374, 376, 378; in the Mississippi River, 377, 379; in the Ohio River, 377; opercle, 372; pelagic habitat of, 372; serration, 372; spines, 372–78; as sport fishes, 373–79; Striped Bass (*Morone saxatilis*), 372–73, 379; tooth patch, 372–78; White Bass (*Morone chrysops*), *43*, 372, 374, 376–79; White Perch (*Morone americana*), 372, 374–76, 378; Yellow Bass (*Morone mississippiensis*), 372, 376, 378–79

terete shape, 184, 206, 210, 220, 226

terminal mouth: barbs and carps (*Cyprinidae*), 138, 140; bowfins (*Amiidae*), 74; catfishes (*Ictaluridae*), 252–58; drums and croakers (*Sciaenidae*), 380; fish identification, 443; gobies (*Gobiidae*), 326; livebearers (*Poeciliidae*), 342; mudminnows (*Umbridae*), 272; pictorial keys, *38*; salmon, trout, chars, and whitefishes (*Salmonidae*), 280, 304; shads and herrings (*Clupeidae*), 90; sharpbellies (*Xenocyprididae*), 148; suckers (*Catostomidae*), 110–12, 118, 122; topminnows and killifishes (*Fundulidae*), 338; true minnows (*Leuciscidae*), 178, 184, 188, 192, 198, 204, 208, 210, 218, 230, 234

Tertiary period, 427

thoracic fins, 344

Threadfin Shad (*Dorosoma petenense*), 90, 94, 96–97

Threespine Stickleback (*Gasterosteus aculeatus*), 422–23

Tiger Muskie, 263

tooth patch: catfishes (*Ictaluridae*), 252–60; fish identification, 446; temperate basses (*Moronidae*), 372–78 topminnows and killifishes (*Fundulidae*): anal fins, 332–38; in backwaters, 336–37; Banded Killifish (*Fundulus diaphanus*), 8, 334–35; belly, 336; Blackstripe Topminnow (*Fundulus notatus*), 338–39; characteristics of, 332–33; in the Des Plaines River, 339; dorsal fins, 332, 334, 336, 338; and drainage, 335, 337, 339; in the Fox River, 339; gill cover, 334; in the Illinois River, 335; in the Kankakee River, 337, 339; in Lake Erie, 339; in Lake Michigan, 335, 337, 339; and larvae, 333; lateral line, 332; lateral scales, 334; in the Ohio River, 339; pelvic fins, 338; pictorial keys, *39*; spines, 332; Starhead Topminnow (*Fundulus dispar*), 8, *11*, 336–37, 342; subspecies of, 334–35; terminal mouth, 338; Western Banded Killifish (*Fundulus diaphanus*), 8, 334–35

Trail Creek, Indiana, 3

trout. *See* salmon, trout, chars, and whitefishes (*Salmonidae*)

Trout-perch (*Percopsis omiscomaycus*), 314–15

trout-perches (*Percopsidae*): adipose fins, 312–14; characteristics of, 312–13; ctenoid scales, 312, 314; cycloid scales, 312; fusiform body, 314; in the Illinois River, 315; in the Kankakee River, 314–15; in Lake Michigan, 314–15; lateral line, 314; pictorial keys, *31*; in pools, 314; and sandbars, 315; Sand Roller (*Percopsis transmontana*), 312–13; spines, 312, 314; subterminal mouth, 312, 314; Trout-perch (*Percopsis omiscomaycus*), 314–15; tubercles, 309

true minnows (*Leuciscidae*): adipose fins, 196; and agriculture, 153, 158, 178, 196; anadromous migration of, 372–73; anal fins, 152, 154, 160, 164, 178–82, 188, 190, 198–210, 214–20, 224–30, 234, 236; in backwaters, 164, 170, 198, 200, 218, 222, 228; as bait, 151, 159, 163, 171, 175–79, 189, 228–31, 237; bands, 152, 156, 158, 172, 190, 200, 204, 206, 210, 214, 218, 222, 224, 234, 236; barbels, 151, 160, *166*, 172, 180–86, 208, 232, 234, 236; belly, 156–59, 168, 170, 174–78, 186, 196, 214, 232–34; and benthic dwellers, 202;

Bigeye Chub (*Hybopsis amblops*), 151; Bigmouth Shiner (*Notropis dorsalis*), *19*, 195, 202–3; Blackchin Shiner (*Notropis heterodon*), 8, 204–5; Blacknose Shiner (*Notropis heterolepis*), 8, 206–7; Bluntnose Minnow (*Pimephales notatus*), 8, 226–28, 230; Brassy Minnow (*Hybognathus hankinsoni*), 168–70; bridle, 172, 218; Bullhead Minnow (*Pimephales vigilax*), 226, 228, 230–31; in the Calumet River, 171, 187, 199; canines, 372; Carmine Shiner (*Notropis percobromus*), 192, 212–13; caudal fins, 175–76, 188, 216; caudal peduncle, 174, 186; caudal spot, 186, 226, 228, 230; Central Stoneroller (*Campostoma anomalum*), 111, 152–55; characteristics of, 150–51; and the Chicago Area Waterway System, 199, 335; in coldwater habitat, 184–85; Colorado Pikeminnow (*Ptychocheilus lucius*), 150; Common Shiner (*Luxilus cornutus*), *15*, 175–77, 187; Creek Chub (*Semotilus atromaculatus*), *14*, 160, 184, 186, 236–37; and dams, 167, 173, 181, 183, 215; in the Des Plaines River, 173, 179, 201, 205, 215, 219, 231; dorsal fins, 150, 152, 156–64, 168–94, 198–210, 214–30, 234, 236; and drainage, 155, 165, 169, 171, 181, 185, 197–205, 209, 211, 221, 227, 231, 237; Emerald Shiner (*Notropis atherinoides*), 192–93, 214; Fathead Minnow (*Pimephales promelas*), 12, 151, 228–30; in the Fox River, 153, 155, 169, 175, 194, 203, 205, 209, 219, 221, 223, 225, 231, 233, 235; frenum, 232, 234; fusiform body, 156, 158, 168–72, 178, 190, 192, 196–204, 208, 216–18, 222, 232, 234; Ghost Shiner (*Notropis buchanani*), 198–99; gills, 160, 162, 188, 198; Golden Shiner (*Notemigonus crysoleucas*), 151, 188–89; Gravel Chub (*Erimystax x-punctatus*), 166–67; Hornyhead Chub (*Nocomis biguttatus*), 159, 175, 186–87, 211, 234, 236; in Hudson Bay, 179, 185, 209, 229; in the Illinois River, 151, 155, 163, 169, 173, 179, 181, 183, 194, 197, 199, 209, 215, 220, 235; Ironcolor Shiner (*Notropis chalybaeus*), *11*, 200–201, 218, 337; juveniles, 161–62, 174–75, 184, 186,

188, 234; in the Kankakee River, 151, 169, 172–73, 179, 195, 197, 200–205, 215–23, 231, 235; keels, 188, *190–220*; Lake Chub (*Couesius plumbeus*), 160–61, 236; in Lake Erie, 183; in Lake Michigan, 150, 155, 161, 165, 183, 193, 197, 199, 205, 208–9, 217, 220–21, 233; Largescale Stoneroller (*Campostoma oligolepis*), 152, 154–55; and larvae, 178, 180, 182, 186, 194, 196, 204, 220, 222, 224, 232, 235; lateral line, 156, 158, 160, 164, 168, 170, 174, 176, 178, 184–88, 194, 198, 202, 206, 214, 216, 220, 224, 228, 234, 236; Longnose Dace (*Rhinichthys cataractae*), 232–34; in marshes, 184, 222–23; median fins, 152; migration of, 173; Mimic Shiner (*Notropis volucellus*), 8, 195, 220–21; in the Mississippi River, 153, 157, 159, 165–66, 172, 175, 177, 183–87, 191–92, 202, 205, 209–12, 217, 221, 227, 231, 235, 237, 335, 337, 339; Mississippi Silvery Minnow (*Hybognathus nuchalis*), 170–71; Northern Pearl Dace (*Margariscus nachtriebi*), 184–85; Northern Redbelly Dace (*Chrosomus eos*), 156–57; in the Ohio River, 153, 159, 165, 167, 175, 180, 187, 192, 197–98, 215, 217, 221, 225, 227, 231, 235, 237; Ozark Minnow (*Notropis nubilus*), *15*, 210–11; Pallid Shiner (*Hybopsis amnis*), 18, 172–73; pectoral fins, 166, 180, 184, 186; pelagic habitat of, 182, 192, 208; pelvic fins, 150, 178, 180, 182, 188, 192, 198, 214; peritoneum, 151, 156, 158, 168, 170, 223, 230; pictorial keys, *37*; and plankton, 156, 184, 192, 220; in pools, 162, 164, 175, 182, 198, 208, 220, 228, 237; predorsal scales, 174, 176; Pugnose Minnow (*Opsopoeodus emiliae*), 222–23; Pugnose Shiner (*Notropis anogenus*), 8, 190–91; Redfin Shiner (*Lythrurus umbratilis*), 178–79; in the Red River, 183, 191, 212; Red Shiner (*Cyprinella lutrensis*), 162–64; riffles, 162, 164, 166, 172–75, 187, 196–97, 216, 224, 232, 234; River Shiner (*Notropis blennius*), 194–95; in the Rock River, 155, 167, 175, 185, 209, 211, 213, 225, 235; Rosyface Shiner (*Notropis rubellus*), 192, 212–15; sandbars, 208;

Sand Shiner (*Notropis stramineus*), 194–95, 202, 216–17, 220; Shoal Chub (*Macrhybopsis hyostoma*), 180–82; Silver Chub (*Macrhybopsis storeriana*), 182–83; Silverjaw Minnow (*Notropis buccatus*), *19*, 196–97, 202; Southern Redbelly Dace (*Chrosomus erythrogaster*), 14, 156–59; spines, 150, 372–78; Spotfin Shiner (*Cyprinella spiloptera*), 162, 164–65; Spottail Shiner (*Notropis hudsonius*), 208–9, 295; Starhead Topminnow (*Fundulus dispar*), 8, *11*, 336–37, 342; in the St. Joseph River, 209, 220–21, 233; Striped Shiner (*Luxilus chrysocephalus*), 174–77; subterminal mouth, 152, 166, 172, *180*, 186, 196, 198, 202, 206, 220, 224, 226, 232; Suckermouth Minnow (*Phenacobius mirabilis*), 224–25; terete shape, 184, 206, 210, 220, 226; terminal mouth, 178, 184, 188, 192, 198, 204, 208, 210, 218, 230, 234; tubercles, 152, 154, 166, 170, 174–86, 192, 214, 224–30, 234, 236; ventral area, 188, 224; and water quality, 164, 167, 196, 205, 214–17, 237; Weed Shiner (*Notropis texanus*), 200, 218–19; Western Blacknose Dace (*Rhinichthys obtusus*), 12, 14, 232, 234–35; and zooplankton, 156, 192, 220
tubercles: barbs and carps (*Cyprinidae*), 136; salmon, trout, chars, and whitefishes (*Salmonidae*), 276–84, 290, 292; trout-perches (*Percopsidae*), 309; true minnows (*Leuciscidae*), 152, 154, 166, 170, 174–86, 192, 214, 224–30, 234, 236
tuna and mackerel (*Scombridae*), 89
Turtle Creek, Wisconsin, 119
turtles, 139
Tyler Creek, Illinois, 15

"Updated Annotated List of Wisconsin's Fishes, An" (Lyons and Schmidt), xi
urban development, 3, 10, 14
US Army Corps, 6, 61, 120, 124, 296, 302, 307, 364, 437
US Fish and Wildlife Service, 307

vegetation: aquatic, 8–9, 13, 50, 72, 76, 113, 122, 138, 141, 162, 189–90, 200, 204–6, 222, 228, 230, 256, 266–72, 334, 336, 347, 351–60, 363, 366, 388–400, 404–

vegetation (*continued*)

5, 408, 429, 449; backwaters, 18, 66, 76, 200, 222, 228, 248, 262, 264, 268, 318, 336–37, 349, 353, 360, 392; Chicago Region, 2–3; flooded areas, 2, 18, 120, 267; forests, 2; muddy areas, 168; native plants, 12; ponds, 150, 156, 228, 244, 336, 353, 360, 363, 406, 424; pools, 68; sloughs, 65, 76, 113, 190, 264, 270, 394, 398; streams, 13–15, 18, 112, 150, 162, 172, 189–90, 200, 204, 206, 230, 244, 264–67, 270–73, 318, 326, 334, 342, 347, 349, 353, 357–60, 363, 366, 394–95, 399, 406, 424, 429; swamps, 120, 360; uprooting, 141; wetlands, 9, 113, 244, 270, 273, 318

ventral area: fish identification, 443–44, 447; lampreys (*Petromyzontidae*), 56; loaches (*Cobitidae*), 240; pictorial keys, *29, 32, 35*; pikes (*Esocidae*), 266; sharpbellies (*Xenocyprididae*), 142; suckers (*Catostomidae*), 114; true minnows (*Leuciscidae*), 188, 224

vents, 47, 84, 86

vermiculation, 362

Walleye (*Sander vitreus*), 311, 384–85, 406, 414–17

Warmouth (*Lepomis gulosus*), 8, 352–53

warmwater streams, 6

waste, 4–5

water quality: and barbs and carps (*Cyprinidae*), 136, 139; and catfishes (*Ictaluridae*), 257; Clean Water Act, x, 5, 139; and darters and perches (*Percidae*), 389, 391, 401–5, 409; degradation of, 5; and drums and croakers (*Sciaenidae*), 383; and gars (*Lepisosteidae*), 70; and gobies (*Gobiidae*), 327; and lampreys (*Petromyzontidae*), 47, 55; and mudminnows (*Umbridae*), 273; seasonal changes in, 11; and shads and herrings (*Clupeidae*), 91, 94; and suckers (*Catostomidae*), 99–105, 115, 129–30; and sunfishes (*Centrarchidae*), 347, 349, 357, 359, 363–67; and true minnows (*Leuciscidae*), 164, 167, 196, 205, 214–17, 237

Weed Shiner (*Notropis texanus*), 200, 218–19

Welland Canal, Canada, 57, 93

Western Banded Killifish (*Fundulus diaphanus*), 8, 334–35

Western Blacknose Dace (*Rhinichthys obtusus*), 12, 14, 232, 234–35

Western Creek Chubsucker (*Erimyzon claviformis*), *14*, 110–12

Western Mosquitofish (*Gambusia affinis*), 341–43

Western Sand Darter (*Ammocrypta clara*), 386–87

wetlands: agriculture, 9; backwaters, 6, 10–12, 318, 393; cold headwater streams, 13–14; connections, 4, 117; ephemeral streams, 12–13; Great Lakes basin, 4; Lake Michigan, 6, 11; meltwater, 8; perennial streams, 15–17; rivers, 17–18, *19–21*; sidestreams, 6, 10; sloughs, 6, 113, 270; vegetation, 9, 113, 244, 270, 273, 318

White Bass (*Morone chrysops*), *43*, 372, 374, 376–79

White Crappie (*Pomoxis annularis*), 368–70

whitefishes. *See* salmon, trout, chars, and whitefishes (*Salmonidae*)

White Perch (*Morone americana*), 372, 374–76, 378

White Sucker (*Catostomus commersonii*), 106, 108–9

Wilhelm, Gerould, xi

Wilmington Dam, Illinois, 91

Wolf Lake, Illinois, 223

World's Fair in Chicago, 139, 297

Yellow Bass (*Morone mississippiensis*), 372, 376, 378–79

Yellow Bullhead (*Ameiurus natalis*), 246–47, 249

Yellow Perch (*Perca flavescens*), 161, 311, 327, 385, 406–7

Yellow River, Indiana, 18, 173, 175, 215

Yukon Territory, Canada, 281

Zebra Mussel (*Dreissena polymorpha*), 407

zooplankton: and lampreys (*Petromyzontidae*), 46; and paddlefishes (*Polyodontidae*), 62; and salmon, trout, chars, and whitefishes (*Salmonidae*), 279, 307; and shads and herrings (*Clupeidae*), 96; and sunfishes (*Centrarchidae*), 369, 371; and true minnows (*Leuciscidae*), 156, 192, 220